The Corporate Social Responsibility Reader

In the age of global capitalism, shareholders and profits are not the only concerns of modern business corporations. Debates surrounding economic and environmental sustainability, and increasing intense media scrutiny, mean that businesses have to show ethical responsibility to stakeholders beyond the boardroom. A commitment to corporate social responsibility may help the wider community. It could also protect an organization's brand and reputation.

Including key articles and original perspectives from academics, NGOs and companies themselves, *The Corporate Social Responsibility Reader* is a welcome and insightful introduction to the important issues and themes of this growing field of study. The book addresses:

- The changing relationships between business, state and civil society
- The challenges to business practice
- What businesses should be responsible for, and why
- Issues of engagement, transparency and honesty
- The boundaries of CSR – can businesses ever be responsible?

Case studies examine major international corporations like Coca-Cola and Starbucks, while broader articles discuss thematic trends and issues within the field. This comprehensive but eclectic collection provides a wonderful overview of CSR and its place within the contemporary social and economic landscape. It is essential reading for anyone studying business and management, and its ethical dimensions.

Jon Burchell is a lecturer in the Management School at the University of Sheffield, UK. His research focuses on the impact of social and environmental concerns upon business strategy. In particular, the impact of CSR and the role of stakeholders in shaping and defining the concept of a 'responsible business', the development and application of sustainable development, and the challenge of anti-corporate campaigns.

The Corporate Social
Responsibility Reader

Edited by

Jon Burchell

 Routledge
Taylor & Francis Group

LONDON AND NEW YORK

First published 2008
by Routledge
2 Park Square, Milton Park, Abingdon, Oxon OX14 4RN

Simultaneously published in the USA and Canada
by Routledge
270 Madison Ave, New York, NY 10016

Routledge is an imprint of the Taylor & Francis Group, an informa business

Typeset in Perpetua and Bell Gothic by
RefineCatch Limited, Bungay, Suffolk
Printed and bound in Great Britain by
TJ International Ltd, Padstow, Cornwall

British Library Cataloguing in Publication Data
A catalogue record for this book is available from the British Library

Library of Congress Cataloging in Publication Data
The corporate social responsibility reader / edited by Jon Burchell.
    p. cm.
 1. Social responsibility of business.   I. Burchell, Jon, 1970–
 HD60.C6914 2007
 658.4′08 – dc22   2007037013

ISBN10: 0–415–42433–X (hbk)
ISBN10: 0–415–42434–8 (pbk)

ISBN13: 978–0–415–42433–2 (hbk)
ISBN13: 978–0–415–42434–9 (pbk)

Contents

CHAPTER FIVE
Engagement, transparency and trust: a new style of interaction?   **185**

Acknowledgements

The publishers would like to thank the following for permission to reprint their material:

Adidas for permission to reprint its 'Guidelines in Employment Standards'.

Association of Chartered Certified Accountants for permission to reprint R. Cowe and M. Hopkins, 'Corporate Social Responsibility: Is There a Business Case?' (2003).

Blackwell Publishing for permission to reprint M. Blowfield and J. G. Frynas, 'Setting New Agendas: Critical Perspectives on Corporate Social Responsibility in the Developing World', *International Affairs*, Vol. 81, No. 3 (2005).

Business for Social Responsibility for permission to reprint Allen L. White, 'Fade, Integrate or Transform? The Future of CSR' (*c.* 2006).

Cadbury Schweppes for permission to reprint 'Our CSR Vision and Strategy' from *Cadbury Schweppes 2006 CSR Report*.

Christian Aid for permission to reprint 'Living Its Values: Coca-Cola in India'. Taken from *Behind the Mask: The Real Face of CSR*.

Clean Clothes Campaign for permission to reprint 'Code of Labour Practices for the Apparel Industry Including Sportswear'. Website: www.cleanclothes.org.

CorporateWatch for permission to reprint 'Corporate Psychology: Killing from Behind a Desk' taken from *Corporate Laws and Structures* (2004). Website: www.corporatewatch.org.uk.

CSR Network for permission to reprint 'CSR Reporting: Examining the Unpalatable Issues' (2005). Website: www.csrnetwork.com.

Earthscan for permission to reprint K. Dent, 'The Contradictions in Codes: The Sri-Lankan Experience', in R. Jenkins *et al.* (2002) *Corporate Responsibility and Labour Rights*; D. Doane, 'Good Intentions – Bad Outcomes? The Broken Promise of CSR Reporting', in A. Henriques and J. Richardson (2004) *The Triple Bottom Line*; and S. Zadek, 'How Civil can Corporations Be?' from *The Civil Corporation* (2004).

Ebury Press for permission to reprint D. Gorman, 'Starbucks', taken from *Dave Gorman's Googlewack Adventure*.

The Economist for permission to reprint C. Crook, 'The Good Company', *The Economist*, 20 January 2005.

Elsevier Press for permission to reprint A. Carroll, 'The Pyramid of Corporate Social Responsibility: Toward the moral management of Organizational Stakeholders', *Business Horizons* (July–August 1991).

Global Reporting Initiative for permission to reprint Reporting Principles taken from *Sustainability Reporting Guidelines* (2006).

Greenleaf Publishing for permission to reprint A. T. Lawrence, 'The Drivers of Stakeholder Engagement: Reflections on the Case of Royal Dutch/Shell' in J. Andriof *et al.* (2002) *Unfolding Stakeholder Thinking*.

HarperCollins Publishers Ltd. for permission to reprint N. Klein, 'The Unbearable Lightness of Cavite' taken from *No Logo* (2001).

Institute for Economic Affairs for permission to reprint D. Henderson, 'Companies, Commitment and Collectivism' taken from *Misguided Virtue: False Notions of Corporate Social Responsibility*.

International Institute for Sustainable Development for permission to reprint A. Najam, D. Runnals and M. Halle, 'Environment and Globalization: Five Propositions' (2007).

McSpotlight for permission to reprint 'What's Wrong with McDonald's' (2006). Website: www.mcspotlight.org.

George Monbiot for permission to reprint 'Still Drilling?', *Guardian*, 13 June 2006.

New York Times for permission to reprint M. Friedman, 'The Social Responsibility of Business is to Increase its Profits', *New York Times Magazine*, 13 September 1970.

OECD Publishing for permission to reprint 'The OECD Guidelines for Multinational Enterprises'.

Polity Press for permission to reprint D. Held and A. McGrew, 'Globalization and the New Political Circumstances of World Order' taken from *Governing Globalization* (2002).

Simon and Schuster for permission to reprint J. Bakan, 'The Externalizing Machine' taken from *The Corporation* (2004).

SustainAbility Ltd for permission to reprint 'Ten Key Messages' taken from *Buried Treasure: Uncovering the Business Case for Corporate Sustainability* (2001).

United Nations Global Compact Office for permission to reprint 'The United Nations Global Compact: Advancing Corporate Citizenship'.

Vodafone for permission to reproduce 'Mobile Phones, Masts and Health' from *Vodafone CSR Report* (2006).

World Business Council for Sustainable Development for permission to reprint 'Why Now?' taken from *From Challenge to Opportunity: The Role of Business in Tomorrow's Society*.

ZNet for permission to reprint V. Shiva, 'Globalization and its Fall Out'. Website: www.Zmag.org (2003).

Introduction[1]

■   Jon Burchell

THE INCREASING DEBATES surrounding global climate change, concern over the pursuit of constant economic growth over sustainable production practices, corporate scandals involving major multinationals such as Enron and the subsequent questioning of the regulatory structures and morality of global capitalism, all suggest that the complex relationship between business, the state and civil society is undergoing change. The debate, on this occasion, is being conducted under the rubric of Corporate Social Responsibility (CSR), Stakeholder Management and Corporate Citizenship.

The development of CSR strategies has been particularly pressing for brand-based, multinational companies such as Nike, Shell and Gap. Greater public concern over the activities of such corporations has highlighted the importance of protecting the brand image, and the need to demonstrate a corporation's socially responsible attitude in its interactions with consumers and suppliers in order to maintain its social capital (see Nahapiet and Ghoshal 1998). The urgency of responding to criticisms and negating potentially damaging publicity has heightened awareness regarding the apparent advantages of an effective CSR strategy.

Debates about the social responsibilities of corporations are by no means new. Research and policy has long been concerned with addressing what the role of the private firm should be, whose interests it should serve and how. Traditional perspectives have often focused upon the claim that shareholders represented the predominant interest to be served by firms and that by serving them, firms inevitably serve society. As Friedman (1962: 33) stated:

> There is one and only one social responsibility of business – to use its resources and engage in activities designed to increase its profits as long as it stays within the rules of the game.[2]

However, some writers have approached firms' obligations in a significantly more complex manner, suggesting that far from only being answerable to their shareholders, firms are engaged in interactions with civil society, as well as nation states and global organisations. In this context, how they organise, how inclusive they are, with whom they enter into dialogue and so on is negotiable (see e.g. Bowen 1953; Bell 1976; Hutton 1995).

The pace and degree to which the language and practice of CSR have been embraced represents a significant contemporary development regarding redefining the relationship between capital and civil society (Andriof *et al.* 2002; Weiser and Zadek 2000). Within this process, a number of key changes are helping to shape the dialogue surrounding CSR; first, the state is stepping back from corporatism and is less willing to directly shape and provide for the needs of its citizenry (Cox 1999). Second, capital is increasingly globalizing and supposedly dominant in its relations with both the state and civil society (Sklair 2001). Third, marketing strategies of major multinationals have increasingly focused upon attaching lifestyles and values to cement the importance of the brand above the actual commodities being sold (Klein 2000). Fourth, and as a possible reaction to the two previous points, consumers are becoming more powerful and derive increasing meaning and value from what they consume, attaching principles to products and producers (Bauman 1998; Klein 2000). And fifth, there is a growing emphasis upon sustainable development and the demands for business to adopt more stringent sustainable practices (Burchell and Lightfoot 2003).

Under these pressures the relationships between business, the state and civil society are changing. As Andriof and McIntosh (2001: 17) suggest:

> Consumers and employees are now well informed about the challenges facing the world, they have little faith in governments' ability to change things, they acknowledge the corporation as the most powerful social construct of the present era and, most importantly, they are willing to reward corporations who are responsive to their concerns.

Under these circumstances, there is increasing demand for greater clarity regarding the nature of corporate responsibility. Given that the parameters and boundaries of this new discourse are still evolving, how this changing environment is debated and managed, how positions are communicated, analysed and shaped, what the new obligations and responsibilities of the actors are and what approaches and substantive rationalities the different parties use, will arguably shape the business environment and civil society for the foreseeable future. For all sides, therefore, the opportunity to shape the debates surrounding the social responsibilities of business, and the means and extent to which business should undertake the role of the 'Corporate Citizen', have significant implications.

This Reader seeks to provide an initial introduction to many of the key issues and themes that are emerging within the CSR field. The book explores the many differing debates, approaches and strategies that surround the emergence of socially responsible business practice. It examines the pressures encouraging companies to adopt more ethical business strategies, the types of practices and strategies which different companies have sought to develop in this field, and the potential advantages that are identified for a socially responsible business.

The debate surrounding the role of business in society, through its very nature, involves a broad range of different voices and opinions. This is not just a discussion by business for business. It is also not just an academic exercise in understanding a changing management environment. The current and future role of business in a globalized society has social, political and environmental ramifications. It is within this broader context that the readings in this book should be considered. In seeking to reflect such diverse voices, clearly some key writings have had to be omitted. In this sense, the readings included in this book should not be taken as a definitive collection of the major works within the CSR field. Rather, it seeks to provide the reader with a critical overview, as seen from a range of diverse perspectives, regarding the current state of CSR activity. Within the book you will therefore find extracts from academic texts, company documents, comment from non-governmental organizations (NGOs) and business organizations, CSR frameworks and guidelines.

The selections have also been chosen for their individual merit as thought-provoking pieces; articles that challenge the reader to consider what the role of business in society should be and how far the development of CSR represents a concerted effort by the business community to tackle these responsibilities seriously. I have often felt that the field of CSR is a continuing puzzle. For every occasion in which one starts to identify merit and true value in the actions of companies, another article appears which makes one question whether there is any real commitment behind the responsible business language and raises a cynical eyebrow towards the concept of CSR. Personally, I can still not decide exactly what value to attribute to the development of CSR (a position that often causes significant confusion for my students who would like to be handed a definitive answer!). However, CSR has provided an opportunity to discuss and challenge and engage in debates surrounding the contemporary and future relationship between business, the state and civil society. This book, and the readings contained within it, is designed to encourage readers to engage in this debate and develop their own perspectives.

Chapter one seeks to develop a contextual understanding of the emergence of CSR. The chapter focuses on the changing pressures that have led to a reassessment of the relationship between business and civil society. It highlights the emerging challenges that confront contemporary business and discusses a range of pressures which have helped to shift the balance of power between business, the state and civil society; most notably the onset of globalization and the environmental challenges of creating a sustainable society.

Chapter two focuses upon critical perspectives on contemporary business activity. In the light of increased public protest and emerging corporate scandals, recent years have witnessed heightened hostility towards businesses and in particular the role of multinational corporations. The chapter focuses on the question 'What is wrong with contemporary global business?', highlighting some of the critics of the contemporary business environment and the claims that too much power and influence is being wielded by modern corporations.

Chapter three focuses on the question of what exactly we should expect companies to be responsible for. It highlights some of the foundation stones within the concept of CSR and corporate citizenship, the debates surrounding the role of business in modern society and the claims that businesses need to recognize their social responsibilities in order to develop and survive. In doing so, it starts to develop a picture of a sustainable, responsible business.

Chapter four examines some of the codes and guidelines within the CSR field that have emerged in recent years. Given the broad range of definitions and concepts that have been placed under the rubric of CSR, frameworks have been sought which help companies to identify what activities they should focus on and how they should seek to report and measure their progress in these areas. A number of such codes and frameworks are examined in this chapter, to provide a picture of what are perceived as the central tenets of responsible business activity and the merits of these frameworks in helping companies achieve these.

Chapter five focuses upon examining the attempts by companies to put some of the CSR principles, ideas and strategies into practice. At the heart of much of the CSR activity has been a call for greater transparency and honesty in the actions of modern corporations, and with it, a closer engagement with a stakeholder community which often extends way beyond the traditional concerns of shareholders. As the notion of stakeholder management has come to the fore, companies have increased the extent to which they seek to create an ongoing dialogue with their stakeholders in providing greater clarity and transparency regarding their actions. This chapter highlights some of these processes of engagement, focusing on both positive and negative perceptions of stakeholder dialogue and company CSR reporting.

The final chapter seeks to raise some questions regarding the future of CSR and responsible business practice. In doing so, it focuses on readings that question whether CSR is merely another passing management strategy or whether it is a sustainable concept that will shape the future direction in which companies interact with the societies within which they operate. Does CSR really provide the foundation stone for significant change in the ethical and environmental practices of business or, in seeking to appease critical voices, is CSR actually damaging the primary responsibilities of the business community?

NOTES

1   A similar introductory overview may be found in Burchell and Cook 2006.
2   See also Levitt 1958.

REFERENCES

Andriof, J. and M. McIntosh (2001) 'Introduction', in J. Andriof and M. McIntosh (eds) *Perspectives on Corporate Citizenship,* Sheffield, Greenleaf Publishing, pp. 13–24.

Andriof, J., B. Waddock, S. Husted and S. Rahman (2002) *Unfolding Stakeholder Thinking: Theory, Responsibility and Engagement,* Sheffield, Greenleaf Publishing.

Bauman, Z. (1998) *Work, Consumption and the New Poor,* Milton Keynes, Open University Press.

Bell, D. (1976) *The Coming of Post-industrial Society,* New York, Basic Books.

Bowen, H.R. (1953) *The Social Responsibilities of the Businessman,* New York, Harper and Row.

Burchell, J. and J. Cook (2006) 'Confronting the Corporate Citizen: Expanding the Challenges of Corporate Social Responsibility', *International Journal of Sociology and Social Policy,* Vol. 26, Nos 3/4, pp. 121–137.

Burchell, J. and S. Lightfoot (2003) 'The EU and Sustainable Development: What Next After Johannesburg', in J. Barry and B. Baxter (eds) *Europe, Globalisation and the Challenge of Sustainability,* London, Routledge.

Cox, R. (1999) 'Civil Society at the Turn of the Millennium', *Review of International Studies,* Vol. 25, pp. 3–28.

Friedman, M. (1962) *Capitalism and Freedom,* London, University of Chicago Press.

Hutton, W. (1995) *The State We're In,* London, Jonathan Cape.

Klein, N. (2000) *No Logo,* London, Flamingo.

Levitt, T. (1958) 'The Danger of Social Responsibility', *Harvard Business Review,* Vol.36, No.5, pp. 41–50.

Nahapiet, J. and S. Ghoshal (1998) 'Social Capital, Intellectual Capital and the Organisational Advantage', *Academy of Management Review,* Vol.23, No.2, pp. 242–266.

Sklair, L. (2001) *The Transnational Capitalist Class,* Oxford, Blackwell.

Weiser, J. and S. Zadek (2000) *Conversations With Disbelievers: Persuading Companies to Address Social Challenges,* Report Published by the Ford Foundation.

CHAPTER ONE

Globalization, sustainable development and the changing business environment

IN UNDERSTANDING THE nature and growth of the concept of CSR it is first necessary to consider what changes and pressures have emerged that have influenced the ways in which business functions or at least is perceived to function. The suggestion here is that certain pressures are emerging which are shifting the interaction and balance of power between the state, business and civil society, and it is this shift in roles and responsibilities that is raising new questions regarding what roles and responsibilities business is undertaking within this new set-up. In particular, this chapter focuses on two key concepts which appear to be at the heart of this process of change: namely the evolution of globalization and the environmental push towards sustainable development.

GETTING TO GRIPS WITH GLOBALIZATION

Both terms, 'globalization' and 'sustainable development', represent a wide-ranging disparate set of ideas when examined closely. In both cases the exact nature of the process and the potential impact are open to a vast array of differing interpretations. In the case of globalization the impact is viewed in both positive and negative terms. In general globalization may be seen to reflect the underlying processes in modern society which have seen a strengthening of social interaction and connections that stretch beyond the traditional confines of the nation state. While the concept has a relatively long history, the increasing impact of globalization largely coincided with the period since the early 1970s which has witnessed a growing connection, both political and economic, across nations especially within the developed West. As Held and McGrew (2000) note in their discussion of globalization, the impact of this process has been felt in terms of economic, political and social implications.

In seeking to provide evidence of the increased globalized nature of contemporary society, theorists point to a broad range of different phenomena which have combined to create closer interaction across national boundaries. First, we have seen in recent years a dramatic change in the nature of global communications and media networks. The dramatic evolution of information technology and the growth and reach of communication tools such as the internet have without doubt changed the manner in which we communicate whether in business or in social terms. On a personal level, we are now able to interact with people across the globe through real-time conversations, e-mail interactions, the emergence of mobile phone technology and so on. Distance is no longer a severe restraint on the types of relationships we can develop and the level of information to which we have access. Increasingly, virtual interactions through cyber space are superseding actual physical encounters.

For the business community, obviously, the evolution of modern communications technology has had a significant impact on the nature of business activity in contemporary society. Recent years have witnessed a dramatic expansion of the global financial system in which financial transactions can be undertaken on a global scale within a few brief seconds. The fluctuating fortunes of the major international money markets are today closely tied to one another, with global economic consequences. The collapse of a number of South East Asian economies during the 1990s gave a dramatic example of this process with repercussions felt across the globe. In addition, the reduction in the importance of physical location has been a vital factor in the increased role, power and influence of large-scale multinational companies (MNCs) which now command a broad level of international global trade. Companies are no longer forced to locate production and management together. Within the global marketplace, companies now have greater flexibility to relocate production to more advantageous locations with the promise of broader international markets.

The shift towards a more global level of interaction and a global business community has also resulted in the increasing influence of a number of international institutions functioning beyond the level of the individual nation state. Most notable of these developments have been the emergence of the European Union as a key economic actor and the growth in influence of the World Trade Organization, the International Monetary Fund, the United Nations and the World Bank.

All these developments have had a significant impact on the way in which business activity is conducted in modern society. Greater networking of global economies has provided significant opportunities for financial investment. The growth in MNCs has been accompanied by a global distribution of products and brands with many companies such as Nike, McDonald's and Walt Disney becoming globally recognized. Clearly the process of globalization has undoubtedly opened up a broad range of challenges and opportunities for the business community.

Globalization has also, however, brought with it a number of problems and negative impacts. Critics of the nature of contemporary global trade argue that while, for some, globalization has brought significant benefits, for others it has led to a vast power and wealth imbalance which has left many in poverty and exclusion from the supposed global society. Vandana Shiva, for example, suggests that economic insecurity and exclusion for many within the global economy has been a significant factor in the increased levels of terrorism witnessed within modern society. Others, such as Klein (2000), focus upon the increasingly homogenized nature of modern society brought about through the mass branding of all aspects of contemporary life. Authors such as these, as will be discussed further in the next chapter, pushed these inequalities to the fore by highlighting the poor working conditions within which many of the products for companies such as Nike, The Gap and Walt Disney were being made.

GLOBALIZATION AND THE ENVIRONMENT

Another key aspect of the evolution of globalization has been the impact that these processes have had upon the natural environment. Since the 1960s we have witnessed a growing popular concern regarding the damage human activities may be having to the natural environment, precipitated by a never-ending stream of environmental disasters. In the late 1950s local inhabitants of Minimata in Japan developed lead poisoning from eating fish caught in the bay. Investigations found the cause of this disaster to be pollution leaked into the bay from a chemical factory owned by the Chisso Corporation. The corporation denied any links between the illnesses and its factory and continued to leak mercury into the bay until the late 1960s when public pressure finally brought about government action. In 1967 the *Torrey Canyon* oil-tanker ran aground, spilling its cargo of crude oil, creating a 270-square-mile oil-slick and contaminating 120 miles of Cornish coastline. The company and the British government both found themselves relatively powerless in their efforts to clear up the oil-slick, and millions watched on television as the oil devastated large areas of pristine coastline and killed swathes of wild animals. In 1984, in Bhopal, India, 3000 local residents died and many more became subsequently ill when an explosion at the Union Carbide pesticide plant sent a plume of toxic gas into the air. The Bhopal Medical Appeal estimates that approximately 20,000 people have since died as a result of the accident.

While these events in many ways reflected localized environmental problems, other events highlighted the growing global nature of the environmental challenge. In the Ukraine the explosion of the Chernobyl nuclear reactor in April 1986 released a radioactive cloud which spread radiation across a vast area of Northern Europe, devastating the livelihoods of farmers throughout the area. Furthermore, during the 1980s and 1990s scientists began to identify evidence of an increasing hole in the earth's ozone layer, and a pattern of global warming, brought on, they argued, by the increasing societal emission of greenhouse gases. It appeared increasingly that society's growing reliance on industrialization and economic growth was having a severely detrimental impact on the natural environment. Stead and Stead (2004: 26), for example, summarize the current pressures on the natural world as follows:

> Some 2.4 billion people currently live in water-stressed nations, and that figure will likely increase by about 50 per cent over the next twenty-five years. Somewhere between 10 per cent and 20 per cent of the world's cropland is degraded because of soil erosion, salinization and so forth. There are between 300 million and 500 million tons of hazardous wastes generated and disposed of each year worldwide. Global carbon emissions increased approximately 9 per cent in the 1990s, reaching 68 billion tons per year by 2000. These are just a few of the patterns indicating that current human activity is ecologically unsustainable.

Understandably, at the heart of much of the concern over the potential environmental crisis lay a questioning of the role of business in creating these problems. Environmental campaigners argued that the nature of modern industrial society had inevitably led to a process of destruction of the natural world, arguing that the constant pursuit of economic growth, increased consumption and high-risk technological developments could not be maintained within a planet containing finite resources. The environment, it was argued, could not merely be regarded as a business externality. Under increasing pressure from civil society campaign groups, environmental researchers and local populations, governments began to respond to the environmental agenda, seeking to create a level of international agreement regarding the future protection of the natural world and to find a way to balance economic growth with environmental protection. The central concept to emerge from this process has been that of sustainable development, defined by the Brundtland Commission as 'development that meets the needs of the present without compromising the ability of future generations to meet their own needs' (WCED 1987: 43).

At the heart of this concept lies an awareness that society must identify a new course which can balance the demands of society, the economy and the environment more effectively than has been witnessed in the past. While there has been growing acceptance for the idea of a more sustainable society, the precise processes through which we are to get there have been far more contentious. Sustainable development remains a relatively open and contested concept with many varying definitions. For some theorists such as Arne Naess (1989) and Edward Goldsmith (1972), for example, sustainable development can only be achieved through significant structural changes within contemporary society. The change in attitude required to meet the sustainability target, it is argued, requires a radical rethinking of both economic and political structures and a fundamental shift in the nature of industrialization and capitalist production processes in which the driving force of economic growth is replaced. At the other end of the spectrum, by contrast, theorists such as David Pearce *et al.* (1989) argue that it is possible to integrate growth and environmental protection into one economic system. While economic growth, he argues, is necessary as the driving force of modern society, it is possible to use economic tools to protect the environment by utilizing them to introduce economic costs into the overall costs of production. Clearly, therefore, sustainable development, and in particular the process of achieving a sustainable system, remains a contestable process. Without doubt the direction in which sustainable development strategy evolves will strongly influence the type of environment within which future businesses will have to function. Therefore, it is no surprise to see the business community responding with its own interpretation and approach to the environmental issue.

ADAPTING TO THE CHALLENGES

Clearly, therefore, the modern globalized world has brought with it a range of new relationships and opportunities but also problems and challenges. For many analysts it appeared that the supposed global marketplace was creating significant opportunities for some while sustaining increasingly poor conditions for the majority. These concerns over the environment and the ethical actions of modern multinationals have produced increased public criticism and resulted during the 1990s in a succession of high-profile large-scale 'anti-corporate' and 'anti-capitalist' protests outside meetings of the WTO, the World Bank and the G8 in locations across the globe from Seattle to Genoa.

At the heart of most of these campaigns has been a concern regarding the increasing levels of power being leveraged by multinational corporations and the unethical practices being highlighted from within the international business community. In particular, there is a questioning of the power relationship between business and governments and concern that the balance of power is tipping dangerously far towards business.

The central question one needs to confront in terms of this changing relationship is what control and restrictions can a nation state confer on a multinational business? And under what conditions might a nation state find itself compromised in this relationship? This issue has become increasingly important as a number of the larger multinationals now control an economic turnover that is larger than that of many nation states themselves. In what ways then might a company be able to exert pressure upon a national government? As mentioned earlier, globalization has made it far easier for companies to locate different aspects of their business in different locations across the globe. In particular we have witnessed a dramatic transferral of production processes to countries with lower wage demands and more relaxed labour regulations. Under these circumstances there is a significant level of competition from countries seeking to encourage companies to locate in their country. This can undoubtedly provide companies with significant leverage when seeking advantageous conditions, and indeed, the threat that a company may relocate if governments seek to introduce legislation that may hamper its business is a definite tool in the MNCs' armoury. Similarly, as the environmental disasters of the past thirty years have highlighted, pollution is no respecter of national boundaries. Any amount of national environmental legislation can only take the move towards a sustainable society so far. Global environmental problems require global, international solutions; solutions that cannot be provided by individual nation states alone.

Pressures such as these have led some commentators to suggest that nation states are increasingly being stripped of any real power in the modern global economy. Indeed, Daniel Bell (1976) suggests that nation states are becoming too small for the big problems in life and too big for the small problems, leaving them with the trappings and ceremony of authority but with very little actual power. Under these conditions it is not merely the relationship between business and government that is changing. In a similar manner, we are arguably seeing some interesting changes in the relationships between civil society and both business and government.

The readings in this chapter reflect many of the initial themes and concerns outlined above. Held and McGrew provide an introductory overview to the nature of modern globalized society, pointing to both its positive and negative attributes. The second reading from the International Institute for Sustainable Development highlights the connections between the processes of globalization and the emerging environmental challenges that have accompanied it, focusing on the close connections between the two. The third reading ties closely to many of the themes we will be discussing in Chapter two. Vandana Shiva highlights the potential dangers for society emerging from the continuing globalization process. She suggests that globalization is creating an ever-expanding gulf in wealth and power across the globe, with significant repercussions for society.

The fourth reading is a more light-hearted look at the impact of globalization through the eyes of writer Dave Gorman. While on a peculiar trip around the world he comes face to face with the impact of the global brand in Seattle.

GUIDE FOR FURTHER READING

There is a wealth of literature on the issues of globalization and sustainable development from a whole range of differing perspectives. In addition to the readings selected here see also Bell, D. (1976) *The Coming of Post-industrial Society*, New York, Basic Books; Kofman, E. and G. Youngs (eds) (1996) *Globalization: Theory and Practice*, London, Pinter; Held, D. and A. McGrew (eds) (2000) *The Global Transformations Reader*, Cambridge, Polity Press; Holliday, C., S. Schmidheiny and P. Watts (eds) (2002) *Walking the Talk: The Business Case for Sustainable Development*, Sheffield, Greenleaf; Lee, K., A. Holland and D. McNeill (2000) *Global Sustainable Development in the 21st Century*, Edinburgh, Edinburgh University Press.

For some web-based information try the following:

- www.globalization101.org – An introduction to many of the key issues and questions surrounding globalization by the Centre for Strategic and International Studies.
- www.ifg.org – The international forum on globalization. Provides a wealth of resources, links and research around the central themes of globalization.
- www.earthsummit2002.org – Stakeholder forum's world summit website giving background and detailed assessments of the ideas and outcomes from the Johannesburg summit.
- www.sustainable-development.gov.uk – The UK government's sustainable development website.

REFERENCES

Bell, D. (1976) *The Coming of Post-industrial Society*, New York, Basic Books.

Goldsmith, E. (1972) *A Blueprint for Survivial*, London, Penguin.

Held, D. and A. McGrew (eds) (2000) *The Global Transformations Reader*, Cambridge, Polity Press.

Klein, N. (2000) *No Logo*, London, Flamingo.

Naess, A. (1989) *Ecology, Community and Lifestyle: Outline of an Ecosophy*, Cambridge, Cambridge University Press.

Pearce, D., A. Markandya and E.B. Barbier (1989) *Blueprint for a Green Economy*, London, Earthscan.

Stead, W. and J.G. Stead (2004) *Sustainable Strategic Management*, Armonk, NY, ME Sharpe.

WCED (1987) *Our Common Future. The Report of the Brundtland Commission*, Oxford, Oxford University Press.

David Held and Anthony McGrew

GLOBALIZATION

Introduction

IN HIS REPORT to the special Millennium Summit, UN Secretary-General Kofi Annan sought to define a new role for the United Nations at the centre of 'global governance' (UN Secretary-General, 2000). Since the UN's creation in 1945 a vast nexus of global and regional institutions has evolved, surrounded by a proliferation of non-governmental agencies and advocacy networks seeking to influence the agenda and direction of international public policy. As Kofi Annan's remarks acknowledged, though world government remains a fanciful idea, there does exist an evolving global governance complex – embracing states, international institutions, transnational networks and agencies (both public and private) – which functions, with variable effect, to promote, regulate or intervene in the common affairs of humanity. Over the last five decades, its scope and impact have expanded dramatically such that its activities have become significantly politicized, as global protests against the World Trade Organization attest. Few architects of the UN system could have envisaged that postwar multilateralism would be transformed into the 'complex multilateralism' of the twenty-first century (O'Brien *et al.*, 2000). Whether the rhetoric of global governance conceals an underlying historical continuity in the geopolitical management of world affairs remains, however, the focus of intense theoretical and political controversy. [. . .]

Globalization and the new political circumstances of world order

Any discussion of global governance must start with an understanding of the changing fabric of international society. Woven into this are the complex processes known as globalization. Globalization refers to a historical process which transforms the spatial organization of social relations and transactions, generating transcontinental or inter-regional networks of interaction and the exercise of power (Held *et al.*, 1999). Different historical forms of globalization can be identified, including the epoch of world discovery in the early modern period, the era of European empires and the present era shaped by the neoliberal global economic project. These different historical forms of globalization are characterized by distinctive spatio-temporal and organizational attributes; that is, particular patterns of extensity, intensity, velocity and impact in global relations, flows and networks, alongside different degrees of institutionalization, modes of stratification and reproduction. Although contemporary globalization has elements in common with its past phases, it is distinguished by unique spatio-temporal and organizational features, creating a world in which the extensive reach of global relations and networks is matched by their relative high intensity, high velocity and high impact propensity across many facets of social life, from the economic to the environmental.

To understand the implications of globalization for the governance of world affairs it is necessary to specify some of the key domains of activity and interaction in and through which global processes are evolving. The focus here is on the economic, the environmental and the political. The focus is on the economic because it is clearly a principal driving force of contemporary globalization, and no account of the nature and form of globalization can be pursued without reference to it. The focus is on the environment because it illustrates most acutely the changing scale of market failure and the new global risks faced not just by individual political communities but also by humankind as a whole. And the focus is on politics, law and security in order to highlight the changing form and context of state power, and the pressing agenda of global public issues that require more extensive and intensive forms of global regulation.

Economic globalization

Today, all countries are engaged in international trade, and in nearly all the value of trade accounts for significant proportions of their national income. The historical evidence shows that international trade has grown to unprecedented levels, both absolutely and relatively in relation to national income. Among the OECD (Organization for Economic Cooperation and Development) states, trade levels today (measured as a share of GDP) are much greater than they were in the late nineteenth century, the belle époque of world trade growth. World trade (merchandise and services) in 1999 was valued at over $6.8 trillion, with exports having grown, as a percentage of world output, from 7.9 per cent in 1913 to 17.2 per cent in 1998 (Maddison, 2001; WTO, 2001).

As barriers to trade have fallen across the world, markets have become global for many goods and, increasingly, services. No economy can any longer be insulated from global competition. While national economies taken together can gain overall from increased trade, the gains are highly uneven. There are clear winners and losers, both between and within countries. An increased proportion of trade between developed and developing countries, for example, can hurt low-skilled workers in developed countries while simultaneously increasing the income of higher skilled workers. National governments may protect and compensate those who are vulnerable as a result of structural change, but increased demands on and costs of the welfare state tend to be resisted by employers in the trading industries vulnerable to global competition (Garrett, 1998; Rodrik, 1997). The politics of trade creates complex and sometimes unstable political coalitions.

While global exports and trading relations are more important than ever in the world economy, transnational production is even more significant. Foreign direct investment reached three times as many countries in 2000 as it did in 1985 (UNCTAD, 2001, p. 4). Today, 60,000 multinational corporations (MNCs), with nearly 820,000 foreign subsidiaries, sell goods and services worth $15,680 billion across the globe each year, and employ twice as many people today compared with 1990 (UNCTAD, 2001). Multinational corporations have taken economic interconnectedness to new levels. They account for about 25 per cent of world production and 70 per cent of world trade, while their sales are equivalent to almost half of world GDP (Held *et al.*, 1999; UNCTAD, 2001). A quarter to a third of world trade is intrafirm trade between branches of multinationals.

The bulk of the assets of multinationals are typically found in OECD countries and in a relatively small number of developing ones (see Held and McGrew, 2000, pp. 25–7). Of total world foreign direct investment in 2000, 95 per cent went to 30 countries (UNCTAD, 2001, p. 5). Nevertheless, over the last few decades developing economies' shares of foreign investment flows (inwards and outwards) and of world exports have increased considerably (Castells, 1998; UNCTAD, 2001; UNDP, 1998). The newly industrializing economies (NIEs) of East Asia and Latin America have become an increasingly important destination for OECD investment and an increasingly significant source of OECD imports: São Paulo, it is sometimes said, is Germany's largest industrial city (Dicken, 1998). By the late 1990s almost 50 per cent of the world's total of manufacturing jobs were located in developing economies, while over 60 per cent of the exports of developing countries to the industrialized world were manufactured goods, a twelve-fold increase in less than four decades (UNDP, 1998). Contemporary economic globalization, albeit highly unevenly spread, is not just an OECD phenomenon, but embraces all continents and regions.

Alongside transnational production networks, the power of global finance has become central to economic globalization. World financial flows have grown exponentially, especially since the 1970s. Daily turnover on the foreign exchange markets exceeds $1.2 trillion, and billions of dollars of financial assets are traded globally, particularly through derivative products (BIS, 2001). Few countries today are insulated from the fluctuations of global financial markets, although their relationship to these markets differs markedly between North and South.

The 1997 East Asian crisis forcibly illustrated the impact of global financial markets. The financial disruption triggered by the collapse of the Thai baht demonstrated new levels of economic connectedness. The Asian 'tiger' economies had benefited from the rapid increase of financial flows to developing countries in the 1990s and were widely held to be positive examples to the rest of the world. But the heavy flows of short-term capital, often channelled into speculative activity, could be quickly reversed, causing currencies to fall dramatically and far in excess of any real economic imbalances. The inability of the prevailing international financial regime (the International Monetary Fund, Bank for International Settlements, etc.) to manage the turmoil created a wide-ranging debate on its future institutional architecture.

A further important structural change is arising from recurrent exchange rate crises, which have become, since the 1990s, a dominant feature of the current system. Fixed exchange rates are ceasing to be a viable policy option in the face of global capital flows of the current scale and intensity. Between 1990 and 1999 the percentage of countries operating floating exchange rate regimes increased from 21 per cent to 41 per cent

(*Financial Times*, 8 Jan. 2002, p. 10). The choice faced by countries is increasingly between floating rates and monetary union – shown by the launch of the euro and discussion of dollarization in Latin America.

It is easy to misrepresent the political significance of the globalization of economic activity. National and international economic management remains feasible (Held *et al.*, 1999; Hirst and Thompson, 1999). Many states continue to be immensely powerful and to enjoy access to a formidable range of resources, infrastructural capacity and technologies of coordination and control. The continuing lobbying of states and intergovernmental organizations (for example, the World Trade Organization (WTO)) by MNCs confirms the enduring importance of states to the mediation and regulation of global economic activity. Yet economic globalization has significant and discernible impacts which alter the balance of resources, economic and political, within and across borders, requiring more sophisticated and developed systems of global and regional regulation (see the discussion below, pp. 16–19).

Global environmental change

Economic globalization has had a substantial impact on the environment, although it is by no means the sole cause of global environmental problems. From the outset, it is important to distinguish a number of different forms of global environmental change. They include:

- encounters between previously separated ecological systems of different parts of the world;
- the overspill of the effects of environmental degradation from one state to another (involving the creation, for example, of environmental refugees);
- transboundary pollution and risks (such as acid rain and nuclear power);
- transportation and diffusion of wastes and polluting products across the globe (toxic waste trade, global relocation of dirty industries);
- pollution and degradation of the global commons (the oceans and the atmosphere);
- and, finally, the formation of global institutions, regimes, networks and treaties that seek to regulate all these forms of environmental degradation.

It needs to be stressed that until the early to mid-twentieth century most forms of environmental damage – at least those that could be detected – were concentrated in particular regions and locales. Since then, the globalization of environmental degradation has accelerated as a result of a number of critical factors: fifty years of resource-intensive, high-pollution growth in the countries of the OECD; the industrialization of Russia and other states of the former Soviet Union and of Eastern Europe; the rapid industrialization of many parts of the South; and a massive rise in the global population. In addition, it is now possible to understand risk and environmental change more deeply and with much greater accuracy: for instance, the consequences of the steady build-up of damaging gases in the earth's atmosphere (carbon dioxide, methane, nitrous and sulphur oxides, CFCs).

In response to the intensification of, and publicity surrounding, environmental issues, there has been an interlinked process of cultural and political globalization. This can be exemplified by the emergence of new scientific and epistemic communities; new environmental movements organized transnationally and with transnational concerns; and new international institutions, regimes and conventions such as those agreed in 1992 at the Earth Summit in Brazil and in subsequent follow-up meetings. Unfortunately, none of the latter have as yet been able to acquire sufficient political influence, domestic support or international authority to do more than (at best) limit the worst excesses of some of the global environmental threats.

Not all environmental problems are global, of course; such a view would be highly misleading. Nonetheless, there has been a striking shift in the physical and environmental conditions – that is, in the extent, intensity and rapid transmission of environmental problems – affecting human affairs in general. These processes have moved politics dramatically away from an activity which crystallizes first and foremost around state and interstate concerns. It is clearer than ever that the fortunes of political communities and peoples can no longer be simply understood in exclusively national or territorial terms. In the context of intense global and regional interconnectedness, the very idea of political community as an exclusive, territorially delimited unit is at best unconvincing and at worst anachronistic. In a world in which global warming connects the long-term fate of many Pacific islands to the actions of tens of millions of private motorists across the globe, the conventional territorial conception of political community appears profoundly inadequate. Globalization weaves together, in highly complex and abstract systems, the fates of households, communities and peoples in distant regions of the globe (McGrew, 1997, p. 237). While it would be a mistake to conclude that political communities are without distinctive degrees of division or cleavage at their borders, they are clearly shaped by multiple cross-border interaction networks and power systems. Thus questions are raised both about the fate of the idea of political community, and about the appropriate level for the effective regulation of human affairs: the national, the regional or the global. The proper locus of politics and the articulation of the public interest becomes a puzzling matter.

Political globalization

Economic and environmental globalization has not occurred in a political vacuum; there has been a shift in the nature and form of political organization as well. The distinctive form this has taken in the contemporary period is the emergence of 'global politics' – the increasingly extensive form of political networks and activity. Political decisions and actions in one part of the world can rapidly acquire worldwide ramifications. Sites of political action and/or decision-making can become linked through rapid communications into complex networks of political interaction. Associated with this 'stretching' of politics is a frequent intensification or deepening of global processes such that 'action at a distance' permeates the social conditions and cognitive worlds of specific places or policy communities (Giddens, 1990). Consequently, developments at the global level – whether economic, social or environmental – can have almost instantaneous local consequences and vice versa.

The idea of global politics challenges the traditional distinctions between the domestic and the international, the territorial and the non-territorial, and the inside and the outside, as embedded in conventional conceptions of 'the political' (see Held et al., 1999, chs 1, 2 and 8). It also highlights the richness and complexity of the interconnections that transcend states and societies in the global order. Global politics today, moreover, is anchored not just in traditional geopolitical concerns but also in a large diversity of economic, social and ecological questions. Pollution, drugs, human rights and terrorism are among an increasing number of transnational policy issues which cut across territorial jurisdictions and existing political alignments, and which require international cooperation for their effective resolution.

Nations, peoples and organizations are linked, in addition, by many new forms of communication, which range across borders. The revolution in microelectronics, in information technology and in computers has established virtually instantaneous world-wide links which, when combined with the technologies of the telephone, television, cables, satellites and jet transportation, have dramatically altered the nature of political communication. The intimate connection between 'physical setting', 'social situation' and politics, which distinguished most political associations from premodern to modern times, has been ruptured; the new communication systems create new experiences, new modes of understanding and new frames of political reference independently of direct contact with particular peoples, issues or events. The speed with which the events of 11 September 2001 ramified across the world and made mass terrorism a global issue is one poignant example.

The development of new communication systems generates a world in which the particularities of place and individuality are constantly represented and reinterpreted through regional and global communication networks. But the relevance of these systems goes far beyond this, for they are fundamental to the possibility of organizing political action and exercising political power across vast distances (Deibert, 1997). For example, the expansion of international and transnational organizations, the extension of inter-national rules and legal mechanisms – their construction and monitoring – have all received an impetus from the new communication systems, and organizations of all sorts depend on them as a means to further their aims.

In mapping these developments, it is important to explore the way in which the sovereign state now lies at the intersection of a vast array of international regimes and organizations that have been established to manage whole areas of transnational activity (trade, financial flows, crime and so on) and collective policy problems. The rapid growth of transnational issues and problems has involved a spread of layers of political regulation both within and across political boundaries. It has been marked by the transformation of aspects of territorially based political decision-making, the development of regional and global organizations and institutions, and the emergence of regional and global law.

This can be illustrated by a number of developments, including, most obviously, the rapid emergence of multilateral cooperation and international organizations. New forms of multilateral and transnational politics have evolved, involving governments, inter-governmental organizations (IGOs) and a wide variety of transnational pressure groups and international non-governmental organizations (INGOs). At the beginning of the twentieth century there were just 37 IGOs and 176 INGOs, whereas in 1996 there were 1,830 IGOs and 38,243 INGOs (UIA, 1997). In addition, there has been a very substantial development in the number of international treaties in force, as well as in the number of international regimes, altering the situational context of states (Held *et al.*, 1999, chs 1–2).

To this pattern of extensive political interconnectedness can be added the dense web of activity of the key international policy-making forums, including the summits of the UN, the G7 (Group of seven leading industrial nations), the IMF, WTO, EU, APEC (Asia-Pacific Economic Cooperation), ARF (the regional forum of ASEAN, the Association of South East Asian Nations) and MERCOSUR (Southern Cone Common Market – in Latin

America), as well as many other official and unofficial meetings. In the middle of the nineteenth century, there were two or three interstate conferences or congresses a year; today the number totals over 4,000. National government is increasingly locked into an array of global, regional and multilayered systems of governance – and can barely monitor it all, let alone stay in command.

Political communities can no longer be thought of, if they ever could with any validity, simply as discrete worlds or as self-enclosed political spaces; they are enmeshed in complex structures of overlapping forces, relations and networks. Clearly, these are structured by inequality and hierarchy. However, even the most powerful among them – including the most powerful states – do not remain unaffected by the changing conditions and processes of regional and global enmeshment. In particular, the idea of a political community of fate – of a self-determining collectivity – can no longer be located meaningfully only within the boundaries of a single nation-state. Some of the most fundamental forces and processes which determine the nature of life chances within and across political communities are now beyond the reach of individual nation-states.

The political world at the start of the twenty-first century is marked by a significant series of new types of political externality or 'boundary problem'. In the past, of course, nation-states principally resolved their differences over boundary matters by pursuing reasons of state backed by diplomatic initiatives and, ultimately, by coercive means. But this geopolitical logic appears singularly inadequate and inappropriate to resolve the many complex issues, from economic regulation to resource depletion and environmental degradation, which engender – at seemingly ever greater speeds – an intermeshing of 'national fortunes'. In all major areas of government policy, the enmeshment of national political communities in regional and global processes involves them in intensive issues of transboundary coordination and control. Political space for the development and pursuit of effective government and the accountability of political power is no longer coterminous with a delimited national territory. National communities themselves by no means make and determine decisions and policies exclusively for themselves when they decide on such issues as the regulation of health, conserving the environment and combating terrorism; and national governments by no means simply determine what is right or appropriate exclusively for their own citizens.

These new political circumstances present a unique challenge to a world order designed in accordance with the Westphalian principle of exclusive sovereign rule over a bounded territory and its associated geopolitical mechanisms for governing world affairs.

From geopolitics to global governance?

Globalization poses, with renewed immediacy, the question of how world affairs are, and should be, governed (Smouts, 2001). At issue is whether the thickening institutional density, expanding jurisdiction, intensifying transnational politics and deepening impact of suprastate regulation denotes a qualitative – structural – shift in how global affairs and transboundary problems are governed. For Rosenau, and many others, these developments represent the evolving infrastructure of a fragile system of global governance – a new complex multilateralism (Rosenau, 1999). Just how far this system embodies a radical break with traditional geopolitical modes of regulating world order (hegemony and the balance of power), or whether indeed it is displacing or supplementing them, remains the source of continuing disagreement (Cox, 1997; Gill, 2000; Keohane and Nye, 2000; Rosenau, 1999, 2000a; Ruggie, 1998). Sceptics, such as Gilpin, doubt that there is any substance to these claims, arguing that global governance is at best pure rhetoric, at worst a utopian aspiration (Gilpin, 2001).

Several factors have encouraged this burgeoning discourse on global governance. First, the end of the Cold War brought to a close the era of stalemate politics within the UN and associated agencies. This created the prospect of a more active and effective international governance. It also enabled a more inclusive form of multilateralism than had been feasible in a politically and economically divided world. Moreover, it contributed to the dwindling legitimacy accorded to hierarchical or hegemonic modes of regulating world order. These modes are contested by a diverse range of transnational pressure groups, social movements and protest movements. Second, as already noted, the intensification of globalization has increased the demand for multilateral cooperation and the provision of global public goods, including financial stability, the setting of common standards in ever more areas, and environmental protection. A new infrastructure of global regulation has evolved, reaching ever more deeply into the domestic affairs of states and societies, and it remains central to the promotion and management of globalization. Third, during the last three decades there has been a significant reconfiguration of state power and authority. Governing has become a more complex and volatile process. Realizing cherished domestic political goals, delivering core policy programmes and resolving domestic crises increasingly involve the state in a negotiated order between diverse agencies, both public and private, within and beyond the state (Bergesen and Lunde, 1999). Governance, as a concept of analysis, refers to this process of social coordination with a public purpose – a process in which the state plays a strategic but not necessarily the dominant role (Pierre and Peters, 2000).

Given the absence of a world government, the concept of global governance provides a language for describing the nexus of systems of rule-making, political coordination and problem-solving which transcend states and societies (Rosenau, 2000a, 2000b). It is particularly relevant to describing the structures and processes of governing beyond the state where there exists no supreme or singular political authority. Theoretically, it is much more than simply a descriptive term: it constitutes a broad analytical approach to addressing the central questions of political life under conditions of globalization, namely: who rules, in whose interests, by what mechanisms and for what purposes?

Global governance: towards a new world order?

As an analytical approach, global governance rejects the conventional state-centric conception of world politics and world order. The principal unit of analysis is taken to be global, regional or transnational systems of authoritative rule-making and implementation. As Rosenau comments,

> By locating rule systems at the heart of our theoretical formulations, we can trace and assess the processes of governance wherever they may occur. That is, through focusing on rule systems we will not be confined to the world of states and will be empowered to explore issues and processes in terms of the way in which authority is created, dispersed, consolidated or otherwise employed to

exercise control with respect to the numerous issues and processes that states
are unable or unwilling to address.

(2000a, p. 188)

At the analytical core of the global governance approach is a concern with understanding
and explaining the political significance of global, regional and transnational authority
structures (Boli, 1999; Smouts, 2001).

Accordingly, the focus is on the evolving system of (formal and informal) political
coordination – across multiple levels from the local to the global – among public authorities (states and IGOs) and private agencies seeking to realize common purposes or resolve
collective problems. Although this system transcends the classic postwar form of multilateralism, it is far from a 'unified global system underpinned by global law enforcement'
(Cable, 1999, p. 54). It differs dramatically from the concept of world government in
that it does not presuppose the idea of a central global public authority, which legislates
for the common affairs of humanity. On the contrary, it is defined by diverse sources of
rule-making, political authority and power.

Several observations are made in the literature concerning the institutional architecture of global governance:

1   It is *multilayered* in the sense that it is constituted by and through the structural
     enmeshment of several principal infrastructures of governance: the suprastate (such
     as the UN system), the regional (EU, MERCOSUR, ASEAN, etc.), the transnational
     (civil society, business networks and so on), and the substate (community associ-
     ations, and city governments) (Scholte, 2000). Sandwiched between these layers is
     national government.
2   It is often described as polyarchic or *pluralistic* since there is no single locus of
     authority. This is not to imply any equality of power between the participants but
     simply to acknowledge that political authority is decidedly fragmented.
3   It has a *variable geometry* in so far as the relative political significance and regulatory
     capacities of these infrastructures vary considerably around the globe and from issue
     to issue.
4   The system is *structurally complex*, being composed of diverse agencies and networks
     with overlapping (functional and/or spatial) jurisdictions, not to mention differen-
     tial power resources and competencies.
5   Far from national governments being sidelined in this system, they become increas-
     ingly crucial as *strategic sites* for suturing together these various infrastructures of
     governance and legitimizing regulation beyond the state.

A central characteristic of global governance, emphasized particularly in the existing
literature, is the reconfiguration of authority between the various layers or infrastructures
of governance. This is evident in the expanding jurisdiction and competencies of both
suprastate (for instance, the World Intellectual Property Organization (WIPO)) and sub-
state institutions (such as devolved governments and autonomous regions). Although
there is considerable variance from sector to sector – compare for instance the global
impact of the IMF and the International Labour Organization (ILO) – for the most part
the activities of suprastate bodies reach ever more deeply into the internal life of states,
from food standards to banking regulation. Indeed, the most recent and comprehensive

study of global regulation concluded that 'today most citizens greatly underestimate the extent to which most nations' shipping laws are written at the IMO [International Maritime Organization] in London, air safety laws at the ICAO [International Civil Aviation Organization] in Montreal, food standards at the FAO [Food and Agriculture Organization] in Rome, intellectual property rights in Geneva at the WTO/WIPO . . . motor vehicles standards by the ECE [Economic Commission for Europe] in Geneva', to mention but a few sectors (Braithwaite and Drahos, 1999, p. 488).

This relocation and delegation of political authority between the various layers of governance has created what some refer to as a 'new medievalism' since it resembles the complexity of competing jurisdictions, porous administrative boundaries and multiple levels of political authority which characterized medieval Europe. Global governance embodies a complex patchwork of overlapping jurisdictions, generating ambiguities about the principal location of authority and political responsibility. This is particularly evident where conflicts of legal or regulatory principles occur – should global, regional, national or local rules take precedence and how is this to be decided? In the context of the European Union, with a developed supranational legal infrastructure, such conflicts are resolved through juridical mechanisms. At the global level, such mechanisms are largely absent, but where they exist in some form (as with the WTO dispute machinery or WIPO machinery on patents) they provoke concerns about democratic accountability, legitimacy and subsidiarity.

Such concerns are reinforced by what in the study of global governance is sometimes referred to as the privatization of global regulation, that is, a redrawing of the boundaries between public authority and private power. From technical standards to the disbursement of humanitarian assistance and official aid through non-governmental organizations (NGOs), private agencies have become increasingly influential in the formulation and implementation of global public policy. The International Accounting Standards Committee establishes global accounting rules, while the major bond rating agencies make critical judgements about the credit status of governments and public and private organizations around the globe. Much of this privatized governance occurs in the shadow of global public authorities, but to the extent to which corporate and private interests have captured the agendas of such bodies, like those of the WTO, the International Organization of Securities Commissions (IOSCO) and others, there is a fusion of public and private power. The current salience of public–private partnerships, such as the Global AIDS Fund and the Global Compact, articulates the expanding influence of private interests in the formulation as well as the delivery of global policies. Contemporary global governance involves a relocation of authority from public to quasi-public, and to private, agencies.

Associated with this relocation of authority is a shift in the principal modalities of global rule-making and implementation. Although much of the formal business of global governance is conducted within and through established international organizations, a growing literature indicates that significant aspects of the formulation and implementation of global public policy occur within an expanding array of political networks: transgovernmental (such as the Basel Committee on Banking Supervision (BCBS) and the Financial Action Task Force (FATF)), trisectoral (public, corporate, and NGOs), and transnational (such as Médecins Sans Frontières). These networks – which can be ad hoc or institutionalized – have become increasingly important in coordinating the work of experts and functionaries within governments, international organizations, and the corporate and the NGO sectors (further examples are the Global Water Partnership, the World

Commission on Dams, the Global Alliance for Vaccines and Immunization). They function to set policy agendas, disseminate information, formulate rules, establish and implement policy programmes – from measures against money laundering taken by the FATF to global initiatives to counter AIDS. Many of these networks are of a purely bureaucratic nature, but they have also become mechanisms through which civil society and corporate interests are effectively embedded in the global policy process. In part, the growth of these networks is a response to the overload and politicization of multilateral bodies, but it is also an outcome of the growing technical complexity of global policy issues and the communications revolution.

To the extent that a global communications infrastructure has facilitated the evolution of global policy networks, so too it has underwritten the effective worldwide mobilization of protest against the agencies of global governance. This contestation takes many political forms other than direct action, from advocacy (as with the Campaign to Ban Landmines, Jubilee 2000), through surveillance of corporate activities in order to police voluntary codes of conduct (CorpWatch), to resisting the terms of economic globalization (campaigns to outlaw child labour or sweatshop practices). Transnational civil society is integral to the politics of global governance.

For the advocates of the global governance perspective, geopolitical management of global affairs is becoming less plausible (and legitimate) as the sole governing principle of world order. In a highly interconnected world of diverse nation-states, in which non-state actors also wield enormous influence, hierarchical forms of managing global affairs are losing their efficacy and legitimacy.

References

Bergesen, H. and L. Lunde (1999) *Dinosaurs or Dynamos? The United Nations and the World Bank at the Turn of the Century*, London: Earthscan.

BIS (2001) *Quarterly Report, December*, Geneva: Bank For International Settlements.

Boli, J. (1999) 'Conclusion: world authority structures and legitimations', in J. Boli and G. M. Thomas (eds), *Constructing World Culture: International Nongovernmental Organizations since 1875*, Stanford: Stanford University Press.

Braithwaite, J. and P. Drahos (1999) *Global Business Regulation*, Cambridge: Cambridge University Press.

Cable, V. (1999) *Globalization and Global Governance*, London: Royal Institute of International Affairs.

Castells, M. (1998) *End of the Millennium*, Oxford: Blackwell.

Cox, R. W. (ed.) (1997) *The New Realism: Perspectives on Multilateralism and World Order*, London: Macmillan.

Deibert, R. (1997) *Parchment, Printing and Hypermedia*, New York: Cornell University Press.

Dicken, P. (1998) *Global Shift*, London: Paul Chapman.

Garrett, G. (1998) *Partisan Politics in the Global Economy*, Cambridge: Cambridge University Press.

Giddens, A. (1990) *The Consequences of Modernity*, Cambridge: Polity.

Gill, S. (2000) 'New constitutionalism, democratization and global political economy', *Peace Research Abstracts*, 37.

Gilpin, R. (2001) *Global Political Economy*, Princeton: Princeton University Press.

Held, D. and A. McGrew (eds) (2000) *The Global Transformations Reader*, Cambridge: Polity.

Held, D., A. McGrew, D. Goldblatt and J. Perraton (1999) *Global Transformations: Politics, Economics and Culture*, Cambridge: Polity.

Hirst, P. and G. Thompson (1999) *Globalization in Question*, Cambridge: Polity.

Keohane, R. and J. Nye (2000) 'Introduction', in J. Nye and J. Donahue (eds), *Governance in a Globalizing World*, Washington DC: Brookings Institution.

McGrew, A. (1997) 'Democracy beyond borders? Globalization and the reconstruction of democratic theory and practice', in A. G. McGrew (ed.), *The Transformation of Democracy? Globalization and Territorial Democracy*, Cambridge: Polity.

Maddison, A. (2001) *The World Economy: A Millennial Perspective*, Paris: OECD.

O'Brien, R., A. M. Goetz, J. A. Scholte and M. Williams (2000) *Contesting Global Governance: Multilateral Economic Institutions and Global Social Movements*, Cambridge: Cambridge University Press.

Pierre, J. and B. G. Peters (2000) *Governance, Politics and the State*, London: Palgrave.

Rodrik, D. (1997) *Has Globalization Gone Too Far?* Washington DC: Institute for International Economics.

Rosenau, J. N. (1999) 'Toward an ontology for global governance', in M. Hewson and T.J. Sinclair (eds), *Approaches to Global Governance Theory*, Albany: State University of New York Press.

Rosenau, J. N. (2000a) 'Change, complexity, and governance in globalizing space', in J. Pierre (ed.), *Debating Governance: Authority, Steering, and Democracy*, Oxford: Oxford University Press.

Rosenau, J. (2000b) 'Governance in a globalizing world', in Held and McGrew 2000.

Ruggie, J. (1998) *Constructing the World Polity*, London: Routledge.

Scholte, J. A. (2000) *Globalization: A Critical Introduction*, London: Macmillan.

Smouts, M.-C. (2001) 'International cooperation: from coexistence to world governance', in M.-C. Smouts (ed.), *The New International Relations*, London: Hurst.

UIA (1997) *Yearbook of International Organizations*, Brussels: Union of International Associations.

UN Secretary-General (2000) *Renewing the United Nations*, New York: United Nations (www.un.org).

UNCTAD (2001) *World Investment Report*, Geneva: UNCTAD.

UNDP (1998) *Globalization and Liberalization*, New York: UNDP.

WTO (2001) *World Trade Report*, Geneva: World Trade Organization.

Adil Najam, David Runnals and Mark Halle

ENVIRONMENT AND GLOBALIZATION
Understanding the linkages

ALTHOUGH THE CONTEMPORARY debate on globalization has been contentious, it has not always been useful. No one doubts that some very significant global processes—economic, social, cultural, political and environmental—are underway and that they affect (nearly) everyone and (nearly) everything. Yet, there is no agreement on exactly how to define this thing we call "globalization," nor on exactly which parts of it are good or bad, and for whom. For the most part, a polarized view of globalization, its potential and its pitfalls has taken hold of the public imagination. It has often been projected either as a panacea for all the ills of the world or as their primary cause. The discussion on the links between environment and globalization has been similarly stuck in a quagmire of many unjustified expectations and fears about the connections between these two domains.

Although the debates on the definition and importance of globalization have been vigorous over time, we believe that the truly relevant policy questions today are about who benefits and who does not; how the benefits and the costs of these processes can be shared fairly; how the opportunities can be maximized by all; and how the risks can be minimized.

In addressing these questions, one can understand globalization to be a complex set of dynamics offering many opportunities to better the human condition, but also involving significant potential threats. Contemporary globalization manifests itself in various ways, three of which are of particular relevance to policy-makers. They also comprise significant environmental opportunities and risks.

1   **Globalization of the economy.** The world economy globalizes as national economies integrate into the international economy through trade; foreign direct investment; short-term capital flows; international movement of workers and people in general; and flows of technology.[1] This has created new opportunities for many; but not for all. It has also placed pressures on the global environment and on natural resources, straining the capacity of the environment to sustain itself and exposing human dependence on our environment.[3] A globalized economy can also produce

---

Box 1 Defining globalization

What is globalization?

There are nearly as many definitions of globalization as authors who write on the subject. One review, by Scholte, provides a classification of at least five broad sets of definitions:[2]

Globalization as internationalization. The "global" in globalization is viewed "as simply another adjective to describe cross-border relations between countries." It describes the growth in international exchange and interdependence.

Globalization as liberalization. Removing government-imposed restrictions on movements between countries.

Globalization as universalization. Process of spreading ideas and experiences to people at all corners of the earth so that aspirations and experiences around the world become harmonized.

Globalization as westernization or modernization. The social structures of modernity (capitalism, industrialism, etc.) are spread the world over, destroying cultures and local self-determination in the process.

Globalization as deterritorialization. Process of the "reconfiguration of geography, so that social space is no longer wholly mapped in terms of territorial places, territorial distances and territorial borders."

---

globalized externalities and enhance global inequities.[4] Local environmental and economic decisions can contribute to global solutions and prosperity, but the environmental costs, as well as the economic ramifications of our actions, can be externalized to places and people who are so far away as to seem invisible.

2   **Globalization of knowledge.** As economies open up, more people become involved in the processes of knowledge integration and the deepening of non-market connections, including flows of information, culture, ideology and technology.[5] New technologies can solve old problems, but they can also create new ones. Technologies of environmental care can move across boundaries quicker, but so can technologies of environmental extraction. Information flows can connect workers and citizens across boundaries and oceans (e.g., the rise of global social movements as well as of outsourcing), but they can also threaten social and economic networks at the local level. Environmentalism as a norm has become truly global, but so has mass consumerism.

3   **Globalization of governance.** Globalization places great stress on existing patterns of global governance with the shrinking of both time and space; the expanding role of non-state actors; and the increasingly complex inter-state interactions.[6] The global nature of the environment demands global environmental governance, and indeed a worldwide infrastructure of international agreements and institutions has emerged and continues to grow.[7] But many of today's global environmental

problems have outgrown the governance systems designed to solve them.[8] Many of these institutions, however, struggle as they have to respond to an ever-increasing set of global challenges while remaining constrained by institutional design principles inherited from an earlier, more state-centric world.

The relationship between the environment and globalization—although often overlooked —is critical to both domains.[9] The environment itself is inherently global, with life-sustaining ecosystems and watersheds frequently crossing national boundaries; air pollution moving across entire continents and oceans; and a single shared atmosphere providing climate protection and shielding us from harsh UV rays. Monitoring and responding to environmental issues frequently provokes a need for coordinated global or regional governance. Moreover, the environment is intrinsically linked to economic development, providing natural resources that fuel growth and ecosystem services that underpin both life and livelihoods. Indeed, at least one author suggests that "the economy is a wholly-owned subsidiary of the ecology."[10]

While the importance of the relationship between globalization and the environment is obvious, our understanding of how these twin dynamics interact remains weak. Much of the literature on globalization and the environment is vague (discussing generalities); myopic (focused disproportionately only on trade-related connections); and/or partial (highlighting the impacts of globalization on the environment, but not the other way around).

It is important to highlight that not only does globalization impact the environment, but the environment impacts the pace, direction and quality of globalization. At the very least, this happens because environmental resources provide the fuel for economic globalization, but also because our social and policy responses to global environmental challenges constrain and influence the context in which globalization happens. This happens, for example, through the governance structures we establish and through the constellation of stakeholders and stakeholder interests that construct key policy debates. It also happens through the transfer of social norms, aspirations and ideas that criss-cross the globe to formulate extant and emergent social movements, including global environmentalism.

In short, not only are the environment and globalization intrinsically linked, they are so deeply welded together that we simply cannot address the global environmental challenges facing us unless we are able to understand and harness the dynamics of globalization that influence them. By the same token, those who wish to capitalize on the potential of globalization will not be able to do so unless they are able to understand and address the great environmental challenges of our time, which are part of the context within which globalization takes place.

The dominant discourse on globalization has tended to highlight the promise of economic opportunity. On the other hand, there is a parallel global discourse on environmental responsibility. A more nuanced understanding needs to be developed—one that seeks to actualize the global opportunities offered by globalization while fulfilling global ecological responsibilities and advancing equity. Such an understanding would, in fact, make sustainable development a goal of globalization, rather than a victim. As a contribution towards this more nuanced understanding of these two dynamics, we will now outline five propositions related to how environment and globalization are linked and how they are likely to interact.

Table 1 Environment and globalization: some examples of interaction

How does globalization affect the environment?	Means of influence	How does environment affect globalization?
— *Scale* and composition of economic activity changes, and consumption increases, allowing for more widely dispersed externalities. — *Income* increases, creating more resources for environmental protection. — *Techniques* change as technologies are able to extract more from nature but can also become cleaner.	**Economy**	— Natural *resource scarcity and/or abundance* are *drivers of globalization*, as they incite supply and demand forces in global markets. — The need for *environmental amelioration* can extract costs from economy and siphon resources away from development goals.
— Global interactions *facilitate exchange of environmental knowledge and best practices*. — *Environmental consciousness* increases with emergence of global environmental networks and civil society movements. — Globalization facilitates the spread of existing *technologies* and the emergence of new technologies, often replacing existing technologies with more extractive alternatives; greener technologies may also be spurred. — Globalization helps spread a homogenization of *consumption*-driven aspirations.	**Knowledge**	— Signals of environmental stress travel fast in a compressed world, *environmentally degraded and unsustainable locations* become marginalized from trade, investment, etc. — Sensibilities born out of environmental stress can push towards *localization* and *non-consumptive development* in retaliation to the thrust of globalization. — Environmental stress can trigger alternative technological paths, e.g., dematerialization, alternative energy, etc., which may not have otherwise emerged. — Environmentalism becomes a global *norm*.
— Globalization makes it increasingly difficult for states to rely only on *national regulation* to ensure the well-being of their citizens and their environment. — There is a *growing demand and need for global regulation*,	**Governance**	— Environmental standards *influence patterns of trade and investment* nationally and internationally. — The nature of environmental challenges requires the incorporation of environmental

especially for the means to enforce existing agreements and build upon their synergies to improve environmental performance.

— Globalization facilitates the involvement of a growing *diversity of participants and their coalitions* in addressing environmental threats, including market and civil society actors.

governance into other areas (e.g., trade, investment, health, labour, etc.).

— Stakeholder participation in *global environmental governance*—especially the participation of NGOs and civil society—has become a model for other areas of global governance.

The five propositions

By way of exploring the linkages between environment and globalization, let us posit five key propositions on how these two areas are linked, with a special focus on those linkages that are particularly pertinent for policy-making and policy-makers. The purpose of these propositions is to highlight the possible implications of the dominant trends. This is neither an exhaustive list nor a set of predictions. It is rather an identification of the five important trajectories which are of particular importance to policy-makers because (a) these are areas that have a direct bearing on national and international policy and, (b) importantly, they *can* be influenced by national and international policy.

PROPOSITION #1:
The rapid acceleration in global economic activity and our dramatically increased demands for critical, finite natural resources undermine our pursuit of continued economic prosperity.

The notion that rising pressures on, and dwindling stocks of, critical natural resources can dramatically restrain the motors of economic growth is not new.[11] What *is* new, however, is the realization that the spectacular economic expansion we have been seeing has made the resource crunch a pressing reality that could easily become the single biggest challenge to continued economic prosperity.

The premise of the proposition is fairly simple. First, natural resources—oil, timber, metals, etc.—are the raw materials behind much of global economic growth. Second, there is ultimately a finite amount of these resources available for human use. Third, and importantly, the quantum of resources being used has grown exponentially in recent years, especially with the spectacular economic expansion of large developing economies— such as India and China—and increasing global prosperity. Fourth, we are already witnessing increasing global competition for such resources; and not just market, but geopolitical forces are being mobilized to ensure continued supplies and controls over critical resources.[12]

Add these facts together and you arrive at a realization that sooner rather than later the degradation of ecological processes—especially fragile ecological systems that are central to the preservation of our essential life systems—could cause a major hiccup in continued global economic growth, and possibly become the single most important threat to the continuation of current globalization trajectories.[13] The dynamic is not new, but it has suddenly become more real and more immediate. Growth, of course, is a paradox in the context of sustainable development.[14] We need growth in order to meet the needs of people, especially the poorest among us; but permanent global growth is impossible in a finite system. Studies demonstrate that we already exceed the productive capacity of nature by 25[15] to 30 per cent,[16] and that 60 per cent[17] of the ecosystems are currently overused.

Although scares about "limits to growth"[18] have proved less than credible in the past, simple economic logic (and available trends) argues that, as competition for scarce natural resources increases, prices will be driven up—and sooner than we might have assumed. In the past, technology has—and in the future, it certainly could—help to alleviate some of these pressures by developing new solutions and by more widely deploying existing technological solutions. However, the prospects of higher demand, growing prices and dwindling stocks are already propelling new races for control over key resources. The race is now on not just for oil, but for metals, minerals, timber and even for recyclable waste.[19] For many developing countries endowed with critical resources in high demand, this provides an opportunity to harness the power of globalization and pull themselves out of poverty. Past experience suggests that national and global economies have not been particularly good at allowing for the benefits of resources to flow down to the poor;[20] the challenge today is to find the ways and means to do exactly that.

. . .

Together, and in the context of galloping economic growth in Asia and elsewhere, these and other such findings suggest that mounting environmental degradation could impose very significant costs on globalization and economic growth. But they also hold the promise that an improved environment is central to human well-being in ecological as well as in economic terms.

PROPOSITION #2:
The linked processes of globalization and environmental degradation pose new security threats to an already insecure world. They impact the vulnerability of ecosystems and societies, and the least resilient ecosystems. The livelihoods of the poorest communities are most at risk.

With globalization, when insecurity increases and violence erupts, the ramifications become global in reach. The forces of globalization, when coupled with those of environmental degradation, expand concepts of threat and security, both individually and through their connections. We have already begun recognizing new global threats from non-state groups and individuals, and security is now being defined more broadly to include, among other, wars between and within states; transnational organized crime; internal displacements and migration; nuclear and other weapons; poverty; infectious disease; and environmental degradation.[21]

To take one pressing example, the World Resources Institute (WRI) reports that[22]

> Water scarcity is already a major problem for the world's poor, and changes in
> rainfall and temperature associated with climate change will likely make this

worse. Even without climate change, the number of people affected by water scarcity is projected to increase from 1.7 billion today to 5 billion by 2025.[23] In addition, crop yields are expected to decline in most tropical and subtropical regions as rainfall and temperature patterns change with a changing climate.[24] A recent report by the Food and Agriculture Organization estimates that developing nations may experience an 11 per cent decrease in lands suitable for rain-fed agriculture by 2080 due to climate change.[25] There is also some evidence that disease vectors such as malaria-bearing mosquitoes will spread more widely.[26] At the same time, global warming may bring an increase in severe weather events like cyclones and torrential rains.

All of this imperils human security, which in turn drives societal insecurity and, in many cases, violence. Placed in the context of globalization, violence and insecurity can spill out since now they can travel further, just as people, goods and services can.

. . .

PROPOSITION #3:
The newly prosperous and the established wealthy will have to come to terms with the limitations of the ecological space in which both must operate, and also with the needs and rights of those who have not been as lucky.

Consider the following:

- Emerging economies now dominate and drive global growth.[27] Last year their combined output accounted for more than half of total world GDP.
- China has become a major importer of just about all natural resources. It is now also the world's largest importer of recyclable waste material.[28]
- "About 700,000 Chinese tourists visited France last year and the number is climbing annually. By 2020, the World Tourism Organization estimates, 100 million Chinese will make foreign trips each year."[29]
- Mittal Steel, a company born in India, with its recent hostile takeover of Arcelor, is now the world's largest and most global steel company.[30] While the company's financial headquarters is in Europe, much of the company's growth has been in emerging markets—India and China, but also Latin America and elsewhere in Asia.
- "By one calculation, there are now more than 1.7 billion members of 'the consumer class'—nearly half of them in the developing world. A lifestyle and culture that became common in Europe, North America, Japan and a few other pockets of the world in the twentieth century is going global in the twenty-first."[31] "China and India alone claim more than 20 per cent of the global [consumer class] total—with a combined consumer class of 362 million, more than in all of Western Europe."[32]

The point of the above is that the key decisions that will affect—and are already affecting—the trajectories of globalization as well as environmental processes are no longer solely Northern. They are increasingly coming from a few large developing countries, especially China and India, but also a handful of other large developing countries. A palpable excitement accompanies this dramatic rise, but there are challenges as well as opportunities.

The dramatic growth in these new economies has forced them to think about the management of that growth, including its environmental dimensions. In many cases, they are doing so on their own terms and in the context of their own specific realities. China, for example, has embarked on substantial environmental programs. Some immediate programs are fueled by the upcoming Olympic Games to be held in China[33] but many are much longer-term initiatives that emerge from an explicit realization by China that the costs of environmental degradation are a major strain on the country's prospects for continued prosperity, and threaten to affect its standing in the world.

The rapid rise of this set of erstwhile developing countries should also trigger reflection within established industrialized economies on the questions of growth and consumption. It is not viable—nor was it ever—to urge consumption restraint on the newly prosperous while continuing on paths of high consumption oneself. While the question of consumption will be discussed more specifically later, the point to be made here is that the newly prosperous as well as those who have been affluent for much longer will now have to come to terms with the limitations of the ecological space in which both must operate and also with the needs and rights of those who have not been as lucky.

. . .

PROPOSITION #4:

Consumption—in both North and South—will define the future of globalization as well as the global environment.

To put this proposition most bluntly, the central challenge to the future of environment and globalization is consumption, not growth. Fueled by the aspirational "norms" of consumption[34] that also become globalized through, in part, the global media and advertising, consumption changes magnify the footprints of growth. For example, while global population doubled between 1950 and 2004, global wood use more than doubled, global water use roughly tripled, and consumption of coal, oil, and natural gas increased nearly five times[35]

A focus on consumption immediately draws our attention to the challenge of inequity. That challenge cannot be brushed aside. A simple but powerful illustration suggests that on average, in 2000, one American consumed as much energy as 2.1 Germans, 12.1 Colombians, 28.9 Indians, 127 Haitians or 395 Ethiopians.[36] These numbers are, of course, stylized but they do help make the point that we live in a massively unequal world and that these inequities are central to the future of globalization as well as the environment. Also, one should note that national averages hide massive consumption inequity within nearly all societies. The very affluent within developing countries over-consume just as the poor within affluent countries under-consume.

The scope of the challenge is highlighted by the *2006 Living Planet Report*[37] which points out that, based on current projections, humanity will be using two planets' worth of natural resources by 2050—if those resources have not run out by then. Humanity's ecological footprint—the demand people place upon the natural world—has increased to the point where the Earth is unable to keep up in the struggle to regenerate. The key to resolving this challenge is to de-link consumption from growth, and growth from development:[38] to provide the poor with the opportunity to increase their use of resources even as the affluent reduce their share so that a sustainable level and global equity can be achieved.[39]

. . .

PROPOSITION #5:
Concerns about the global market and global environment will become even more inter-
    twined and each will become increasingly dependent on the other.

Although still unrecognized by many, it is nonetheless a fact that a large proportion of existing global environmental policy is, in fact, based on creating, regulating and managing markets. The most obvious examples are direct trade-related instruments like the Con-vention on International Trade in Endangered Species of wild fauna and flora (CITES) or the Basel Convention on Trade in Hazardous Waste. But even less obvious instruments such as the Climate Convention (especially through its emission trading provisions) or the Biodiversity Convention (through, for example, the Cartagena Protocol on living modi-fied organisms) operate within created or existing marketplaces and markets are a central element of their design and implementation.

    For their part, the managers of market interactions—most prominently in the area of international trade, but also in investment, subsidies, etc.—have also belatedly come to the conclusion that they cannot divorce market policies from environmental policy for long. To take international trade as an example, we see that a significant part of inter-national trade is in environment-related goods—ranging from trade in resources such as timber or fish to flowers and species, and much more. Moreover, trade in just about all goods has environmental relevance in the manufacture, transport, disposal and use of those goods. The Preamble to the Marrakech Agreements establishing the World Trade Organization (WTO) recognizes this clearly. And following its lead, the Doha Round of WTO negotiations has also acknowledged this intrinsic connection by placing environ-ment squarely on the trade negotiation agenda.[40] Although those negotiations are currently stalled, the principle of the inclusion of environmental concerns on the trade agenda is no longer in question and is not in doubt.

    Importantly, there is a synergy in the stated goals of the trade and the environment system. Both claim to work in the context of, and for the attainment of, sustainable development.[41] Given that international trade is a principal motor of globalization, one can argue that sustainable development should be considered an ultimate goal of globalization, just as it is the stated end-goal of the international trading system.

    This integration of environment into trade policy and trade into environmental policy will only intensify. The hope, of course, is that not only the two policy issues, but also the two policy arenas, will interact more than they have to date; that each will recognize that they share the meta-goal of sustainable development; and that both will seek to reach that goal through collaboration. One must start, therefore, with the acceptance that policies that impact markets go beyond the WTO (e.g., supply chains, regional and bilateral arrangements, etc.) just as policies that impact the environment go beyond UNEP (e.g., national and local initiatives, private sector and civil society initiatives, etc.). Our concern here, therefore, is larger than to the future of WTO and UNEP; it is how environmental and market dynamics interact to reap the potential of globalization and environmental improvement.

. . .

Avenues for action: what can we do?

Better global governance is the key to managing both globalization and the global environment. More importantly, it is also the key to managing the relationship between the two. The processes of environment and globalization are sweepingly broad, sometimes overwhelming, but they are not immune to policy influence. Indeed, the processes as we know them have been shaped by the policies that we have—or have not—put in place in the past. Equally, the direction that globalization, the global environment and the inter-action of the two will take in the years to come will be shaped by the policy decisions of the future. Governance, therefore, is the key avenue for action by decision-makers today.

However, it is also quite clear that both globalization and environment challenge the current architecture of the international system as it now exists. Both dynamics limit a state's ability to decide on and control key issues affecting it. Globalization does it largely by design as states commit to liberalize trade and embrace new technologies. The environment challenges the system by default as ecosystem boundaries rarely overlap with national boundaries and ecological systems are nearly always supra-state. The role of the state in the management of the international system has to evolve to respond to the evolution of the challenges facing it.

This evolution is already happening, but often in painful, even contorted, ways. Having outgrown its old structure, the international system is designing a new, more inclusive one.[42] Many problems have been identified in the current system of global governance: it is too large; it is chronically short of money and yet also wasteful of the resources it has; it has expanded in an ad hoc fashion; it lacks coordination and a sense of direction; it is often duplicative and sometimes different organizations within the system work at cross-purposes to each other, etc. In terms of environment and globalization, we see three important goals for the global governance system as it exists today.

Managing institutional fragmentation: Although there already exist organs within the system to address most problems thrown up by environment and globalization, the efforts of these institutions are fragmented and lack coordination or coherence. The efforts and the instruments for making the "system" work as a whole either do not exist or are under-utilized. The institutional architecture that we have remains focused on precise issues even though the pressing challenges of our times—particularly those related to environment and globalization—relate to the connections between issues (e.g., labour and trade; environment and investment; food and health, etc.). There is a pressing need, therefore, for meaningful global governance reform that creates viable and workable mechanisms for making existing institutions work together more efficiently and effectively than they have so far.

Broadening the base of our state-centric system: Despite some headway over the last two decades, the essential architecture of the international governance system remains state-centric, even though neither the problems nor the solutions are any longer so. In terms of environment and globalization dynamics, one now finds civil society and market actors playing defining roles in establishing the direction and sequence of events. Whether it is companies creating new global norms and standards through their procurement and supply chains, or NGOs establishing voluntary standards in areas such as forestry or organic products, we see that policy in practice is no longer the sole domain of the inter-state system. It should be acknowledged that both civil society and business are beginning to be integrated into global governance mechanisms—for example, through their presence and participation in global negotiations and summits and through closer interactions with environmentally progressive businesses. This process needs to be deepened and accelerated, and meaningful ways need to be found to incorporate them as real partners in the global governance enterprise.

Establishing sustainable development as a common goal: The post-World War II international organizational architecture was originally designed to avoid another Great War. In terms of what the system does and in terms of the types of goals that it has set for itself (e.g., the Millennium Development Goals; stabilization of atmospheric concentrations of CO_2; eradication of diseases such as Malaria; control of HIV/AIDS, etc.), the system has evolved to a broader understanding of what we mean by "security" as well as of what its own role is. Yet, it is not always clear that the entire system of global governance is moving towards a common goal. This creates undue friction between the organizations that make up the system and results in disjointed policies.

To the extent that a new common global goal has emerged, it is sustainable development. Not only is sustainable development quintessentially about the linkages between environment and globalization, it is also a goal that has increasingly been adopted by various elements of the global system. For example, it is not only the overarching goal of all environmental organizations and instruments, it is also now a stated goal of the World Trade Organization, the Food and Agriculture Organization and many others.

Notes

1   Bhagwati, 2004; IMF, 2002.
2   Scholte, 2000:15–17.
3   Georgiescu-Roegen, 1971.
4   Daly, 1993; Bauman, 1998; Shiva, 2005.
5   Jelin, 2000; Held, 2003; Mittelman and Othman (eds.), 2001.
6   UNSG, 2000; UNDP, 2002.
7   Weiss, 1999; Roch and Perez, 2005.
8   Najam *et al.*, 2004; Najam *et al.*, 2006.
9   Speth (ed.), 2003; Wijen *et al.* (eds.), 2005.
10   Nelson, 2002. Popularly attributed to Paul Hawken.
11   Even 18th century scientists were preoccupied with the effects of resource scarcity on the future improvement of society, e.g., see Malthus, 1798.
12   Bromley, 2006; Sturm and Wackernagel, 2003; Roughneen, 2006; Godoy, 2006.
13   See Young *et al.*, 2006, for the effects of globalization on the resilience, vulnerability and adaptability of socio-ecological systems. See Pirages and Cousins, 2005, for the evolution of the "new limits to growth."
14   The authors are thankful to Phillipe Roch for this insight and some of the text on growth in this and other sections.

15   See http://www.footprintnetwork.org.
16   WWF, 2006.
17   Millennium Ecosystem Assessment, 2005.
18   See Meadows, 1972; Meadows *et al.*, 2004, for the concept of "limits." The concept as originally presented was widely challenged (see Simon, 1981), but as a general concept it is widely accepted that there are ultimate limits to all finite resources. Also see Georgiescu-Roegen, 1971.
19   See for example Lees, 2006. The race also increases our interest in mining the oceans and the skies.
20   On "resource curse" thesis and implications see Auty, 1993; Lay *et al.*, 2006; for policy solutions see WRI, 2005.
21   UNSG, 2004.
22   See discussion in WRI *et al.*, 2005: Chapter 1 "Nature, Power and Povery," 17.
23   IPCC, 2001:9 in WRI, 2005.
24   IPCC, 2001:84 in WRI, 2005.
25   FAO, 2005:2 in WRI, 2005.
26   IPCC, 2001:455 in WRI, 2005.
27   Measured at PPP, *The Economist*, 2006.
28   Sun *et al.*, 2004; Terazono *et al.*, 2004.
29   Smith, 2006.
30   BBC, 2006.
31   See "The Rise and Spread of the Consumer Class" at http://www.worldwatch.org/node/810-.
32   See Chapter 1, "The State of Consumption Today," Worldwatch State of the World 2004.
33   Saltmarsh, 2006.
34   See e.g., Durning, 1992.
35   State of the World 2006:44.
36   See Sierra Club Web site; http://www.sierraclub.org/population/consumption/.
37   WWF, 2006.
38   See e.g., Daly, 1996.
39   Schor, 1991.
40   For full text of these documents see http://www.wto.org. See preamble in Marrakech Agreement Establishing the World Trade Organization, as well as Article XX chapeau and sub-points for environmental exceptions in the General Agreement on Tariffs and Trade.
41   Najam, 2004; Halle, 2005.
42   Najam, Papa and Taiyab, 2006.

Bibliography

Auty, R.M., 1993. *Sustaining Development in Mineral Economies: The Resource Curse Thesis.* London, U.K.: Routledge.

Bauman, Z., 1998. "On Glocalization: Or Globalization for Some, Localization for Others." *Thesis Eleven*, 54, 37–49.

BBC News, 2006. "Mittal Steel Unveils Arcelor Bid." January 27.

Bhagwati, J., 2004. *In Defense of Globalization.* New York: Oxford University Press.

Bromley, D., 2006. "Toward Understanding Global Tension: Natural Resources and Competing Economic Histories." *Resource Policies: Effectiveness, Efficiency, and Equity*. 2006 Berlin Conference on the Human Dimensions of Global Environmental Change 17–18 November.

Daly, H.E., 1993. "The Perils of Free Trade." *Scientific American*. (November): 50–57.

Daly, H.E., 1996. *Beyond Growth*. Boston; Beacon Press.

Durning, A., 1992. *How Much is Enough? The Consumer Society and the Future of the Earth*. New York: W.W. Norton and Company.

Economist, The, 2006. "Economist Survey: World Economy." September 14.

Food and Agriculture Organization (FAO), 2005. "Impact of Climate Change, Pests and Diseases on Food Security and Poverty Reduction." Background document for the Special Event at the 31st Session of the Committee on World Food Security. 23–26 May.

Georgiescu-Roegen, Nicholas, 1971. *The Entropy Law and the Economic Process*. Cambridge, MA: Harvard University Press.

Godoy, J., 2006. "China Reaches into Europe's Resource-Rich 'Backyard.'" *Inter Press Service News Agency*, November 15.

Halle, M., 2005. *Where Are We in the Doha Round?* Winnipeg, Canada: International Institute for Sustainable Development. Available at: http://www.iisd.org.

Held, D., 2003. "Cosmopolitanism: Taming Globalization." In Held, D. and A. G. McGrew (eds.) *The Global Transformations Reader*. 2nd ed. Cambridge, U.K.: Polity Press.

Intergovernmental Panel on Climate Change (IPCC), 2001. *Third Assessment Report: Working Group II: Impacts, Adaptation and Vulnerability*. Oxford: Oxford Univeristy Press.

International Monetary Fund (IMF), 2002. *Globalization: A Framework for IMF Involvement*. IMF Issues Brief of March 15. Washington, DC: IMF.

Jelin, E., 2000. "Towards a Global Environmental Citizenship?" *Citizenship Studies*, Volume 4(1).

Lay, J., R. Thiele and M. Wiebelt, 2006. *Resource Booms, Inequality and Poverty: The Case of Gas in Bolivia*. Kiel Working Paper No. 1287. Kiel, Germany: The Kiel Institute for the World Economy.

Lees, G., 2006. "India and China Compete for Burma's Resources." *World Politics Watch Exclusive*. August 21.

Malthus, T., 1798. *An Essay on the Principle of Population, as it Affects the Future Improvement of Society*. With Remarks on the Speculations of Mr. Godwin, M. Condorcet, and Other Writers. London, Printed for J. Johnson, in St. Paul's Church Yard.

Meadows, D.H. *et al.*, 1972. *The Limits to Growth*. New York: Universe Books.

Meadows, D.H., J. Randers and D.L. Meadows, 2004. *Limits to Growth: The Thirty-Year Update*. White River Jct., VT: Chelsea Green Publishing Company.

Millennium Ecosystem Assessment, 2005. *Ecosystems and Human Well-Being: Synthesis Reports*. Washington DC: MA, WRI and Island Press.

Mittelman, J.H. and N. Othman (eds.), 2001. *Capturing Globalisation*. London, U.K.: Routledge.

Najam, A., 2004. "Trade and Environment Negotiations after Doha: Southern Priorities and Options." In *Sustainable Development: Bridging the Research/Policy Gaps in Southern Contexts* edited by Sustainable Development Policy Institute, Pakistan. Pp. 183–195. Karachi: Oxford University Press.

Najam, A., M. Papa and N. Taiyab, 2006. *Global Environmental Governance: A Reform Agenda*. Winnipeg: IISD.

Nelson, G. 2002. *Beyond Earth Day: Fulfilling the Promise*. Madison, WI: University of Wisconsin Press.

Pirages, D. and K. Cousins, 2005. *From Resource Scarcity to Ecological Security: Exploring New Limits to Growth*. Cambridge, MA: MIT Press.

Roch, P. and F.X. Perez, 2005. "International Environmental Governance: Striving for a Comprehensive, Coherent, Effective and Efficient International Environmental Regime." *Colorado Journal of International Environmental Law and Policy,* 16(1).

Roughneen, S., 2006. "Influence Anxiety: China's Role in Africa." *ISN Security Watch*. May 15.

Saltmarsh, M. "Getting in early as China cleans up." *International Herald Tribune*. January 8, 2006.

Scholte, J.A., 2000. *Globalization: A Critical Introduction*. New York: Palgrave.

Schor, J., 1991. "Global Equity and Environmental Crisis: An Argument for Reducing Working Hours in the North." *World Development*. Volume 19(1).

Shiva, V., 2005. *Globalization's New Wars: Seed, Water and Life Forms*. New Delhi: Women Unlimited.

Simon, J.L., 1981. *The Ultimate Resource*. Princeton, NJ: Princeton University Press.

Smith, C., 2006. "Chinese Speak the International Language of Shopping." November 7, *The New York Times*.

Speth, J.G. (ed.), 2003. *Worlds Apart: Globalization and the Environment*. Washington D.C.: Island Press.

Sturm, A. and M. Wackernagel, 2003. *The Winners and Losers in Global Competition: Why Eco-Efficiency Reinforces Competitiveness: A Study of 44 Nations*. Ashland, OH: Purdue University Press.

Sun, X., E. Katsigris and A. White, 2004, "Meeting China's Demand for Forest Products: An Overview," in *International Forestry Review*, 6(3–4):227–236.

Terazono, A., A. Yoshida, J. Yang, Y. Moriguchi and S. Sakai, 2004. "Material Cycles in Asia: Especially the Recycling Loop between Japan and China," in *Material Cycles and Waste Management,* 6(2):82–96.

UNDP, 2002. *Global Reports: An Overview of Their Evolution*. New York: UNDP Office of Development Studies.

UNSG, 2000. *We the Peoples: The Role of the United Nations in the 21st Century*. Report of the Secretary-General. See Chapter 1 on "Globalization and Governance." New York: United Nations A/54/2000.

UNSG, 2004. Report of the U.N. Secretary-General's High Level Panel on Threats, Challenges and Change *A More Secure World: Our Shared Responsibility*. New York: United Nations A/59/565.

Weiss, E.B., 1999. "The Emerging Structure of International Environmental Law." In Vig, N. and R. Axelrod (eds.) *The Global Environment: Institutions, Law, and Policy*. Washington DC: CQ Press.

Wijen, F., K. Zoeteman and J. Pieters (eds.), 2005. *A Handbook of Globalisation and Environmental Policy*. Cheltenham, U.K. and Northampton, MA: Edward Elgar Publishing Limited.

WRI, UNDP, UNEP and the World Bank, 2005. *World Resources 2005: The Wealth of the Poor: Managing Ecosystems to Fight Poverty*. Washington DC: WRI.

WWF, 2006. *Living Planet Report 2006*. Gland, Switzerland: WWF.

Young, O. *et al.* (2006) "The Globalization of Socio-Ecological Systems: An Agenda for Scientific Research" *Global Environmental Change* 16(3).

Vandana Shiva

GLOBALIZATION AND ITS FALL OUT

Neither prosperity nor peace

GLOBALIZATION WAS IMPOSED on the world with a promise of peace and prosperity. Instead we are faced with war and economic crisis. Not only has prosperity proved elusive, the minimal economic securities of people and countries are fast disappearing.

Hunger deaths have started to occur in countries such as Argentina where hunger was never a problem, and starvation has returned to countries like India which had driven away famine like the one of 1942 which killed 2 million people under colonial, and provided food security through public policy shaped by the democratic process of an independent and sovereign country. Even the rich economies of U.S., Europe and Japan are facing a decline. Globalization has clearly failed to improve the well being of citizens or countries.

It has helped some corporations increase their profits and markets, but many corporations like AOL/Time Warner and Enron whose non-sustainable growth was based on deregulation accompanying globalization have themselves either gone bankrupt or lost their value. Following the globalization path is proving to be a recipe for non-sustainability for the rich and impoverishment and destitution for the poor.

Peace was the other promise of globalization but terrorism and war is what we have inherited. Peace was to be a result of increased global prosperity through globalization. Increased poverty is the unfolding reality. And economic insecurity and exclusion is creating conditions for the rise of terrorism and fundamentalism.

Economic and political exclusion, and the erosion of national economic sovereignty is making many young men turn to terrorism and violence as a way of achieving their goals. The erosion of economic nationalism and the growth of economic security is also providing fertile ground for the rise of right-wing fundamentalist politics, with parties using the reality of economic insecurity to fan the flames of cultural insecurity, and filling the vacuum left by the collapse of economic nationalism and economic sovereignty with the pseudo nationalist agenda of "cultural nationalism".

At the global level, the rhetoric of "clash of civilizations", and the war against Islam performs the same function as the exclusivist political agendas of cultural nationalism and fundamentalist ideology at the national level.

The convergence of fundamentalism

Two forms of fundamentalism seem to be converging and becoming mutually reinforcing and mutually supportive.

The first is the market fundamentalism of globalization itself. This fundamentalism redefines life as commodity, society as economy, and the market as the means and end of the human enterprise. The market is being made the organizing principle for the provisioning of food, water, health, education and other basic needs, it is being made the organizing principle for governance, it is being made the measure of our humanity.

Our being human is no longer predicated on the fundamental human rights enshrined in all constitutions and in the U.N. declaration of human rights. It is now conditional on our ability to "buy" our needs on the global marketplace in which the conditions of life – food, water, health, knowledge – have become the ultimate commodities controlled by a handful of corporations. In the market fundamentalism of globalization, everything is a commodity, everything is for sale. Nothing is sacred, there are no fundamental rights of citizens and no fundamental duties of governments.

The market fundamentalism of globalization and the economic exclusion inherent to it is giving rise to, and being reinforced and supported by, politics of exclusion emerging in the form of political parties based on "religious fundamentalism"/xenophobia/ethnic cleansing and reinforcement of patriarchies and castism. The culture of commodification has increased violence against women, whether it is in the form of rising domestic violence, increasing cases of rape, an epidemic of female foeticide, and increased trafficking in women.

Globalization as a patriarchal project has reinforced patriarchal exclusions. Atrocities against dalits have also seen an increase as a result of globalization, with higher castes enjoying new power with their integration into the global marketplace and also wanting to usurp the resources of the poor and marginalized, especially dalits and tribals, for commercial exploitation. Land reform laws which made the land rights of dalits inalienable have been undone. An attempt is under way to undo the constitutional protection of tribal land rights under Schedule V of the Constitution.

Women, dalits, tribals, minorities are special victims of the social and economic impact of globalization. New movements of solidarity such as the Indian People's Campaign against W.T.O. are forging new alliances between diverse movements. However, people's movements are being overtaken by the emerging politics of exclusion.

Economic insecurity makes citizens vulnerable to politics based on exclusion. For those in power, or seeking power, a politics of exclusion is becoming a political necessity. It becomes necessary for filling the vacuum created by the demise of economic sovereignty and the welfare state and substituting a politics based on economic rights with politics identity.

It becomes necessary for deflecting public attention away from the negative impact of globalization and explaining the lack of jobs and livelihoods, and the lack of basic needs satisfaction which result from economic globalization in terms of competition for scarce jobs and resources from "minorities" and "immigrants". Fundamentalism and xenophobia emerge as handmaidens of corporate globalization, dividing, diverting and distracting people, and thus providing insularity and immunity to the globalization project.

In India, every vote since 1991 has been a vote against globalization and trade liberalization which is creating 10 million new unemployed people every year, is pauperizing the peasantry and disenfranchising the marginalized. This changed in 2002 with the Gujarat elections which followed the massacre of 2000 Muslims and the violent engineering of the electoral agenda away from basic needs to a majority–minority conflict and contest. The arithmetic guaranteed victory to the party which had created a divide between the majority and minority communities and sown mutual fear and hatred through rapes and killings. This violent and exclusivist agenda is now being developed for all forthcoming elections.

And while the killings were underway, and national concern was focussed on fighting communalism and fundamentalism, the globalization agenda was put on fast forward. GMOs were given clearance, Patent laws were changed to allow patents on life, a new water policy was introduced based on water privatization, and new policies were introduced to dismantle farmers' livelihood security and people's food security. The 2003 budget has further pushed the globalization agenda, using the diversion of communal and religious divide to dissipate democratic opposition.

In the U.S. and U.K., the war against Iraq has become a convenient diversion from issues of globalization and the rise in unemployment and economic insecurity. A politics of hate is becoming the indirect support for the failed and failing project of globalization.

We need a new politics of solidarity and peace which simultaneously addresses violence and exclusion inherent to globalization, the violence of terrorism and fundamentalism and the violence of war. The different forms of violence and different forms of fundamentalism have common roots, and need a common response. Globalization is intolerant of economic decentralization, economic democracy and economic diversity. Terrorism and fundamentalism are intolerant of cultural diversity. And the war machine is intolerant of the "other" and of peaceful resolution of conflict.

The response to globalization is the protection and defense of our diverse economies at local and national levels. The response to fundamentalism is celebrating our cultural diversities. The response to war is the recognition that the "other" is not a threat but the very precondition of our being.

Imagine how different the world would be if it was based on a philosophy of mutual interdependence instead of the current dominant philosophy which is based on "If I have to be, you must be exterminated" – or "Your existence is a threat to my existence".

In the world based on interdependence rather than domination, exclusion, extermination, Monsanto would not push a TRIPS agreement that treats the farmers whose seeds Monsanto has patented at "thieves". Monsanto, Syngenta, Ricetec and other Biopirates would recognize that their breeding is based on prior breeding by farmers.

If Biotech corporations could see that humanity depends on biodiversity, and food security needs pollinators and diverse plant species, they would not deploy genetically engineering Bt crops which kill bees and butterflies, they would not create herbicide-resistant plants and wipe out plant diversity.

If President Bush could see the Tigris and Euphrates and the Mesopotamian civilization as ancestors and recognize our common roots in a common evolution, he would not be rushing in to wipe out the historical roots with unmanned bombs and weapons of mass destruction.

If those who control capital could see that their wealth embodies nature's creativity and people's labour, they would not be creating rules of trade that destroy nature and the livelihoods.

The fundamentalism of the market and the fundamentalism of ideologies of hate and intolerance are rooted in fear – fear of the other, fear of the capacity and creativity of the other, fear of the sovereignty of the other.

We are witnessing the worst expressions of organized violence of humanity against humanity because we are witnessing the wiping out of philosophies of inclusion, compassion and solidarity. This is the highest cost of globalization – it is destroying our very capacity to be human. Rediscovering our humanity is the highest imperative to resist and reverse this inhuman project. The debate on globalization is not about the market or the economy. It is about remembering our common humanity. And the danger of forgetting the meaning of being human.

Dave Gorman

STARBUCKS

FAR FROM BEING sleepless in Seattle, I was sleepful. I slept solidly for sixteen hours – twice as long as popular opinion recommends – and woke to feel groggy, confused and, confusingly, sleepier than I was before I slept.

I don't understand how too much sleep does that to you. It's not like it's possible to eat a meal that makes you feel hungrier or drink so much water your thirst is aggravated not quenched, but somehow a sleep-overdose can make you sleepy.

I contemplated going back to sleep but managed to talk myself out of it. After all, I'd established that sleep made me feel sleepier so surely getting some more sleep would only make matters worse and the mattress more attractive. Using that logic I tricked myself into getting up. Forgetting my room was on the ground floor I pulled back the curtains to see a bright but crisp afternoon in progress and a very surprised gardener looking back at a naked Englishman pulling back his curtains, if you'll pardon the expression. I immediately whipped the curtains shut again. My brain clearly wasn't up to thinking speed yet. Sleep really did seem like an attractive option but I fought the urge and decided a shot of caffeine was what I needed.

I looked around the room for the obligatory tea and coffee making facilities but they didn't appear to be there. To begin with I was convinced I must be mistaken – surely tea and coffee are a given in every hotel – but when I opened up a drawer to find a note saying, *'Guests wishing to read a Bible should please contact reception who will be happy to lend you a copy kindly donated by the Gideon organisation'*, I knew I was in a hotel that was extraordinarily sparing with 'extras'.

Reluctantly I got dressed and went out in search of the caffeine my system craved. It wasn't hard to find. In fact, it's entirely possible that my hotel room was the only decaffeinated 100 square feet in all of Seattle. Immediately next door to the hotel I found a Starbucks, so I ordered myself a double espresso and settled into a comfy armchair in the window from where I could see another branch of Starbucks directly opposite and a third branch a few hundred yards to my right, which was itself just next door to a

Seattle Coffee Company outlet, who also had a second branch two hundred yards to my left.

'Why are there so many coffee places?' I asked the young guy who came by collecting empty cups and wiping down tables.

'What do you mean?' he asked, clearly completely nonplussed by my question.

'Is this like . . . *the coffee district* or something?' I asked. He looked back at me, even more confused than before, 'you know, like Chinatown, only . . . for coffee?'

'Dude, this is Seattle,' he said, tossing his long blond locks back over his shoulders; 'we drink coffee in Seattle. It's what we do.'

'Yes,' I said, as undudely as I could, 'I drink coffee too. It just seems odd to me that I'm sitting in a Starbucks and I can see two other Starbucks *and* two Seattle Coffee Companies. That's a lot of coffee for a small stretch of street.'

He put his tray of dirty cups down on the table with an angry clank and pulled his hands up to his hips. I'd obviously said something to upset him. His nostrils flared.

'It's called choice, dude,' he snapped defensively. 'It's how we do things in America. If you don't like it you can always leave.'

Whoa. There was me having what I thought was an idle chat about the extravagant number of coffee shops in one street and somehow he thought I was taking a vicious sideswipe at him, his lifestyle, his country, his flag and, who knows, his mother. The sheer absurdity of his overreaction meant an involuntary chuckle slipped past my lips but that made his nostrils flare again, so I bit my lip instead.

'I'm not having a go at anything or anyone,' I said, containing my smile. 'I've just never seen three Starbucks so close to each other before. It seems odd, that's all.'

'Like I say,' he said, '*this* is Seattle.'

'Yes. I get that now,' I said, although I still didn't really 'get' the logic at all. 'I didn't mean any offence. It just seems to me that five coffee shops offers *less* choice than, say, one coffee shop and four . . . other things.'

'Dude,' he said, the word sounding like fingernails on a blackboard to me now, 'choice is choice. Someone can choose to drink coffee in *this* Starbucks or in *that* Starbucks . . .'

'Or,' I said helpfully indicating number three, 'in *that* one.'

'Exactly,' he said. 'Choice.' And with that, he picked up his tray and went back to his duties.

Moments later he pulled the apron from around his waist and with a high five to one of his colleagues, signed off work for the day. I watched in amazement as he walked out of the shop, crossed the road, entered a different Starbucks and ordered himself a coffee. I strongly suspected there was a bit too much caffeine coursing through that young man's veins. I looked at my double espresso and, concerned about taking a similar overdose, I decided to leave what was left and be on my way.

My next googlewhacks, John and Chris, were going to pick me up at the hotel around seven o'clock which meant I still had a couple of hours to kill. I decided I'd do so by visiting the Space Needle because that seemed to be *the* iconic Seattle landmark. Not visiting it would be like not visiting Graceland in Memphis and only an idiot would let that happen.

CHAPTER TWO

Challenging the corporation

Critical perspectives on contemporary corporate activity

IN RECENT YEARS we have witnessed a dramatic growth in campaigning against multinational corporations. Organizations such as Nike, The Gap and McDonald's have increasingly come under the media spotlight due to campaigns by pressure groups regarding their environmental and labour rights records. At the same time the demise of corporations such as Enron, and the unethical practices that these cases have highlighted, have raised public concern regarding the nature and activities of the modern multinational corporation.

It is not just the corporations themselves that have come under intense scrutiny. As well as protests against the individual companies, we have also seen mass demonstrations organized to coincide with meetings of some of the key international economic institutions. In December 1999 70,000 campaigners converged on the American city of Seattle to protest outside the meeting of the World Trade Organization. In 2000 30,000 people participated in demonstrations to coincide with the meeting of the International Monetary Fund and World Bank in Washington, while 20,000 protested outside a similar meeting in Prague in the same year. As concern grew, so did the level of protest. In Nice 100,000 protestors campaigned outside the EU summit, while in Genoa in 2001 300,000 people converged on the G8 summit. Clearly therefore it has not been just the business community that has been concerned with the social, ethical and environmental record of contemporary business institutions.

In this chapter we look at the background to this rising challenge to the contemporary corporation, a challenge which has without doubt had a significant contribution to the speed with which the concept of corporate social responsibility has evolved in recent years and the issues around which it has revolved. We shall consider the issues that have been at the heart of the campaigns and question why protestors are targeting companies rather than governments in seeking change. In addition, we will look at some of the key theoretical approaches to understanding these events provided by theorists and commentators.

IDENTIFYING THE PROBLEMS

A range of issues lie at the heart of many of the campaigns and protests in recent years. In trying to break down these issues a number of recurrent themes are central to explaining why these problems are emerging now. As already noted, at the heart of much of the campaign activity is the role, actions and power of the multinational corporations. While there is specific concern regarding the individual practices of these organizations, a broader concern has been voiced regarding the scale and the economic power and influence which these companies are able to wield. Indeed, the statistical evidence raises some important implications. Susan George highlights the potential power of these organizations, noting that of the top 100 economic entities in the world, 51 are corporations while only 49 are states. She goes on to suggest that only 500 corporations account for approximately two-thirds of all world trade (George 2001: 13). Similarly, John Pilger (2002) notes that the GDP of General Motors is now bigger than that of Thailand or Norway. Undoubtedly, it is argued, with that level of economic power comes a significant level of political influence.

Concerns are raised regarding the ability of these large-scale multinationals to shape the economic and political conditions under which they will locate production in any particular country. In addition to the economic implications of so much trade being controlled by so few organizations, it is also argued that despite their size, multinationals are not actually responsible for a specifically high level of employment across the globe. Statistics suggest that 60,000 multinationals only employ approximately 60 million people worldwide. This makes them responsible for employing less than 10 per cent of the available workforce (George 2001: 13). Critics argue that this imbalance demonstrates that multinationals are taking a lot out of the globalized economy but effectively putting relatively little back in.

Another aspect that has been a key dimension to the emergence of anti-corporate and anti-capitalist protesting has been the creation of export processing zones (EPZs) across the developing world. Effectively, EPZs were created with the idea of encouraging inward investment from large multinationals into developing nations. By offering incentives and supportive conditions within which to locate production, it was argued, the level of inward investment and employment would help growth and increase skills within the labour force. To enable these forms of incentivized conditions, EPZs are often operated outside of existing national regulations and laws. To encourage companies to use these zones for manufacturing, governments have allowed companies to be exempt from customs duties and, in some cases, beyond the enforcement of minimum wage regulations.

The operations and activities within many EPZs across the globe have been a primary focal point for much of the ethical trading campaigning that has emerged against large-scale clothing and apparel manufacturers. Critics of the EPZs argue that there is little evidence to suggest that the proposed benefits of operating these zones extends anywhere beyond the direct benefits to the companies actually operating within them. It is suggested that the claims for wider potential benefits emerging from the operation of EPZs have so far been largely illusory. Instead of being a catalyst for further development and increased employment and training opportunities, critics suggest that the EPZs have merely created the most basic forms of low-wage and low-skilled employment, often with no union recognition and no basic protection for workers' rights. Indeed, an International Labour Organization report into the impact of EPZs in 1998 argued that

> Few governments have managed to implement policies to ensure that zone investors transfer technology and skills to local industry and workers, with the result that the human capital base remains low.
>
> (ILO 1998)

Manufacturing industries are not the only focal point for public concern over the power of the contemporary multinational corporation. Much of the protest activity has been directed at the increasing power and influence of financial institutions and the widening gap that is emerging between rich and poor. At the heart of much of this campaigning is a concern that the current economic system does nothing to help poorer nations remove themselves from poverty. The huge support and media attention garnered by the Make Poverty History and Drop the Debt campaigns raised the issue of Third World debt to the top of the political agenda. Campaigners argued that without the cancellation of many of these debts, poorer nations would never be able to create the infrastructure and opportunities which would allow them to enter the global marketplace and trade on a fair and balanced level. Under current conditions, it is argued, poorer countries are forced into very one-sided arrangements which often involve the opening up of their markets to external investment and trade while they themselves have their access to Western markets largely controlled and restricted. The concept of free trade, it is suggested, remains a distant hope given such an imbalanced power relationship.

Campaigners argue that unless a process of fair trade is adopted we will continue to see a further widening of the gap between rich and poor. Given that the poorest 10 per cent of the world's population currently participates in less than 0.5 per cent of the world's trade and that the poorest 20 per cent of the population now receives less than 1 per cent of global wealth (see George 2001; Roddick 2001), there is clearly a strong incentive to create change and significant pressure on the business community to be a key player in that process of change rather than one of the primary beneficiaries of a one-sided and unequal system of global trade.

What has proved interesting about the emergence of the anti-capitalist protests in recent years is the breadth of organizations and the diverse range of people who have found themselves involved in the campaign process. The campaigners who converged on cities such as Seattle and Prague reflected a broad range of specific issues and concerns, including trade unions, environmental campaigners, human rights groups, religious organizations as well as the more radical anarchistic organizations upon which the popular media and Western governments focused most of the attention and subsequently placed the blame for the levels of violence and disruption which accompanied these protests. However, a more far-reaching process was in evidence during these campaigns. Different groups started to realize that although the specific issues which had led them to the protests may have been different, the underlying causes of these problems all seemed to stem back, in their opinion, to the same structures and organizations, at the root of which lay the global corporate world.

For critics of the current global economic and industrial climate, these problems and pressures were exemplified by the attempted introduction of the Multilateral Agreement on Investment (MAI) in the late 1990s. Designed as an attempt to create a broad global agreement on the processes of foreign direct investment, the OECD argued that the MAI sought to create a process for 'Fair and non-discriminatory treatment for foreign investors, high standards of investment protection and an effective dispute settlement mechanism' (www.oecd.org/daf/cmis/mai/maindex).

However, the MAI proposals sparked significant criticism from a broad range of social NGOs who saw the agreement as a key symbolic step in shifting the balance of power towards big business and away from national government and civil society. The World Development Movement, for example, argued that 'citizens will lose long-standing and fundamental democratic rights while multinational companies will be given sweeping new powers, including the ability to sue governments and local authorities'.

Similarly, Oxfam (1998) described the MAI as an 'increase to the rights of investors vis-à-vis states and citizens without a parallel transfer of social and environmental responsibilities'. Further, they argued, the MAI would 'seriously limit the ability of governments to regulate investment in the public interest and transfer control over investment decisions from governments to unaccountable companies' (Oxfam 1998: 2).

Regardless of the actual aims or proposed impacts that the MAI was supposed to have on world trade, the proposed agreement certainly became a symbol for what many groups perceived as the increasingly powerful position being gained by multinational companies and their attempts to remove all restrictions on their activities. The MAI thus became perceived by many as a battleground for maintaining some level of control over global business.

The campaigns surrounding the meetings of the World Bank, IMF and WTO, and the dissent over the proposals contained within the MAI, gave the impetus for alternative visions of a globalized world. These ideas began to take a more coherent form during the meeting of the World Social Forum in Porto Alegre in January 2001. Timed to contrast with the meeting of the World Economic Forum being held in Davos, the World Social Forum saw 3000 delegates from over 100 countries converge to develop a platform for an alternative vision for the structure of the global marketplace. At the heart of this prescription lay an attempt 'To seek concrete responses to the challenges of building "another world", one where the economy would serve people and not the other way around' (www.forumsocial mundial.org.br).

The Forum argued that under current global capitalism, the demands of the free market and financial considerations were considered the only measures of worth. To contrast with this prescription the WSF placed greater emphasis upon prioritizing fair trade over free trade, the restriction on financial investment and the shutting down of tax havens, greater protection for the natural environment, and the cancellation of Third World debt, which, they argued, would never allow developing nations to compete evenly within the global marketplace. In addition, the Forum argued that corporations should be legally and financially responsible for their actions.

UNDERSTANDING THE BACKLASH AGAINST COMPANIES

Accompanying the activities and events outlined above, we have also witnessed a broad range of literature looking at the role and activities of the contemporary corporation and attempting to understand why companies are coming under increasing scrutiny from civil society regarding their actions and responsibilities. One of the most influential of these texts has been Naomi Klein's (2000) *No Logo*, an extract from which appears in this Reader (2.2). Klein maps out the processes through which, she argues, large brands are colonizing people's lives. Traditional cultural and political space, she claims, is being removed and replaced by neatly packaged, branded equivalents. Brands sell to the individual a lifestyle image, a vision of how individuals should perceive themselves and their lifestyles. In the contemporary global marketplace, she suggests, the individual product is no longer the central feature. Rather, the brand and its ubiquitous image provide the driving force for development. As she suggests, 'Nike, Microsoft and Starbucks have sought to become the chief communicators of all that is good and cherished in our culture' (Klein 2000:131).

Klein, however, argues that our belief in these brands has been damaged in recent years through the series of exposés that have resulted in a growing questioning of the behaviour and processes underlying the growth of these global brands. In particular, the evidence of exploitation of the third world workforce, the damage caused to the natural world, and the aggressive practices of many of these companies has caused considerable concern. In this regard, Klein discusses in depth the 'clustering' process used by Starbucks to gain a competitive edge in a particular location, McDonald's regular use of legal threat to both deflect criticism in cases such as the McLibel trial in the UK, and to solidify its brand name in cases such as the 26-year battle against a man called Ronald McDonald who ran a small local restaurant in Illinois. Public awareness of processes such as these, she argues, weakens our faith in the brands which we have come to trust. Furthermore, and in some cases more influentially, she suggests that our commitment to a brand may almost subconsciously make us feel complicit in their activities.

In many ways McDonald's, and more generally the fast-food industry as a whole, have come to symbolize the negative aspects of the homogenized globalized marketplace. Ritzer (1993), for example, describes a process of McDonaldization within society, whereby 'the principles of the fast-food restaurant are coming to dominate more and more sectors of American society as well as of the rest of the world' (Ritzer 1993: 1). He suggests that the processes evident within the McDonald's production and consumption patterns are being transferred into many other aspects of our everyday lives. McDonaldization thus becomes a byword for uniformity of production, predictability, calculation and control. Eric Schlosser's (2002) book *Fast Food Nation* continues this notion, suggesting that the processes of the fast-food industry are transforming not just the nature of food, but also our landscape, economy, workforce and culture. The very nature of the large-scale production processes required to support the fast-food industry, he argues, has radically reshaped the way in which food is manufactured, distributed and consumed.

The readings selected for this chapter have been chosen to give a flavour of the critiques of the modern corporation that we have outlined in this discussion. Two of the readings are taken from theoretical critiques, while the other two provide examples of the ideas and arguments emerging from within the anti-corporate campaign movements.

The first reading is an extract from Joel Bakan's book *The Corporation*. In this book, Bakan seeks to understand the nature and processes underlying the evolution of the modern corporation. Interestingly Bakan makes a startling comparison between the character traits of the corporation and the psychological profile of a psychopath, arguing that both share an inability to act upon moral obligations not to cause harm to others and both are compelled to undertake actions for selfish ends. The second reading is an extract from *No Logo* by Naomi Klein which we discussed earlier. The third reading comes from an organization called CorporateWatch and looks at the structures and laws which, it argues, provide the framework within which corporations are able to act with little or no responsibility to others.

The final reading in many ways may be seen as one of the catalysts of much of the recent campaigning and anti-corporate activity that we have witnessed in recent times. The 'What's Wrong with McDonald's' leaflet was the basis upon which McDonald's launched its legal campaign against two London Greenpeace activists. In what became known as McLibel, the longest libel case in British legal history, McDonald's sued Dave Morris and Helen Steel over the contents of the leaflet. Symbolically, the case became very much a David versus Goliath affair, in which a small, locally produced and distributed leaflet became the subject of international discussion. Support for the two defendants led to the creation of McSpotlight, an international website, while coverage of the trial itself put McDonald's food and production processes under the media spotlight. The final judgment produced a mixed outcome, with the judge deciding that the defendants had libelled McDonald's and ordering them to pay £60,000 damages. However, he also ruled that the defendants had been correct in their claims that the company exploited children with their advertising, produced 'misleading' advertising, were 'culpably responsible' for cruelty to animals, were 'antipathetic' to unionization and paid their workers low wages.

In March 1999 the Court of Appeal made further rulings that it was fair comment to say that McDonald's employees worldwide 'do badly in terms of pay and conditions', and true that 'if one eats enough McDonald's food, one's diet may well become high in fat etc., with the very real risk of heart disease' (Mcspotlight.org). While the two defendants have yet to pay any damages to McDonald's, the damage to the company's reputation from both the outcome and the process of the trial itself has had far deeper repercussions, and has undoubtedly led other companies to consider more carefully the risks involved in becoming the target of mass demonstration over company ethics, responsibility and practice.

GUIDE TO FURTHER READING

There are many other authors who have developed interesting critiques of modern business practice or who have tried to understand the rise of the anti-capitalist and anti-corporate campaigns of recent years. In particular, see Monbiot, G. (2000) *Captive State: The Corporate Takeover of Britain*, Oxford, Pan Macmillan; Pilger, J. (2002) *The New Rulers of the World*, London, Verso; Roddick, A. (2001) *Take It Personally: How Globalisation Affects You and Powerful Ways to Challenge It*, London, Thorsons; Hertz, N. (2001) *The Silent Takeover: Global Capitalism and the Death of Democracy*, London, Heinemann; Schlosser, E. (2002) *Fast Food Nation*, London, Penguin.

WEB-BASED RESOURCES

The internet has become a powerful tool for campaign organizations and as a result there is a wealth of useful information available from the web. As a starting point try:

- www. cleanclothes.org – Clean Clothes Campaign website. Focuses upon campaigns around the clothing industry.
- www.mcspotlight.org – Originally developed as a support tool during the McLibel trial, this website has expanded way beyond just an interest in McDonald's.
- www.corporatewatch.org – UK-based anti-corporate campaigning organization.
- www.forumsocialmundial.org.br – Website of the World Social Forum.

REFERENCES

George, S. (2001) 'Corporate Globalisation', in E. Bircham and J. Charlton (eds) *Anticapitalism: A Guide to the Movement*, London, Bookmarks.

ILO (1998) *Labour and Social Issues Relating to Economic Processing Zones*, Geneva, ILO.

Klein, N. (2000) *No Logo*, London, HarperCollins.

Oxfam (1998) *The Multilateral Agreement on Investment: Potential Impacts on Local Economic Development*, London, Oxfam.

Pilger, J. (2002) *The New Rulers of the World*, London, Verso.

Ritzer, G. (1993) *The McDonaldization of Society*, Berkeley, University of California Press.

Roddick, A. (2001) *Take It Personally: How Globalisation Affects You and Powerful Ways to Challenge It*, London, Thorsons.

Schlosser, E. (2002) *Fast Food Nation*, London, Penguin.

Joel Bakan

THE EXTERNALIZING MACHINE

AS A PSYCHOPATHIC creature, the corporation can neither recognize nor act upon moral reasons to refrain from harming others. Nothing in its legal makeup limits what it can do to others in pursuit of its selfish ends, and it is compelled to cause harm when the benefits of doing so outweigh the costs. Only pragmatic concern for its own interests and the laws of the land constrain the corporation's predatory instincts, and often that is not enough to stop it from destroying lives, damaging communities, and endangering the planet as a whole. Enron's implosion, and the corporate scandals that followed, were, ironically, violations of corporations' own self-interest, as it was shareholders, the very people—indeed, the only people—corporations are legally obliged to serve, who were chief among its victims. Far less exceptional in the world of the corporation are the routine and regular harms caused to *others*—workers, consumers, communities, the environment—by corporations' psychopathic tendencies. These tend to be viewed as inevitable and acceptable consequences of corporate activity—"externalities" in the coolly technical jargon of economics.

"An externality," says economist Milton Friedman, "is the effect of a transaction . . . on a third party who has not consented to or played any role in the carrying out of that transaction." All the bad things that happen to people and the environment as a result of corporations' relentless and legally compelled pursuit of self-interest are thus neatly categorized by economists as externalities—literally, other people's problems.[1] Friedman cites as a mundane example the case of a person whose shirt is dirtied by the smoke emissions from a power plant. That person pays a price—the cost of cleaning the dirty shirt and the inconvenience of wearing it—that flows directly from the power plant's operations. The corporation that owns the power plant, in turn, gains benefits by saving money through not building higher smokestacks, installing better filters, finding a less populated location in which to operate, or taking other costly measures that might avoid dirtying people's shirts.[2]

Beyond the dirty shirt example, however, corporate externalities have "enormous effects on the world at large," as Friedman points out.[3] Though they can be positive—jobs are created and useful products developed by corporations in pursuit of their self-interest—it is no exaggeration to say that the corporation's built-in compulsion to externalize its costs is at the root of many of the world's social and environmental ills. That makes the corporation a profoundly dangerous institution, as Patricia Anderson painfully learned.

In the dark early hours of Christmas Day 1993, Patricia Anderson was driving home from midnight mass, her four children in the backseat of her 1979 Chevrolet Malibu car, the youngest six years old and the eldest fifteen. She stopped at a red light, and as she waited for it to change, a car slammed into the back of her car, causing it to burst into flames. Anderson and her children suffered horrible and disfiguring second- and third-degree burns (the driver of the other car, who was drunk at the time, got away with minor injuries). Three of the children were burned over 60 percent of their bodies, and one of them had to have her hand amputated. Anderson, though thankful no one was killed – "I just thank God that me and my kids survived," she said—sued General Motors, blaming the company for the explosion and fire. The fuel tank on her Malibu, her lawyers argued, had been insufficiently protected from the impact of the collision.[4]

After a lengthy trial the jury found that GM had dangerously positioned the fuel tank to save costs, and Los Angeles Superior Court Judge Ernest G. Williams later upheld its verdict (though he reduced the damages). "The court finds that clear and convincing evidence demonstrated that defendants' fuel tank was placed behind the axle on automobiles of the make and model here in order to maximize profits—to the disregard of public safety," he wrote, which put GM in breach of applicable laws. The fuel tank on Ms. Anderson's 1979 Malibu was eleven inches from the rear bumper. The fuel tank on the previous year's Malibu, a larger vehicle, had been twenty inches from the rear bumper. A 1969 directive at the company had recommended fuel tanks be at least seventeen inches from the rear bumper. Also, on the 1979 model there was no metal brace to separate the fuel tank from the rear of the car, a standard feature on the previous year's model.[5]

The evidence in the trial showed that General Motors had been aware of the possibility of fuel-fed fires when it had designed the Malibu and some of its other models as well. Six fuel-fed fire suits had been filed against the company in the late 1960s, twenty-five more in the early 1970s, and in May 1972, a GM analyst predicted that there would be another sixty by the mid-1970s. On June 6, 1973, around the time GM began planning the new smaller Malibu that Patricia Anderson was driving, GM management asked an engineer from the company's Advance Design department, Edward C. Ivey, to analyze fuel-fed fires in GM vehicles. He submitted his report, "Value Analysis of Auto Fuel Fed Fire Related Fatalities," shortly thereafter.[6]

In the report, Ivey multiplied the five hundred fuel-fed fire fatalities that occurred each year in GM vehicles by $200,000, his estimate of the cost to GM in legal damages for each potential fatality, and then divided that figure by 41 million, the number of GM vehicles operating on U.S. highways at the time. He concluded that each fuel-fed fatality cost GM $2.40 per automobile. The calculation appeared like this in the memorandum:

$$\frac{500 \text{ fatalities} \times \$200,000/\text{fatality}}{41,000,000 \text{ automobiles}} = \$2.40/\text{automobile}$$

The cost to General Motors of ensuring that fuel tanks did not explode in crashes, estimated by the company to be $8.59 per automobile, meant the company could save $6.19 ($8.59 minus $2.40) per automobile if it allowed people to die in fuel-fed fires rather than alter the design of vehicles to avoid such fires.[7]

The jury, as the judge indicated, found General Motors' behavior to be morally reprehensible and against applicable laws because it had put profits above public safety. It awarded Anderson and her children (and a friend who had also been riding in the car) compensatory damages totaling $107 million and punitive damages of $4.8 billion, an unprecedented amount in a product-liability case. The total amount of the award was reduced to $1.2 billion in a later settlement, and General Motors filed an appeal of the lower court's decision in the California Court of Appeals.[8] In support of that appeal, the U.S. Chamber of Commerce, a representative and leading voice of big business, weighed in with a brief that reflected the general acceptance of cost-benefit analysis in corporate decision making. The jury's decision, according to the Chamber, was an "illegitimate result," one that is "deeply troubling" for its message "that manufacturers should not engage in cost-benefit analyses when they design products" and for its implication that cost-benefit analysis is "'despicable' in itself." Cost-benefit analysis, the Chamber said, is a "hallmark of corporate good behavior"; "the logic underlying it is unimpeachable."[9]

The Chamber of Commerce is right that cost-benefit analyses are at the heart of corporate decision making. "The manufacturer [in a case like *Anderson v. General Motors*] may defend its decision by showing that the net increase in safety would be outweighed by the increase in cost and/or loss of utility of the alternative design,"[10] as one legal scholar has stated. The corporation's institutional makeup, its compulsion to serve its own financial interests above everything else, requires executives to make only those decisions that create greater benefits than costs for their corporations. Executives have no authority to consider what harmful effects a decision might have on other people, such as Patricia Anderson and her children, or upon the natural environment, unless those effects might have negative consequences for the corporation itself. "Once the executive is at work," according to philosopher Alisdair MacIntyre, "the aims of the . . . corporation must be taken as a given . . . tasks characteristically appear to him as merely technical. He has to calculate the most efficient, the most economical way of mobilizing the existing resources to produce the benefits . . . at the lowest costs. The weighing of costs against benefits is not just his business, it is business."[11]

Though Edward Ivey acknowledged in his report that "a human fatality is really beyond value, subjectively," that "it is really impossible to put a value on human life," he knew it was equally impossible for him *not* to put a value on a human life for the purpose of his analysis. As an analyst who had been asked to provide useful information for a corporate decision about the costs and benefits associated with placement of fuel tanks, his task was to value human life in "an objective matter," as he put it in the report, and that meant assessing its dollar value.[12]

The jury in Patricia Anderson's case, on the other hand, refused to operate by the corporation's institutional presumptions. It chose, instead, to judge General Motors from the standpoint of human moral decency. That was its mistake, according to the Chamber of Commerce in its submission to the California appeals court. Jurors, it says, are "not well-positioned to make accurate risk-utility assessments in cases involving complex engineering issues"; they are "sometimes led astray by the fact that they see before them the injured plaintiff"; they "tend to balk at any attempt to put a dollar value on human life";

they are too easily led by skillful plaintiff's lawyers to feel the "traditional public sense of the sanctity of life" and to view "risk-utility balancing as unspeakable callousness." The jurors in the case, in other words, mistakenly valued life for its own sake—for reasons of family, love, friendship, joy, and all the other intangibles that make life worthwhile. They were, the Chamber of Commerce implies, all too human in judging General Motors as inhuman and for refusing to turn life into a numbers game.[13]

General Motors is not unique, however. In all corporate decision making, life's intangible richness and fragility are made invisible by the abstract calculations of cost-benefit analyses, something Charles Kernaghan learned firsthand on a visit to a garbage dump in the Dominican Republic.

Following garbage trucks to dumps and then sifting through what they leave behind, is helpful, Kernaghan has found, for discovering the locations of factories in the new global economy, and for finding out what goes on inside of them. The factories, which Kernaghan monitors as director of the National Labor Committee, an organization with a mandate to stop American corporations from using sweatshop labor, are located in impoverished countries where labor is cheap and easy to exploit. Thanks to the greater flexibility corporations now have with liberalized international trade laws and new communications and transportation technologies, such factories do the bulk of light manufacturing for the industrialized West. Their locations are a secret, closely guarded by the predominantly U.S. and European corporations that use them. "They hide these factories and sweatshops all over the world," says Kernaghan, and refuse requests for the factories' names and addresses "because they know it's easier to exploit teenagers behind locked metal gates, with armed guards, behind barbed wire."[14]

Kernaghan struck gold on one of his garbage dump forays when, in the Dominican Republic, he found copies of Nike's internal pricing documents in a box that had been left by one of the garbage trucks. The documents contained calculations every bit as chilling as those in Edward Ivey's report. Their purpose was to maximize the amount of profit that could be wrung out of the girls and young women who sew garments for Nike in developing-world sweatshops. Production of a shirt, to take one example, was broken down into twenty-two separate operations: five steps to cut the material, eleven steps to sew the garment, six steps to attach labels, hang tags, and put the shirt in a plastic bag, ready to be shipped. A time was allotted for each task, with units of ten thousandths of a second used for the breakdown. With all the units added together, the calculations demanded that each shirt take a maximum of 6.6 minutes to make—which translates into 8 cents' worth of labor for a shirt Nike sells in the United States for $22.99.[15]

"The science of exploitation" is how Kernaghan describes the pricing documents. Their cold calculations, he says, mask the suffering and misery of the work they demand. The typical factory Kernaghan visits in a country such as Honduras or Nicaragua, China or Bangladesh, is surrounded by barbed wire. Behind its locked doors, mainly young women workers are supervised by guards who beat and humiliate them on the slightest pretext and who fire them if a forced pregnancy test comes back positive. Each worker repeats the same action—sewing on a belt loop, stitching a sleeve—maybe two thousand times a day. They work under painfully bright lights, for twelve- to fourteen-hour shifts, in overheated factories, with too few bathroom breaks and restricted access to water (to reduce the need for more bathroom breaks), which is often foul and unfit for human consumption in any event. "They don't want you to have feelings, they don't want you to dream," says

Kernaghan of the factories' owners. The young women "work to about twenty-five, at which point they're fired because they're used up. They're worn out. Their lives are already over. And the company has replaced them with another crop of young girls."[16]

Despite everything he has seen on his developing-world beat—and some of it is almost surreal, like the school bus marked "Southampton School District" that he saw on a Honduras highway taking kids to work at a factory to stitch garments for The Gap— Kernaghan still recalls that his most disconcerting moment was at the corner of Fifty-first Street and Madison Avenue in Manhattan in the mid-1990s. There the labor activist was huddled behind a building, hiding out with a frightened sixteen-year-old girl, a diminutive sweatshop worker from Honduras named Wendy Díaz. Their eyes were trained on the doorway of the cardinal of St. Patrick's Cathedral's house across the street. The two were "frightened to death," says Kernaghan, of what was about to happen.[17]

Kernaghan and Díaz had first met at a food stand on the Pan-American Highway in Honduras, about one hundred yards from the factory where Díaz worked. Díaz and a group of young workers, aggrieved by the horrible working conditions at the factory, had contacted Kernaghan and asked to meet with him. Kernaghan agreed to meet the women at the food stand. Close to fifty of them showed up for the meeting. They found a spot behind a wooden fence where no one would see them—or so they thought. "All of a sudden, we're about to start the meeting," says Kernaghan, "when in walk three guys, very tough-looking guys." The women jumped to their feet, told Kernaghan the men were spies, and quickly began to disperse.

As they left, however, some of the women surreptitiously passed to Kernaghan, under a table, their pay stubs from the factory, which they had concealed in their hands. "I took my hand out after everyone had left," he recalls, "and in the palm of my hand was the face of Kathie Lee Gifford," imprinted on the pay stub to identify the label the women were working for. Now, for the first time, Kernaghan knew who reaped the benefit of the work done by Wendy Díaz and her coworkers at the Global Fashions factory. It was Wal-Mart, the megaretailer that sold Kathie Lee Gifford's line of clothing. So Kernaghan contacted Wal-Mart and Gifford and badgered them into meeting with him. The cardinal's home at St. Patrick's Cathedral was chosen as a neutral site for the meeting, which is what brought Kernaghan and Díaz to the corner of Fifty-first Street and Madison Avenue.[18]

The two arrived early, but they panicked before Gifford showed up, overcome by the prospect of an acrimonious encounter with a big celebrity. So they ran across the street to hide. When Gifford showed up for the meeting, flanked by an entourage of men in dark suits, they watched as she approached the entrance to the cardinal's residence. Eventually, they summoned enough courage to leave their hideout and join the meeting. Once there, Díaz told her story to Gifford: how she had worked, from the time she was thirteen years old, stitching together apparel for American companies in Honduran sweatshops—the thirteen-hour workdays, the pitiful wages, the humiliation and physical beatings by guards, how she would go to bed hungry each night after running home through dark streets with her friends, whistling and singing, in the hope rapists would leave them alone. "It was the most amazing thing I'd seen," says Kernaghan. "This powerful celebrity leans over and says, 'Wendy, please believe me, I didn't know these conditions existed. And now that I do, I'm going to work with you, I'm going to work with these other people and it'll never happen again.' "[19]

An agreement was drafted and signed with Kathie Lee Gifford that night, says Kernaghan. In it Gifford promised to stop using sweatshops, to pay decent wages to her workers, and to allow independent inspectors into her factories to ensure compliance with human rights and labor laws.

Yet Kernaghan is certain that Wal-Mart still uses sweatshop labor in developing countries, despite its initiation of third-party monitoring of its suppliers. He points out that Wal-Mart has roughly 4,400 supplier factories in China and that a large proportion of these are almost surely sweatshops. His claim is supported by a *Business Week* investigation that found that as late as 1999, Kathie Lee handbags were being made in a Chinese factory where employees worked fourteen-hour days, seven days a week, thirty days a month, for an average wage of 3 cents an hour, and were beaten, fined, and fired if they complained about it.[20] It is therefore not surprising that when Kernaghan signed the agreement with Gifford he was skeptical about whether it would result in significant change. He surmises that the corporate reaction to such a document would have been "What are you nuts? We're going to pay a living wage? That's not how the system works."[21]

Nor could it be how the system works. The corporation, like the psychopathic personality it resembles, is programmed to exploit others for profit. That is its only legitimate mandate. From that perspective, Wendy Díaz, and the millions of other workers across the globe who are driven by poverty and starvation to work in dreadful conditions for shocking wages, are not human *beings* so much as human *resources*. To the morally blind corporation, they are tools to generate as much profit as possible. And "the tool can be treated just like a piece of metal—you use it if you want, you throw it away if you don't want it," says Noam Chomsky. "If you can get human beings to become tools like that, it's more efficient by some measure of efficiency . . . a measure which is based on dehumanization. You have to dehumanize it. That's part of the system."[22]

That does not mean the people who run corporations are inhuman. Indeed, "these people would make great neighbors . . . when you meet with them in person they're quite decent," Kernaghan says of the corporate executives he has met on his beat. They must, however, serve the corporation's dehumanizing mandate. "The structure," says Kernaghan, "the whole system, just drags everybody with it." At the heart of that structure is a simple dynamic: a corporation "tends to be more profitable to the extent it can make other people pay the bills for its impact on society," as businessman Robert Monks describes it. "There's a terrible word that economists use for this called 'externalities.' "[23]

"The corporation," says Monks, "is an externalizing machine, in the same way that a shark is a killing machine. . . . There isn't any question of malevolence or of will; the enterprise has within it, and the shark has within it, those characteristics that enable it to do that for which it was designed." As a result, says Monks, the corporation is "potentially very, very damaging to society." Monks is not among the usual suspects of activists, radicals, and intellectuals who criticize the corporation. He is, to the contrary, one of America's most important and influential businessmen, a business insider who is as inside as an insider can be. Monks has helped reform and run numerous Fortune 500 companies and banks, served as adviser to Republican administrations, and ran twice as a Republican candidate for a Senate seat in Maine (both times unsuccessfully). He founded and heads an international investment firm. From his vantage point within the corporate world, Monks worries about what he sees in the modern business corporation.[24]

Monks recalls the moment he first realized what was wrong with the corporation. Lodged in a motel room in a small town where he had stopped for the night during an early-1970s election campaign, he awoke with a start in the middle of the night, his eyes aflame with irritation. When he got up to look out the window, he was shocked by what he saw—mounds of white foam floating down the river on whose banks the motel was perched. Monks went back to sleep and the next morning asked a clerk what had happened during the night. "Well, look," the clerk told him, "every night the paper company sends the stuff down the river. . . . Don't you understand, that's how we get rid of the effluent from the paper mills." Monks knew a lot of people in the town—the mayor, the people who worked in the mills, the mill owners. "And," he says, "I knew that there wasn't a person in there who wanted to have the river polluted, not a person. And yet here we're living in a world where it's happening every night."[25]

Monks realized at that moment, he says, that the corporation, an institution to which he had devoted his life, was in fact a "doom machine." "The difficulty with the corporate entity," he now believes, "is that it has a dynamic that doesn't take into account the concerns of flesh-and-blood human people who form the world in which it exists"; that "in our search for wealth and for prosperity, we created a thing that's going to destroy us."[26]

Ray Anderson, another highly successful businessman, agrees with Monks. He describes the corporation as a "present day instrument of destruction" because of its compulsion to "externalize any cost that its unwary or uncaring public will allow it to externalize." Like Monks, Anderson, founder and chairman of Interface, Inc., the world's largest commercial carpet manufacturer, had a late-career epiphany about the institution to which he had devoted his life. Until that moment, he says, he never "gave a thought to what we were taking from the earth or doing to the earth in the making of our products." Today, he believes, "the notion that we can take and take and take and take, waste and waste, and waste and waste, without consequences is driving the biosphere to destruction."[27]

Anderson remembers the moment when his beliefs about the corporation shifted. It was the summer of 1994. Environmentalism had become a mainstream worry, and Interface, Inc.'s customers had begun to inquire about what the company was doing for the environment. "We didn't have answers," recalls Anderson, "the real answer was 'Not very much.'" At the time Anderson was not bothered by his lack of answers, but others in his company were. In response to their concerns, he created a task force to investigate the company's worldwide environmental position, and he agreed to give a speech describing his own personal environmental vision.[28]

The difficulty, Anderson quickly realized, was that "I didn't have an environmental vision. . . . I began to sweat," he recalls. "Oh my, what to say?" Desperate for material and inspiration, he began to read a book about ecology. There he came across the phrase "the death of birth," a description of species extinction. "It was a point of a spear into my chest," he now recalls, "and I read on, and the spear went deeper, and it became an epiphanal experience, a total change of mind-set for myself and a change of paradigm." "We're all sinners, we're all sinners," says Anderson today of his position as a corporate chief. "Someday people like me will end up in jail." But he now rejects as dangerously misguided the beliefs he once shared with the large majority of business leaders—"that nature is unlimited, the earth . . . a limitless source for raw material, a limitless sink into which we can send our poisons and waste"; "that the relevant timeframe is my lifetime, maybe my working life, but certainly not more than my lifetime"; and that the market's invisible hand will take care of everything. The market alone cannot provide sufficient constraints on corporations' penchant to cause harm, Anderson now believes, because it is "blind to . . . externalities, those costs that can be externalized and foisted off on somebody else."[29]

All businesspeople understand that corporations are designed to externalize their costs. What makes Monks and Anderson unique is that they fear the consequences of this design, rather than celebrating its virtue. The corporation, as they say, is deliberately programmed, indeed legally compelled, to externalize costs without regard for the harm it may cause to people, communities, and the natural environment. Every cost it can unload onto someone else is a benefit to itself, a direct route to profit. Patricia Anderson's family's burns—externalities; Wendy Díaz's exploitation and misery—externalities. These and a thousand other points of corporate darkness, from Bhopal and the *Exxon Valdez* to epidemic levels of worker injury and death and chronic destruction of the environment, are the price we all pay for the corporation's flawed character.[30]

Notes

1   The creation of externalities by corporations relates directly to the legal rule that corporations must always act in ways that serve their own best interests, i.e., that maximize their shareholders' wealth. As corporate law scholar Janis Sarra stated in an interview: "Corporate law, as it is currently constructed in the Anglo-American para-digm, requires that corporate officers take account of short-term costs and long-term costs *to the corporation*, but not to anyone else. Anything that is not considered such a cost is called an externality and includes the costs of corporate harms that are borne by workers, small creditors, consumers, or community members. If a corporation makes a decision that will harm the land or have some sort of long-term effect on fishing waters of First Nations people or results in environmental contamination of communities, those kinds of costs are external to the corporation and do not need to be accounted for in the corporation's decision. These externalities also do not need to be costed on the corporate balance sheet because only the profit is recorded, but not the costs to others. That is how corporate law is currently constructed."

2   Interview with Milton Friedman.

3   Ibid.

4   "Record $4.9 Billion Award Against GM for Dangerous Fuel Tanks," www.cnn.com, July 9, 1999; Milo Geyelen, "How a Memo Written 26 Years Ago Is Costing General Motors Dearly," *The Wall Street Journal*, September 29, 1999, 1.

5   Geyelen, "How a Memo Written 26 Years Ago Is Costing General Motors Dearly."

6   Ibid.

7   The $8.19 figure comes from other GM documents, not the Ivey Report. For a descrip-tion, see, "GM Fuel Tanks," www.safetyforum.com; Public Citizen, "Profits over Lives—Long-Hidden Documents Reveal GM Cost-Benefit Analyses Led to Severe Burn Injuries; Disregard for Safety Spurred Large Verdict," July 19, 1999, available www.citizen.org/congress/civjus/tort/.

8   The case is currently embroiled in procedural wrangling and has not yet been heard by the California Court of Appeal.

9   *Patricia Anderson v. General Motors*, Brief of Chamber of Commerce of the United States as *amicus curiae* in support of the Appellant, California Court of Appeal for the Second Appellate District—Division Four, 3 ("illegitimate"), 1 ("troubling" and "manufactur-ing"), 3 ("despicable"), 8 ("hallmark"), 10 ("unimpeachable").

10   Meiring de Villiers, "Technological Risk and Issue Preclusion: A Legal and Policy Critique," *Cornell Journal of Law and Public Policy* 9 (2000): 523, as cited in the Chamber of Commerce Brief, p. 9.

11   MacIntyre, A. (1977) "Utilitarianism and Cost-Benefit Analysis: An Essay on the Relevance of Moral Philsophy to Bureaucratic Theory." In K. Sayre (ed.) Values in the Electrical Power Industry, Notre Dame, University of Notre Dame Press.

12   Ivey Report (print version on file with the author).

13   Chamber of Commerce Brief, 10. ("Skillful" and "sanctity," citing Gary T. Schwartz, Deterrence and Punishment in the Common Law of Punitive Damages: A Comment (1982) 56 5.Cal L. Rev. 133, p. 152.)

14   Interview with Charles Kernaghan.

15   Ibid.

16   Ibid.

17   Ibid.

18   Ibid.

19   Ibid.

20   Dexter Roberts and Aaron Bernstein, "Inside a Chinese Sweatshop: 'A Life of Fines and Beating,' " *BusinessWeek Online*, October 2, 2000. According to the report, "Since 1992, Wal-Mart has required its suppliers to sign a code of basic labor standards. After exposés in the mid-1990s of abuses in factories making Kathie Lee products, which the chain carries, Wal-Mart and Kathie Lee both began hiring outside auditing firms to inspect supplier factories to ensure their compliance with the code. Many other companies that produce or sell goods made in low-wage countries do similar self-policing, from Toys 'R' Us to Nike and Gap. While no company suggests that its auditing systems are perfect, most say they catch major abuses and either force suppliers to fix them or yank production.

     "What happened at Chun Si [the factory making Kathie Lee handbags] suggests that these auditing systems can miss serious problems—and that self-policing allows companies to avoid painful public revelations about them." See also the National Labor Committee's Web site, www.nlcnet.org, for complete and up-to-date information on major U.S. companies' use of sweatshops throughout the developing world. Examples of successful resistance to sweatshops can also be found at the site.

21   Roberts and Bernstein, "Inside a Chinese Sweatshop."

22   Interview with Noam Chomsky.

23   Interviews with Charles Kernaghan and Robert Monks.

24   Interview with Robert Monks. See also Robert Monks, *The Emperor's Nightingale: Restoring the Integrity of the Corporation in the Age of Shareholder Activism* (Reading, Mass.: Addison-Wesley, 1998); Hilary Rosenberg, *A Traitor to His Class: Robert A. G. Monks and the Battle to Change Corporate America* (New York: John Wiley and Sons, 1999).

25   Interview with Robert Monks.

26   Ibid.

27   Interview with Ray Anderson.

28   Ibid.

29   Ibid. The book was Paul Hawkens, *The Ecology of Commerce* (New York: HarperCollins, 1993), in which the author quotes E. O. Wilson's phrase "the death of birth."

30   For some further examples of externalities, see Russell Mokhiber and Robert Weissman, *Corporate Predators: The Hunt for Mega-Profits and the Attack on Democracy* (Monroe, Maine: Common Courage Press, 1999); M. F. Hawkins, *Unshielded: The Human Cost of the Dalkon Shield* (Toronto: University of Toronto Press, 1997).

Naomi Klein

THE UNBEARABLE LIGHTNESS OF CAVITE
Inside the free-trade zones

DESPITE THE CONCEPTUAL brilliance of the "brands, not products" strategy, production has a pesky way of never quite being transcended entirely: *somebody*
has to get down and dirty and make the products the global brands will hang their
meaning on. And that's where the free-trade zones come in. In Indonesia, China, Mexico,
Vietnam, the Philippines and elsewhere, export processing zones (as these areas are also
called) are emerging as leading producers of garments, toys, shoes, electronics, machinery,
even cars.

If Nike Town and the other superstores are the glittering new gateways to the branded
dreamworlds, then the Cavite Export Processing Zone, located ninety miles south of
Manila in the town of Rosario, is the branding broom closet. After a month visiting similar
industrial areas in Indonesia, I arrived in Rosario in early September 1997, at the tail end
of monsoon season and the beginning of the Asian economic storm. I'd come to spend a
week in Cavite because it is the largest free-trade zone in the Philippines, a 682-acre
walled-in industrial area housing 207 factories that produce goods strictly for the export
market. Rosario's population of 60,000 all seemed to be on the move; the town's busy,
sweltering streets were packed with army jeeps converted into minibuses and with
motorcycle taxis with precarious sidecars, its sidewalks lined with stalls selling fried rice,
Coke and soap. Most of this commercial activity serves the 50,000 workers who rush
through Rosario on their way to and from work in the zone, whose gated entrance is
located smack in the middle of town.

Inside the gates, factory workers assemble the finished products of our branded
world: Nike running shoes, Gap pajamas, IBM computer screens, Old Navy jeans. But
despite the presence of such illustrious multinationals, Cavite – and the exploding number
of export processing zones like it throughout the developing world – could well be the
only places left on earth where the superbrands actually keep a low profile. Indeed, they
are positively self-effacing. Their names and logos aren't splashed on the façades of the
factories in the industrial zone. And here, competing labels aren't segregated each in its

own superstore; they are often produced side by side in the same factories glued by the very same workers, stitched and soldered on the very same machines. It was in Cavite that I finally found a piece of unswooshed space, and I found it, oddly enough, in a Nike shoe factory.

I was only permitted one visit inside the zone's gates to interview officials – individual factories, I was told, are off limits to anyone but potential importers or exporters. But a few days later, with the help of an eighteen-year-old worker who had been laid off from his job in an electronics factory, I managed to sneak back to get the unofficial tour. In the rows of virtually identical giant shed-like structures, one factory stood out: the name on the white rectangular building said "Philips," but through its surrounding fence I could see mountains of Nike shoes piled high. It seems that in Cavite, production has been banished to our age's most worthless status: its factories are unbrandable, unswooshworthy; producers are the industrial untouchables. Is this what Phil Knight meant, I wondered, when he said his company wasn't about the sneakers?

Manufacturing is concentrated and isolated inside the zone as if it were toxic waste: pure, 100 percent production at low, low prices. Cavite, like the rest of the zones that compete with it, presents itself as the buy-in-bulk Price Club for multinationals on the lookout for bargains – grab a really big shopping cart. Inside, it's obvious that the row of factories, each with its own gate and guard, has been carefully planned to squeeze the maximum amount of production out of this swath of land. Windowless workshops made of cheap plastic and aluminum siding are crammed in next to each other, only feet apart. Racks of time cards bake in the sun, making sure the maximum amount of work is extracted from each worker, the maximum number of working hours extracted from each day. The streets in the zone are eerily empty, and open doors – the ventilation system for most factories – reveal lines of young women hunched in silence over clamoring machines.

In other parts of the world, workers live inside the economic zones, but not in Cavite: this is a place of pure work. All the bustle and color of Rosario abruptly stops at the gates, where workers must show their ID cards to armed guards in order to get inside. Visitors are rarely permitted in the zone and little or no internal commerce takes place on its orderly streets, not even candy and drink vending. Buses and taxicabs must drop their speed and silence their horns when they get into the zone – a marked change from the boisterous streets of Rosario. If all of this makes Cavite feel as if it's in a different country, that's because, in a way, it is. The zone is a tax-free economy, sealed off from the local government of both town and province – a miniature military state inside a democracy.

As a concept, free-trade zones are as old as commerce itself, and were all the more relevant in ancient times when the transportation of goods required multiple holdovers and rest stops. Pre-Roman Empire city-states, including Tyre, Carthage and Utica, encouraged trade by declaring themselves "free cities," where goods in transit could be stored without tax, and merchants would be protected from harm. These tax-free areas developed further economic significance during colonial times, when entire cities – including Hong Kong, Singapore and Gibraltar – were designated as "free ports" from which the loot of colonialism could be safely shipped back to England, Europe or America with low import tariffs.[1] Today, the globe is dotted with variations on these tax-free pockets, from duty-free shops in airports and the free banking zones of the Cayman Islands to bonded warehouses and ports where goods in transit are held, sorted and packaged.

Though it has plenty in common with these other tax havens, the export processing zone is really in a class of its own. Less holding tank than sovereign territory, the EPZ is an area where goods don't just pass through but are actually manufactured, an area, furthermore, where there are no import and export duties, and often no income or property taxes either. The idea that EPZs could help Third World economies first gained currency in 1964 when the United Nations Economic and Social Council adopted a resolution endorsing the zones as a means of promoting trade with developing nations. The idea didn't really get off the ground, however, until the early eighties, when India introduced a five-year tax break for companies manufacturing in its low-wage zones.

Since then, the free-trade-zone industry has exploded. There are fifty-two economic zones in the Philippines alone, employing 459,000 people – that's up from only 23,000 zone workers in 1986 and 229,000 as recently as 1994. The largest zone economy is China, where by conservative estimates there are 18 million people in 124 export processing zones.[2] In total, the International Labor Organization says that there are at least 850 EPZs in the world, but that number is likely much closer to 1,000, spread through seventy countries and employing roughly 27 million workers.[3] The World Trade Organization estimates that between $200 and $250 billion worth of trade flows through the zones.[4] The number of individual factories housed inside these industrial parks is also expanding. In fact, the free-trade factories along the U.S. Mexico border – in Spanish, *maquiladoras* (from *maquillar*, "to make up, or assemble") – are probably the only structures that proliferate as quickly as Wal-Mart outlets: there were 789 maquiladoras in 1985. In 1995, there were 2,747. By 1997, there were 3,508 employing about 900,000 workers.[5]

Regardless of where the EPZs are located, the workers' stories have a certain mesmerizing sameness: the workday is long – fourteen hours in Sri Lanka, twelve hours in Indonesia, sixteen in Southern China, twelve in the Philippines. The vast majority of the workers are women, always young, always working for contractors or subcontractors from Korea, Taiwan or Hong Kong. The contractors are usually filling orders for companies based in the U.S., Britain, Japan, Germany or Canada. The management is military-style, the supervisors often abusive, the wages below subsistence and the work low-skill and tedious. As an economic model, today's export processing zones have more in common with fast-food franchises than sustainable developments, so removed are they from the countries that host them. These pockets of pure industry hide behind a cloak of transience: the contracts come and go with little notice; the workers are predominantly migrants, far from home and with little connection to the city or province where zones are located; the work itself is short-term, often not renewed.

As I walk along the blank streets of Cavite, I can feel the threatening impermanence, the underlying instability of the zone. The shed-like factories are connected so tenuously to the surrounding country, to the adjacent town, to the very earth they are perched upon, that it feels as if the jobs that flew here from the North could fly away again just as quickly. The factories are cheaply constructed and tossed together on land that is rented, not owned. When I climb up the water tower on the edge of the zone and look down at the hundreds of factories, it seems as if the whole cardboard complex could lift up and blow away, like Dorothy's house in *The Wizard of Oz*. No wonder the EPZ factories in Guatemala are called "swallows."

Fear pervades the zones. The governments are afraid of losing their foreign factories; the factories are afraid of losing their brand-name buyers; and the workers are afraid of losing their unstable jobs. These are factories built not on land but on air.

"It should have been a different Rosario"

The air the export processing zones are built upon is the promise of industrialization. The theory behind EPZs is that they will attract foreign investors, who, if all goes well, will decide to stay in the country, and the zones' segregated assembly lines will turn into lasting development: technology transfers and domestic industries. To lure the swallows into this clever trap, the governments of poor countries offer tax breaks, lax regulations and the services of a military willing and able to crush labor unrest. To sweeten the pot further, they put their own people on the auction block, falling over each other to offer up the lowest minimum wage, allowing workers to be paid less than the real cost of living.

In Cavite, the economic zone is designed as a fantasyland for foreign investors. Golf courses, executive clubs and private schools have been built on the outskirts of Rosario to ease the discomforts of Third World life. Rent for factories is dirt cheap: 11 pesos per square foot – less than a cent. For the first five years of their stay, corporations are treated to an all-expenses-paid "tax holiday" during which they pay no income tax and no property tax. It's a good deal, no doubt, but it's nothing compared to Sri Lanka, where EPZ investors stay for ten years before having to pay any tax.[6]

The phrase "tax holiday" is oddly fitting. For the investors, free-trade zones are a sort of corporate Club Med, where the hotel pays for everything and the guests live free, and where integration with the local culture and economy is kept to a bare minimum. As one International Labor Organization report puts it, the EPZ "is to the inexperienced foreign investor what the package holiday is to the cautious tourist." Zero-risk globalization. Companies just ship in the pieces of cloth or computer parts – free of import tax – and the cheap, non-union workforce assembles it for them. Then the finished garments or electronics are shipped back out, with no export tax.

The rationale goes something like this: *of course* companies must pay taxes and strictly abide by national laws, but just in this one case, on this one specific piece of land, for just a little while, an exception will be made – for the cause of future prosperity. The EPZs, therefore, exist within a kind of legal and economic set of brackets, apart from the rest of their countries – the Cavite zone, for example, is under the sole jurisdiction of the Philippines' federal Department of Trade and Industry; the local police and municipal government have no right even to cross the threshold. The layers of blockades serve a dual purpose: to keep the hordes away from the costly goods being manufactured inside the zone, but also, and perhaps more important, to shield the country from what is going on inside the zone.

Because such sweet deals have been laid out to entice the swallows, the barriers around the zone serve to reinforce the idea that what is happening inside is only temporary, or is not really happening at all. This collective denial is particularly important in Communist countries where zones house the most Wild West forms of capitalism this side of Moscow: this is *definitely* not really happening, *certainly* not here where the government in power maintains that capital is the devil and workers reign supreme. In her book *Losing Control?*, Saskia Sassen writes that the zones are a part of a process of carving up nations so that "an actual piece of land becomes denationalized . . ."[7] Never mind that the boundaries of these only-temporary, not-really-happening, denationalized spaces keep expanding to engulf more and more of their actual nations. Twenty-seven million people worldwide are now living and working in brackets, and the brackets, instead of being slowly removed, just keep getting wider.

It is one of the zones' many cruel ironies that every incentive the governments throw in to attract the multinationals only reinforces the sense that the companies are economic tourists rather than long-term investors. It's a classic vicious cycle: in an attempt to alleviate poverty, the governments offer more and more incentives; but then the EPZs must be cordoned off like leper colonies, and the more they are cordoned off, the more the factories appear to exist in a world entirely separate from the host country, and outside the zone the poverty only grows more desperate. In Cavite, the zone is a kind of futuristic industrial suburbia where everything is ordered; the workers are uniformed, the grass manicured, the factories regimented. There are cute signs all around the grounds instructing workers to "Keep Our Zone Clean" and "Promote Peace and Progress of the Philippines." But walk out of the gate and the bubble bursts. Aside from the swarms of workers at the start and end of shifts, you'd never know that the town of Rosario is home to more than two hundred factories. The roads are a mess, running water is scarce and garbage is overflowing.

Many of the workers live in shantytowns on the outskirts of town and in neighboring villages. Others, particularly the youngest workers, live in the dormitories, a hodgepodge of concrete bunkers separated from the zone enclave by only a thick wall. The structure is actually a converted farm, and some rooms, the workers tell me, are really pigpens with roofs slapped on them.

The Philippines' experience of "industrialization in brackets" is by no means unique. The current mania for the EPZ model is based on the successes of the so-called Asian Tiger economies, in particular the economies of South Korea and Taiwan. When only a few countries had the zones, including South Korea and Taiwan, wages rose steadily, technology transfers occurred and taxes were gradually introduced. But as critics of EPZs are quick to point out, the global economy has become much more competitive since those countries made the transition from low-wage industries to higher-skill ones. Today, with seventy countries competing for the export-processing-zone dollar, the incentives to lure investors are increasing and the wages and standards are being held hostage to the threat of departure. The upshot is that entire countries are being turned into industrial slums and low-wage labor ghettos, with no end in sight. As Cuban president Fidel Castro thundered to the assembled world leaders at the World Trade Organization's fiftieth-birthday celebration in May 1998, "What are we going to live on? . . . What industrial production will be left for us? Only low-tech, labor-intensive and highly contaminating ones? Do they perhaps want to turn a large part of the Third World into a huge free trade zone full of assembly plants which don't even pay taxes?"[8]

As bad as the situation is in Cavite, it doesn't begin to compare with Sri Lanka, where extended tax holidays mean that towns can't even provide public transportation for EPZ workers. The roads they walk to and from the factories are dark and dangerous, since there is no money for streetlights. Dormitory rooms are so overcrowded that they have white lines painted on the floor to mark where each worker sleeps – they "look like car parks," as one journalist observed.[9]

Jose Ricafrente has the dubious honor of being mayor of Rosario. I met with him in his small office, while a lineup of needy people waited outside. A once-modest fishing village, his town today has the highest per capita investment in all of the Philippines – thanks to the Cavite zone – but it lacks even the basic resources to clean up the mess that the factories create in the community. Rosario has all the problems of industrialization – pollution, an exploding population of migrant workers, increased crime, rivers of sewage – without any of the benefits. The federal government estimates that only 30 of the zone's 207 factories pay any taxes at all, but everybody else questions even that low figure. The mayor says that many companies are granted extensions of their tax holiday, or they close and reopen under another name, then take the free ride all over again. "They fold up before the tax holiday expires, then they incorporate to another company, just to avoid payment of taxes. They don't pay anything to the government, so we're in a dilemma right now," Ricafrente told me. A small man with a deep and powerful voice, Ricafrente is loved by his constituents for the outspoken positions he took on human rights and democracy during Ferdinand Marcos's brutal rule. But the day I met him, the mayor seemed exhausted, worn down by his powerlessness to affect the situation in his own backyard.[10] "We cannot even provide the basic services that our people expect from us," he said, with a sort of matter-of-fact rage. "We need water, we need roads, we need medical services, education. They expect us to deliver all of them at the same time, expecting that we've got money from taxes from the places inside the zone."

The mayor is convinced that there will always be a country – whether Vietnam, China, Sri Lanka or Mexico – that is willing to bid lower. And in the process, towns like Rosario will have sold out their people, compromised their education system and polluted their natural resources. "It should be a symbiotic relationship," Ricafrente says of foreign investment. "They derive income from us, so the government should also derive income from them. . . . It should have been a different Rosario."

Working in brackets

So, if it's clear by now that the factories don't bring in taxes or create local infrastructures, and that the goods produced are all exported, why do countries like the Philippines still bend over backward to lure them inside their borders? The official reason is a trickle-down theory: these zones are job-creation programs and the income the workers earn will eventually fuel sustainable growth in the local economy.

The problem with this theory is that the zone wages are so low that workers spend most of their pay on shared dorm rooms and transportation; the rest goes to noodles and fried rice from vendors lined up outside the gate. Zone workers certainly cannot dream of affording the consumer goods they produce. These low wages are partly a result of the fierce competition for factories coming from other developing countries. But, above all, the government is extremely reluctant to enforce its own labor laws for fear of scaring away the swallows. So labor rights are under such severe assault inside the zones that there is little chance of workers earning enough to adequately feed themselves, let alone stimulate the local economy.

The Philippine government denies this, of course. It says that the zones are subject to the same labor standards as the rest of Philippine society: workers must be paid the minimum wage, receive social security benefits, have some measure of job security, be dismissed only with just cause and be paid extra for overtime, and they have the right to form independent trade unions. But in reality, the government views working conditions in the export factories as a matter of foreign trade policy, not a labor-rights issue. And since the government attracted the foreign investors with promises of a cheap and docile workforce, it intends to deliver. For this reason, labor department officials turn a blind eye to violations in the zone or even facilitate them.

Many of the zone factories are run according to iron-fist rules that systematically break Philippine labor law. Some employers, for instance, keep bathrooms padlocked except during two fifteen-minute breaks, during which time all the workers have to sign in and out so management can keep track of their nonproductive time. Seamstresses at a factory sewing garments for the Gap, Guess and Old Navy told me that they sometimes have to resort to urinating in plastic bags under their machines. There are rules against talking, and at the Ju Young electronics factory, a rule against smiling. One factory shames those who disobey by posting a list of "The Most Talkative Workers."

Factories regularly cheat on their workers' social security payments and gather illegal "donations" from workers for everything from cleaning materials to factory Christmas parties. At a factory that makes IBM computer screens, the "bonus" for working hours of overtime isn't a higher hourly wage but doughnuts and a pen. Some owners expect workers to pull weeds from the ground on their way into the factory; others must clean the floors and the washrooms after their shifts end. Ventilation is poor and protective gear scarce.

Then there is the matter of wages. In the Cavite zone, the minimum wage is regarded more as a loose guideline than as a rigid law. If $6 a day is too onerous, investors can apply to the government for a waiver on that too. So while some zone workers earn the minimum wage, most – thanks to the waivers – earn less.[11]

Not low enough: squeezing wages in China

Part of the reason the threat of factory flight is so tangible in Cavite is that compared with China, Filipino wages are very high. In fact, everyone's wages are high compared with China. But what is truly remarkable about that is that the most egregious wage cheating goes on inside China itself.

Labor groups agree that a living wage for an assembly-line worker in China would be approximately US87 cents an hour. In the United States and Germany, where multinationals have closed down hundreds of domestic textile factories to move to zone production, garment workers are paid an average of US$10 and $18.50 an hour, respectively.[12] Yet even with these massive savings in labor costs, those who manufacture for the most prominent and richest brands in the world are still refusing to pay workers in China the 87 cents that would cover their cost of living, stave off illness and even allow them to send a little money home to their families. A 1998 study of brand-name manufacturing in the Chinese special economic zones found that Wal-Mart, Ralph Lauren, Ann Taylor, Esprit, Liz Claiborne, Kmart, Nike, Adidas, J.C. Penney and the Limited were only paying a fraction of that miserable 87 cents – some were paying as little as 13 cents an hour.

The only way to understand how rich and supposedly law-abiding multinational corporations could regress to nineteenth-century levels of exploitation (and get caught repeatedly) is through the mechanics of subcontracting itself: at every layer of contracting, subcontracting and homework, the manufacturers bid against each other to drive down the price, and at every level the contractor and subcontractor exact their small profit. At the end of this bid-down, contract-out chain is the worker – often three or four times removed from the company that placed the original order – with a paycheck that has been trimmed at every turn. "When the multinationals squeeze the subcontractors, the subcontractors squeeze the workers," explains a 1997 report on Nike's and Reebok's Chinese shoe factories.[13]

Notes

1   Richard S. Thoman, *Free Ports and Foreign Trade Zones* (Cambridge: Cornell Maritime Press, 1956).
2   These are International Labor Organization figures as of May 1998 but in "Behind the Label: 'Made in China,' " by Charles Kernaghan, March 1998, the figures on China's zone are much higher. Kernaghan estimates that there are 30 million inside the zones, and that there are 400 – as opposed to 124 – special economic zones inside China.
3   The International Labor Organization's Special Action Program on Export Processing Zones. Source: Auret Van Heerden.
4   This estimate was provided by Michael Finger at the World Trade Organization in a personal correspondence. No official figures are available.
5   Figures for 1985 and 1995 provided by the WTO. Figures for 1997 supplied by the Maquila Solidarity Network/Labor Behind the Label Coalition, Toronto.
6   *World Accounting Report*, July 1992.
7   Saskia Sassen, *Losing Control? Sovereignty in an Age of Globalization* (New York: Columbia University Press, 1996), 8–9.
8   "Castro Dampens WTO Party," *Globe and Mail*, 20 May 1998.
9   Martin Cottingham, "Cut to the Bone," *New Statesman & Society*, 12 March 1993, 12.
10 Personal interview, 2 September 1997.
11 The Workers' Assistance Center, Rosario.
12 "Globalization Changes the Face of Textile, Clothing and Footwear Industries," International Labor Organization press release, 28 October 1996.
13 "Working Conditions in Sports Shoe Factories in China Making Shoes for Nike and Reebok," by Asia Monitor Resource Centre and Hong Kong Christian Industrial Committee, September 1997.

CorporateWatch

CORPORATE PSYCHOLOGY
Killing from behind a desk

The corporate mind

IF WE AGREE that the corporation is not a human being, the question arises: what is it? Viewed from within in political terms, the answer is simple. The corporation is a dictatorship, or at best an oligarchy, run as a centrally planned economy with an extensive bureaucracy. Workers within the system have few rights, they are increasingly under tight surveillance, and the penalty for disobedience is loss of livelihood (less extreme than the imprisonment or torture used by political dictators, but nonetheless terrifying). Rebellion is made less likely by bread and circuses (wages plus benefits of every kind from subsidized canteens and works outings to private health insurance and expense-account lunches), coupled with sheer fatigue, and by the shortage of different models to aspire to. It's true that workers, unlike subjects of a political dictatorship, are generally free to emigrate, but most of the possible destinations are run the same way.

The analogy goes further: like most dictatorships, corporations foster a self-serving ideology; seek ever more power and control; are intensely fearful of attacks from outside; and cannot tolerate dissent (witness the disproportionate reactions to protests against world trade summits).

The analogy breaks down, however, because whereas the political dictatorship is run to the wishes of an individual or ruling party elite, in the corporate system the CEO and board of directors are themselves merely tools of the system.

But where is the core of the system? Here lies the true power and true vulnerability of the corporation, because at its centre is a power vacuum: the shareholders own, and supposedly have control, but they do not actually control: the board and CEO actually control, but theoretically owe their power to the shareholders. As a result, the buck doesn't stop – no-one has the ultimate duty to think about what the corporation should do and be: the only imperative is the directors' duty to act in the best interests of the company, which means the best interests of the shareholders, which means profit. If this leads the directors or managers to have to act against their conscience, well, that's their duty to shareholders. When shareholders see the company acting in ways their conscience would otherwise reject, well, the directors run the company, it's their responsibility.

This situation has itself grown out of a centuries-long development in company law and practice. Selfish individuals have no doubt contributed to this, but others who truly believe themselves to be decent and well-intentioned are also caught up in the corporate web. The vacuum at the heart of the corporation harnesses its managers' and employees' intelligence to aims which their consciences would otherwise abhor. Far from calling itself a human being, the corporation for all its power is a mindless predator, a super-brute, with a single, self-centred, self-expanding aim – to act in its own best interests.

Corporate psychology – killing from behind a desk

Who are the people who manufacture torture equipment, advertise cigarettes to children, bribe dictators, discharge toxic waste into the environment, order goods from sweat-shops? Even the most rabid of anti-corporate activists doesn't believe that everyone working for Union Carbide in 1984 was an evil psychopath who laughed when chronic neglect of safety procedures led to the company's Bhopal factory blowing up, spewing poison gas and killing 10,000 people. But if decision-makers and employees of criminal corporations are much like the rest of us – they love their families, enjoy watching football or walking the dog, worry about old age and the state of the world – how can they collaborate in the things their company does?

Dan Gretton, an activist and writer working at Platform in London, has researched this. While psychological research hasn't gone far in examining the backstage perpetrators of corporate crime, it has looked at the psychology of torture and genocide in human history, most particularly at the Holocaust. Gretton's project, entitled 'Killing us Softly', takes this research and shows how it applies to the everyday workings of corporate crime: if ordinary, otherwise sane people could find themselves collaborating in the greatest evil the world has ever seen and psychologically adapt to it (and the research shows that they could and did) less extreme versions of the same psychological traits or mechanisms could allow them to do the same in less extreme situations, where killing is a consequence rather than the aim of an operation.

There is no attempt here to compare the *crimes* of corporate employees to those of the Holocaust: while one should not underestimate the number of victims of corporate crime (the figures on babies dying through inappropriate feeding with infant milk formula run into the millions, yet the companies involved continue their irresponsible marketing), the level of individual guilt involved is orders of magnitude lower. This section attempts simply to show how the very extremity of the crimes of the Holocaust revealed the psychological mechanisms of the administrative criminal which continue to contribute to lesser crimes. Corporate crime itself had a role in the Holocaust: commercial companies manufactured extermination equipment and poison gas and used concentration camp slave labour.

Gretton has identified six crucial mechanisms by which otherwise 'moral' people come to collaborate:

- **incrementalism**
  The hundreds of steps, often accompanied by increasing responsibility and reward, by which people gradually become accustomed to participation.
- **normalization**
  The existence of a culture in which the crimes are considered not only normal but necessary, and where continued exposure makes people accustomed to them. Gretton discusses how young doctors became 'normalized' to selecting victims for the gas chambers at Auschwitz. 'In the beginning it was almost impossible. Afterward it became almost routine.' Doctors became 'insiders', doing the work but drowning their basic objections in group drinking and ritualized outbursts of disgust.
- **linguistic dehumanization**
  Changing the way people are referred to from sentient beings to objects or abstract concepts: this can be found almost anywhere one looks, from the SS descriptions of trainloads of doomed Jews as 'cargo', to the infamous US military description of civilian war dead as 'collateral damage' to the slave owner calling his slaves 'hands' to the corporate euphemism of 'downsizing'.
- **avoidance of physical violence**
  Perhaps more a side-effect of than a precondition for collaboration, this trait was observed in Nazis including Adolf Eichmann and Franz Stangl when they came to trial. The men displayed disproportionate reactions to allegations that they had themselves beaten or shot at prisoners, suggesting that they fetishized the evil of physical violence to reduce their own guilt over their much larger crimes of administrative killing.
- **distancing**
  Not just physical distancing but mental distancing, this phenomenon is often linked with the linguistic dehumanization described above – the people affected by the act are never seen as individuals but as a mass – 'the Jews', 'the natives', 'the enemy'. In the corporate context, one can find a version of this mechanism in the concentration on speculative long-term or large-scale outcomes – 'Nigeria will benefit from oil development [so it doesn't matter if a few people die]', 'agriculture must become more efficient [even if this means forcing half the farmers off their land and into poverty]' – by looking far into a bright distance the decision-maker avoids seeing what is crushed under their feet.
- **compartmentalization of the mind**
  Perhaps the most crucial mechanism: this is a well-documented phenomenon in which people put parts of their lives in different categories. Powerful people often display a capacity to exercise affectionate and moral qualities at home, but somewhere on the journey to work human and ethical values are put away into a safe box to allow them to act according to the requirements of the job. The oil company executive who has just authorized the forced 'development' of a chunk of Nigeria, who then goes home and plays with his grandchildren believes his conscience is clear because he has closed off the connection between the different parts of his world. Thus Gretton has found a doctor working at Auschwitz in 1942 who wrote journal entries recording the weather and the excellence of the food in between brief notes on mass executions and the extraction of human tissue from living bodies for

experiments. A slightly different aspect of compartmentalization can be seen in the phenomenon of the person who is 'only doing my job': even when that job is assembling detonators for cluster bombs, they manage not to see themselves as contributing to killing.

For corporate decision-makers, there is also a simple practical mechanism at work – they are extremely unlikely to be held personally responsible for the consequences of their company's acts. There is less motivation to consider the consequences of one's acts if you know no-one will ever punish you for them.

Gretton's project explores a concept developed during the 1961 trial of Adolf Eichmann, architect of the Holocaust – the concept of the *Schreibtischtäter*, which Gretton translates as 'desk-murderer' – a person who does not kill themselves, but who, from behind the scenes, in a quiet office, organizes or orders actions which result in killing. There is some sign of a formal adoption of this view of the perpetrator in the statutes of the International Criminal Court which specifically include ordering or facilitating crimes. The fact that this concept of holding distant decision-makers responsible for the consequences of their actions has not significantly spread into national law perhaps reveals another basic problem of human psychology, or ethics – we find it very difficult to assign responsibility for serious crimes spread across a large group of people or a variety of bodies. For example, hundreds of people will be involved in the decisions which lead to the building of an oil pipeline. When the poorly-trained armed police hired to guard the pipeline route start shooting the evicted locals when they protest, hundreds of people, some of them thousands of miles away, share the responsibility. The way the law has traditionally operated offers little means to bring them to justice – who of the hundreds can be held responsible? Are they all guilty of murder or manslaughter and liable to face the full penalties? Or should a share of responsibility only merit a share of punishment? We haven't answered these questions yet – they're scarcely being asked. This is partly the flip-side of our legal system's and our culture's fetishization of physical violence, as discussed above: the psychological mechanisms permitting and condoning corporate crime operate not only in corporate decision-makers but in all of us.

> I am the clerk, the technician, the mechanic, the driver.
> They said, Do this, do that, don't look left or right,
> don't read the text. Don't look at the whole machine. You
> are only responsible for this one bolt. For this one rubber-stamp.
> This is your only concern. Don't bother with what is above you.
> Don't try to think for us. Go on, drive. Keep going. On, on.
>
> Answer them, said he to himself, said the little man,
> the man with a head of his own. Who is in charge? Who knows
> where this train is going?
> Where is their head? I too have a head.
> Why do I see the whole engine,
> Why do I see the precipice–
> is there a driver on this train?
> The clerk driver technician mechanic looked up.
> He stepped back and saw – what a monster.

Can't believe it. Rubbed his eyes and – yes,
it's there all right. I'm all right. I do see
the monster. I'm part of the system.
I signed this form. Only now I am reading the rest of it.

(from 'I am your spy' by Mordechai Vanunu, the technician who blew the whistle on Israel's secret nuclear weapons programme in 1986. Vanunu has spent the seventeen years since then in prison, mostly in solitary confinement. http://www.vanunu.freeserve.co.uk)

McSpotlight

WHAT'S WRONG WITH McDONALD'S?

McDONALD'S SPEND OVER $1.8 billion every year worldwide on advertising and promotions, trying to cultivate an image of being a 'caring' and 'green' company that is also a fun place to eat. Children are lured in (dragging their parents behind them) with the promise of toys and other gimmicks. But behind the smiling face of Ronald McDonald lies the reality – McDonald's only interest is money, making profits from whoever and whatever they can, just like all multinational companies. McDonald's Annual Reports talk of 'Global Domination' – they aim to open more and more stores across the globe – but their continual worldwide expansion means more uniformity, less choice and the undermining of local communities.

Promoting unhealthy food

McDonald's promote their food as 'nutritious', but the reality is that it is junk food – high in fat, sugar and salt, and low in fibre and vitamins. A diet of this type is linked with a greater risk of heart disease, cancer, diabetes and other diseases. Their food also contains many chemical additives, some of which may cause ill-health, and hyperactivity in children. Don't forget too that meat is the cause of the majority of food poisoning incidents. In 1991 McDonald's were responsible for an outbreak of food poisoning in the UK, in which people suffered serious kidney failure. With modern intensive farming methods, other diseases – linked to chemical residues or unnatural practices – have become a danger to people too (such as BSE).

Exploiting workers

Workers in the fast food industry are paid low wages. McDonald's do not pay overtime rates even when employees work very long hours. Pressure to keep profits high and wage costs low results in understaffing, so staff have to work harder and faster. As a consequence, accidents (particularly burns) are common. The majority of employees are people who have few job options and so are forced to accept this exploitation, and they're compelled to 'smile' too! Not surprisingly staff turnover at McDonald's is high, making it virtually impossible to unionize and fight for a better deal, which suits McDonald's who have always been opposed to Unions.

Robbing the poor

Vast areas of land in poor countries are used for cash crops or for cattle ranching, or to grow grain to feed animals to be eaten in the West. This is at the expense of local food needs. McDonald's continually promote meat products, encouraging people to eat meat more often, which wastes more and more food resources. Seven million tons of grain fed to livestock produces only 1 million tons of meat and by-products. On a plant-based diet and with land shared fairly, almost every region could be self-sufficient in food.

Damaging the environment

Forests throughout the world – vital for all life – are being destroyed at an appalling rate by multinational companies. McDonald's have at last been forced to admit to using beef reared on ex-rainforest land, preventing its regeneration. Also, the use of farmland by multinationals and their suppliers forces local people to move on to other areas and cut down further trees.

McDonald's are the world's largest user of beef. Methane emitted by cattle reared for the beef industry is a major contributor to the 'global warming' crisis. Modern intensive agriculture is based on the heavy use of chemicals which are damaging to the environment.

Every year McDonald's use thousands of tons of unnecessary packaging, most of which ends up littering our streets or polluting the land buried in landfill sites.

Murdering animals

The menus of the burger chains are based on the torture and murder of millions of animals. Most are intensively farmed, with no access to fresh air and sunshine, and no freedom of movement. Their deaths are barbaric – 'humane slaughter' is a myth. We have the choice to eat meat or not, but the billions of animals massacred for food each year have no choice at all.

Censorship and McLibel

Criticism of McDonald's has come from a huge number of people and organizations over a wide range of issues. In the mid-1980s, London Greenpeace drew together many of those strands of criticism and called for an annual World Day of Action against McDonald's. This takes place every year on 16th October, with pickets and demonstrations all over the world. McDonald's, who spend a fortune every year on advertising, are trying to silence world-wide criticism by threatening legal action against those who speak out. Many have been forced to back down because they lacked the money to fight a case. But Helen Steel and Dave Morris, two supporters of London Greenpeace, defended themselves in a major UK High Court libel trial. No legal aid is available so they represented themselves. McDonald's engaged in a huge cover up, refusing to disclose masses of relevant documents. Also, the defendants were denied their right to a jury. Despite all the cards being stacked against them, Helen and Dave turned the tables and exposed the truth by putting McDonald's business practices on trial. Protests against the $30 billion a year fast-food giant continue to grow. It's vital to stand up to intimidation and to defend free speech.

What you can do

Together we can fight back against the institutions and the people in power who dominate our lives and our planet, and we can create a better society without exploitation. Workers can and do organize together to fight for their rights and dignity. People are increasingly aware of the need to think seriously about the food we and our children eat. People in poor countries are organizing themselves to stand up to multinationals and banks which dominate the world's economy. Environmental and animal rights protests and campaigns are growing everywhere. Why not join in the struggle for a better world. Talk to friends and family, neighbours and workmates about these issues. Please copy and circulate this leaflet as widely as you can.

CHAPTER THREE

Just what should business be responsible for?

Understanding the concept of CSR

A S CHAPTER TWO highlights, companies have clearly found themselves under intense scrutiny regarding their practices and actions. The more these debates have emerged on the political agenda the more complex the roles and responsibilities of companies seem to be becoming. In response to these challenges the business community has emerged with a strong defence of its position and activities. Indeed, in many cases it has sought to engage with many of the criticisms being channelled towards it and to seek ways in which to address the concerns of civil society and place its activities into a more socially responsible context. Inevitably, therefore, we have witnessed a growing debate regarding what exactly the roles and responsibilities of business should be. Where does business responsibility begin and end? Where are the dividing lines between business responsibility and both state and individual responsibility? In addition, who should business be accountable to?

In this chapter we take a closer look at the concept of corporate responsibility and ask just what should business be responsible for? We look at the history of responsible business practice, and the evolution and debates that surround the concept of corporate social responsibility. In particular, we consider whether or not it is actually in a company's best interest to be socially responsible.

THE HISTORY OF RESPONSIBLE BUSINESS PRACTICE

Despite the negative picture portrayed in the readings in Chapter two, there is strong evidence to suggest that not all of the business community has acted with complete disregard for any form of moral or ethical standpoint and with no sense of corporate social responsibility. Indeed, one can point to a number of examples where industrialists have tied their entrepreneurial activity closely to philanthropic, religious or political commitments to societal welfare. Sir Titus Salt, for example, constructed a village in the late nineteenth century to provide self-contained living space for the people working in his woollen mills as well as offering a school, hospital, library, shops and fresh drinking water and gas supplies to its inhabitants. In addition, he sought to introduce production processes that cut down the levels of smoke being produced by the mills themselves. In a similar vein companies such as Cadburys point to the Quaker roots of the company and the values these instilled in the operations from its very early formative years.

Examples such as Salt's highlight an important consideration in our discussion of corporate responsibility. While undoubtedly there was a significant level of social commitment in Salt's actions, there was also an important underlying business rationale. His socially responsible decisions also brought with them a number of important business benefits. Building a village that surrounded his mill meant that his staff were all located close to their work. Providing health and educational facilities similarly helped to produce a healthier and more productive workforce and created an effective environment in which to train the next generation of workers. What examples, such as Salt's, highlighted, therefore, from a very early stage of industrialization, was that there was a very strong connection between social and economic activity.

The postwar reconstruction era placed far greater emphasis upon the state as provider of welfare and support for its citizens. The emergence of a welfare state and the public ownership of key utilities and industries helped to largely draw a distinguishing line between the responsibilities of business and those of the state. However, this distinction came under intense pressure during the 1980s, and the New Right policies of Margaret Thatcher in the UK and Ronald Reagan in the USA. The 1980s witnessed a dramatic transition in the responsibilities of both business and state. During this period, the political emphasis focused upon narrowing the responsibilities of the state and the reintroduction of market forces into many fields and industries which had previously been under public/state control. In this way, many public utilities such as water, electricity, public transport and so on became open to free market competition through privatization and deregulation. At the same time, there was a stronger emphasis throughout government policy upon using the management skills and approaches of private business to help turn around the fortunes of key public services such as education and the health service. Privatization, deregulation and the emergence of public–private partnerships, therefore, marked a transition in which the dividing lines between private business and public responsibility were becoming far more blurred.

As was outlined in Chapter one, the increasing power and influence of private business that accompanied globalization during the 1980s and 1990s was paralleled by increasing concern for the impact of modern business practice on the state of the natural environment. This challenge to business was highlighted during the Rio Earth Summit in 1992. The Rio Summit undoubtedly saw the business community on the back foot regarding its social and environmental performance. During the discussions at Rio the United Nations considered the introduction of an international code of conduct for multinational companies, which would place far stricter controls on environmental protection, labour standards and consumer rights among other issues.

Under such intense scrutiny the international business community responded with its own voluntary set of proposals for action coordinated via the World Business Council for Sustainable Development. At its heart was the notion of corporate social responsibility as being the business response to the challenge of sustainable development. It was argued that through education, the sharing of best practice and the recognition of the business opportunities that CSR offered, the business community would respond effectively to the environmental and social challenges highlighted at Rio, without the need for detailed regulation and control. Business, it was claimed, could use its knowledge and skills to work with governments and civil society to improve environmental standards and to increase social conditions. It would undertake its responsibilities in these areas voluntarily and without the need for strict control or a regulated framework.

However, a broad range of questions remained unanswered concerning how one should define a business's social responsibilities, exactly what business should be responsible for, to whom it should be responsible and how this process was to be undertaken and enforced.

DEFINING CORPORATE RESPONSIBILITY

While we may be moving into a period in which we have greater expectations of companies adopting socially responsible strategies and practices, we are far from developing a wholly clear understanding regarding what exactly the notion of corporate responsibility entails. At present the range of definitions available are accompanied by a broad set of language and concepts to match. While some businesses talk about corporate social responsibility, others frame the process in terms of sustainable business practice, corporate citizenship or even corporate accountability. In recent years there has also been a move towards corporate responsibility, taking the emphasis away from just the social dimension implied by corporate social responsibility. (For a more detailed discussion regarding the differing perspectives on CSR see Vogel 2005; Lockett *et al.* 2006; McWilliams *et al.* 2006.)

The diverse concepts and broad array of definitions largely reflect the differing approaches and activities that come under the rubric of CSR. For this reason, it can often be more fruitful to try to identify the central themes and foundations of responsible business practice rather than seeking one all-encompassing definition. Michael Hopkins, for example, places an emphasis upon the stakeholder dimension of the concept within his definition, arguing that 'CSR is concerned with treating the stakeholders of the firm ethically or in a responsible manner' (Hopkins 2003: 1). Lord Holme (1999) expands on this ethical dimension to the concept while also connecting it closely to the economic role of business, suggesting that corporate responsibility is 'the continuing commitment by business to behave ethically and contribute to economic development while improving the quality of life of the workforce and their families as well as of the local community and society at large'.

At the heart of many of the differing definitions of CSR is a commitment from companies to produce some form of social or environmental benefit, which goes beyond merely the basic compliance with the law (see Davis 1973; Carroll 1979; McWilliams and Siegel 2001). Companies engaged in CSR activity should therefore be seeking to focus not just on the economic benefits of their actions but also on the ethical and environmental impacts of their activities on the broad range of different stakeholders who are affected by their activities. Blowfield and Frynas (2005: 503) suggest that CSR should best be viewed as an umbrella term for a variety of theories and practices rather than as one distinct, clearly defined concept. The key aspects of this umbrella concept, they argue, are that

1   Companies have a responsibility for their impact on society and the natural environment, sometimes beyond legal compliance and the liability of individuals.
2   Companies have a responsibility for the behaviour of others with whom they do business (e.g. within supply chains).
3   Business needs to manage its relationship with wider society, whether for reasons of commercial viability or to add value to society.

Within this approach, therefore, CSR represents an overall set of values or a framework within which companies should seek to position themselves. However, there is no direct prescription for how exactly these responsibilities should be reflected or enacted. As the definitional examples above demonstrate, there remains significant scope for interpretation; especially when it comes to identifying who the stakeholders may be, what constitutes an improvement in quality of life as well as issues of being able to accurately define what a company's positive or negative impacts might be. Understandably, therefore, there has been significant debate regarding exactly how a responsible business should behave.

WHAT IS RESPONSIBLE BUSINESS PRACTICE?

At the heart of the challenge of creating an effective process of corporate social responsibility there lies a significant paradox for companies to tackle. Milton Friedman, in his famous article reproduced in this chapter, highlights this paradox effectively by noting that 'only people can have responsibilities' (Friedman 1970: 17). He goes on to state that

> In a free enterprise, private property system, a corporate executive is an employee of the owners of the business. He has direct responsibility to his employers. That responsibility is to conduct the business in accordance with their desires, which generally will be to make as much money as possible.

If this is the primary responsibility of the executives, Friedman argues, what right has the executive to undertake any form of socially orientated activity with the company's, and, by definition, the owners', money? In Friedman's view, the only truly socially responsible action that a company can take is to strive to be as profitable and successful as possible while conforming to the basic rules of society. However, many theorists have challenged the basic premises upon which Friedman's analysis is based, both in terms of who a company has responsibilities to, and also with regard to whether being socially responsible actually necessitates a loss of profits.

In contrast to Friedman's approach, other theorists have argued that companies have responsibilities not only to their shareholders. In fact they have responsibilities to a far broader range of people who, through various channels, may be seen to have a stake in the company itself. Carroll argues that 'the concept of stakeholder personalizes social or societal responsibilities by delineating the specific groups or persons business should consider in its CSR orientation' (Carroll 1979). Stakeholders, therefore, constitute any individuals or groups who have a 'stake' or interest in the decisions and actions of a company. This includes the shareholders as mentioned earlier, but also incorporates consumers, campaign organizations concerned as to the impact of the company, local residents where the company is sited, governments and employees among others. A company's socially responsible practices should therefore seek to reflect the concerns and demands of not just its shareholders but this broader group of stakeholders to which it is accountable. Without their support, it is argued, these companies have no licence to operate.

A BUSINESS CASE FOR CSR?

The other questionable assumption from Friedman's discussion is whether undertaking socially responsible practices necessitates a reduction in the company's profits. By direct contrast, much work in the CSR sphere focuses upon highlighting how companies can actually become more successful through CSR. At the heart of this has been the development of a 'business case' for being socially responsible centred around trying to demonstrate that social responsibility and profitability are not mutually exclusive concepts.

As the reading by Cowe and Hopkins (2003) demonstrates, there are a number of potential ways in which becoming more socially responsible can actually be beneficial for a company, creating what many theorists identify as a 'win-win' situation. It is argued that companies can actually build shareholder value by understanding and tackling their impacts upon society. This added value can come from a range of different spheres including enhanced reputation, access to ethical investments, improved recruitment and retention of staff, the encouragement of innovation, and learning and improved risk management. As Cowe and Hopkins highlight, there is clear potential for companies to use corporate responsibility as a key part of their company brand and identity. However, despite plenty of anecdotal material, there is little concrete evidence to show a direct link between increased profits and socially responsible practices.

In many cases, it might also be that the financial gains are far more long term in contrast to the initial potential costs involved in changing company practices. There are also question marks over whether the potential benefits of CSR are the same for all types of companies. While many of the positives are fairly obvious for large-scale, brand-based companies selling directly to the public where image and reputation is key, the same incentives are not necessarily apparent for smaller companies or those companies whose markets are less in the public eye.

For the time being therefore the jury is still out regarding exactly what is required of a responsible business and the potential impacts adopting such a strategy may have on a company. The readings selected in this chapter have been chosen to reflect this diversity of opinion and to highlight the challenges that CSR poses to both the business community, its critics and its stakeholders.

The first reading is Milton Friedman's famous article from the *New York Times* in which he outlines the reasons why the only social responsibility of business should be to focus upon increasing its profits. The second reading is an extract from an article by

Archie Carroll in which he highlights the broader challenge for companies of recognizing and responding to a stakeholder community which stretches far beyond the traditional confines of its shareholders. The other three readings all reflect the debates within the business community regarding what exactly a business should be responsible for and what benefits may accrue from a CSR strategy. The third reading comes from the World Business Council for Sustainable Development and highlights why businesses need to address the CSR agenda. The fourth and fifth readings both focus upon aspects of the business case for CSR, highlighting the different dimensions within which an effective CSR strategy can be beneficial to a company.

GUIDE TO FURTHER READING

Writing in this field ranges from theoretical discussions regarding the nature of business ethics and social responsibility to more hands-on guides for companies seeking to get to grips with the notion of CSR. As a starting point see Andriof, J. and M. McIntosh (2001) *Perspectives on Corporate Citizenship*, Sheffield, Greenleaf; Hopkins, M. (2003) *The Planetary Bargain: Corporate Social Responsibility Matters*, London, Earthscan; Elkington, J. (1997) *Cannibals With Forks: The Triple Bottom Line of 21st Century Business*, Oxford, Capstone; Crane, A. and D. Matten (2004) *Business Ethics*, Oxford, Oxford University Press; Cannon, T. (1994) *Corporate Responsibility: Roles and Responsibilities: A Textbook on Business Ethics, Governance, Environment*, London, Prentice Hall.

WEB-BASED RESOURCES

There is now a broad range of organizations providing guidance on CSR-related issues, and their websites provide some very interesting practical guides and examples to reflect how the concept is being developed and used. Of particular note are:

- www.bitc.org.uk – Business in the Community. Membership organization focused upon encouraging businesses to improve their impacts on society through corporate responsibility strategies.
- www.wbcsd.ch – Website of the World Business Council for Sustainable Development.
- www.iblf.org – International Business Leaders Forum. Charity set up to promote responsible business practice.
- www.bsr.org – Business for Social Responsibility. Leading research and consultancy organization in the CSR field.

REFERENCES

Blowfield, M. and J.G. Frynas (2005) 'Setting New Agendas: Critical Perspectives on Corporate Social Responsibility in the Developing World', *International Affairs*, Vol. 81, No.3, pp. 499–513.

Carroll, A. (1979) 'A Three-dimensional *Conceptual Model of Corporate Performance'*, *Academy of Management Review*, Vol. 4, No. 4, pp. 497–505.

Cowe, R. and M. Hopkins (2003) *Corporate Social Responsibility: Is There a Business Case?*, London, ACCA.

Davis, K. (1973) 'The Case for and Against Business Assumption of Social Responsibilities', *The Academy of Management Journal*, Vol. 16, No. 2, pp. 312–322.

Friedman, M. (1970) 'The Social Responsibility of Business is to Increase its Profits', *New York Times Magazine*, 13 September.

Holme, Lord (1999) 'Corporate Social Responsibility', Speech given at conference organized by Norsk Hydro, 28 April.

Hopkins, M. (2003) *The Planetary Bargain: Corporate Social Responsibility Matters*, London, Earthscan.

Lockett, A., J. Moon, and W. Visser (2006) 'Corporate Social Responsibility in Management Research: Focus, Nature, Salience and Sources of Influence', *Journal of Management Studies*, Vol. 43, No. 1, pp. 115–136.

McWilliams, A. and D.S. Siegal (2001) 'Corporate Social Responsibility: A Theory of the Firm Perspective', *Academy of Management Review*, Vol. 26, No. 1, pp. 117–127.

McWilliams, A., D.S. Siegel, and P.M. Wright (2006) 'Corporate Social Responsibility: Strategic Implications', *Journal of Management Studies*, Vol. 43, No. 1, pp. 1–18.

Vogel, D. (2005) *The Market for Virtue: The Potential and Limits of Corporate Social Responsibility*, New York, Brookings Institution Press.

Milton Friedman

THE SOCIAL RESPONSIBILITY OF BUSINESS IS TO INCREASE ITS PROFITS

WHEN I HEAR businessmen speak eloquently about the "social responsibilities of business in a free-enterprise system," I am reminded of the wonderful line about the Frenchman who discovered at the age of 70 that he had been speaking prose all his life. The businessmen believe that they are defending free enterprise when they declaim that business is not concerned "merely" with profit but also with promoting desirable "social" ends; that business has a "social conscience" and takes seriously its responsibilities for providing employment, eliminating discrimination, avoiding pollution and whatever else may be the catchwords of the contemporary crop of reformers. In fact they are—or would be if they or anyone else took them seriously—preaching pure and unadulterated socialism. Businessmen who talk this way are unwitting puppets of the intellectual forces that have been undermining the basis of a free society these past decades.

The discussions of the "social responsibilities of business" are notable for their analytical looseness and lack of rigor. What does it mean to say that "business" has responsibilities? Only people can have responsibilities. A corporation is an artificial person and in this sense may have artificial responsibilities, but "business" as a whole cannot be said to have responsibilities, even in this vague sense. The first step toward clarity in examining the doctrine of the social responsibility of business is to ask precisely what it implies for whom.

Presumably, the individuals who are to be responsible are businessmen, which means individual proprietors or corporate executives. Most of the discussion of social responsibility is directed at corporations, so in what follows I shall mostly neglect the individual proprietor and speak of corporate executives.

In a free-enterprise, private-property system, a corporate executive is an employe of the owners of the business. He has direct responsibility to his employers. That responsibility is to conduct the business in accordance with their desires, which generally will be to make as much money as possible while conforming to the basic rules of the society, both those embodied in law and those embodied in ethical custom. Of course, in some cases his employers may have a different objective. A group of persons might establish a corporation for an eleemosynary purpose—for example, a hospital or a school. The manager of such a corporation will not have money profit as his objective but the rendering of certain services.

In either case, the key point is that, in his capacity as a corporate executive, the manager is the agent of the individuals who own the corporation or establish the eleemosynary institution, and his primary responsibility is to them.

Needless to say, this does not mean that it is easy to judge how well he is performing his task. But at least the criterion of performance is straightforward, and the persons among whom a voluntary contractual arrangement exists are clearly defined.

Of course, the corporate executive is also a person in his own right. As a person, he may have many other responsibilities that he recognizes or assumes voluntarily—to his family, his conscience, his feelings of charity, his church, his clubs, his city, his country. He may feel impelled by these responsibilities to devote part of his income to causes he regards as worthy, to refuse to work for particular corporations, even to leave his job, for example, to join his country's armed forces. If we wish, we may refer to some of these responsibilities as "social responsibilities." But in these respects he is acting as a principal, not an agent; he is spending his own money or time or energy, not the money of his employers or the time or energy he has contracted to devote to their purposes. If these are "social responsibilities," they are the social responsibilities of individuals, not of business.

What does it mean to say that the corporate executive has a "social responsibility" in his capacity as businessman? If this statement is not pure rhetoric, it must mean that he is to act in some way that is not in the interest of his employers. For example, that he is to refrain from increasing the price of the product in order to contribute to the social objective of preventing inflation, even though a price increase would be in the best interests of the corporation. Or that he is to make expenditures on reducing pollution beyond the amount that is in the best interests of the corporation or that is required by law in order to contribute to the social objective of improving the environment. Or that, at the expense of corporate profits, he is to hire "hardcore" unemployed instead of better-qualified available workmen to contribute to the social objective of reducing poverty.

In each of these cases, the corporate executive would be spending someone else's money for a general social interest. Insofar as his actions in accord with his "social responsibility" reduce returns to stock-holders, he is spending their money. Insofar as his actions raise the price to customers, he is spending the customers' money. Insofar as his actions lower the wages of some employes, he is spending their money.

The stockholders or the customers or the employes could separately spend their own money on the particular action if they wished to do so. The executive is exercising a distinct "social responsibility," rather than serving as an agent of the stockholders or the customers or the employes, only if he spends the money in a different way than they would have spent it.

But if he does this, he is in effect imposing taxes, on the one hand, and deciding how the tax proceeds shall be spent, on the other.

This process raises political questions on two levels: principle and consequences. On the level of political principle, the imposition of taxes and the expenditure of tax proceeds are governmental functions. We have established elaborate constitutional, parliamentary and judicial provisions to control these functions, to assure that taxes are imposed so far as possible in accordance with the preferences and desires of the public—after all, "taxation without representation" was one of the battle cries of the American Revolution. We have a system of checks and balances to separate the legislative function of imposing taxes and enacting expenditures from the executive function of collecting taxes and administering expenditure programs and from the judicial function of mediating disputes and interpreting the law.

Here the businessman—self-selected or appointed directly or indirectly by stockholders—is to be simultaneously legislator, executive and jurist. He is to decide whom to tax by how much and for what purpose, and he is to spend the proceeds—all this guided only by general exhortations from on high to restrain inflation, improve the environment, fight poverty and so on and on.

The whole justification for permitting the corporate executive to be selected by the stockholders is that the executive is an agent serving the interests of his principal. This justification disappears when the corporate executive imposes taxes and spends the proceeds for "social" purposes. He becomes in effect a public employe, a civil servant, even though he remains in name an employe of a private enterprise. On grounds of political principle, it is intolerable that such civil servants—insofar as their actions in the name of social responsibility are real and not just window-dressing—should be selected as they are now. If they are to be civil servants, then they must be selected through a political process. If they are to impose taxes and make expenditures to foster "social" objectives, then political machinery must be set up to guide the assessment of taxes and to determine through a political process the objectives to be served.

This is the basic reason why the doctrine of "social responsibility" involves the acceptance of the socialist view that political mechanisms, not market mechanisms, are the appropriate way to determine the allocation of scarce resources to alternative uses.

On the grounds of consequences, can the corporate executive in fact discharge his alleged "social responsibilities"? On the one hand, suppose he could get away with spending the stockholders' or customers' or employes' money. How is he to know how to spend it? He is told that he must contribute to fighting inflation. How is he to know what action of his will contribute to that end? He is presumably an expert in running his company—in producing a product or selling it or financing it. But nothing about his selection makes him an expert on inflation. Will his holding down the price of his product reduce inflationary pressure? Or, by leaving more spending power in the hands of his customers, simply divert it elsewhere? Or, by forcing him to produce less because of the lower price, will it simply contribute to shortages? Even if he could answer these questions, how much cost is he justified in imposing on his stockholders, customers and employes for this social purpose? What is his appropriate share and what is the appropriate share of others?

And, whether he wants to or not, can he get away with spending his stockholders', customers' or employes' money? Will not the stockholders fire him? (Either the present ones or those who take over when his actions in the name of social responsibility have reduced the corporation's profits and the price of its stock.) His customers and his employes can desert him for other producers and employers less scrupulous in exercising their social responsibilities.

This facet of "social responsibility" doctrine is brought into sharp relief when the doctrine is used to justify wage restraint by trade unions. The conflict of interest is naked and clear when union officials are asked to subordinate the interest of their members to some more general social purpose. If the union officials try to enforce wage restraint, the consequence is likely to be wildcat strikes, rank-and-file revolts and the emergence of strong competitors for their jobs. We thus have the ironic phenomenon that union leaders—at least in the U.S.—have objected to Government interference with the market far more consistently and courageously than have business leaders.

The difficulty of exercising "social responsibility" illustrates, of course, the great virtue of private competitive enterprise—it forces people to be responsible for their own actions and makes it difficult for them to "exploit" other people for either selfish or unselfish purposes. They can do good—but only at their own expense.

Many a reader who has followed the argument this far may be tempted to remonstrate that it is all well and good to speak of government's having the responsibility to impose taxes and determine expenditures for such "social" purposes as controlling pollution or training the hard-core unemployed, but that the problems are too urgent to wait on the slow course of political processes, that the exercise of social responsibility by businessmen is a quicker and surer way to solve pressing current problems.

Aside from the question of fact—I share Adam Smith's skepticism about the benefits that can be expected from "those who affected to trade for the public good"—this argument must be rejected on grounds of principle. What it amounts to is an assertion that those who favor the taxes and expenditures in question have failed to persuade a majority of their fellow citizens to be of like mind and that they are seeking to attain by undemocratic procedures what they cannot attain by democratic procedures. In a free society, it is hard for "good" people to do "good," but that is a small price to pay for making it hard for "evil" people to do "evil," especially since one man's good is another's evil.

I have, for simplicity, concentrated on the special case of the corporate executive, except only for the brief digression on trade unions. But precisely the same argument applies to the newer phenomenon of calling upon stockholders to require corporations to exercise social responsibility (the recent G.M. crusade, for example). In most of these cases, what is in effect involved is some stockholders trying to get other stockholders (or customers or employes) to contribute against their will to "social" causes favored by the activists. Insofar as they succeed, they are again imposing taxes and spending the proceeds.

The situation of the individual proprietor is somewhat different. If he acts to reduce the returns of his enterprise in order to exercise his "social responsibility," he is spending his own money, not someone else's. If he wishes to spend his money on such purposes, that is his right, and I cannot see that there is any objection to his doing so. In the process, he, too, may impose costs on employes and customers. However, because he is far less likely than a large corporation or union to have monopolistic power, any such side effects will tend to be minor.

Of course, in practice the doctrine of social responsibility is frequently a cloak for actions that are justified on other grounds rather than a reason for those actions.

To illustrate, it may well be in the long-run interest of a corporation that is a major employer in a small community to devote resources to providing amenities to that community or to improving its government. That may make it easier to attract desirable employes, it may reduce the wage bill or lessen losses from pilferage and sabotage or have other worthwhile effects. Or it may be that, given the laws about the deductibility of corporate charitable contributions, the stockholders can contribute more to charities they favor by having the corporation make the gift than by doing it themselves, since they can in that way contribute an amount that would otherwise have been paid as corporate taxes.

In each of these—and many similar—cases, there is a strong temptation to rationalize these actions as an exercise of "social responsibility." In the present climate of opinion, with its widespread aversion to "capitalism," "profits," the "soulless corporation" and so on, this is one way for a corporation to generate goodwill as a by-product of expenditures that are entirely justified in its own self-interest.

It would be inconsistent of me to call on corporate executives to refrain from this hypocritical window dressing because it harms the foundations of a free society. That would be to call on them to exercise "social responsibility"! If our institutions, and the attitudes of the public make it in their self-interest to cloak their actions in this way, cannot summon much indignation to denounce them. At the same time, can express admiration for those individual proprietors or owners of closely held corporations or stockholders of more broadly held corporations who disdain such tactic as approaching fraud.

Whether blameworthy or not the use of the cloak of social responsibility, and the nonsense spoken in its name by influential and prestigious businessmen, does clearly harm the foundations of a free society. I have been impressed time and again by the schizophrenic character of many businessmen. They are capable of being extremely far-sighted and clearheaded in matters that are internal to their businesses. They are incredibly shortsighted and muddle-headed in matters that are outside their businesses but affect the possible survival of business in general. This short-sightedness is strikingly exemplified in the calls from many businessmen for wage and price guidelines or controls or incomes policies. There is nothing that could do more in a brief period to destroy a market system and replace it by a centrally controlled system than effective governmental control of prices and wages.

The short-sightedness is also exemplified in speeches by businessmen on social responsibility. This may gain them kudos in the short run. But it helps to strengthen the already too prevalent view that the pursuit of profits is wicked and immoral and must be curbed and controlled by external forces. Once this view is adopted, the external forces that curb the market will not be the social consciences, however highly developed, of the pontificating executives; it will be the iron fist of Government bureaucrats. Here, as with price and wage controls, businessmen seem to me to reveal a suicidal impulse.

The political principle that underlies the market mechanism is unanimity. In an ideal free market resting on private property, no individual can coerce any other, all cooperation is voluntary, all parties to such cooperation benefit or they need not participate. There are no "social" values, no "social" responsibilities in any sense other than the shared values and responsibilities of individuals. Society is a collection of individuals and of the various groups they voluntarily form.

The political principle that underlies the political mechanism is conformity. The individual must serve a more general social interest—whether that be determined by a church or a dictator or a majority. The individual may have a vote and a say in what is to be done, but if he is overruled, he must conform. It is appropriate for some to require others to contribute to a general social purpose whether they wish to or not.

Unfortunately, unanimity is not always feasible. There are some respects in which conformity appears unavoidable, so I do not see how one can avoid the use of the political mechanism altogether.

But the doctrine of "social responsibility" taken seriously would extend the scope of the political mechanism to every human activity. It does not differ in philosophy from the most explicitly collectivist doctrine. It differs only by professing to believe that collectivist ends can be attained without collectivist means. That is why, in my book *Capitalism and Freedom*, I have called it a "fundamentally subversive doctrine" in a free society, and have said that in such a society, "there is one and only one social responsibility of business—to use its resources and engage in activities designed to increase its profits so long as it stays within the rules of the game, which is to say, engages in open and free competition without deception or fraud."

Archie B. Carroll

THE PYRAMID OF CORPORATE SOCIAL RESPONSIBILITY
Toward the moral management of organizational stakeholders

FOR THE BETTER part of 30 years now, corporate executives have struggled with the issue of the firm's responsibility to its society. Early on it was argued by some that the corporation's sole responsibility was to provide a maximum financial return to shareholders. It became quickly apparent to everyone, however, that this pursuit of financial gain had to take place within the laws of the land. Though social activist groups and others throughout the 1960s advocated a broader notion of corporate responsibility, it was not until the significant social legislation of the early 1970s that this message became indelibly clear as a result of the creation of the Environmental Protection Agency (EPA), the Equal Employment Opportunity Commission (EEOC), the Occupational Safety and Health Administration (OSHA), and the Consumer Product Safety Commission (CPSC).

These new governmental bodies established that national public policy now officially recognized the environment, employees, and consumers to be significant and legitimate stakeholders of business. From that time on, corporate executives have had to wrestle with how they balance their commitments to the corporation's owners with their obligations to an ever-broadening group of stakeholders who claim both legal and ethical rights.

This reading will explore the nature of corporate social responsibility (CSR) with an eye toward understanding its component parts. The intention will be to characterize the firm's CSR in ways that might be useful to executives who wish to reconcile their obligations to their shareholders with those to other competing groups claiming legitimacy. This discussion will be framed by a pyramid of corporate social responsibility. Next, we plan to relate this concept to the idea of stakeholders. Finally, our goal will be to isolate the ethical or moral component of CSR and relate it to perspectives that reflect three major ethical approaches to management—immoral, amoral, and moral. The principal goal in this final section will be to flesh out what it means to manage stakeholders in an ethical or moral fashion.

Evolution of corporate social responsibility

What does it mean for a corporation to be socially responsible? Academics and practitioners have been striving to establish an agreed-upon definition of this concept for 30 years. In 1960, Keith Davis suggested that social responsibility refers to businesses' "decisions and actions taken for reasons at least partially beyond the firm's direct economic or technical interest." At about the same time, Eells and Walton (1961) argued that CSR refers to the "problems that arise when corporate enterprise casts its shadow on the social scene, and the ethical principles that ought to govern the relationship between the corporation and society."

In 1971 the Committee for Economic Development used a "three concentric circles" approach to depicting CSR. The inner circle included basic economic functions—growth, products, jobs. The intermediate circle suggested that the economic functions must be exercised with a sensitive awareness of changing social values and priorities.

The outer circle outlined newly emerging and still amorphous responsibilities that business should assume to become more actively involved in improving the social environment.

The attention was shifted from social responsibility to social responsiveness by several other writers. Their basic argument was that the emphasis on responsibility focused exclusively on the notion of business obligation and motivation and that action or performance were being overlooked. The social responsiveness movement, therefore. emphasized corporate action, proaction, and implementation of a social role. This was indeed a necessary reorientation.

The question still remained, however, of reconciling the firm's economic orientation with its social orientation. A step in this direction was taken when a comprehensive definition of CSR was set forth. In this view, a four-part conceptualization of CSR included the idea that the corporation has not only economic and legal obligations, but ethical and discretionary (philanthropic) responsibilities as well (Carroll 1979). The point here was that CSR, to be accepted as legitimate, had to address the entire spectrum of obligations business has to society, including the most fundamental—economic. It is upon this four-part perspective that our pyramid is based.

In recent years, the term corporate social performance (CSP) has emerged as an inclusive and global concept to embrace corporate social responsibility, responsiveness, and the entire spectrum of socially beneficial activities of businesses. The focus on social performance emphasizes the concern for corporate action and accomplishment in the social sphere. With a performance perspective, it is clear that firms must formulate and implement social goals and programs as well as integrate ethical sensitivity into all decision making, policies, and actions. With a results focus, CSP suggests an all-encompassing orientation toward normal criteria by which we assess business performance to include quantity, quality, effectiveness, and efficiency. While we recognize the vitality of the performance concept, we have chosen to adhere to the CSR terminology for our present discussion. With just a slight change of focus, however, we could easily be discussing a CSP rather than a CSR pyramid. In any event, the long-term concern is what managers do with these ideas in terms of implementation.

The pyramid of corporate social responsibility

For CSR to be accepted by a conscientious business person, it should be framed in such a way that the entire range of business responsibilities are embraced. It is suggested here that four kinds of social responsibilities constitute total CSR: economic, legal, ethical, and philanthropic. Furthermore, these four categories or components of CSR might be depicted as a pyramid. To be sure, all of these kinds of responsibilities have always existed to some extent, but it has only been in recent years that ethical and philanthropic functions have taken a significant place. Each of these four categories deserves closer consideration.

Economic responsibilities

Historically, business organizations were created as economic entities designed to provide goods and services to societal members. The profit motive was established as the primary incentive for entrepreneurship. Before it was anything else, business organization was the basic economic unit in our society. As such, its principal role was to produce goods and services that consumers needed and wanted and to make an acceptable profit in the process. At some point the idea of the profit motive got transformed into a notion of maximum profits, and this has been an enduring value ever since. All other business responsibilities are predicated upon the economic responsibility of the firm, because without it the others become moot considerations. Table 1 summarizes some important statements characterizing economic responsibilities. Legal responsibilities are also depicted in Table 1, and we will consider them next.

Table 1 Economic and legal components of corporate social responsibility

Economic components (responsibilities)	Legal components (responsibilities)
1 It is important to perform in a manner consistent with maximizing earnings per share.	1 It is important to perform in a manner consistent with expectations of government and law.
2 It is important to be committed to being as profitable as possible.	2 It is important to comply with various federal, state, and local regulations.
3 It is important to maintain a strong competitive position.	3 It is important to be a law-abiding corporate citizen.
4 It is important to maintain a high level of operating efficiency.	4 It is important that a successful firm be defined as one that fulfills its legal obligations.
5 It is important that a successful firm be defined as one that is consistently profitable.	5 It is important to provide goods and services that at least meet minimal legal requirements.

Legal responsibilities

Society has not only sanctioned business to operate according to the profit motive; at the same time business is expected to comply with the laws and regulations promulgated by federal, state, and local governments as the ground rules under which business must operate. As a partial fulfillment of the "social contract" between business and society, firms are expected to pursue their economic missions within the framework of the law. Legal responsibilities reflect a view of "codified ethics" in the sense that they embody basic notions of fair operations as established by our lawmakers. They are depicted as the next layer on the pyramid to portray their historical development, but they are appropriately seen as coexisting with economic responsibilities as fundamental precepts of the free enterprise system.

Ethical responsibilities

Although economic and legal responsibilities embody ethical norms about fairness and justice, ethical responsibilities embrace those activities and practices that are expected or prohibited by societal members even though they are not codified into law. Ethical responsibilities embody those standards, norms, or expectations that reflect a concern for what consumers, employees, shareholders, and the community regard as fair, just or in keeping with the respect or protection of stakeholders' moral rights.

In one sense, changing ethics or values precede the establishment of law because they become the driving force behind the very creation of laws or regulations. For example, the environmental, civil rights, and consumer movements reflected basic alterations in societal values and thus may be seen as ethical bellwethers foreshadowing and resulting in the later legislation. In another sense, ethical responsibilities may be seen as embracing newly emerging values and norms society expects business to meet, even though such values and norms may reflect a higher standard of performance than that currently required by law. Ethical responsibilities in this sense are often ill-defined or continually under public debate as to their legitimacy, and thus are frequently difficult for business to deal with.

Superimposed on these ethical expectations emanating from societal groups are the implied levels of ethical performance suggested by a consideration of the great ethical principles of moral philosophy. This would include such principles as justice, rights, and utilitarianism.

The business ethics movement of the past decade has firmly established an ethical responsibility as a legitimate CSR component. Though it is depicted as the next layer of the CSR pyramid, it must be constantly recognized that it is in dynamic interplay with the legal responsibility category. That is, it is constantly pushing the legal responsibility category to broaden or expand while at the same time placing ever higher expectations on businesspersons to operate at levels above that required by law. Table 2 depicts statements that help characterize ethical responsibilities. The table also summarizes philanthropic responsibilities, discussed next.

Philanthropic responsibilities

Philanthropy encompasses those corporate actions that are in response to society's expectation that businesses be good corporate citizens. This includes actively engaging

Table 2 Ethical and philanthropic components of corporate social responsibility

Ethical components (responsibilities)	Philanthropic components (responsibilities)
1 It is important to perform in a manner consistent with expectations of societal mores and ethical norms.	1 It is important to perform in a manner consistent with the philanthropic and charitable expectations of society.
2 It is important to recognize and respect new or evolving ethical moral norms adopted by society.	2 It is important to assist the fine and performing arts.
3 It is important to prevent ethical norms from being compromised in order to achieve corporate goals.	3 It is important that managers and employees participate in voluntary and charitable activities within their local communities.
4 It is important that good corporate citizenship be defined as doing what is expected morally or ethically.	4 It is important to provide assistance to private and public educational institutions.
5 It is important to recognize that corporate integrity and ethical behavior go beyond mere compliance with laws and regulations.	5 It is important to assist voluntarily those projects that enhance a community's "quality of life."

in acts or programs to promote human welfare or goodwill. Examples of philanthropy include business contributions to financial resources or executive time, such as contributions to the arts, education, or the community. A loaned-executive program that provides leadership for a community's United Way campaign is one illustration of philanthropy.

The distinguishing feature between philanthropy and ethical responsibilities is that the former are not expected in an ethical or moral sense. Communities desire firms to contribute their money, facilities, and employee time to humanitarian programs or purposes, but they do not regard the firms as unethical if they do not provide the desired level. Therefore, philanthropy is more discretionary or voluntary on the part of businesses even though there is always the societal expectation that businesses provide it.

One notable reason for making the distinction between philanthropic and ethical responsibilities is that some firms feel they are being socially responsible if they are just good citizens in the community. This distinction brings home the vital point that CSR includes philanthropic contributions but is not limited to them. In fact, it would be argued here that philanthropy is highly desired and prized but actually less important than the other three categories of social responsibility. In a sense, philanthropy is icing on the cake—or on the pyramid, using our metaphor.

The pyramid of corporate social responsibility is depicted in Table 3. It portrays the four components of CSR, beginning with the basic building block notion that economic performance undergirds all else. At the same time, business is expected to obey the law because the law is society's codification of acceptable and unacceptable behavior. Next is business's responsibility to be ethical. At its most fundamental level, this is the obligation to do what is right, just, and fair, and to avoid or minimize harm to stakeholders

Table 3 Stakeholder responsibility matrix

	Types of CSR			
Stakeholders	Economic	Legal	Ethical	Philanthropic
Owners	–	–	–	–
Customers	–	–	–	–
Employees	–	–	–	–
Community	–	–	–	–
Competitors	–	–	–	–
Suppliers	–	–	–	–
Social activist groups	–	–	–	–
Public at large	–	–	–	–
Others	–	–	–	–

(employees, consumers, the environment, and others). Finally, business is expected to be a good corporate citizen. This is captured in the philanthropic responsibility, wherein business is expected to contribute financial and human resources to the community and to improve the quality of life.

No metaphor is perfect, and the CSR pyramid is no exception. It is intended to portray that the total CSR of business comprises distinct components that, taken together, constitute the whole. Though the components have been treated as separate concepts for discussion purposes, they are not mutually exclusive and are not intended to juxtapose a firm's economic responsibilities with its other responsibilities. At the same time, a consideration of the separate components helps the manager see that the different types of obligations are in a constant but dynamic tension with one another. The most critical tensions, of course, would be between economic and legal, economic and ethical, and economic and philanthropic. The traditionalist might see this as a conflict between a firm's "concern for profits" versus its "concern for society," but it is suggested here that this is an oversimplification. A CSR or stakeholder perspective would recognize these tensions as organizational realities, but focus on the total pyramid as a unified whole and how the firm might engage in decisions, actions, and programs that substantially fulfill all its component parts.

In summary, the total corporate social responsibility of business entails the simultaneous fulfillment of the firm's economic, legal, ethical, and philanthropic responsibilities. Stated in more pragmatic and managerial terms, the CSR firm should strive to make a profit, obey the law, be ethical, and be a good corporate citizen.

Upon first glance, this array of responsibilities may seem broad. They seem to be in striking contrast to the classical economic argument that management has one responsibility: to maximize the profits of its owners or shareholders. Economist Milton Friedman, the most outspoken proponent of this view, has argued that social matters are not the concern of businesspeople and that these problems should be resolved by the unfettered workings of the free market system. Friedman's argument loses some of its punch, however, when you consider his assertion in its totality. Friedman posited that management is "to make as much money as possible while conforming to the basic rules of society, both those embodied in the law and those embodied in ethical custom" (Friedman 1970). Most people focus on the first part of Friedman's quote but not the second part. It seems clear from this statement that profits, conformity to the law, and ethical custom embrace three components of the CSR pyramid—economic, legal, and ethical. That only leaves the philanthropic component for Friedman to reject. Although it may be appropriate for an economist to take this view, one would not encounter many business executives today who exclude philanthropic programs from their firms' range of activities. It seems the role of corporate citizenship is one that business has no significant problem embracing. Undoubtedly this perspective is rationalized under the rubric of enlightened self interest.

We next propose a conceptual framework to assist the manager in integrating the four CSR components with organizational stakeholders.

CSR and organizational stakeholders

There is a natural fit between the idea of corporate social responsibility and an organization's stakeholders. The word "social" in CSR has always been vague and lacking in specific direction as to whom the corporation is responsible. The concept of stakeholder personalizes social or societal responsibilities by delineating the specific groups or persons business should consider in its CSR orientation. Thus, the stakeholder nomenclature puts "names and faces" on the societal members who are most urgent to business, and to whom it must be responsive.

By now most executives understand that the term "stakeholder" constitutes a play on the word stockholder and is intended to more appropriately describe those groups or persons who have a stake, a claim, or an interest in the operations and decisions of the firm. Sometimes the stake might represent a legal claim, such as that which might be held by an owner, an employee, or a customer who has an explicit or implicit contract. Other times it might be represented by a moral claim, such as when these groups assert a right to be treated fairly or with due process, or to have their opinions taken into consideration in an important business decision.

Management's challenge is to decide which stakeholders merit and receive consideration in the decision-making process. In any given instance, there may be numerous stakeholder groups (shareholders, consumers, employees, suppliers, community, social activist groups) clamoring for management's attention. How do managers sort out the urgency or importance of the various stakeholder claims? Two vital criteria include the stakeholders' legitimacy and their power. From a CSR perspective, their legitimacy may be most important. From a management efficiency perspective, their power might be of central influence. Legitimacy refers to the extent to which a group has a justifiable right to be making its claim. For example, a group of 300 employees about to be laid off by a plant-closing decision has a more legitimate claim on management's attention than the local chamber of commerce, which is worried about losing the firm as one of its dues-paying members. The stakeholder's power is another factor. Here we may witness significant differences. Thousands of small, individual investors, for example, wield very little power unless they can find a way to get organized. By contrast, institutional investors and large mutual fund groups have significant power over management because of the sheer magnitude of their investments and the fact that they are organized.

With these perspectives in mind, let us think of stakeholder management as a process by which managers reconcile their own objectives with the claims and expectations being made on them by various stakeholder groups. The challenge of stakeholder management is to ensure that the firm's primary stakeholders achieve their objectives while other stake-holders are also satisfied. Even though this "win-win" outcome is not always possible, it does represent a legitimate and desirable goal for management to pursue to protect its long-term interests.

This matrix is intended to be used as an analytical tool or template to organize a manager's thoughts and ideas about what the firm ought to be doing in an economic, legal, ethical, and philanthropic sense with respect to its identified stakeholder groups. By carefully and deliberately moving through the various cells of the matrix, the manager may develop a significant descriptive and analytical data base that can then be used for purposes of stakeholder management. The information resulting from this stakeholder/responsibility analysis should be useful when developing priorities and making both long-term and short-term decisions involving multiple stakeholder's interests.

To be sure, thinking in stakeholder responsibility terms increases the complexity of decision making and may be extremely time consuming and taxing, especially at first. Despite its complexity, however, this approach is one methodology management can use to integrate values—what it stands for—with the traditional economic mission of the organization. In the final analysis, such an integration could be of significant usefulness to management. This is because the stakeholder/responsibility perspective is most con-sistent with the pluralistic environment faced by business today. As such, it provides the opportunity for an in-depth corporate appraisal of financial as well as social and economic concerns. Thus, the stakeholder/responsibility perspective would be an invaluable founda-tion for responding to the firm's stakeholder management question about strategies, actions, or decisions that should be pursued to effectively respond to the environment business faces.

References

Carroll, A. (1979) 'A Three-dimensional *Conceptual Model of Corporate Performance*', *Academy of Management Review*, Vol. 4, No. 4, pp. 497–505.

Davis, K. (1960) 'Can Business Afford to Ignore its Social Responsibilities?', *California Management Review*, 2.3: 70–76.

Eells, R. and C. Walton (1961), *Conceptual Foundations of Business* (Homewood, ill.: Richard D. Irwin).

Friedman, M. (1970) 'The, Social Responsibility of Business is to Increase its Profits', *New York Times Magazine*, 13 September.

World Business Council for Sustainable Development
WHY NOW?

Why now? Why are we proposing a fresh approach?

Why offer a manifesto for the global companies of the future? Why argue for a fresh approach now, when companies are seeing profits grow and business expand?

Our answer is that we are coming into contact with some of the world's most challenging issues. This presents us with an obligation to act, as well as opportunities to channel our energies into business activities that address these challenges and contribute to human progress.

Given the scale and reach of business, we have the potential to make a major difference. WBCSD member companies alone have a combined turnover of over US$5.5 trillion, with products and services that touch the lives of three billion people a day.

In examining our role, we start from the basis that the fundamental purpose of business is to provide continually improving goods and services for increasing numbers of people at prices that they can afford. This is a purpose that we need to relate to today's challenges. For example, in a world facing serious pollution and the threats of rising temperatures, water shortages, and crop failures, can we improve our goods in ways that address environmental issues? In seeking to provide goods and services to increasing numbers of people, can we reach out to the three billion who today live in poverty and the three billion expected to be added to the world's population by 2050? These six billion people are potential customers, employees, and suppliers.

We should not see such signals as someone else's problem, but as risks for our businesses, which we have a role in addressing, along with governments and international bodies.

Dealing with such issues makes business sense. It is directly in our interest to avoid operating on a polluted planet in which billions are too poor to afford the products we create.

Issues such as poverty, the environment, and globalization also raise short-term challenges. As we write, the world has just experienced a year that has set new records in losses from natural disasters. This has intensified public awareness of poverty and concern over the environment, already at a high pitch following a G8 summit that focused on these issues.

Trust in businesses is at a low ebb, with only four in ten saying they trust global corporations. It could take very little to turn this combination of distrust of business and concern over the world's future into widespread anger. The time is therefore right for progressive businesses to demonstrate not only that we understand and share public concerns, but that we are doing more and more about them.

The model that we have put forward can help companies create business opportunities out of tackling the world's major issues. While many businesses can point to specific activities as evidence that they are already applying such a model, we believe that to apply it at scale, and at the heart of business strategy, is extremely demanding. However, the prize is worth the effort. We stand to gain increased profitability for companies and significant benefits for society, along with a growing recognition of the good that businesses can do.

What's new? How does this approach relate to the current debate on the role of business?

We welcome the current debate on the role of business in society. However, much of this debate revolves around a misleading distinction between pursuing shareholder value and demonstrating corporate social responsibility (CSR).

The shareholder value school argues that the sole legitimate purpose of business is to focus on creating shareholder wealth. The less well-defined CSR school calls for operating the core business in a responsible way, sometimes through philanthropy, sometimes through voluntarily going beyond the demands of legislation, for example in health, safety, or environmental standards.

However, as Ian Davis, Worldwide Managing Director of McKinsey and Company, has observed, both views obscure the real relationship of business to so-called external issues, and it is time the debate was recast.

Business does good by doing business

Any successful company will both create shareholder value and operate responsibly. In fact these amount to the same thing. Most companies benefit society simply by doing business. We meet customers' needs for goods and services. We create jobs. We pay wages and salaries. We provide for employees and families through pensions and health plans. We innovate to create products that contribute to human progress. We pay taxes that fund public services and infrastructure. We create work for millions of suppliers, many of them small- and medium-sized companies. Our search for competitive advantage leads to efficiency, and thus to reduced consumption of resources, less pollution, and higher quality products.

The purpose of any business that seeks to be sustainable has to be more than generating short-term shareholder value. Simply by adding the word *long-term* to *shareholder value*, we embrace everything necessary for the survival and success of the company. This includes building trust among communities and maintaining a healthy environment in which to do business.

All of these benefits are created in the normal course of responding to market signals.

Smart businesses pick up societal signals

Progressive businesses are now widening their horizons as they look for opportunities and are gaining competitive advantage by responding to societal signals as well as market signals. For example, a company that acts to promote human welfare is helping to build its future market and workforce. A company that acts to protect the environment is helping to preserve the natural capital upon which its operations depend and possibly gaining early-mover advantage in the more highly-regulated markets of the future. Such companies realize that ignoring these issues means – at best – missing early indicators of future profitability and – at worst – risking the company's market valuation and reputation.

The products are the purpose – the profits are the prize

In responding to societal signals, companies are now looking more widely and imaginatively at the fundamental purpose of providing continually improving goods and services to increasing numbers of customers at prices they can afford. They are improving their products in ways that serve societal ends, and they are increasing customer numbers by reaching out to new markets in developing and emerging economies.

In this view of the role of business, shareholder value is seen as the measure of success in fulfilling the more fundamental purpose of providing improving goods and services that today's and tomorrow's consumers want.

As a result of responding to societal signals, many companies are now active in areas often considered the domain of governments: providing basic goods such as health, education, and pensions; advocating a framework to tackle climate change; or addressing poverty through corporate strategy.

R. Cowe and M. Hopkins

CORPORATE SOCIAL RESPONSIBILITY
Is there a business case?

The nature of the business case for CSR

PROVING THAT CSR benefits shareholder value is the Holy Grail of those who promote greater responsibility, because sceptical managers would be easily convinced of the advantages if they could be shown clear, irrefutable evidence. Such hard proof remains elusive, although the next section shows there is a growing body of circumstantial evidence.

It has not yet been possible to make a strong, causal, quantitative link between CSR actions and financial indicators such as share price, stock market value, return on assets, and economic value added (EVA). Some correlations have been shown to exist, but that does not necessarily demonstrate a causal link. A good correlation could simply occur by chance – although no correlation is obviously not a good sign! In the absence of hard data, most analyses have focused on qualitative rather than quantitative relationships.[1] They touch on risks and opportunities, on revenues and costs, reputation and access to capital. For example, one study[2] identified business benefits in eight areas:

- reputation management
- risk profile and risk management
- employee recruitment, motivation and retention
- investor relations and access to capital
- learning and innovation
- competitiveness and market positioning
- operational efficiency and
- licence to operate.

Another study attempted to match traditional indicators of business performance against aspects of sustainable development:[3]

- shareholder value
- revenue
- operational efficiency
- access to capital
- customer attraction
- brand value and reputation
- human and intellectual capital
- risk profile
- innovation and
- licence to operate.

Six main issues are common to most analyses of potential risks and opportunities.

- Equity created in a company's reputation or brand can be easily harmed or even lost by irresponsible behaviour. This is particularly true for companies whose brand equity depends on company reputation rather than specific brand attributes, e.g. oil companies, retailers and telecoms operators. Reputation is built on intangibles such as trust, reliability, quality, consistency, credibility, relationships and transparency, as well as tangibles such as investment in people, diversity and the environment. High-profile crises can be particularly damaging, e.g. Shell's experience in the mid-1990s with the Brent Spar oil platform and troubles in Nigeria, exposés of labour conditions in supply chains of companies such as Nike and Gap, and Monsanto's calamitous confrontations over genetically modified food ingredients.

- Access to finance is an issue for several reasons. Banks are increasingly aware of CSR risks in their customer relationships, making them wary of dubious projects such as environmentally damaging and socially disruptive dams. More and more equity investors are also alert to SEE risks . . . the market for specific SRI is still relatively small but is increasing rapidly, as demonstrated by the creation of new financial indexes such as FTSE4Good and the Dow Jones Sustainability Index (DJSI). These developments, and government action putting new requirements on pension funds, are pushing SRI into the mainstream. The result is that investors are increasingly interested in ranking major international companies according to their environmental and social performance.

- CSR issues can be important in attracting, retaining and motivating employees. This is particularly true in sensitive industries such as oil and chemicals, where companies report that graduate recruits are concerned to ensure that potential employers have responsible policies. Companies which cannot demonstrate that will struggle to recruit the best talent and are likely to suffer higher costs of recruitment and retention.

- Following from that, CSR can assist innovation, creativity, learning and the growth of intellectual capital. Intellectual capital is increasingly important to business success in most sectors, and well-motivated employees are likely to contribute more to a company's growth in these areas.

- Better risk management can be achieved by the analysis of relations with external stakeholders, which is typically part of CSR. Factors such as new technologies, and changing societal, regulatory and market expectations, drive companies to take a broader perspective when analysing the range of risks they may encounter.

Expensive and time-consuming lawsuits, as well as lost investments, are forcing companies to take a more proactive stance to establish the necessary guidelines and processes that minimize those kinds of risk. Given the increase in cross-border business relationships and the threat of cross-border litigation, boards also have to consider the risk management standards of business partners and even suppliers. CSR helps compliance with regulation and avoidance of legal sanctions. For example, the building of relationships with host governments, communities and other stakeholders can enhance a company's reputation and credibility and be of vital importance.

● There is a wider impact as public expectations grow of greater corporate social responsibility linked to the heightened public debate on the benefits and shortcomings of globalization and the perceived role of business in this process. To reverse the loss of trust which has accelerated since the early 1990s, the business world as a whole needs to demonstrate that it is broadly benefiting society and working to improve impacts in all areas.

All of these potential benefits carry a cost. To date there have been no in-depth benefit-cost analyses of CSR in a corporation, although such exercises are likely to be undertaken in the future. The items that would need to be included in such an exercise are listed in Table 1.

Table 1 CSR and profits: likely benefits and costs

Stakeholder group	Benefits	Costs
Directors	More independent non-executive directors	More meetings and briefings
Shareholders	Increased investment from socially responsible investors	Increased costs of reporting and transparency
Managers	Better HR policies lead to increased motivation; More awareness of ethical issues from focus group sessions lead to more confidence about employees	Increased training in ethics; Focus group sessions and reporting
Employees	Better HR polices lead to increased motivation; Good ethical conduct by superiors leads to improved productivity; Fewer labour relations disputes; Fewer strikes; Better working conditions; Good CSR company leads to easier recruitment of high fliers and young people; Reduced costs of recruitment	Inclusion of ethics training; More intra-company communications; More effort on labour relations; Will need to implement human rights policies

continued on p. 104

Table 1 (cont.)

Stakeholder group	Benefits	Costs
Customers	Increased attractiveness to concerned consumers; Fewer disputes; Advertising can cite CSR image; Enhanced reputation; Brand equity recognition	Cost of goods may increase in the short term
Sub-contractors/ suppliers	Better quality inputs; Less harmful effect on "public image"	Cost of inputs may increase in short term
Community	More willingness to accept new investments; Improved public image	Requires continual interaction with communities; Will need to produce CSR report; Will need to monitor internal activities; Implement human rights policy
Government	More confidence in company; Fewer legal battles; No new potentially harmful legislation; More favourable trading regime; More willing to accept expansion or downsizing	Costs of adhering to new regulations may increase
Environment	Fewer legal battles; Improved public image; Contribute to sustainability of company	Investment in environmental damage control

Source: MHC International Ltd, www.mhcinternational.com

Segmenting CSR

These benefits and costs are unlikely to be uniform across businesses. They will vary by sector, by size and nature of company, and by geographic location. For example, some industries and types of operation carry much more significant risks – the clearest examples are oil, chemicals, and supply chains in developing countries. This group of activities is most likely to be exposed to scrutiny by powerful and well-informed NGOs with access to the media. Other industries may well escape NGO (and therefore media) scrutiny for long periods – although risks always exist if companies are not behaving responsibly.

Multinationals are, on the whole, more likely than small companies to be targeted by critics and exposed in the media . . . this does not mean that CSR is irrelevant for SMEs, but they are less likely to face the kind of risks which threaten multinationals. It should be said, however, that local media can have as great an impact on a local company as the global media can have on multinationals. Smaller companies may also be more susceptible to employee dissatisfaction, because the employer/employee relationship is more intimate, and ending employment with a small company may carry less significant consequences than leaving a multinational which promises a developing career path.

It is also clear that consumer pressures are less likely to be felt by businesses which do not sell direct to the public. This does not make non-consumer companies immune, as Monsanto found out to its cost. Nor does it mean that smaller companies which supply consumer businesses are immune from these pressures – in fact, they can be magnified through the supply chain efforts of the retailer or brand owner.

Even with a multinational, geographic location affects which issues are most important. In South Africa, for example, black empowerment and HIV/Aids are critical. In the US child labour is likely to have the highest profile, while in northern Europe employee and environmental issues are at the top of most lists.

It is also true that issues change over time. An individual event – such as the Brent Spar incident or Premier Oil's involvement in Burma – can propel a previously insignificant issue to the top of the public agenda. That is why companies need to remain alert to the changing environment, just as they need to understand their own particular strengths and vulnerabilities throughout their organizations.

Limitations

Proponents of CSR, like all evangelists, are wont to overemphasize the potential benefits. This can be counterproductive. If managers can see that the claimed benefits are overblown, they are likely to react negatively and possibly underestimate the actual benefits which could accrue to their company.

It is important to understand the limitations, because ultimately managers are measured on financial returns and CSR activity which does not support financial returns will not be sustainable. Understanding the limitations will also help managers find ways to extend the limits and to extract more value from CSR.

The limits of where CSR benefits companies have not been extensively researched, but one publication[4] has attempted to set out a useful analysis. The authors base their argument on the power of shareholders and the paramount need to deliver shareholder value.

That means companies cannot engage in CSR activity which might seriously hit shareholder returns, even in the short term. Their argument then rests on the extent to which CSR can enhance shareholder value. They point to the relative insignificance of socially responsible investors in the City, and ethical consumers in the mass market. This is likely to restrain the potential benefits to be gained from those stakeholder groups. In some cases, such as the production of highly polluting cars, most consumers would be actively opposed to discontinuing these ranges. Similarly, in many cases CSR is likely to be low down most employees' list of priorities, meaning that companies which are not regarded as particularly responsible still manage to recruit sufficient able graduates and other staff. The authors conclude:

> The business case is powerful at an individual company level and on specific
> issues . . . There appear to be some issues where the business case is either

weak or non-existent, and others where there can be no business case until market conditions are changed.

Awareness of such limitations should help managers find ways to combine CSR with shareholder value, rather than blindly pursuing either one or the other.

Empirical evidence to date

There is a growing body of empirical evidence on the relationship between CSR and business success. But, as with most business research, it is inconclusive and short on quantitative support. There is much opinion research among individual stakeholder groups such as employees and consumers, reporting claims by significant proportions of each group that they are influenced by companies' social responsibility.[5] Such research is weakened, however, by the fact that respondents are likely to overstress what they believe would be seen as responsible behaviour. For example, there is a clear gap between consumers' ethical claims and their actual shopping behaviour.[6]

More convincing evidence can be found by examining corporate behaviour and per-formance, although this can also be complex. One early examination of the evidence hit on a key problem with much of the research that is available. In a paper for the US Conference Board,[7] Zadek and Chapman examined whether there is a link between cor-porate social and financial performance, drawing on evidence in the UK and elsewhere in Europe. They found that much of the evidence was made suspect by the interests of those undertaking it, or was flawed by weak methodology. Definition, measurement and data problems existed in assessing both social responsibility and financial performance. Never-theless, they concluded that there was some evidence of a relationship between corporate social and financial performance.

There are two strands to the research on CSR. The first, as in the example below, looks at corporate performance, as measured by conventional financial indicators such as profitability. The second examines share price performance, and especially the perform-ance of portfolios selected on socially responsible grounds. For example, one of the authors studied the link between the top UK companies in terms of responsibility rankings and their stock market performance.[8] The results showed a weak inverse correlation between the CSR ranking and share price, which means that a high CSR ranking was slightly worse for a company's share price than a low one. From the end of 1994 to the end of 1996 the FTSE 100 share index rose by 29%. Eleven of the 25 biggest UK firms saw their share price rise by more than this, but they were not necessarily the most responsible companies. Share price gains significantly in excess of the FTSE 100 rise were seen by HSBC (ranked 8th on social responsibility but with a share price rise of 84.4%), Glaxo Wellcome (ranked 2nd with a share price gain of 43.2%) and British Airways (ranked 6th and a share price gain of 69.6%). This was a limited study but one conclusion stands out, and has also emerged repeatedly from other research: CSR does not lead to significant share price underperformance.

Similarly, several studies have examined the US Domini Social Index, which dates back to 1990, and have concluded that its outperformance cannot be explained only by the investment style or characteristics. But in an analysis for UBS Warburg,[9] Larry Chen found that many studies purporting to show outperformance of screened funds can be challenged because they are too small, too partial, too narrow or methodologically flawed. For example, the Domini Index is biased towards large cap and hightech stocks, which explained its outperformance.

Faced with these conflicts, Mr Chen concluded that, while there was no cast-iron link between social responsibility and outperformance, nobody had proved the reverse either. He concluded: "Contrary to theory, most academic studies show that incorporating social screening into a portfolio does not necessarily have detrimental effects on performance. Studies suggested that SRI portfolios have about the same risk-adjusted returns as their normal counterparts."

The latest academic study,[10] by a team based at Maastricht University in the Netherlands, supports this neutral position. After complex analysis of 103 funds from the US, UK and Germany, it concludes: "Even after controlling for investment style we find no significant differences in risk-adjusted returns between ethical and conventional funds."

This neutral conclusion is actually quite dramatic, given the conviction among most investment professionals that non-financial criteria must damage returns.

Collins and Porras's "Built to Last" evidence

Graves and Waddock of Boston College, USA, carried out one of the most interesting pieces of work[11] in recent years on corporate – as opposed to share price – performance. They based their work on analysing a number of "visionary" companies identified in the book *Built to Last*[12] by Collins and Porras. The book highlighted the performance characteristics – and significant positive performance differences – between companies they termed visionary or "built to last" (BTL) and a control group of comparison companies. The study was based on data from the founding of each company to the early 1990s, with some companies in business for as long as 100 years. Collins and Porras compared 18 large-capitalization "visionary" companies identified in a survey of chief executives to a set of companies matched to these by industry and time of founding – and highly successful according to conventional measures.

Collins and Porras showed that the visionary companies performed well for shareholders over long periods. Moreover, they found a striking long-term financial performance difference between the visionary (BTL) and comparison (non-BTL) companies. BTL companies dramatically outperformed the comparison group in terms of market performance, generating more than six times the returns of the comparison group and fifteen times the general market.

Graves and Waddock examined the extent to which these visionary companies achieved their extraordinary performance by working productively and positively with other primary stakeholders such as customers, employees, communities and the environment, i.e. are BLT companies more likely than non-BLT companies to be CSR companies? To assess this question, Graves and Waddock used five stakeholder-related measures based on the criteria used by Kinder, Lydenberg and Domini, the US ethical investment group. Graves and Waddock examined the relationship between 1991 and 1997, using a variety of financial and stock market measures. They did indeed find a relationship between BLT and CSR:

> Not only do these companies continue to perform better for shareholders in financial and market terms, but they also carry less debt, which can be viewed

as a measure of risk, and they evidence significantly better treatment of a range of stakeholders. These data thus provide more evidence for what is termed the "good management hypothesis" that companies that treat their stakeholders well are well-managed companies. That is, we posit – and these results confirm – that there is a positive relationship between the overall quality of management of a firm and the way it treats its critical stakeholders.

These findings have been confirmed most recently in research by academics at DePaul University.[13] They examined the overall financial performance of the 2001 "Best Citizen" companies according to *Business Ethics* magazine, based on eight statistical criteria, including total return, sales growth and profit growth over one-year and three-year periods. The Best Citizens scored ten percentile points higher than the mean ranking of the remainder of the S&P 500 companies.

In a comprehensive review of academic research on both sides of the Atlantic for the insurer CIS, the UK green think-tank Forum for the Future has reviewed a wide range of evidence for both share performance and underlying corporate performance.[14]

It discovered that a clear majority of studies since the 1970s had found a positive link between CSR and corporate performance, as Figure 1 demonstrates.

The report concluded that the weight of evidence suggested positive links between CSR and corporate performance, and found against the presumption that SRI would damage portfolio returns and/or increase risk. But, like others, this research accepted that causal connections were difficult to prove:

> The evidence shows that there is a potential SEE effect that appears to offset the cost of lower diversification in a screened SRI portfolio.
>
> While this may not prove the case for higher returns, it certainly seems to show that screened investing does not imply lower returns.
>
> While the majority of studies carried out from the 1970s to the 1990s found evidence of a correlation between CSR performance and financial performance, it is difficult to disentangle cause from effect. But while assessment of past research rejects the claim that being green and socially responsible always pays, more recent evidence shows that CSR can create shareholder value for some issues, in some industries, with some firms and for some

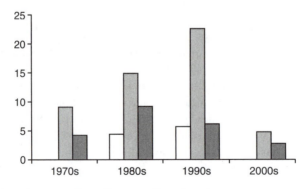

Figure 1 Correlations in research studies over four decades

Source: Forum for the Future

management strategies. As with SRI investing, the question is not does CSR pay, but when does CSR pay?

BT's analysis of the business case

BT has carried out one of the most compelling statistical exercises examining the links between CSR and business performance. The BT method did not attempt to quantify shareholder benefit directly. Instead, it addressed the position of the company in the marketplace. Its analysis is based on the relationship between various factors and satisfaction levels among its 19m residential customers, with results based on tens of thousands of customer interviews in regular polling over 80 months. BT identified four key drivers of customer satisfaction (see Figure 2), the most important being direct contact with the company when reporting faults, making complaints and so on. But reputation and image were also found to be a major determinant of customer satisfaction, and over a quarter of the overall figure for image and reputation was attributable to CSR-related activities.

BT's quantitative analysis suggests that its customers perceive a 1% change in issues such as trust, employee care and social responsibility as of much greater importance than a 1% change in call and rental charges. The figures express the relationships as a ratio. So, for example, if BT's overall image and reputation rose by 1%, its customer satisfaction rating would rise by 0.42%.

If, as the BT studies strongly suggest, CSR activities play a role via image and reputation in maintaining or building the group's market share in a competitive market, then CSR will defend or build shareholder value. In other business sectors, the CSR contribution to customer satisfaction might be greater or smaller, but it can be assumed that similar relationships would be found in other companies with similar mass consumer bases, e.g. banking.

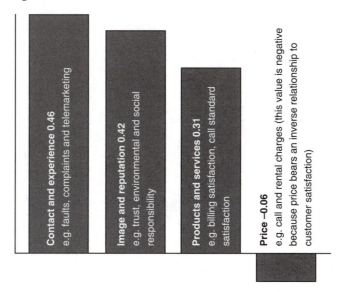

Figure 2 BT's four drivers of customer satisfaction

Source: BT

Notes

1   Based on World Economic Forum (Jan. 2002) *Global Corporate Citizenship: The Leadership Challenge*, Geneva, Switzerland: WEF.

2   Arthur D. Little (2001) "The Business Case for Corporate Citizenship", Cambridge CB4 0DW, UK.

3   SustainAbility/UNEP (2001) *Buried Treasure: Uncovering the Business Case for Corporate Sustainability*, Paris: UNEP.

4   Roger Cowe and Jonathon Porritt (2002) *Government's Business: Enabling Corporate Sustainability*, Forum for the Future, London.

5   E.g. *The Ethical Employee*, Work Foundation, London, 2002, reported a third of UK employees would leave their current employer because of a poor CSR record; MORI CSR poll, summer 2002, found a quarter of consumers described themselves as "ethical", with one in six actively boycotting or choosing products because of ethical reputation.

6   See Cowe and Williams (2000) *Who Are the Ethical Consumers?*, The Cooperative Bank, Manchester.

7   Simon Zadek and Jenny Chapman (1998) "Revealing the Emperor's Clothes: How Social Responsibility Counts", unpublished paper prepared for the Conference Board, London, p. 1.

8   Michael Hopkins (1999) *The Planetary Bargain: Corporate Social Responsibility Comes of Age*, Macmillan Press.

9   *Sustainbility Investment: The Merits of Socially Responsible Investing*, UBS Warburg, London, 2001.

10   Bauer, Koedijk and Otten (2002) "International Evidence on Ethical Mutual Fund Performance and Investment Style", Maastricht University, 2002.

11   S. Graves and S. Waddock (1999) "Beyond Built to Last . . . Stakeholder Relations in "Built-to-Last" Companies", Boston College Carroll School of Management, Chestnut Hill, MA.

12   James C. Collins and Jerry I. Porras (1994) *Built to Last: Successful Habits of Visionary Companies*, New York: HarperBusiness.

13   Verschoor and Murphy, "Strategic Finance", January 2002.

14   *Sustainability Pays*, Co-operative Insurance Society, 2002.

SustainAbility

TEN KEY MESSAGES
Conclusions and recommendations

SUSTAINABILITY'S BUSINESS CASE quest has left us optimistic – and hungry for more. Evidence in favour of the business case continues to build and is particularly strong in certain areas of business performance. However, there still remains a significant gap between what is intuitively logical and what one can prove. The enormous social and environmental values at stake suggest to us that business case research must take an even higher priority.

In this section, we summarize the key messages we take from our journey thus far, and outline a number of next steps. As we said at the outset, we view this as a long-term effort, and will periodically revisit these findings in *Buried Treasure Online*.

Ten key messages

1 Positive impact

The jury is in – overall, corporate SD performance has a positive impact on business success.

As we have shown, there is an impressive and growing body of research analysing the business case for sustainable development. To date, the large majority of the research supports at least a weak to moderate correlation between SD and business performance.

The first key message for companies is that a strategic focus on SD performance aligns well with mainstream business purpose.

2 Brand and reputation

Of the ten measures of business success, brand value and reputation is the measure that appears to be most positively linked to corporate SD performance.

. . .

[T]his link is strongest as an inverse relationship. In other words, poor SD performance – across one or more dimensions – can be more strongly associated with damage to brand value and reputation than superior SD performance can be linked to its enhancement.

Nonetheless, as we discuss below, the weight of evidence for this measure is anecdotal rather than research-based, in large part due to the difficulties in quantifying impact on brand value and reputation.

The links between aspects of SD performance and human and intellectual capital and risk profile are well supported by existing research.

The link to innovation can also be made, but mainly for the two corporate environmental performance dimensions. However, the direction of these links is often unclear. At times innovation brings about environmental advances, while in other cases it is an environmental focus that triggers a drive towards innovation.

The second key message is that a business case analysis should not focus exclusively on financial measures.

3 Environmental process

Of the ten dimensions of SD performance, overall environmental performance (in particular, environmental process focus) is supported by the strongest business case.

Stakeholder focus on corporate environmental performance emerged early as one of the most significant aspects of overall corporate responsibility. As such, it is hardly surprising that it is now the most developed, most researched and best-measured dimension – and is supported by the strongest business case.

Yet there are good reasons to expect that this lead will continue, even as other SD dimensions receive more attention. In many industries, a company's environmental performance has strong and direct links to its cost profile (one of the principal arguments behind eco-efficiency) due to the relationship to resource use, waste processing costs, liabilities and regulatory compliance cost.

At the same time, it is likely that the increasingly accepted business case for environmental performance will also work to strengthen the business case for other SD dimensions.

The third key message is that corporate environmental performance should continue to play a prominent role in any SD business case assessment.

4 Financial results

Positive links between SD performance and verified financial results are supported by business case research.

. . .

[T]here are numerous ways to measure business success, and our choice of ten specific measures supports this diversity.

Nonetheless, business decision-makers generally pay more attention to measures which directly relate to financial results, rather than softer measures. One reason is that there is an additional layer of uncertainty added with some of the softer measures of business success, such as licence to operate. In other words, even if the business case shows a strong link between SD performance and a softer measure, a sceptic could then argue that the softer business success measure is in itself only weakly related to the real interest – financial results.

Fortunately, business case research supports a positive link between corporate SD performance and the single most watched measure of business success: shareholder value. In particular, good performance in the environmental process focus dimension has been shown to generate superior shareholder value.

Other key financial results, such as operational efficiency, revenues and access to capital, are also positively influenced by corporate SD performance, according to current research.

The fourth key message is that the business case can be developed without having to exclusively rely on indirect or intangible measures of business success.

5 *Multiple measures*

The business case is strongest when multiple measures of business success are considered.

Business case researchers – and companies themselves – typically focus on the impact SD has on one particular measure of business performance (often a financial result measure), and base their overall business case on the strength of this particular link.

. . .

[H]owever, the full business case message comes out only when the multi-dimensional nature of business success is considered. A focus on one measure exclusively only presents a partial picture of the business case, as different SD dimensions will typically affect different measures of business success.

The fifth key message is to take a more holistic view of business success – considering both financial results and financial drivers (which influence future financial results).

6 *Business strategy*

The business case is strongest when companies incorporate SD performance into mainstream business strategy.

Not surprisingly, the potential business benefits associated with superior SD performance are more likely to materialize if and when SD performance is evaluated in the same way as other business decisions. Many companies have found that the very isolation of corporate environmental performance from core business planning has been a major shortcoming, limiting both what can be achieved environmentally (because core decision-making lies elsewhere in the company) and the links to business success.

The sixth key message is that business case analysis should lead – rather than follow – a decision to improve SD performance.

7 Chicken and egg

The chicken and egg question – 'Are responsible companies more prosperous, or are prosperous companies more responsible?' – cannot yet be put aside.

As anyone with a passing familiarity with correlation analysis knows, it is impossible to infer the direction of causation. This has plagued business case researchers from the outset. Despite the growing evidence of links to business success, it has been impossible to prove that SD performance drives business performance, rather than the reverse. The more academic, multi-company research studies suffer particularly from this ambiguity.

Fortunately, the growing body of case-study evidence, supported by the company business case believers, provides a sound basis for believing that the direction is, at minimum, two ways. At the company level, there are countless examples of cost savings or other business benefits directly attributable to tangible SD-related decisions.

The seventh key message is that companies should look closely at their own business model and other companies' experience to better understand the mechanism by which improved SD performance can contribute to business success.

8 Sensitivity testing

The business case is likely to strengthen in coming years, based on current trends.

. . .

[T]here are a number of trends at work that could significantly strengthen the business case in coming years. Some of the strongest levers are regulatory, such as the gradual shift toward economic instruments that provide a direct financial incentive for continuous improvement.

As we have shown, however, the potential number of positive influences are wide-ranging, and include measurable things like downward pressure on prices for more sustainable inputs, as well as more intangible factors, such as tightening links between SD performance and corporate reputation.

The eighth key message is that business case analysis should be dynamic, with results tested for sensitivity to various plausible scenarios.

9 Work in progress

The business case debate is still raging, and the current state of research supplies only partial answers.

The link between SD and business performance is well documented in a few cases, but on the whole remains rather speculative. This is due to any of a number of factors, such as:

— The fact that positive links are generally weak to moderate, rather than strong;
— Gaps in the research, particularly for the social dimensions of SD performance and certain less obvious measures of business success;

— The continuing difficulty of attributing direction of causation; and
— The lack of high quality business case assessments by companies themselves.

The ninth key message is that companies should use external evidence to supplement, rather than drive, an in-depth analysis of their own particular situation.

10 Research gap

The biggest research gap plaguing the business case question as a whole is the lack of robust, generally accepted measures of corporate SD performance . . . there is a pressing need to provide better measurement tools.

One challenge that confronts business case advocates is the charge that certain intangible dimensions of SD performance, such as human rights or ethics, values and principles, cannot be measured. Without underestimating the challenge, it is interesting to recall that similar arguments were heard in the 1980s with respect to measurement of corporate environmental performance, an area which now benefits from considerable work on key performance indicators (KPIs).

The focus on KPIs has played, and will continue to play, an invaluable part in making corporate SD performance more measurable. Some companies have gone far to develop company-specific KPIs, which are rigorously defined and measured. The next challenge is to press for greater harmonization across sectors – and throughout industry more generally.

The tenth key message is that companies should follow – and add to – the debate on sustainable development KPIs as a central part of their business case strategy.

Where to from here?

As we noted at the outset, searching for the business case buried treasure is an ongoing quest, and we view this report as one output of a long-term effort.

Research gaps

The **Sustainable Business Value © Matrix** makes clear that many specific research gaps remain. With respect to measures of business performance, little rigorous, academic-style analysis has been done to link SD performance with:

- Revenue
- Access to capital
- Brand value and reputation
- Innovation
- Licence to operate.

Indeed, only 36 of the 100 cells in the matrix are supported by strong evidence (shown as solid colours). In many cases, this lack of formal research is attributable to a number of factors, such as:

- The difficulty in measuring performance of certain SD dimensions, as discussed above;
- An initial assumption that there is not likely to be a strong relationship between a particular dimension and business performance; and
- The as yet incomplete state of the corporate SD performance field in general, and the business case debate in particular.

Turning to this last point, we next identify some interesting – and as yet unanswered – business case questions for each of our ten measures of business success.

Unanswered questions

Shareholder value

- Within industry sectors, how do the environmental and social footprints of companies that are strong performers in terms of shareholder value-added compare with those of weak performers, over the short-, medium- and long-term?
- How does the emerging generation of CFOs see the links between shareholder value and sound TBL performance?

Revenue

- How have business supply chain efforts and partner screening affected revenue prospects for companies with strong SD performance?
- What are the patterns of revenue growth in companies and value webs that are seen to be net positive contributors in terms of the triple bottom line?
- What are the specific areas in the SD-driven dimensions where revenue-creating opportunities could be massive?

Operational efficiency

- How have eco-efficiency benefits evolved over the past decade?
- How would a global carbon trading system affect particular companies and industries?

Access to capital

- To what extent do the SD screening requirements of capital providers (from the World Bank to commercial banks) help boost the success rates of funded projects?
- What events make investors abandon a stock? How do these events relate to SD?
- Which capital providers are most advanced in linking TBL screening to long-term risk issues? Are there tools that have been developed in, for example, the overseas aid and development area that could have useful applications in the mainstream capital markets? If so, what would it take to make these tools market-friendly? Who has already tried to bridge this gap and with what results?

Customer attraction

- What are the long-run trends in terms of the willingness of consumers and customers to spend time in identifying TBL-friendly products and services?
- If concerned ethical or green consumers or customers are more loyal, as is often argued, what is this extra loyalty worth in specific markets and to specific companies?
- Why is there a discrepancy between the willingness of consumers to purchase sustainable products expressed in polls and actual purchasing behaviour?

Brand value and reputation

- What is the quantified importance of brand value and reputation to the other business performance measures?
- To what extent do TBL-driven programmes designed to boost brand value and reputation offset problems in other areas? For example, does BP's 'Beyond Petroleum' campaign offset their refinery explosions in Scotland or situation in Angola; does Shell's *Profits and Principles* offset their situation in Nigeria; or does Ford's corporate citizenship initiative offset the impact on its reputation from the Firestone tyre recall issue?
- How do brand and reputation managers in leading companies assess the business case in their mainstream activities, and what can we learn in the SD area?

Human and intellectual capital

- To what extent do the sorts of people who are now high priority recruits in new economy businesses perceive and consider TBL values and priorities?
- To what extent – and how – do TBL issues affect the likelihood of potential new recruits to accept job offers and, once in, to stay?
- What is the value to employees, calculated in salary terms, of a company's strong SD performance?

Risk profile

- How does the use of new B2B approaches over the internet (e.g. online tendering) mesh with emerging TBL requirements? Are e-tendering processes more or less likely to pick up and reward good TBL performers, and exclude or downgrade poor or riskier performers?
- To what extent do companies relying on online tendering verify what potential suppliers tell them about critical TBL issues?

Innovation

- What is the social, economic and environmental footprint of the 'New Economy'?
- To what extent do SD professionals bring a defensive, anti-innovation approach to the work of companies, and to what extent are they able to think 'out of the box'?
- To what extent – and how – are companies involving their R&D department in the sustainability agenda?

Licence to operate

- How do TBL factors link to the licence to operate (and the licence to innovate) in various sectors, markets and world regions?
- How do the best companies ensure that they detect potential threats to their licences at an early stage?

CHAPTER FOUR

Regulating corporations

The role and impact of codes and guidelines

AS THE PREVIOUS chapter highlighted, while we may be beginning to get a picture of the nature of CSR and how it may prove beneficial to businesses, we are still some way short of getting a clear understanding of exactly what constitutes an effective CSR strategy. Companies may be aware that they should act on the CSR agenda, but how do they decide what to do and how to approach the development of an effective responsibility strategy?

In trying to shape the way in which CSR is developing we have witnessed a dramatic rise in the number of frameworks and codes which now surround the CSR field. These guidelines have emerged from a broad variety of sources and reflect a diversity of stylistic approaches to CSR issues. On one level one can identify a proliferation of individual company codes of conduct and company value statements, outlining for that specific organization the standards by which they expect their employees, and often their suppliers, to function. On a broader level, there are now also a range of external, auditable standards which companies can seek to attain to reflect their commitment within the social and environmental fields. We have also witnessed a growing engagement between business, governments and non-governmental organizations (NGOs) working together to try to establish a series of benchmark statements which reflect an acceptable picture of what an environmentally and socially responsible business should be striving to achieve. As Leipziger (2003: 19) suggests:

> There is no single code or standard, no panacea that will lead to corporate responsibility. Each company is different, with its own challenges, corporate culture, unique set of stakeholders and management systems. Corporate responsibility is a journey for which there is no single map but hundreds of guides. Codes and standards are maps that can be combined in new ways for different journeys.

This chapter focuses on the different guidelines and frameworks which have been developed to provide a benchmark for companies seeking to develop a CSR strategy. It identifies the different types of frameworks and codes which exist, and the rationale behind their development. We shall look at the value of these tools in moving companies towards a greater commitment to CSR and also the problems and weaknesses that some of these frameworks present.

Leipziger identifies a continuum within the CSR field which runs from values and principles through codes of conduct and norms to standards (Leipziger 2003: 36). As companies seek to progress through this continuum the challenges become greater. While values and principles outline the qualities that are desirable towards achieving a specific outcome they remain more of a goal to be pursued rather than anything that can be effectively measured and assessed. By contrast codes provide a set of rules for action and behaviour. Codes however often remain specific to an individual company or industry and are usually enforced through internal company scrutiny. By contrast, norms and standards have a far more expansive purpose applying broadly across geographic regions and industry sectors. In this way they are not solely the realm of an individual company or indeed the business sector itself, but become a more broad-ranging, consensual multi-stakeholder process.

In response to many of the campaigns and criticisms levelled at business in recent years, companies have been quick to provide their stakeholders with a clear guideline on what they should be able to expect of them, often through the publication of a company code of conduct. These codes of conduct have been particularly prevalent for manufacturing companies with supply chains extending to developing nations. The highlighting of sweatshop conditions, the use of child labour and the lack of union representation within factories has raised many questions about how large multinationals conduct their business operations and how the items that we purchase as consumers in the West are actually being produced. Eric Clark (2007: 253) describes one such example in China, in his study of the toy industry:

> Between shifts the workers, mostly young women, their faces set in exhaustion, shuffle from building to building. Shifts can last fifteen hours a day or more, seven days a week – unlawful but far from uncommon in the peak of toy making season. Inside the fetid dormitories, their only living space, and often packed illegally with as many as twenty-two to a room, they collapse into curtained off bunks. . . . We are under a day's flying time from New York, much less from Los Angeles. But the toy aisles of Walmart and Toys R Us, and happy American kids in the television toy commercials could be a hundred years and a million miles away.

Retail companies such as Nike and The Gap have responded to criticisms such as these by placing greater emphasis on ensuring that all their suppliers adhere to the companies' codes of conduct, which clearly outline what is expected of their suppliers and what is deemed appropriate and acceptable behaviour.

Company codes of conduct function as an effective statement of intent in many ways. They provide a clear, formalized statement of a company's values and commitments and represent a framework within which that company seeks to be judged. By establishing and monitoring a code of conduct, it is argued, consumers and investors alike can be assured that the individual company is functioning within a socially responsible and ethically sound framework. In terms of supply chain management, they also allow a company to set a clear standard to which any of its suppliers should adhere.

While company codes of conduct provide a level of commitment towards responsible business practice, practical experience has suggested that ensuring that codes of conduct are maintained and applied is a far greater challenge than the creation of the codes themselves. While a company may indeed expect all of its employees and suppliers to abide by its standards, ensuring that codes of conduct are actually maintained and enforced is a far more difficult process to monitor. While companies strive to ensure greater compliance through unannounced factory visits and inspections, many critics suggest that many breaches of these codes go undetected. In some cases, it is argued, the contractual pressure of large manufacturing targets and low-cost prices set by the multinationals leave the manufacturers with little option but to break the company codes on issues such as working hours, forced overtime and pay levels.

Returning to Eric Clark's analysis of the toy industry, he highlights the problems of enforcing codes of conduct, even when these codes are being monitored by external auditing companies.

> It is a perverse fact that just as auditing of factories has developed, so too has anti-auditing – factories have become more sophisticated and proficient at hiding the truth about conditions. A 24-year-old worker at the Shenzhen factory told the *Los Angeles Times*, 'Mattel has no way to know the truth about what really goes on here. Every time there is an inspection, the bosses tell us what lies to say.'
>
> (Clark 2007: 276).

The publication of a code of conduct does however provide a commitment from a company to a certain standard of behaviour; commitments which the companies themselves have not been the only organizations monitoring. Campaign groups such as the Clean Clothes Campaign have utilized codes of conduct to challenge company behaviour on the basis of their own standards. In their 'Nike Case File' the Clean Clothes Campaign quotes directly from Nike's Code of Conduct regarding wages and conditions for workers and then challenges these commitments in relation to wages for workers in Indonesia, Vietnam and El Salvador. A similar level of scrutiny is undertaken regarding the Code of Conduct's commitments on overtime, rights to collective bargaining and many other aspects (www.cleanclothes.org/companies/nikecase99–11–1.htm).

While codes of conduct act as at least a starting point, therefore, they cannot necessarily provide the necessary assurance that companies are maintaining the level of socially responsible behaviour to which they aspire, or which other stakeholders expect of them. In addition, they are only applicable to the individual company. For a supplier dealing with a range of companies, this could result in their having to comply with a diverse set of standards and codes of conduct, all of which vary from one company to another in different dimensions and requirements. The alternative approach therefore is to seek some form of common standards and requirements that all companies should be committed to.

KEY FRAMEWORKS FOR ACTION

As we have already mentioned, there currently exists a plethora of standards and frameworks which companies may seek to adhere to within the CSR field. Clearly a detailed
examination of all of these approaches is far beyond the realms of this introductory Reader.
The readings selected provide a way of introduction to some of the key frameworks and their
primary focal points. The most influential frameworks within this field may be identified as
follows:

- The UN Global Compact
- Global Reporting Initiative
- OECD Guidelines for Multinationals
- ILO Conventions
- ISO 14000 Series
- Global Sullivan Principles
- Accountability 1000s
- Social Accountability 8000

The development of these frameworks and standards certainly increase the pressure on
companies to engage in the debates around corporate social responsibility and evaluate
their own performance. In some ways, they have even created a level of competition among
companies seeking to gain recognition for their activities through compliance with a broad
range of standards and involvement with a diverse set of CSR initiatives. Engagement
with externally driven and verified frameworks undoubtedly provides more credibility to a
company's CSR commitment than merely internally derived codes and value statements.

However, it is important to question whether or not benchmarks and frameworks really
do enough to ensure the socially and environmentally responsible behaviour of business.
In particular it raises two key questions. First, as these frameworks represent only guides
or benchmarks in most cases, do they actually commit companies to any real substantive
changes in their activities? If, as some critics suggest, companies are able to 'cherry pick'
which frameworks they adhere to and which standards they seek to attain, does this really
mean that we are getting to the heart of their social and environmental impact? To what
extent does this process allow companies to avoid the issues that are really challenging to
them and focus upon the ones within which they can instigate change most easily? The
second concern is that while those who sign up to these frameworks are committing themselves to a level of social and environmental change, what happens to those companies who,
for whatever reason, choose not to engage? Other than a level of peer pressure, there is little
to coerce companies into the CSR process if they do not feel it will be of value or relevance
to them.

Problems such as these lead to one of the central debates within the CSR field: namely
the question of whether or not regulation is required to enforce a level of social responsibility on all companies. The business community has always been largely vocal in its dislike of
the concept of regulating CSR. Given the diversity of issues and themes contained within the
CSR field and the heterogeneous nature of businesses, they argue, it is almost impossible to
create a 'one-size-fits-all' model of responsible business practice. The current voluntary

approach, it is argued, allows companies to apply the central principles of CSR to their particular setting and context. Others, however, suggest that voluntary approaches alone will never ensure the level of compliance that is required to improve the ethical standards of business worldwide. Allowing companies to self-regulate in this field, it is argued, is problematic, since it allows companies to choose whether or not to engage with this agenda and to what extent. Harris Gleckman and Riva Krut (1994: 8–9), for example, argue that corporate self-regulation is actually an oxymoron. Thus, they claim:

> Potential polluters cannot make 'laws' (i.e. regulate) and order 'sanctions' (i.e. authorise penalties and fines) that are against self-interest. Further, state regulation presumes that there is a political process that defines a level of pollution and regulations are issued to disperse this standard equitably over the generators of pollution. No individual 'self-regulator' can determine the publicly approved level of pollution or allocate itself the correct amount of pollution.

In a similar manner, Richter's (2001) study of the impact of codes of conduct on the infant foods industry highlights similar problems with self-regulation. She identifies an important power dimension within the process which, she argues, raises significant question marks over the value of such voluntary approaches. She suggests that

> To ensure that regulation is in the best interests of society, the most basic step seems to be aware always of the critical distinction between the party to be regulated and the parties involved in the process of drawing up the regulation and making it effective.
>
> (Richter 2001: 207)

Codes and frameworks within the CSR field therefore clearly represent a moving and evolving field in which much is in the eye of the beholder. The readings in this chapter are designed to give the reader a feel for some of the differing approaches to this complex field and to get a taste for the types of issues that feature heavily within the process. However, when considering these approaches it is important to keep in mind a number of vital critical questions as Leipziger highlights in the introduction to *The Corporate Responsibility Code Book*. She suggests:

> Albert Einstein wrote that 'not everything that counts can be counted; and not everything that can be counted counts.' This sentence provides a useful commentary on codes of conduct and principles and a useful refrain for readers who should question the tools presented in this volume. Do these tools allow an organisation to count and consider what is most relevant in its sector, to its stakeholders? Do the tools count that which does not need to be counted?
>
> (Leipziger 2003: 21)

Undoubtedly companies are today providing far more detailed information regarding their activities and social and environmental impacts. However, as the readings in this chapter and the discussion of CSR reporting and stakeholder dialogue in the following chapter demonstrate, there is still considerable debate regarding whether or not the information being provided is enough from which to make a truly accurate assessment of company activity and impact.

To give a taste of the types of issues and themes being tackled by codes of conduct and frameworks, a number of examples are highlighted within the readings for this chapter. Three frameworks are highlighted, with extracts from the United Nations Global Compact, OECD Guidelines for Multinationals and the Global Reporting Initiative Sustainability Reporting Guidelines. Adidas' 'Guidelines on Employment Standards' has also been included as an example of a company code as well as the more rigorous and detailed code for the apparel industry being proposed by the Clean Clothes Campaign. Finally, a more critical perspective on codes of conduct is provided within the extract from Kelly Dent's article on 'The Contradiction in Codes'.

GUIDE TO FURTHER READING

For a general guide to all of the main codes and frameworks in the CSR field see Leipziger, D. (2003) *The Corporate Responsibility Code Book*, Sheffield, Greenleaf. In addition, see Fussler, C., A. Cramer and S. van der Vegt (eds) (2004) *Raising the Bar: Creating Value with the UN Global Compact Held*, Sheffield, Greenleaf; Grayson, D. and A. Hodges (2004) *Corporate Social Opportunity: 7 Steps to Make CSR Work for your Business*, Sheffield, Greenleaf; Jenkins, R., R. Pearson and G. Seyfang (2002) *Corporate Responsibility and Labour Rights*, London, Earthscan; Richter, J. (2001) *Holding Corporations Accountable: Corporate Conduct, International Codes and Citizen Action*, London, Zed Books.

WEB-BASED RESOURCES

All of the major frameworks have accompanying websites that provide useful information on the key issues and themes and the application of these frameworks to the business setting. See, for example:

- www.unglobalcompact.org – Website for the UN Global Compact.
- www.ilo.org – International Labour Organization. Focused on working towards the promotion of decent working conditions throughout the world.
- www.thesullivanfoundation.org/gsp – The Global Sullivan Principles.
- www.sa-intl.org – Social Accountability International. Promoting human rights in the workplace.

REFERENCES

Clark, E. (2007) *The Real Toy Story: Inside the Ruthless Battle for Britain's Youngest Consumers*, London, Black Swan.

Gleckman, H. and R. Krut (1994) *The Social Benefits of Regulating International Business*, Geneva, UNRISD.

Leipziger, D. (2003) *The Corporate Responsibility Code Book*, Sheffield, Greenleaf.

Richter, J. (2001) *Holding Corporations Accountable: Corporate Conduct, International Codes and Citizen Action*, London, Zed Books.

OECD

THE OECD GUIDELINES FOR MULTINATIONAL ENTERPRISES

Preface

1. **THE OECD** *Guidelines for Multinational Enterprises* (the *Guidelines*) are recommendations addressed by governments to multinational enterprises. They provide voluntary principles and standards for responsible business conduct consistent with applicable laws. The *Guidelines* aim to ensure that the operations of these enterprises are in harmony with government policies, to strengthen the basis of mutual confidence between enterprises and the societies in which they operate, to help improve the foreign investment climate and to enhance the contribution to sustainable development made by multinational enterprises. The *Guidelines* are part of the OECD *Declaration on International Investment and Multinational Enterprises* the other elements of which relate to national treatment, conflicting requirements on enterprises, and international investment incentives and disincentives.

2. International business has experienced far-reaching structural change and the *Guidelines* themselves have evolved to reflect these changes. With the rise of service and knowledge-intensive industries, service and technology enterprises have entered the international marketplace. Large enterprises still account for a major share of international investment, and there is a trend toward large-scale international mergers. At the same time, foreign investment by small- and medium-sized enterprises has also increased and these enterprises now play a significant role on the international scene. Multinational enterprises, like their domestic counterparts, have evolved to encompass a broader range of business arrangements and organisational forms. Strategic alliances and closer relations with suppliers and contractors tend to blur the boundaries of the enterprise.

3. The rapid evolution in the structure of multinational enterprises is also reflected in their operations in the developing world, where foreign direct investment has grown rapidly. In developing countries, multinational enterprises have diversified beyond primary production and extractive industries into manufacturing, assembly, domestic market development and services.

4.   The activities of multinational enterprises, through international trade and invest-ment, have strengthened and deepened the ties that join OECD economies to each other and to the rest of the world. These activities bring substantial benefits to home and host countries. These benefits accrue when multinational enterprises supply the products and services that consumers want to buy at competitive prices and when they provide fair returns to suppliers of capital. Their trade and investment activities contribute to the efficient use of capital, technology and human and natural resources. They facilitate the transfer of technology among the regions of the world and the development of technolo-gies that reflect local conditions. Through both formal training and on-the-job learning enterprises also promote the development of human capital in host countries.

5.   The nature, scope and speed of economic changes have presented new strategic challenges for enterprises and their stakeholders. Multinational enterprises have the opportunity to implement best practice policies for sustainable development that seek to ensure coherence between social, economic and environmental objectives. The ability of multinational enterprises to promote sustainable development is greatly enhanced when trade and investment are conducted in a context of open, competitive and appropriately regulated markets.

6.   Many multinational enterprises have demonstrated that respect for high standards of business conduct can enhance growth. Today's competitive forces are intense and multinational enterprises face a variety of legal, social and regulatory settings. In this context, some enterprises may be tempted to neglect appropriate standards and prin-ciples of conduct in an attempt to gain undue competitive advantage. Such practices by the few may call into question the reputation of the many and may give rise to public concerns.

7.   Many enterprises have responded to these public concerns by developing internal programmes, guidance and management systems that underpin their commitment to good corporate citizenship, good practices and good business and employee conduct. Some of them have called upon consulting, auditing and certification services, contributing to the accumulation of expertise in these areas. These efforts have also promoted social dialogue on what constitutes good business conduct. The *Guidelines* clarify the shared expectations for business conduct of the governments adhering to them and provide a point of refer-ence for enterprises. Thus, the *Guidelines* both complement and reinforce private efforts to define and implement responsible business conduct.

8.   Governments are co-operating with each other and with other actors to strengthen the international legal and policy framework in which business is conducted. The post-war period has seen the development of this framework, starting with the adoption in 1948 of the Universal Declaration of Human Rights. Recent instruments include the ILO Declaration on Fundamental Principles and Rights at Work, the Rio Declaration on Environment and Development and Agenda 21 and the Copenhagen Declaration for Social Development.

9.   The OECD has also been contributing to the international policy framework. Recent developments include the adoption of the Convention on Combating Bribery of Foreign Public Officials in International Business Transactions and of the OECD Principles of Corporate Governance, the OECD Guidelines for Consumer Protection in the Context of Electronic Commerce, and ongoing work on the OECD Guidelines on Transfer Pricing for Multinational Enterprises and Tax Administrations.

10.   The common aim of the governments adhering to the *Guidelines* is to encourage

the positive contributions that multinational enterprises can make to economic, environmental and social progress and to minimise the difficulties to which their various operations may give rise. In working toward this goal, governments find themselves in partnership with the many businesses, trade unions and other non-governmental organisations that are working in their own ways toward the same end. Governments can help by providing effective domestic policy frameworks that include stable macroeconomic policy, non-discriminatory treatment of firms, appropriate regulation and prudential supervision, an impartial system of courts and law enforcement and efficient and honest public administration. Governments can also help by maintaining and promoting appropriate standards and policies in support of sustainable development and by engaging in ongoing reforms to ensure that public sector activity is efficient and effective. Governments adhering to the *Guidelines* are committed to continual improvement of both domestic and international policies with a view to improving the welfare and living standards of all people.

I Concepts and principles

1   The *Guidelines* are recommendations jointly addressed by governments to multinational enterprises. They provide principles and standards of good practice consistent with applicable laws. Observance of the *Guidelines* by enterprises is voluntary and not legally enforceable.

2   Since the operations of multinational enterprises extend throughout the world, international co-operation in this field should extend to all countries. Governments adhering to the *Guidelines* encourage the enterprises operating on their territories to observe the *Guidelines* wherever they operate, while taking into account the particular circumstances of each host country.

3   A precise definition of multinational enterprises is not required for the purposes of the *Guidelines*. These usually comprise companies or other entities established in more than one country and so linked that they may co-ordinate their operations in various ways. While one or more of these entities may be able to exercise a significant influence over the activities of others, their degree of autonomy within the enterprise may vary widely from one multinational enterprise to another. Ownership may be private, state or mixed. The *Guidelines* are addressed to all the entities within the multinational enterprise (parent companies and/or local entities). According to the actual distribution of responsibilities among them, the different entities are expected to co-operate and to assist one another to facilitate observance of the *Guidelines*.

4   The *Guidelines* are not aimed at introducing differences of treatment between multinational and domestic enterprises, they reflect good practice for all. Accordingly, multinational and domestic enterprises are subject to the same expectations in respect of their conduct wherever the *Guidelines* are relevant to both.

5   Governments wish to encourage the widest possible observance of the *Guidelines*. While it is acknowledged that small and medium-sized enterprises may not have the same capacities as larger enterprises, governments adhering to the *Guidelines* nevertheless encourage them to observe the *Guidelines* recommendations to the fullest extent possible.

6   Governments adhering to the *Guidelines* should not use them for protectionist

purposes nor use them in a way that calls into question the comparative advantage of any country where multinational enterprises invest.

7   Governments have the right to prescribe the conditions under which multinational enterprises operate within their jurisdictions, subject to international law. The entities of a multinational enterprise located in various countries are subject to the laws applicable in these countries. When multinational enterprises are subject to conflicting requirements by adhering countries, the governments concerned will co-operate in good faith with a view to resolving problems that may arise.

8   Governments adhering to the *Guidelines* set them forth with the understanding that they will fulfil their responsibilities to treat enterprises equitably and in accordance with international law and with their contractual obligations.

9   The use of appropriate international dispute settlement mechanisms, including arbitration, is encouraged as a means of facilitating the resolution of legal problems arising between enterprises and host country governments.

10   Governments adhering to the *Guidelines* will promote them and encourage their use. They will establish National Contact Points that promote the *Guidelines* and act as a forum for discussion of all matters relating to the *Guidelines*. The adhering Governments will also participate in appropriate review and consultation procedures to address issues concerning interpretation of the *Guidelines* in a changing world.

II General policies

Enterprises should take fully into account established policies in the countries in which they operate, and consider the views of other stakeholders. In this regard, enterprises should:

1   Contribute to economic, social and environmental progress with a view to achieving sustainable development.

2   Respect the human rights of those affected by their activities consistent with the host government's international obligations and commitments.

3   Encourage local capacity building through close co-operation with the local community, including business interests, as well as developing the enterprise's activities in domestic and foreign markets, consistent with the need for sound commercial practice.

4   Encourage human capital formation, in particular by creating employment opportunities and facilitating training opportunities for employees.

5   Refrain from seeking or accepting exemptions not contemplated in the statutory or regulatory framework related to environmental, health, safety, labour, taxation, financial incentives, or other issues.

6   Support and uphold good corporate governance principles and develop and apply good corporate governance practices.

7   Develop and apply effective self-regulatory practices and management systems that foster a relationship of confidence and mutual trust between enterprises and the societies in which they operate.

8   Promote employee awareness of, and compliance with, company policies through appropriate dissemination of these policies, including through training programmes.

9   Refrain from discriminatory or disciplinary action against employees who make *bona fide* reports to management or, as appropriate, to the competent public authorities, on practices that contravene the law, the *Guidelines* or the enterprise's policies.

10   Encourage, where practicable, business partners, including suppliers and sub-contractors, to apply principles of corporate conduct compatible with the *Guidelines*.

11   Abstain from any improper involvement in local political activities.

III Disclosure

1   Enterprises should ensure that timely, regular, reliable and relevant information is disclosed regarding their activities, structure, financial situation and performance. This information should be disclosed for the enterprise as a whole and, where appropriate, along business lines or geographic areas. Disclosure policies of enter-prises should be tailored to the nature, size and location of the enterprise, with due regard taken of costs, business confidentiality and other competitive concerns.

2   Enterprises should apply high quality standards for disclosure, accounting, and audit. Enterprises are also encouraged to apply high quality standards for non-financial information including environmental and social reporting where they exist. The standards or policies under which both financial and non-financial information are compiled and published should be reported.

3   Enterprises should disclose basic information showing their name, location, and structure, the name, address and telephone number of the parent enterprise and its main affiliates, its percentage ownership, direct and indirect in these affiliates, including shareholdings between them.

4   Enterprises should also disclose material information on:

   a)   The financial and operating results of the company.
   b)   Company objectives.
   c)   Major share ownership and voting right.
   d)   Members of the board and key executives, and their remuneration.
   e)   Material foreseeable risk factors.
   f)   Material issues regarding employees and other stakeholders.
   g)   Governance structures and policies.

5   Enterprises are encouraged to communicate additional information that could include:

   a)   Value statements or statements of business conduct intended for public dis-closure including information on the social, ethical and environmental policies of the enterprise and other codes of conduct to which the company subscribes. In addition, the date of adoption, the countries and entities to which such statements apply and its performance in relation to these statements may be communicated.
   b)   Information on systems for managing risks and complying with laws, and on statements or codes of business conduct.
   c)   Information on relationships with employees and other stakeholders.

IV Employment and industrial relations

Enterprises should, within the framework of applicable law, regulations and prevailing labour relations and employment practices:

1 a)   Respect the right of their employees to be represented by trade unions and other bona fide representatives of employees, and engage in constructive negotiations, either individually or through employers' associations, with such representatives with a view to reaching agreements on employment conditions;

  b)   Contribute to the effective abolition of child labour.

  c)   Contribute to the elimination of all forms of forced or compulsory labour.

  d)   Not discriminate against their employees with respect to employment or occupation on such grounds as race, colour, sex, religion, political opinion, national extraction or social origin, unless selectivity concerning employee characteristics furthers established governmental policies which specifically promote greater equality of employment opportunity or relates to the inherent requirements of a job.

2 a)   Provide facilities to employee representatives as may be necessary to assist in the development of effective collective agreements.

  b)   Provide information to employee representatives which is needed for meaningful negotiations on conditions of employment.

  c)   Promote consultation and co-operation between employers and employees and their representatives on matters of mutual concern.

3   Provide information to employees and their representatives which enables them to obtain a true and fair view of the performance of the entity or, where appropriate, the enterprise as a whole.

4 a)   Observe standards of employment and industrial relations not less favourable than those observed by comparable employers in the host country.

  b)   Take adequate steps to ensure occupational health and safety in their operations.

5   In their operations, to the greatest extent practicable, employ local personnel and provide training with a view to improving skill levels, in co-operation with employee representatives and, where appropriate, relevant governmental authorities.

6   In considering changes in their operations which would have major effects upon the livelihood of their employees, in particular in the case of the closure of an entity involving collective lay-offs or dismissals, provide reasonable notice of such changes to representatives of their employees, and, where appropriate, to the relevant governmental authorities, and co-operate with the employee representatives and appropriate governmental authorities so as to mitigate to the maximum extent practicable adverse effects. In light of the specific circumstances of each case, it would be appropriate if management were able to give such notice prior to the final decision being taken. Other means may also be employed to provide meaningful co-operation to mitigate the effects of such decisions.

7   In the context of bona fide negotiations with representatives of employees on conditions of employment, or while employees are exercising a right to organise, not threaten to transfer the whole or part of an operating unit from the country

concerned nor transfer employees from the enterprises' component entities in other countries in order to influence unfairly those negotiations or to hinder the exercise of a right to organise.

8   Enable authorised representatives of their employees to negotiate on collective bargaining or labour-management relations issues and allow the parties to consult on matters of mutual concern with representatives of management who are authorised to take decisions on these matters.

V Environment

Enterprises should, within the framework of laws, regulations and administrative practices in the countries in which they operate, and in consideration of relevant international agreements, principles, objectives, and standards, take due account of the need to protect the environment, public health and safety, and generally to conduct their activities in a manner contributing to the wider goal of sustainable development. In particular, enterprises should:

1   Establish and maintain a system of environmental management appropriate to the enterprise, including:
    a)   Collection and evaluation of adequate and timely information regarding the environmental, health, and safety impacts of their activities.
    b)   Establishment of measurable objectives and, where appropriate, targets for improved environmental performance, including periodically reviewing the continuing relevance of these objectives; and
    c)   Regular monitoring and verification of progress toward environmental, health, and safety objectives or targets.

2   Taking into account concerns about cost, business confidentiality, and the protection of intellectual property rights:
    a)   Provide the public and employees with adequate and timely information on the potential environment, health and safety impacts of the activities of the enterprise, which could include reporting on progress in improving environmental performance; and
    b)   Engage in adequate and timely communication and consultation with the communities directly affected by the environmental, health and safety policies of the enterprise and by their implementation.

3   Assess, and address in decision-making, the foreseeable environmental, health, and safety-related impacts associated with the processes, goods and services of the enterprise over their full life cycle. Where these proposed activities may have significant environmental, health, or safety impacts, and where they are subject to a decision of a competent authority, prepare an appropriate environmental impact assessment.

4   Consistent with the scientific and technical understanding of the risks, where there are threats of serious damage to the environment, taking also into account human health and safety, not use the lack of full scientific certainty as a reason for postponing cost-effective measures to prevent or minimise such damage.

5   Maintain contingency plans for preventing, mitigating, and controlling serious environmental and health damage from their operations, including accidents and emergencies; and mechanisms for immediate reporting to the competent authorities.

6   Continually seek to improve corporate environmental performance, by encouraging, where appropriate, such activities as:

   a)   Adoption of technologies and operating procedures in all parts of the enterprise that reflect standards concerning environmental performance in the best performing part of the enterprise.

   b)   Development and provision of products or services that have no undue environmental impacts; are safe in their intended use; are efficient in their consumption of energy and natural resources; can be reused, recycled, or disposed of safely.

   c)   Promoting higher levels of awareness among customers of the environmental implications of using the products and services of the enterprise; and

   d)   Research on ways of improving the environmental performance of the enterprise over the longer term.

7   Provide adequate education and training to employees in environmental health and safety matters, including the handling of hazardous materials and the prevention of environmental accidents, as well as more general environmental management areas, such as environmental impact assessment procedures, public relations, and environmental technologies.

8   Contribute to the development of environmentally meaningful and economically efficient public policy, for example, by means of partnerships or initiatives that will enhance environmental awareness and protection.

VI Combating bribery

Enterprises should not, directly or indirectly, offer, promise, give, or demand a bribe or other undue advantage to obtain or retain business or other improper advantage. Nor should enterprises be solicited or expected to render a bribe or other undue advantage. In particular, enterprises should:

1   Not offer, nor give in to demands, to pay public officials or the employees of business partners any portion of a contract payment. They should not use sub-contracts, purchase orders or consulting agreements as means of channelling payments to public officials, to employees of business partners or to their relatives or business associates.

2   Ensure that remuneration of agents is appropriate and for legitimate services only. Where relevant, a list of agents employed in connection with transactions with public bodies and state-owned enterprises should be kept and made available to competent authorities.

3   Enhance the transparency of their activities in the fight against bribery and extortion. Measures could include making public commitments against bribery and extortion and disclosing the management systems the company has adopted in order to honour these commitments. The enterprise should also foster openness and dialogue with

the public so as to promote its awareness of and co-operation with the fight against bribery and extortion.

4   Promote employee awareness of and compliance with company policies against bribery and extortion through appropriate dissemination of these policies and through training programmes and disciplinary procedures.

5   Adopt management control systems that discourage bribery and corrupt practices, and adopt financial and tax accounting and auditing practices that prevent the establishment of "off the books" or secret accounts or the creation of documents which do not properly and fairly record the transactions to which they relate.

6   Not make illegal contributions to candidates for public office or to political parties or to other political organisations. Contributions should fully comply with public disclosure requirements and should be reported to senior management.

VII Consumer interests

When dealing with consumers, enterprises should act in accordance with fair business, marketing and advertising practices and should take all reasonable steps to ensure the safety and quality of the goods or services they provide. In particular, they should:

1   Ensure that the goods or services they provide meet all agreed or legally required standards for consumer health and safety, including health warnings and product safety and information labels.

2   As appropriate to the goods or services, provide accurate and clear information regarding their content, safe use, maintenance, storage, and disposal sufficient to enable consumers to make informed decisions.

3   Provide transparent and effective procedures that address consumer complaints and contribute to fair and timely resolution of consumer disputes without undue cost or burden.

4   Not make representations or omissions, nor engage in any other practices, that are deceptive, misleading, fraudulent, or unfair.

5   Respect consumer privacy and provide protection for personal data.

6   Co-operate fully and in a transparent manner with public authorities in the prevention or removal of serious threats to public health and safety deriving from the consumption or use of their products.

VIII Science and technology

Enterprises should:

1   Endeavour to ensure that their activities are compatible with the science and technology (S&T) policies and plans of the countries in which they operate and as appropriate contribute to the development of local and national innovative capacity.

2   Adopt, where practicable in the course of their business activities, practices that permit the transfer and rapid diffusion of technologies and know-how, with due regard to the protection of intellectual property rights.

3 When appropriate, perform science and technology development work in host countries to address local market needs, as well as employ host country personnel in an S&T capacity and encourage their training, taking into account commercial needs.

4 When granting licenses for the use of intellectual property rights or when otherwise transferring technology, do so on reasonable terms and conditions and in a manner that contributes to the long term development prospects of the host country.

5 Where relevant to commercial objectives, develop ties with local universities, public research institutions, and participate in co-operative research projects with local industry or industry associations.

IX Competition

Enterprises should, within the framework of applicable laws and regulations, conduct their activities in a competitive manner. In particular, enterprises should:

1 Refrain from entering into or carrying out anti-competitive agreements among competitors:

   a) To fix prices.
   b) To make rigged bids (collusive tenders).
   c) To establish output restrictions or quotas; or
   d) To share or divide markets by allocating customers, suppliers, territories or lines of commerce.

2 Conduct all of their activities in a manner consistent with all applicable competition laws, taking into account the applicability of the competition laws of jurisdictions whose economies would be likely to be harmed by anti-competitive activity on their part.

3 Co-operate with the competition authorities of such jurisdictions by, among other things and subject to applicable law and appropriate safeguards, providing as prompt and complete responses as practicable to requests for information.

4 Promote employee awareness of the importance of compliance with all applicable competition laws and policies.

X Taxation

It is important that enterprises contribute to the public finances of host countries by making timely payment of their tax liabilities. In particular, enterprises should comply with the tax laws and regulations in all countries in which they operate and should exert every effort to act in accordance with both the letter and spirit of those laws and regulations. This would include such measures as providing to the relevant authorities the information necessary for the correct determination of taxes to be assessed in connection with their operations and conforming transfer pricing practices to the arm's length principle.

The United Nations Global Compact
ADVANCING CORPORATE CITIZENSHIP

THE UNITED NATIONS Global Compact brings companies together with UN agencies, labour, civil society and governments to advance universal environmental and social principles in order to foster a more sustainable and inclusive world economy.

From its origin as an idea proposed by Secretary-General Kofi Annan at the 1999 World Economic Forum in Davos, the Global Compact has become the world's largest and most widely embraced corporate citizenship initiative. Today, over 2,000 companies from more than 80 countries, as well as many international labour and civil society organizations, are engaged in the Global Compact, working to advance ten universal principles in the areas of human rights, labour standards, the environment and anti-corruption. The Global Compact has unmatched strength in the developing world, home to more than half its participating organizations and a majority of the more than 40 country-level networks it has engendered.

In addition to its rapid growth, the Global Compact has achieved significant impact by fostering company engagement on pressing global corporate citizenship issues. The Global Compact's comparative advantage rests in the universality of its ten principles, the international legitimacy and convening power of the United Nations, and the Compact's potential to be a truly global platform with appeal not only in industrialized countries, but also in the developing world.

Many Global Compact participants have changed their practices, codes of conduct and engaged in new ways with stakeholders as they have sought to implement the principles. According to an impact assessment conducted by McKinsey and Company in mid-2004, half of all participating companies report having changed their policies in relation to the Compact's principles. This is a highly encouraging number considering that many companies joined the initiative in the 2003–2004 timeframe and implementation of the principles is, by its nature, a long-range internal management process. For nearly two-thirds of the companies from developing countries, the Global Compact is the first corporate citizenship initiative in which they have engaged, and many do so to learn how to improve their social and environmental performance and thus enhance their ability to enter into supplier relationships with larger global firms.

The Global Compact has adopted a "leadership model" of engagement, where senior executives are expected to drive corporate engagement, initiated by a CEO letter pledging commitment to the Compact's principles, and supported – whenever possible – by the board of directors. This second expectation is designed to root the Global Compact in the governance structure of the enterprise. Global Compact companies are expected to:

1   Embrace, support and enact, within their sphere of influence, a set of core values in the areas of human rights, labour standards, environmental sustainability and anti-corruption; and
2   Engage with other partners in projects that give concrete expression to the Global Compact principles, in addition to advancing the broader development goals of the UN.

As it has grown, the Compact has developed a value proposition for participating companies based on multi-stakeholder dialogue, learning and implementation of multi-sector partnerships. Through activities in these areas, the Global Compact Office has sought to promote the principles and support company efforts to internalize them.

One of the most significant elements in the evolution in the Compact's model during its first five years has been the organic development of country (and regional) networks. These self-generated networks have grown in a variety of ways, but in all cases have been driven by local companies' need to translate the Compact's global principles into local action. In many cases they have actively helped build local participants and some have facilitated learning activities, dialogues and partnership activities with other stakeholders. For example, in 2004–2005, the Global Compact Egypt network held a series of seminars on implementation, while the Global Compact Society India convened a two-day "Global Compact Regional Conclave in South Asia" in Jamshedpur, India, which drew more than 200 participants and focused on the issue of business and poverty.

Country networks have increasingly become the driving force behind the Compact as its participation grows dramatically across the globe. Indeed, it is the only viable way of managing this growth.

The Global Compact is also a historic development in terms of transforming the relationship between the United Nations and the private sector. During and well after the Cold War environment, the United Nations and the international business community often had a strained relationship. Interventionist and ill-fated attempts by the UN to regulate business practices, commodity prices and technology transfers alienated much of the international business community.

The Global Compact, through is voluntary nature and promotion of values-based markets via "responsible global corporate citizenship", has helped redefine the broader relationship between the UN and business. This has been successful in large measure due to a powerful convergence of UN priorities and principles with business interests and objectives. Because of globalization and expanding supply chains, many companies – especially multinational concerns – are confronting a range of social and environmental issues. And they see that the ways in which they address these problems relate to corporate risk management, as well as to the development of stable and growing markets. More broadly, the very model upon which well-functioning markets is based can only succeed if substantial progress is made in alleviating poverty in its many forms.

The ten principles

The Global Compact seeks to foster a more beneficial relationship between business and societies, paying particular attention to the world's poorest people. The initiative seeks to contribute to more sustainable and inclusive global markets by embedding them in shared values. Importantly, the Global Compact's ten principles in the areas of human rights, labour standards, the environment and anti-corruption *enjoy universal consensus*. They are derived from the Universal Declaration of Human Rights, the International Labour Organization's Declaration on Fundamental Principles and Rights at Work, the Rio Declaration on Environment and Development, and the United Nations Convention Against Corruption.

The Global Compact asks companies to embrace, support and enact, within their sphere of influence, the following principles:

Human rights

- Principle 1: Businesses should support and respect the protection of internationally proclaimed human rights; and
- Principle 2: make sure that they are not complicit in human rights abuses.

Labour

- Principle 3: Businesses should uphold the freedom of association and the effective recognition of the right to collective bargaining;
- Principle 4: the elimination of all forms of forced and compulsory labour;
- Principle 5: the effective abolition of child labour; and
- Principle 6: the elimination of discrimination in respect of employment and occupation.

Environment

- Principle 7: Businesses should support a precautionary approach to environmental challenges;
- Principle 8: undertake initiatives to promote greater environmental responsibility; and
- Principle 9: encourage the development and diffusion of environmentally friendly technologies

Anti-corruption

- Principle 10: Businesses should work against all forms of corruption, including extortion and bribery.

Key stakeholders

The Global Compact involves all relevant actors: governments, which define the principles on which the initiative is based; companies, whose actions it seeks to influence; labour, in whose hands the concrete process of global production takes place; civil society organizations (CSOs), representing stakeholder communities; and the United Nations. Other key actors engaged in the Global Compact include: cities, development agencies, academics, business associations and CSR organizations.

It is important to outline two assumptions about the motives of the Compact participants. First, actors believe that it is in their own enlightened self-interest to work towards alleviation of many of the world's most pressing dilemmas. Second, actors have recognized that many of these problems can be addressed only through multi-stakeholder cooperation.

Governments

Governments provide the essential legitimacy and universality to the principles of the Compact. Ultimately, implementation of the principles takes place within the legislative and regulatory frameworks developed by governments. They facilitate the functioning of the Global Compact at both global and national levels. As legislatures, they create an enabling, legal environment in which voluntary initiatives, such as the Global Compact, play a complementary role.

At the global level, they provide the political space for the Secretary-General to experiment with innovative engagement mechanisms involving business, labour and civil society organizations. They also provide financial support to the Global Compact Office and offer overall policy guidance on advancing responsible corporate citizenship in alignment with UN goals.

At the national level, governments support Compact events and the formation of Global Compact country networks. They also help build policies that advance convergence around the Compact and its principles.

Business

The Global Compact is a voluntary initiative promoting responsible global corporate citizenship. It operates on a leadership model in that it aims to bring a critical mass of business leaders on board to build a sustainable movement. A company's CEO, endorsed by the company's board, must take the initiative to write to the Secretary-General stating the organization's commitment to the Global Compact and its principles. Once this commitment is made, a company:

- Sets in motion changes to business operations so that the Global Compact and its principles become part of strategy, culture and day-to-day operations;
- Is expected to publicly advocate the Global Compact and its principles via communications vehicles such as press releases, speeches, etc.; and
- Is expected to publish in its annual financial report or similar document (e.g. sustainability report), a description of the ways in which it is supporting the Global Compact and all ten principles – the so-called Communication on Progress.

The Global Compact Office neither regulates nor monitors a company's activities. The Compact's website carries the names of the companies that have sent letters of support and provides links to relevant reports, including the Communications on Progress. Global Compact network partners facilitate implementation of the ten principles by submitting case studies and case examples, as well as by offering training and tools. They play an important role in encouraging the development of the Communications on Progress (described further in "The Opportunities and Challenges of Scale" section below).

Participating companies also have the opportunity to contribute to a number of Global Compact activities at the global and local levels, through dialogue, learning activities and partnership projects.

The Global Compact's participant base is composed of large multinational and domestic companies, in addition to small- and medium-sized enterprises (SMEs) which represent approximately 35 percent of the total. The relative large number of SMEs is important given that in many developing countries, SMEs represent the majority of employment and effectively constitute the private sector.

Labour

Labour is part of both industry and civil society. It plays a role that is distinct from both business and other elements of civil society, which is why it is recognized as a separate group by the Global Compact.

Internationally recognized labour standards, including the fundamental rights that are part of the Compact's ten principles, are developed in a tripartite process in which business and labour play critical and central roles. They are also heavily involved in the supervisory procedures of the International Labour Organization to try to ensure that labour standards are implemented at the national level.

The organizational structures of the international trade union movement equip it to coherently participate in the Global Compact in a way that covers engagement on both sectoral and general policy issues. Trade unions are representative organizations that have long traditions of internal democracy, transparency and accountability to members.

Civil Society Organizations

Civil Society Organizations (CSOs) add critical dimensions to the Compact's operations. They offer not just their competencies and substantive knowledge, but their problem-solving capacity and practical reach. Also, they can help to provide checks and balances and lend credibility and social legitimacy to the initiative. These characteristics help entrench the Global Compact's principles in a broader social context.

When participating in dialogue, CSOs add value in the areas of relationship building, information sharing, problem solving and consensus building. As project partners, their practical reach and skills are often crucial to the design and implementation of initiatives that give practical meaning to the Compact's principles. These initiatives also help to maximize learning efforts associated with a company's Compact-related activities.

United Nations agencies

The Global Compact is a network. At its core are the Global Compact Office and six UN agencies: Office of the High Commissioner for Human Rights (OHCHR); United Nations Environment Programme (UNEP); International Labour Organization (ILO); United Nations Office on Drugs and Crime (UNODC); United Nations Development Programme (UNDP); and United Nations Industrial Development Organization (UNIDO). The first four act as the "guardians" of the principles, with UNDP serving as an implementing arm and UNIDO providing expertise and resources with respect to the SMEs. The UN agencies participating in the Global Compact have collectively developed terms of reference for an Inter-Agency Team that meets a few times annually to help ensure a high degree of coherence of the activities of the Global Compact Office and the UN agencies, as well as to explore opportunities to pool the expertise and resources of the team's members.

Key initiatives and priorities

Issue leadership is central to establishing the business case for the ten principles. The focus on and action around important issues is the key to motivating participants and scaling up small successes through joint partnerships. To date, policy dialogues have helped create trust among stakeholders by establishing a neutral platform and creating value-added outcomes. Global Compact dialogues have also significantly contributed to achieving a climate of cooperation between business and civil society organizations.

Business and human rights

Human rights are a key priority for the Global Compact Office as there exists a fundamental lack of understanding on the part of many actors concerning the operational meaning of the human rights principles. In part, this is because human rights have traditionally been the concern of states, and international human rights law has generally been addressed to them only.

As more companies come to realize their (legal, moral, commercial) need to address human rights issues within their own operations and activities, they are also confronted with a number of challenges. For example, there is the need to come to grips with the human rights framework and how the company's own activities might relate to it. There is also uncertainty around how to avoid being complicit in human rights abuse and what are the boundaries of companies' human rights responsibility. Therefore, there is a keen demand for tools and guidance to help companies with their internal implementation management firms, pension funds and stock exchanges. The initiative is supported by the chief executive officers of 20 global companies controlling $6 trillion in assets. In addition, the IFC and The World Bank Group have officially endorsed the recommendations. The Global Compact Office worked with several partners to develop the initiative, including the Swiss Government, The Conference Board, Columbia University and UNEP FI. Implementation of the recommendations is currently under way.

A second initiative centers on the world's stock exchanges, seeking to encourage them to influence their listed companies to support the GC, and to consider other ways of partnering with the GC. It is expected that both the stock exchange and financial analyst communities will become significant advocates and drivers in supporting the GC.

Finally, the Global Compact and the United Nations Environment Programme launched the Principles for Responsible Investment initiative, which is currently mobilizing the chief executive officers of the world's largest pension funds to advance responsible investment globally.

Emergency relief

The Global Compact Office played a major role in the development of "Business Contributions to UN Emergency Relief: An Orientation Guide", which was launched in cooperation with the Office for the Coordination of Humanitarian Affairs (OCHA) at a landmark conference in April 2005. The Guide was designed to assist businesses in identifying effective ways to support the UN's emergency relief efforts. As the response to the December 2004 Southeast Asian Tsunami relief effort demonstrated, work is needed to improve the methods for channeling the enormous generosity of the private sector amid global crises.

Business and development

The Global Compact and its vision relate directly to the international development agenda. Indeed, the Compact's two complementary objectives – i) making the ten principles part of business strategy and operations and ii) promoting partnerships – form an effective tool for business to contribute to sustainable development.

By developing and implementing polices in the four areas of the Global Compact – human rights, labour, the environment and anti-corruption – companies are, by definition, contributing to the process of sustainable development.

In addition, by forging partnerships with other stakeholders, businesses have the opportunity to scale up action within and even beyond their direct spheres of influence. The full integration of the ten principles, particularly in low-income countries, accompanied by well-selected partnership projects, can make companies a driving force for development. Already, business has shown how to contribute in areas such as HIV/AIDS in the workplace, small- and medium-sized business development, the provision of training, environmental protection and a host of community projects.

A noteworthy example of action is the Global Compact's Growing Sustainable Business initiative, implemented by UNDP, which has mobilized companies to invest in less developed countries in order to build key economic, social and environmental pillars.

The opportunities and challenges of scale

The Global Compact Leaders Summit in June 2004 provided the initiative with an opportunity to re-engage leaders from all sectors – business, labour, civil society, and government – and set the strategic course and priorities for the coming years. It was the largest-ever gathering of business leaders at the UN. A conference in London later that year brought together the focal points of many country networks, who agreed to better define their governance systems. The adoption of the tenth principle on anti-corruption – announced at the Summit by the Secretary-General – was followed up with a roll-out of tools for implementation. And work with financial markets, both mainstream investment companies (through the globally recognized *Who Cares Wins* initiative) and stock exchanges, represented another major milestone.

While these are important and promising developments, it is clear that the Global Compact must focus more on *action* and *impact*. While the Global Compact today stands as an impressive network of nearly 2,000 companies and other stakeholder organizations, putting the principles into practice remains the overriding challenge. A bold step was taken in 2004–2005 with the introduction of an explicit policy on how companies should describe their implementation of the principles – the Communication on Progress (COP).

The COP policy requires corporate participants to submit, annually, a prominent communication outlining their implementation of the ten principles – or risk being identified as inactive on the Global Compact website. The overall objective is to raise the transparency and public accountability of the initiative. The Global Compact Office communicated directly with all participating chief executives concerning this requirement, while also engaging the many country networks to mobilize local participants in this regard. To further assist in this effort, a Practical Guide to Communication on Progress was published in May 2005.

An overriding challenge moving forward will be to encourage more and more companies to develop this important communication, understanding hurdles that include language issues, as well as fundamental differences in business culture and attitudes with respect to implementation versus communication. Indeed, it is clear that many Global Compact participants have impressive track records in terms of turning the ten principles into practice, but companies – especially in the developing world where notions of "transparency" and "public reporting" are not as common as in the developed world – must be encouraged to communicate their efforts to help raise the overall credibility of the initiative.

The governance of the Global Compact – at both the global and local levels – is also of prime importance. During 2005, consultations on the overall governance – that is, at the global level – of the initiative began with participants and stakeholders. The outcome of these deliberations will be presented to the Secretary-General in summer 2005. At the same time, the governance of country networks is crucial as the Global Compact seeks to manage growth and scale up efforts. It is also at the local level where many of humanity's problems reside, business dilemmas exist and the needs are the greatest. Moving forward, active country networks will seek to scale up activities, while sleepy networks must become more dynamic, or fade away. Country networks will also be critical with respect to protecting the integrity of the initiative and its brand through, for instance, encouraging companies to communicate progress and helping to resolve any issues and concerns related to specific company action.

As the Global Compact embarks on this critical next phase, in several fundamental ways, the nature of the Global Compact will remain the same. The Compact will remain an open and voluntary initiative engaging with a wide spectrum of companies across the globe. Participating companies will continue to undertake to implement the ten universal principles and engage with other social partners in ways that give concrete expression to the core principles. Finally, the primary means for participant engagement will remain focused on learning, dialogue and partnerships.

While the nature of the Global Compact commitment and core activities will be retained, there will be three significant areas of evolution in the Global Compact's model of company engagement: (1) the Compact will focus on the challenges associated with global firms entering emerging markets and national firms in developing countries seeking to participate in the global marketplace; (2) the participation model will shift to greater emphasize the quality of company commitment to the principles; and (3) country networks will begin to formalize their structures and play a greater role in driving the Global Compact's development.

Global Reporting Initiative

SUSTAINABILITY REPORTING GUIDELINES

Introduction

THIS SECTION OF THE *Guidelines* identifies reporting principles essential to producing a balanced and reasonable report on an organisation's economic, environmental, and social performance. The June 2000 *Guidelines* presented a first version of these principles. These were informed by the financial accounting tradition and adapted for reporting on economic, environmental, and social performance with reference to research related to environmental accounting. Now, with the benefit of time and learning through application of the June 2000 *Guidelines*, GRI presents a revised set of principles that combine and extend many of the concepts that appeared under the headings of "underlying principles" and "qualitative characteristics" of GRI-based reports in the June 2000 *Guidelines*.

Those familiar with financial reporting will recognise overlaps between GRI's reporting principles and those used in financial reporting. However, while financial reporting is a key benchmark for developing principles for reporting on economic, environmental, and social performance, significant differences do exist. The principles in this section take these differences into account. They are rooted in GRI's experience over the last four years, blending knowledge from science and learning from practice.

GRI views these principles as integral to its reporting framework, equal in weight to the elements and indicators in Part C of the *Guidelines*. Organisations using the *Guidelines* are expected to apply these principles in their report preparation. Collectively, the principles define a compact between the reporting organisation and report user, ensuring that both parties share a common understanding of the underpinnings of a GRI-based report. They provide an important reference point to help a user interpret and assess the organisation's decisions regarding the content of its report. The principles are designed with the long term in mind. They strive to create an enduring foundation upon which performance measurement will continue to evolve based on new knowledge and learning.

The principles are goals toward which a reporter should strive. Some reporting organisations may not be able to fully apply them in the short term. However, organisations should identify improvement in how rigourously they apply the principles to their reporting process, in much the same way as they identify improvement in the various aspects of economic, environmental, and social performance.

Reports do not need to contain a detailed checklist showing that all principles have been adopted. But they should offer some discussion of how the reporting principles have been applied. This should include both successes and challenges. If a reporting organisation does not seek to apply these principles, it should indicate where such departures exist and why. Discussion of the application (or non-application) of principles may appear in the profile section of the report or in a separate section that addresses the technical aspects involved in preparing the report.

The 11 principles outlined in the following section will help ensure that reports:

- present a balanced and reasonable account of economic, environmental, and social performance, and the resulting contribution of the organisation to sustainable development;
- facilitate comparison over time;
- facilitate comparisons across organisations; and
- credibly address issues of concern to stakeholders.

Organisation of the principles

The principles are grouped in four clusters (see Figure 1). Those that:

- form the framework for the report (transparency, inclusiveness, auditability);
- inform decisions about what to report (completeness, relevance, sustainability context);
- relate to ensuring quality and reliability (accuracy, neutrality, comparability); and
- inform decisions about access to the report (clarity, timeliness).

The principles of transparency and inclusiveness represent the starting point for the reporting process and are woven into the fabric of all the other principles. All decisions about reporting (e.g., how, when, what) take these two principles and associated practices into consideration.

The principles of sustainability context, completeness, and relevance play the key role in determining what to report. Reports should help place the organisation's performance in the broader context of sustainability challenges, risks, and opportunities. The information contained within the report must meet the test of completeness in terms of the reporting boundaries (i.e., entities included), scope (i.e., aspects or issues reported), and time frame. Lastly, reported information should be relevant to the decision-making needs of stakeholders.

The quality and reliability of the report content are guided by the principles of neutrality, comparability, and accuracy. Reports should be comparable over time and across organisations. Information should be sufficiently accurate and reliable to enable its use for decision-making purposes. Equally important, the report should present its content in a balanced and unbiased manner.

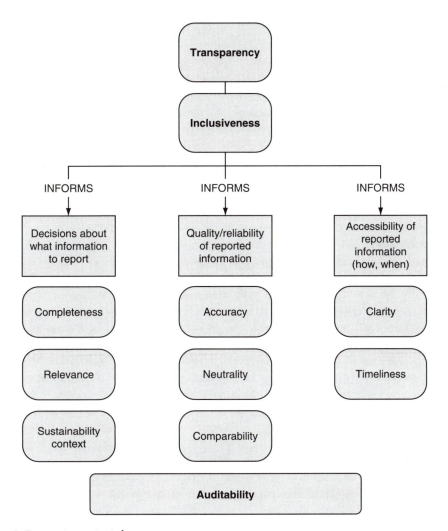

Figure 1 Reporting principles

The principles of clarity and timeliness govern the access and availability of reports. Put simply, stakeholders should receive easily understood information in a time frame that allows them to use it effectively.

Lastly, the principle of auditability relates to several other principles such as comparability, accuracy, neutrality, and completeness. Specifically, this principle refers to the ability to demonstrate that the processes underlying report preparation and information in the report itself meet standards for quality, reliability, and other similar expectations.

Transparency

Full disclosure of the processes, procedures, and assumptions in report preparation are essential to its credibility.

Transparency is an overarching principle and is the centrepiece of accountability. It requires that, regardless of the format and content of reports, users are fully informed of the processes, procedures, and assumptions embodied in the reported information. For example, a report must include information on the stakeholder engagement processes used in its preparation, data collection methods and related internal auditing, and scientific assumptions underlying the presentation of information. This transparency in reporting is an exercise in accountability—the clear and open explanation of one's actions to those who have a right or reason to inquire.

Transparency is central to any type of reporting or disclosure. In the case of financial reporting, over many decades governments and other organisations have created, and continue to enhance, disclosure rules affecting financial reports to increase the transparency of the reporting process. These generally accepted accounting principles and evolving international accounting standards seek to ensure that investors are given a clear picture of the organisation's financial condition, one that includes all material information and the basis upon which this depiction is developed.

GRI seeks to move reporting on economic, environmental, and social performance in a similar direction by creating a generally accepted framework for economic, environmental, and social performance disclosure. As this framework continues to evolve rapidly, general practices will evolve in parallel, based on best practice, best science, and best appraisal of user needs. In this dynamic environment, it is essential that reporting organisations are transparent regarding the processes, procedures, and assumptions that underlie their reports so that users may both believe and interpret reported information. In this sense, transparency transcends any one principle, but affects all.

Inclusiveness

> The reporting organisation should systematically engage its stakeholders to help focus and continually enhance the quality of its reports.

The inclusiveness principle is rooted in the premise that stakeholder views are integral to meaningful reporting and must be incorporated during the process of designing a report. Reporting organisations should seek to engage stakeholders who are both directly and indirectly affected. Aspects of reporting enriched by stakeholder consultation include (but are not limited to) the choice of indicators, the definition of the organisation's reporting boundaries, the format of the report, and the approaches taken to reinforce the credibility of the reported information. Characteristics relevant to designing stakeholder consultation processes include the nature and diversity of products and services, the nature of the reporting organisation's operations and activities, and the geographic range of operations. Stakeholder engagement, like reporting itself, is a dynamic process. Executed properly, it is likely to result in continual learning within and outside the organisation, and to strengthen trust between the reporting organisation and report users. Trust, in turn, fortifies report credibility, itself a key goal of GRI's reporting framework.

The principle of inclusiveness also addresses the diverse needs of stakeholders who use sustainability reports. The range of users of a sustainability report is broader than that of financial reports. Inclusiveness is essential to ensuring that the reporting process and content reflect the needs of these diverse users. Each user group has specific information expectations—at times overlapping with those of other groups, at times distinct. Failure to identify and consult with stakeholders is likely to result in reports that are less relevant to users' needs and thereby less credible to external parties. In contrast, systematic stakeholder engagement enhances receptivity and usefulness across user groups. This engagement may also include soliciting views regarding the utility and credibility of sustainability reports issued by the reporting organisation.

GRI recognises that many reporting organisations have a wide range of potential stakeholders. Any systematic approach to inclusiveness will require an organisation to define an approach for grouping and prioritising stakeholders for purposes of engagement. In the spirit of the inclusiveness and transparency principles, it is important for reporting organisations to clearly and openly explain their approach to defining whom to engage with and how best to engage.

Auditability

> Reported data and information should be recorded, compiled, analysed, and disclosed in a way that would enable internal auditors or external assurance providers to attest to its reliability.

The auditability principle refers to the extent to which information management systems and communication practices lend themselves to being examined for accuracy by both internal and external parties. Reports using the *Guidelines* contain data that is both qualitative and quantitative in nature. In designing data collection and information systems, reporting organisations therefore should anticipate that internal auditing and external assurance processes may be used in the future.

The Verification Working Group

In response to user requests, GRI formed a working group in 1999 to explore issues and options for strengthening the credibility of sustainability reports through various assurance mechanisms. The results of these consultations are reflected in the statements in Part A (Credibility of Reports) and in Annex 4 on assurance processes. The working group also has prepared an advisory assurance strategy paper (available on www.globalreporting.org) for consideration by the GRI Board of Directors. Beginning in September 2002, the Board will consider options for how GRI might continue to play a constructive role in advancing the assurance of sustainability reports.

In preparing reports, organisations should continually ask the question: Is the response to an information query presented in such a way that an internal or external party in the future could examine its accuracy, completeness, consistency, and reliability? Unverifiable statements or data that affect the broad messages contained in a report using the *Guidelines* may compromise its credibility. In addition to accuracy and reliability, the completeness of information may also affect the ability of an auditor to render an assessment.

Completeness

> All information that is material to users for assessing the reporting organisa-
> tion's economic, environmental, and social performance should appear in the
> report in a manner consistent with the declared boundaries, scope, and time
> period.

This principle refers to accounting for and disclosing, in sufficient detail, all information of significant concern to stakeholders within the declared boundaries (i.e., operational, scope, and temporal) of the report. Defining whether such information meets the test of significance to stakeholders should be based on both stakeholder consultation as well as broad-based societal concerns that may not have surfaced through the stakeholder consult-ation process. Such broad-based concerns may derive, for example, from national policy and international conventions.

The completeness principle is three-dimensional:

Operational boundary dimension: Reported information should be complete in relation to the operational boundaries of the reporting organisation, in other words, the range of entities for which the reporting organisation gathers data. These boundaries should be selected with consideration of the economic, environmental, and social impacts of the organisation. Such boundaries may be defined based on financial control, legal ownership, business relationships, and other considerations. The boundaries may vary according to the nature of the reported information. In some cases, the most appropriate boundaries for meeting the expectations outlined by other reporting principles may extend beyond traditional financial reporting boundaries.

Scope dimension: Scope is distinct from boundaries in that an organisation could choose extended reporting boundaries (e.g., report data on all the organisations that form the supply chain), but only include a very narrow scope (e.g., only report on human rights performance). In the context of GRI, "scope" refers to aspects such as energy use, health and safety, and other areas for which the *Guidelines* include indicators and queries. Despite the fact that the reporting boundary may be complete the scope (e.g., human rights aspects only) may not be complete. The process for determining a complete scope may include, for example, the results of lifecycle analysis of products or services and assess-ment of the full range of direct and indirect social or ecological impacts of the reporting organisation. Some of these same tools may also influence decisions about the other

---

Defining boundaries

Defining boundary conditions for reporting on economic, environmental, and social performance is a complex challenge. Complicating factors include the diverse nature of the information and the intimate relationship between the organisation and the larger economic, environmental, and social systems within which it operates. Boundary research is a high priority in GRI's work programme. Discussion papers, exposure drafts and testable protocols will appear during 2002–2003, leading to more systematic and precise treatment of this critical reporting issue.

dimensions of completeness discussed here. The report should disclose all relevant information within the context of the scope (i.e., aspects) covered.

Temporal dimension: Reported information should be complete with reference to the time period declared by the reporting organisation. As far as possible, reportable activities, events, and impacts should be presented for the reporting period in which they occur. This may involve reporting on activities that produce minimal short-term impact, but will have a cumulative effect that may become material, unavoidable, or irreversible in the longer term. Such activities might include, for example, the release of certain bioaccumulative or persistent pollutants. Disclosure of the nature and likelihood of such impacts, even if they may only materialise in the future, comports with the goal of providing a balanced and reasonable representation of the organisation's current economic, environmental, and social performance. In making estimates of future impacts (both positive and negative), the reporting organisation should be careful to make well-reasoned estimates that reflect the best understanding of the likely size, nature, and scope of impacts. Although speculative in nature, such estimates can provide useful and relevant information for decision-making as long as the limitations of the estimates are clearly acknowledged.

Information within the organisation often flows from management systems that operate on a regular, short-term cycle, typically one year. However, a single reporting cycle often is too brief to capture many important economic, environmental, and social impacts. This type of performance, by nature, focuses on the long-term, with forward-looking trends at least as important as lagging, or historical, ones. Thus, reporting organisations should strive to gradually align information systems to account for these forward-looking trends in addition to historical trends.

Relevance

> Relevance is the degree of importance assigned to a particular aspect, indicator, or piece of information, and represents the threshold at which information becomes significant enough to be reported.

Relevance in sustainability reporting is driven by the significance attached to a piece of information to inform the user's decision-making processes. Stakeholders use information on economic, environmental, and social performance in a variety of ways, some of which may differ substantially from that of the reporting organisation. The significance of information can be judged from a number of perspectives; however, in any reporting system, the key perspective is that of the information user. The primary purpose of reporting (as opposed to other types of outreach and communication) is to respond to user information needs in a neutral and balanced manner. Reporting must therefore place a strong emphasis on serving users' specific needs.

In considering relevance, it is important to remain sensitive to differences in how users and reporting organisations apply information. Through stakeholder consultation, a reporting organisation can better understand stakeholders' information needs and how best to respond to them. Ideally, reports should contain information that is useful and relevant to both the reporting organisation and the report users. However, in some cases, information may be relevant to the report user, but may not be of the same value to the reporting organisation. It is important to differentiate between situations where reporting expectations differ and those where information is irrelevant.

Sustainability context

> The reporting organisation should seek to place its performance in the larger context of ecological, social, or other limits or constraints, where such context adds significant meaning to the reported information.

Many aspects of sustainability reporting draw significant meaning from the larger context of how performance at the organisational level affects economic, environmental, and social capital formation and depletion at a local, regional, or global level. In such cases, simply reporting on the trend in individual performance (or the efficiency of the organisation) leaves open the question of an organisation's contribution to the total amount of these different types of capital. For some users, placing performance information in the broader biophysical, social, and economic context lies at the heart of sustainability reporting and is one of the key differentiators between this type of reporting and financial reporting. Moreover, while the ability of an organisation to "sustain" itself is obviously important to a range of stakeholders, it is unlikely that any individual organisation will remain in existence indefinitely. This principle emphasises the sustainability of the broader natural and human environment within which organisations operate.

Where relevant and useful, reporting organisations should consider their individual performance in the contexts of economic, environmental, and social sustainability. This will involve discussing the performance of the organisation in the context of the limits and demands placed on economic, environmental, or social resources at a macro-level. This concept is most clearly articulated in the environmental area in terms of global limits on resource use and pollution levels, but also may be relevant to social and economic issues.

The understanding of how best to link organisational performance with macro-level concerns will continue to evolve. GRI recommends that individual reporting organisations explore ways to incorporate these issues directly into their sustainability reports in order to advance both reporting organisations' and users' understanding of these linkages.

Accuracy

> The accuracy principle refers to achieving the degree of exactness and low margin of error in reported information necessary for users to make decisions with a high degree of confidence.

Economic, environmental, and social indicators can be expressed in many different ways, ranging from qualitative responses to detailed quantitative measurements. The characteristics that determine accuracy vary according to the nature of the information. For example, the accuracy of qualitative information is largely determined by the degree of clarity, detail, and balance in presentation. The accuracy of quantitative information, on the other hand, may depend on the specific sampling methods used to gather hundreds of data points from multiple operating units. The specific threshold of accuracy that is necessary will depend in part on the intended use of the information. Certain decisions will require higher levels of accuracy in reported information than others.

Application of the accuracy principle requires an appreciation of:

- the intentions and decision-making needs of the users; and
- the different conditions under which information is gathered.

As with other principles, it is important to be transparent in how this principle is applied. Explaining the approaches, methods, and techniques that the reporting organisation uses to achieve satisfactory levels of accuracy will help improve the credibility of the report and the acceptance of the reported information.

Neutrality

> Reports should avoid bias in selection and presentation of information and should strive to provide a balanced account of the reporting organisation's performance.

The neutrality principle refers to the fair and factual presentation of the organisation's economic, environmental, and social performance. Embodied in the principle of neutrality is the notion that the core objective behind a reporting organisation's selection and communication of information is to produce an unbiased depiction of its performance. This means presenting an account that includes both favourable and unfavourable results, free from intentional tilt or under- or overstatement of the organisation's performance. The report should focus on neutral sharing of the facts for the users to interpret. Environmental reporting, the precursor to sustainability reporting, has demonstrated this type of gradual evolution from anecdotal and selective disclosure toward a more neutral, factual presentation of data. While reporting practices still vary significantly among reporting organisations, many have recognised that achieving and maintaining credibility among users hinges on the commitment of the reporting organisation to a neutral and fair depiction.

Under the neutrality principle, the *overall* report content must present an unbiased picture of the reporting organisation's performance, avoiding selections, omissions, or presentation formats that are intended to influence a decision or judgement by the user. Where the reporting organisation wishes to present its perspective on an aspect of performance, it should be clear to the reader that such information is separate and distinct from GRI's reporting elements. In the same way that annual financial reports typically contain interpretive material in the front end and financial statements in the back, so too should GRI-based reports strive for a clear distinction between the reporting organisation's interpretation of information and factual presentation.

Comparability

> The reporting organisation should maintain consistency in the boundary and scope of its reports, disclose any changes, and re-state previously reported information.

This principle refers to ensuring that reports on economic, environmental, and social performance support comparison against the organisation's earlier performance as well as against the performance of other organisations. This allows internal and external parties to benchmark performance and assess progress as part of supporting rating activities, investment decisions, advocacy programmes and other activities. Comparability and associated demands for consistency are a pre-requisite to informed decision making by users.

When changes in boundary, scope, and content of reporting occur (including in the design and use of indicators), reporting organisations should, to the maximum extent practicable, re-state current accounts to ensure that time series information and cross-organisational comparisons are both reliable and meaningful. Where such re-statements are not provided, the reporting organisation should disclose such circumstances, explain the reasons, and discuss implications for interpreting current accounts.

Clarity

> The reporting organisation should remain cognizant of the diverse needs and backgrounds of its stakeholder groups and should make information available in a manner that is responsive to the maximum number of users while still maintaining a suitable level of detail.

The clarity principle considers the extent to which information is understandable and usable by diverse user groups. In financial reporting, there is an unspoken assumption concerning the general level of background knowledge and experience of the assumed "primary" user group, namely, investors. No such "primary" user group exists for GRI at this juncture. In fact, it may never exist owing to the diversity of user groups that are consumers of economic, environmental, and social performance information. In using the GRI *Guidelines*, it is reasonable to assume that all users have a working knowledge of at least a portion of the economic, environmental, and social issues faced by the reporting organisation. However, not all user groups will bring the same level of experience—or even the same language—to the reading of the report. Thus, reporting organisations, through assessing stakeholder capabilities, should design reports that respond to the maximum number of users without sacrificing important details of interest to a subset of user groups. Technical and scientific terms should be explained within the report, and clear, suitable graphics should be used where appropriate. Providing information that is not understandable to stakeholders does not contribute to successful engagement. Clarity is therefore an essential characteristic of any reporting effort.

Timeliness

> Reports should provide information on a regular schedule that meets user needs and comports with the nature of the information itself.

The usefulness of information on economic, environmental, and social performance is closely tied to its timely availability to user groups. Timeliness ensures maximum uptake and utility of the information, enabling users to effectively integrate it into their decision-making. As with financial disclosures, reporting on economic, environmental, and social performance is most valuable when users can expect a predictable schedule of disclosures. Special updates can be issued if and when unexpected developments of material interest to users occur.

Reporting organisations should structure disclosures to accord with the nature of the information. Certain environmental information, for example, may be most useful on a quarterly, monthly or continuous ("real time") basis, while other environmental information is most suitable for an annual report. Similarly, reporting on economic performance may parallel financial reporting: annual disclosures can summarise economic performance during the prior 12 months, while quarterly updates can be issued in parallel with quarterly earnings reports to investors. With the menu of new communications technologies available to reporting organisations, adjusting the timing of disclosures to reflect the varying nature of an organisation's impacts is now more feasible than ever before. However, the degree to which any technology approach can be applied depends on stakeholders having access to the necessary technology.

Although a regular flow of information is desirable for meeting certain needs, reporting organisations should commit to a single point in time to provide a consolidated accounting of their economic, environmental, and social performance. This is necessary to meet the fundamental objective of comparability across organisations. As an example, a yearly consolidated report released on a predictable schedule, accompanied by interim updates using electronic media, represents a standard structure that is consistent with the principle of timeliness

Adidas®

GUIDELINES ON EMPLOYMENT STANDARDS

Standards of engagement: authenticity, inspiration, commitment, honesty

THESE ARE COREVALUES of the adidas Group. We measure ourselves by these values and we measure our business partners in the same way.

Consistent with these values, we expect our business partners – contractors, subcontractors, suppliers, and others – to conduct themselves with the utmost fairness, honesty and responsibility in all aspects of their businesses.

The Standards of Engagement are tools that assist us in selecting and retaining business partners who follow work place standards and business practices consistent with our policies and values. As guiding principles, they help identify potential problems so that we can work with business partners to address issues of concern as they arise. Business partners must develop and implement action plans for continuous improvement in factory working conditions. Progress against action plans will be monitored by business partners themselves, our internal monitoring team and external independent monitors.

Specifically, we expect our business partners to operate work places according to the following standards and practices.

General Principle	Business partners must comply fully with all legal requirements relevant to the conduct of their businesses.
Employment Standards	We will do business only with business partners who treat their employees fairly and legally with regard to wages, benefits and working conditions. In particular, the following standards apply:
Forced Labour	Business partners must not use forced labour, whether in the form of prison labour, indentured labour, bonded labour or

otherwise. No employee may be compelled to work through force or intimidation of any form.

Child Labour   Business partners must not employ children who are less than 15 years old or less than the age for completing compulsory education in the country of manufacture, where such age is higher than 15.

Discrimination   Business partners must make recruitment and post-hiring decisions based on ability to do the job, rather than on the basis of personal characteristics or beliefs. Business partners must not discriminate in hiring and employment practices on the grounds of race, national origin, gender, religion, age, disability, marital status, parental status, association membership, sexual orientation or political opinion.

Wages and Benefits   Wages are essential for meeting the basic needs of employees and reasonable savings and discretionary expenditure. In all cases, wages must equal or exceed the minimum wage required by law or the prevailing industry wage, whichever is higher, and legally mandated benefits must be provided. Wages must be paid directly to the employee in cash or check or the equivalent. Information relating to wages must be provided to employees in a form they understand. Advances of, and deductions from, wages must be carefully monitored and comply with law.

In addition to compensation for regular working hours, employees must be compensated for overtime hours at the rate legally required in the country of manufacture or, in those countries where such laws do not exist, at a rate exceeding the regular hourly compensation rate.

Hours of Work   Employees must not be required, except in extraordinary circumstances, to work more than 60 hours per week including overtime or the local legal requirement, whichever is less. Employees must be allowed at least 24 consecutive hours rest within every 7 day period, and must receive paid annual leave.

Freedom of Association and Collective Bargaining   Business partners must recognise and respect the right of employees to join and organise associations of their own choosing and to bargain collectively. Where law specifically restricts the right to freedom of association and collective bargaining, business partners must not obstruct alternative and legal means for independent and free association or collective bargaining. Additionally, business partners must implement systems to ensure effective communication with employees.

Disciplinary Practices   Employees must be treated with respect and dignity. No employee may be subjected to any physical, sexual, psychological or verbal harassment or abuse.

Health and Safety   A safe and hygienic working environment must be provided, and occupational health and safety practices which prevent work-related accidents and injury must be promoted. This includes protection from fire, accidents and toxic substances. Lighting, heating and ventilation systems must be adequate. Employees must have access at all times to sanitary facilities which should be adequate and clean. Business partners must have health and safety policies which are clearly communicated to employees. Where residential facilities are provided to employees, the same standards apply.

Environmental Requirements   Business partners must make progressive improvement in environmental performance in their own operations and require the same of their partners, suppliers and subcontractors. This includes: integrating principles of sustainability into business decisions; responsible use of natural resources; adoption of cleaner production and pollution prevention measures; and designing and developing products, materials and technologies according to the principles of sustainability.

Community Involvement   We will favor business partners who make efforts to contribute to improving conditions in the countries and communities in which they operate.

Promoting labour compliance in the factory

Our ultimate objective is to raise factory conditions to a standard whereby the SOE Team is no longer needed. Factories will maintain high standards without external monitoring. This will ensure the long-term sustainability of the sports goods industry.

The best examples of compliance are where the partner factory internalises the SOE and implements a programme of 'self-monitoring'. A total quality management approach to human resources and personnel policies, procedures and management systems will ensure long-term effective compliance with the SOE. Rather than address compliance on a problem by problem basis, factories which have internalised the SOE view it from a big picture management perspective. Worker organisations have an important role to play in this process of self-monitoring, and management must create communication channels which allow workers to identify problems and help find solutions. Good communication is essential to the internalisation process.

The benefits for factories and other suppliers of establishing a self-monitoring team are:

1   building expertise in the area of compliance and developing best practices;
2   greater and faster success with the SOE because responsibility for compliance efforts are internal rather than being driven from outside the factory;
3   solutions are appropriate to the factory and the local environment;
4   action plans and projects are managed by someone who has a strong understanding of, and interest in, the factory or supplier business, and not by an external 3rd party;
5   working directly with subcontractors to ensure their compliance;
6   the buyer and other stakeholders will have a proper contact for SOE compliance,

just as they do in relation to production or marketing issues. This streamlines the communication process and minimises misunderstandings.

There are some simple steps to follow when developing an internal programme. They are set out below in 3 parts.

Step one of the internalisation process: defining the expectations

Worker–management communication

- There must be a clear and transparent system of worker and management communications. This might include suggestion boxes, workers committees and meetings between management and workers' representatives.
- There should be a system for resolving workplace disputes.
- There should be a system that enables workers to provide input to management.
- There should be a mechanism that allows workers to report harassment and other worker grievances in a confidential manner.
- Where trade unions exist in the factory, a copy of the collective bargaining agreement should be available to all workers and other interested parties.
- There should be an area designated for employee meetings.

General management practices

- A senior manager from the factory should be designated as the internal compliance manager. This person should be senior enough to accept responsibility for the SOE and make management decisions regarding the implementation of local laws and, where required, investments in SOE programmes and projects.
- Written policies which address all parts of the SOE need to be adopted by management.
- The factory rules, health and safety information, and laws regarding workers' rights in respect of wages, working hours and any other legally required information should be posted in local languages throughout the factory.
- New employees should receive an orientation at the time of hiring which includes explanations of the factory's rules, benefits and other entitlements, the factory personnel policies, and health and safety information.
- All supervisors should be trained in local laws and standards, and the appropriate practices to ensure compliance.

Recruitment and human resource practices

Good recruitment and human resources practices include but are not limited to:

- A written manual on employment practices;
- A manager who is directly responsible for the administration of human resources;
- An employee handbook that explains terms and conditions of employment;
- Employment applications which should be completed by all job applicants;
- Written job descriptions for all positions in the factory or supplier business;
- An effective system to verify ages of job applicants and employees;

- If a recruitment agent is used, guidelines should be provided to the agent so that the agent is aware of the business's recruitment expectations and practices of the factory or other supplier;
- If a recruitment agent is used, then there should be a written agreement with the agent that fully explains the hiring practice and sets reasonable recruitment fees;
- Recruitment agents should be able to provide written details of all their labour sources;
- Clear records and vendor descriptions for all suppliers of raw materials should be maintained; and
- Clear records and vendor descriptions for all contractors and subcontractors should be maintained.

Documents and record keeping practices

Good documentation and record keeping includes but is not limited to:

- Employment applications which do not make unlawful requests for personal information;
- Centralised employee files;
- Copies of all documents used to verify employee ages;
- Records of disciplinary actions;
- Current editions of labour codes and local government regulations and requirements;
- Financial records, especially concerning payroll, tax and benefits disbursements;
- Insurance records which show current coverage;
- All applicable local licences for operating a business, and the appropriate inspection reports from the relevant regulatory agencies;
- First aid training records;
- Accident and safety logs;
- Fire drill and evacuation practice logs and reports;
- Machinery inspection reports and preventative maintenance records; and
- adidas SOE audit reports and action plans.

Payroll

Good payroll record keeping includes but is not limited to:

- Current documents from the local government stating the requirements for minimum wage, overtime payments and legally mandated benefits;
- A system that evidences accurate payment to workers for all hours worked, such as time cards, computer records, piece rate tickets or other formal time recording systems, preferably mechanical or computerised;
- A regular and consistent pay period and schedule;
- Computer generated usage slips or receipts for all employees which include details of all hours worked, regular wages, overtime wages, other allowance and benefits, and any deductions; and
- Payroll records on site which are archived for at least three years or the period required under local law where such period is more than 3 years.

Working hours and overtime
Good working hours record keeping includes but is not limited to:

- A posted schedule of the factory working hours;
- A posted policy stating that any overtime should be performed on a voluntary basis;
- A method for tracking the working hours of juvenile employees, ie those employees who are younger than 18 and whose working hours are restricted for their health and safety; and
- There should be a clear system to record overtime hours and to make sure wages for those hours include the overtime premium.

Step two of the internalisation process: picking the internal team and defining their activities

An important part of internal compliance is choosing the correct person(s) for managing the process. An internal compliance team should have the ability to communicate the standards in a manner that is understandable by all employees. The internal team members should have the trust, confidence and respect of the management and other employees. Finally, they should have a familiarity with the operations, practices and policies of the partner factory or supplier.

To ensure success with the internal compliance programme, the internal compliance team needs the support of management. The team will need to involve co-workers in the compliance process, document all of its activities and findings, know the internal processes of the factory, and be knowledgeable about local laws and the adidas SOE. Management should delegate an appropriate level of authority and support to the members of the internal team, and allow them enough time to successfully complete the compliance effort.

An internal team's activities include but are not limited to:

- Conducting reviews of workplace practices;
- Identifying both non-compliance and best practice in the workplace;
- Developing and implementing action plans to resolve instances of non compliance, and then following-up on the progress of the action plans;
- Identifying areas where the supplier can develop proactive systems that promote compliance and then implementing those systems;
- Working with the adidas auditing teams and third party independent monitors reviewing external audits and action plans, and following up on the external action plans;
- Communicating the business partners' best practice policies to all stakeholders;
- Educating management and employees in the relevant laws and regulations, the adidas SOE and how to conduct risk assessments; and
- Auditing contractors, sub-contractors and raw material suppliers.

Step three of the internalisation process: self-monitoring

What tools and resources are needed to do the job of self-monitoring?

- Staff responsible for SOE compliance;
- The national labour code and any local employment laws and regulations;
- The adidas SOE;
- An audit tool – the adidas audit tool is a good starting point;
- An employee interview template setting out questions that should be asked of employees regarding the terms and conditions of their work;
- The adidas Employment Guidelines as a reference guide;
- A template form that the factory may use to regularly report on internal compliance activities – for instance, an annual report to adidas; and
- Training materials for compliance staff regarding monitoring and auditing methods and techniques, together with frequent exposure to training courses which will keep the staff up-to-date on compliance issues.

Clean Clothes Campaign

CODE OF LABOUR PRACTICES FOR THE APPAREL INDUSTRY INCLUDING SPORTSWEAR

I. Introduction

Statement of purpose

The Clean Clothes Campaign is dedicated to advancing the interests of workers in the apparel and sportswear industry and the concerns of consumers who purchase products made and sold by this industry. The Campaign seeks an end to the oppression, exploitation and abuse of workers in this industry, most of who are women. The Campaign also seeks to provide consumers with accurate information concerning the working conditions under which the apparel and sports wear they purchase are made. The Clean Clothes Campaign seeks to achieve its aims through a variety of means including a code of labour practice that would be adopted and implemented by companies, industry associations and employer organisations. The code, which is a concise statement of minimum standards with respect to labour practices, is meant to be accompanied by a commitment by the companies adopting it to take positive actions in applying it. Companies are expected to insist on compliance with the code by any of their contractors, subcontractors, suppliers and licensees organising production that would fall under the scope of the code.

Companies adopting the code will be expected to engage an independent institution established for the purpose of monitoring compliance with the code, in assisting companies in implementing the code and in providing consumers with information concerning the labour practices in the industry.

This code of labour practice sets forth minimum standards for wages, working time and working conditions and provides for observance of all of the core standards of the International Labour Organisation including Conventions 29, 87, 98, 100, 105, 111 and 138. These are minimum standards that are meant to apply throughout the industry and in all countries. The code is not a trade protectionist measure. It is not meant to be used as a means to close the markets of some countries at the expense of workers in other countries.

The code is not meant to be a substitute for international intergovernmental co-operation nor for international legislation. Although the code does seek to afford workers protection from oppression, abuse and exploitation where national laws are inadequate or are not enforced, it does not seek to become a substitute for national laws or the national labour inspectorate. The code is not a substitute for secure and independent trade unions nor should it be used as a substitute for collective bargaining.

Scope of application

The code is intended for retailers as well as manufacturers and all companies positioned in between those in the apparel and sportswear supply chain. It can also be used by industry associations or employer organisations.

The code applies to all of the company's apparel and sportswear products (including sportshoes). The code specifically applies to the following general industrial classification of economic activities within the European Community (NACE) classification codes:

- 436 knitting industry
- 451 manufacture of mass-produced footwear
- 452 production of hand-made footwear
- 453 manufacture of ready-made clothing and accessories
- 454 bespoke tailoring, dressmaking and hatmaking
- 456 manufacture of furs and of fur goods.

Through the code retailers and manufacturers declare their responsibility for the working conditions under which the apparel, sportswear and shoes they sell are produced. This responsibility extends to all workers producing products for the company, regardless of their status or relationship to the company and whether or not they are employees of the company. The code would therefore apply to home-based workers and to workers who are engaged either informally or on a contracted basis.

The code applies to all of the companies' contractors, subcontractors, suppliers and licensees world-wide. The terms 'contractor', 'subcontractor', 'supplier' mean any natural or legal person who contracts with the company and is engaged in a manufacturing process, including CMT (cut-make-and-trim), assembly and packaging, which result in a finished product for the consumer. A licensee means any natural or legal person who contracts with a company to produce or distribute finished products using the name or brand image of that company.

Observance of the code must be an enforceable and enforced part of any agreement between the company and its contractors, subcontractors, suppliers and licensees.

II. Code of labour practices

Introduction

The code provides a concise statement of minimum labour standards together with a pledge by the company to observe these standards and to require its contractors, sub-contractors, suppliers and licensees to observe these standards. The code is concise in order to display it in workplaces and in order to avoid any confusion between basic principles and the application of principles. An independent institution, established to provide independent monitoring of compliance with the code and to assist companies in implementing the code, will provide an auditable check-list of practices and conditions that are consistent with the standards set forth in the code. This independent organisation will also provide a means by which questions over the meaning of the code can be resolved.

The preamble establishes three principles: First, the company accepts responsibility for its workers, including workers involved in contracting and subcontracting agreements. Second, the company pledges to observe the core ILO labour standards and to ensure that workers are provided with living wages and decent working conditions. Third, the company pledges to make observance of the code a condition of any agreements that it makes with contractors and suppliers and to require them to extend this obligation to their subcontractors.

The body of the code is based on the same core ILO conventions including prohibitions against child labour, forced or bonded labour, discrimination, freedom of association and the right to collective bargaining. This is followed by the basic labour conditions – wages, hours and working conditions (including health and safety) and their formulation in the code, also derived from ILO standards.

This section also addresses the issue of regular employment relationships. Increasingly employers avoid the obligations of the employment relationship by treating workers as "independent contractors" when in fact their situation is the same as that of regular employees. The ILO is in the process of developing an international standard on this subject.

The closing section sets out the most important obligations contractors, sub-contractors, suppliers and licensees must undertake in implementing the code and pledges the company to enforce its code using a range of sanctions up to and including termination of any agreements. The closing section pledges all employers concerned to refrain from disciplinary action, dismissal or otherwise discriminating against any worker for providing information concerning observance of the code.

This part also states that the code establishes only minimum standards that must not be used as a ceiling or to discourage collective bargaining. The text of the code, when meant to be posted where workers can see it, shall also include a means by which workers can report failure to comply with the code in a confidential manner.

Preamble

1   (name of company) recognises its responsibilities to workers for the conditions under which its products or services are made and that these responsibilities extend to all workers producing products or services for (name of company) whether or not they are employees of (name of company).

2   Any workers producing products or services manufactured, sold or distributed by (name of company) must be provided with living wages and decent working conditions, and the international labour standards established by Conventions 29, 87, 98, 100, 105, 111 and 138 of the International Labour Organisation must be observed.

3   (name of company) will require its contractors, their subcontractors, suppliers and licensees to provide these conditions and observe these standards when producing or distributing products or components of products for (name of company). (name of company) will, prior to placing orders with suppliers, engaging contractors and subcontractors or granting licenses, assess whether the provisions of this code can be met.

4   For the purposes of this code the term 'contractor', 'subcontractor' or 'supplier' shall mean any natural or legal person who contracts with (name of company), either directly or indirectly via another natural or legal person who contracts with (name of company) and is engaged in a manufacturing process, including CMT (cut-make-and-trim), assembly and packaging, which result in a finished product for the consumer. The term 'licensee' means any natural or legal person who as part of a contractual arrangement with (name of company) uses for any purpose the name of (name of company) or its recognised brand names or images.

Content

- **Employment is freely chosen.**
  There shall be no use of forced, including bonded or prison, labour (ILO Conventions 29 and 105). Nor shall workers be required to lodge "deposits" or their identity papers with their employer.
- **There is no discrimination in employment.**
  Equality of opportunity and treatment regardless of race, colour, sex, religion, political opinion, nationality, social origin or other distinguishing characteristic shall be provided (ILO Conventions 100 and 111).
- **Child labour is not used.**
  There shall be no use of child labour. Only workers above the age of 15 years or above the compulsory school-leaving age shall be engaged (ILO Convention 138). Adequate transitional economic assistance and appropriate educational opportunities shall be provided to any replaced child workers.
- **Freedom of association and the right to collective bargaining are respected.**
  The right of all workers to form and join trade unions and to bargain collectively shall be recognised (ILO Conventions 87 and 98). Workers' representatives shall not be the subject of discrimination and shall have access to all workplaces necessary to enable them to carry out their representation functions (ILO Convention 135 and Recommendation 143). Employers shall adopt a positive approach towards the activities of trade unions and an open attitude towards their organisational activities.
- **Living wages are paid.**
  Wages and benefits paid for a standard working week shall meet at least legal or industry minimum standards and always be sufficient to meet basic needs of workers and their families and to provide some discretionary income.
  Deductions from wages for disciplinary measures shall not be permitted nor shall

any deductions from wages not provided for by national law be permitted without the expressed permission of the worker concerned. All workers shall be provided with written and understandable information about the conditions in respect of wages before they enter employment and of the particulars of their wages for the pay period concerned each time that they are paid.

- **Hours of work are not excessive.**
  Hours of work shall comply with applicable laws and industry standards. In any event, workers shall not on a regular basis be required to work in excess of 48 hours per week and shall be provided with at least one day off for every 7 day period. Overtime shall be voluntary, shall not exceed 12 hours per week, shall not be demanded on a regular basis and shall always be compensated at a premium rate.

- **Working conditions are decent.**
  A safe and hygienic working environment shall be provided, and best occupational health and safety practice shall be promoted, bearing in mind the prevailing knowledge of the industry and of any specific hazards. Physical abuse, threats of physical abuse, unusual punishments or discipline, sexual and other harassment, and intimidation by the employer is strictly prohibited.

- **The employment relationship is established.**
  Obligations to employees under labour or social security laws and regulations arising from the regular employment relationship shall not be avoided through the use of labour-only contracting arrangements, or through apprenticeship schemes where there is no real intent to impart skills or provide regular employment. Younger workers shall be given the opportunity to participate in education and training programmes.

Closing section

Contractors, subcontractors, suppliers and licensees shall undertake to support and co-operate in the implementation and monitoring of this code by:

- providing (name of company) with relevant information concerning their operations;
- permitting inspection at any time of their workplaces and operations by approved inspectors;

  - A. maintaining records of the name, age, hours worked and wages paid for each worker and making these available to approved inspectors on request;
  - A. informing, verbally and in writing, the workers concerned of the provisions of this code; and,
  - A. refraining from disciplinary action, dismissal or otherwise discriminating against any worker for providing information concerning observance of this code.

Contractors, subcontractors, suppliers and licensees found to be in breach of one or more terms of this Code of Labour Practices may lose the right to produce or organise production of goods for (name of company).

Questions as to the interpretation of the meaning of the provisions of this code shall be resolved according to the procedure set forth by an independent institution established for this purpose.

The provisions of this code constitute only minimum standards and conditions for the purpose of preventing exploitation. (name of company) does not intend, will not use, and will not allow any contractor, subcontractor, supplier or licensee to use these minimum standards and conditions as maximum standards or as the only conditions permitted by (name of company) or to serve as the basis for any claim as to what standards or conditions of employment should be provided.

Specific industry standards

Specific industry standards, especially with respect to health and safety (including access to medical services) and workers' accomodation may be incorporated into the code or attached separately and referenced in the code under section # 7 "working conditions are decent". These standards may be formally recognised standards or established best practice.

III. Implementation

Introduction

Implementation refers to the whole range of activities that could be taken by a company to give effect to the Code of Labour Practices. In the past some companies have adopted codes as a public relations response to reports of exploitation but have failed to implement them. Companies adopting the Code of Labour Practices for the apparel and sportswear industry will be expected to agree to certain minimum conditions with respect to implementing the code. One of the most important ways in which a code can be implemented is for it to become an enforceable and enforced part of agreements with contractors, subcontractors, suppliers and licensees.

Implementation and monitoring are often confused. Monitoring, which means to watch or check that the terms of the code are being respected, is one aspect of implementing a code. It is expected that companies adopting the code will in their relationship with their contractors, subcontractors, suppliers and licensees monitor their compliance with the code.

Companies adopting the code are also expected to co-operate and support a system of independent monitoring of compliance with the code. This section concerns the general obligations of the company to implement the code. The obligations of the company with respect to independent monitoring are considered in Part IV.

Obligations of the company to implement the code

- The company agrees to take positive actions to implement the code, to incorporate the code into all of its operations and to make the code an integral part of its overall philosophy and general policy.
- The company will assign responsibility for all matters pertaining to the code within its organisation and inform the independent institution and other relevant bodies where this responsibility is assigned.

- The Board of Directors (or other governing body) of the company shall periodically review the operation of the code, including the reports of internal and external monitoring.
- The company accepts responsibility for observing the code with respect to all employees and workers that it supervises and agrees to:

  - assign responsibility for implementing this code at each place that it owns or controls;
  - ensure that all workers are aware of the contents of the code by clearly displaying an authorised text of the code at all workplaces and by orally informing these employees in a language understood by them of the provisions of the code;
  - refrain from disciplining, dismissing or otherwise discriminating against any employee for providing information concerning observance of this code.

- The company will make observance of the code a condition of all agreements that it enters into with contractors, suppliers and licensees. These agreements will obligate these contractors, suppliers and licensees to require observance of the code in all agreements that they make with their respective subcontractors and suppliers in fulfilling their agreement with the company. Such agreements shall also oblige these contractors, subcontractors, suppliers and licensees to undertake the same obligations to implement the code as found in the preceding point.

Obligations of the company to enforce the code

Observance of the code by contractors, subcontractors and suppliers must be an enforceable and enforced condition of agreement with the company. In order to achieve this:

- The company will ensure that all agreements it enters into concerning the production of apparel and sportswear allow for the termination of the agreement for failure to observe the code by any contractors, subcontractors and suppliers.
- The company shall authorise a procedure with fixed time limits to rectify situations where its code is not being fully observed by a contractor, subcontractor or supplier. The agreement by the contractor, subcontractor or supplier to abide by this procedure would enable the continuation of the agreement with the company. The company shall require contractors or suppliers to institute similar procedures with respect to their contractors, subcontractors or suppliers.
- Such procedures shall be authorised only where:

  - there is a reasonable expectation that the situation will be corrected and that the code will be observed in the future;
  - the period specified for correcting the situation is reasonable;
  - recognisable and unmistakable violations of the code are ceased immediately;
  - such procedures shall not be authorised more than once for the same contractor, subcontractor or supplier for the same or similar failure to comply with the code; and
  - such procedures are consistent with any recommendations or procedures set forth by the independent institution established to assist in implementing this code.

- With respect to child labour, such procedures shall require that there be no further engagement of children and that temporary measures to assist child workers such as the reduction in working time, the provision of educational opportunities and transitional economic support be instituted. In the end, child workers must be replaced by adults and, where possible, from the same family. Procedures should also include measures to assist the children concerned through provision of educational opportunities and transitional economic support.
- Contractors, subcontractors and suppliers must, as part of their agreement with the company, agree to terminate any contract or agreement for the supply or production of goods by any contractor, subcontractor or supplier that they engage not fully observing the code, or they must seek and receive approval from the company to institute a procedure with fixed time limits to rectify situations where the code is not being fully observed.
- Where there is repeated failure to observe or to ensure observance of the code by a particular contractor, subcontractor, supplier or licensee, the agreement should be terminated. Guidelines or procedures for determining when it is necessary to terminate a contract for failure to observe the code shall be set forth by an independent institution established for this purpose.

In situations where it is not clear whether a particular practice constitutes a violation of the code, relevant international labour standards of the International Labour Organisation (ILO) and any recommendations provided by the independent institution established to assist companies in implementing this code shall be sought for guidance.

IV. Independent monitoring, accreditation and certification

Introduction

When a sufficient number of companies, industry associations or employers' organisations have adopted the code of labour practice for the apparel and sportswear industry, then they, in conjunction with appropriate trade union organisations and NGOs, shall establish jointly an independent institution, referred to in this document as "the Foundation".

The purpose of the Foundation shall be to:

- conduct, directly or indirectly through other organisations, the independent monitoring of compliance with the code;
- assist companies in implementing the code; and
- provide a means to inform consumers about observance of the code and more generally about labour conditions in the industry.

To these ends the Foundation shall:

- establish standards for the independent monitoring and for the accreditation of independent monitors;
- train, or to arrange for the training of, independent monitors;
- prepare an auditable checklist of labour practices to be used in monitoring the code;

- conduct or otherwise cause to be conducted independent monitoring of compliance by specific companies with the code of labour practice;
- receive reports of such independent monitoring and make effective recommendations based on these reports to the companies concerned;
- investigate any substantiated reports concerning compliance by participating companies and make effective recommendations based on the findings of such investigations;
- prepare and publish guidelines for participating companies on the implementation of the code;
- provide other technical assistance to companies in implementing the code, including the training of company personnel;
- prepare and publish the authorised version of the code in various languages and in sufficient quantities as required by participating companies;
- establish a means to interpret the provisions of the code, provided that this means is based on the recognised jurisprudence of the International Labour Organisation;
- provide a means by which workers and any others can report on a confidential basis observance of the code;
- establish, based on independent monitoring, a system of certification concerning labour practices which can be used by consumers;
- collect information from any source on working conditions in the apparel and sportswear industry and make this information available to consumers;
- promote the code of labour practice and encourage all companies operating in the industry to adopt it; and
- establish a mechanism that can make effective recommendations with respect to any disputes arising out of the implementation or the certification process.

The Foundation shall be governed by a board consisting of equal representatives of appropriate trade union organisations and NGOs on one hand and of appropriate representatives of retailers and manufacturers on the other hand. The Foundation shall be financed by contributions from participating organisations and by payments for services from contracting companies.

The principal means by which the Foundation shall conduct its work will be based on contracts with specific companies to independently monitor and certify their compliance with the code and by contracts with individuals and organisations to conduct monitoring.

It is understood that the standards for independent monitoring established by the Foundation shall be based on the best practice of the two existing professions that monitor labour practices—the labour inspectorate and the contract-enforcement practices of trade unions. It is also understood that these standards shall include ethical practices for monitors, including respect for any confidential commercial information.

It is also understood that any individuals engaged to conduct monitoring shall receive training for this purpose.

Relation between the company and the Foundation

Companies adopting the code of labour practice for the apparel and sportswear industry shall enter into an agreement with the Foundation. This agreement shall provide for the following:

- the time-frame in which the production in the different facilities should comply with all the standards in the code;
- the information the company has to give to the Monitoring Foundation;
- the payments the company should make to the Monitoring Foundation;
- the procedures for the actual monitoring and the obligations of the different parties; and
- the use of the Foundation contract by the company in its public relations.

With respect to (b) the company assumes the following obligations:

- to maintain full and up-to-date information on all contractors, subcontractors, suppliers and licensees obliged to observe this code, including the nature and location of all workplaces, and to provide this information to the Foundation or its accredited monitors in a timely manner upon request;
- to require contractors, subcontractors, suppliers and licensees to maintain records of the names, ages, hours worked, and wages paid for each worker, and make these records available for inspection by accredited monitors, and to allow the Foundation or its accredited monitors to conduct confidential interviews with workers;
- to ensure that the code is clearly displayed in all places where apparel and sportswear are produced and/or distributed by or under agreement with or for the company and provide authorised texts of the code to contractors and suppliers for their use, and the use by any contractors, subcontractors and suppliers obliged to observe this code. In all cases the text of the code so displayed shall be in languages so that the workers concerned are able to understand it. The text of the code shall be provided to each worker covered by its provisions and all workers so covered shall be orally informed in a language that they can understand of the provisions of the code;
- the code so displayed must provide information to assist workers in reporting violations of the code to the Foundation or its agents taking into account the difficulties that workers will face in doing this and the need for confidentiality in order to protect workers;
- to allow for the necessary access to independent monitors and provide them with any and all relevant information upon demand;
- to ensure and clearly demonstrate that the code is being observed by all parties obliged to observe the code, the company must allow the Foundation and its agents access to all information pertaining to the implementation of the code, and ensure that its contractors, subcontractors and suppliers give similar access to the Foundation and its agents.

Monitoring: basic principles

- monitoring must be by the actual observance of working conditions through unannounced inspection visits ("spot checks") to all workplaces covered by the code;
- the frequency of inspections must be established;
- accredited monitors must be permitted to interview workers on a confidential basis;
- in addition to regular or routine inspections, inspections shall be undertaken at

specific locations following substantiated complaints, where there is sufficient reason to believe that the code is not being observed;

- inspections shall be conducted in a way which does not cause undue disruption to the performance of work in the premises being inspected;
- written reports shall be provided by accredited monitors to all parties and to the participating company concerned following each visit.

The Foundation may seek other sources of information concerning compliance with the code including consulting appropriate trade union organisations, human rights organisations, religious and other similar institutions in order to obtain additional information on a certain company or in order to investigate a certain complaint.

If violations of the code are found, the company must agree to accept the recommendation of the Foundation. This recommendation shall in the first instance be aimed at improving the existing situation. Where such improvement is not possible or satisfactory, then the Foundation can oblige companies to re-negotiate, terminate or refuse to renew their contracts with certain contractors, subcontractors and/or suppliers.

Where companies fail to observe their agreement with the Foundation it is understood that the Foundation may release any relevant information to the public and may terminate the contract between the company and the Foundation.

The independent monitoring process shall form the basis for any public claims by the Foundation or by participating companies as to the operation of the code or concerning the actual labour practices covered by the code.

Kelly Dent

THE CONTRADICTIONS IN CODES
The Sri-Lankan experience

Spotlight on Sri Lanka

SRI LANKA WAS the first South Asian country to change from import substitution, which included protective tariffs, and import controls to an export-oriented economy. In 1977, under then President Jayawardena, regulations protecting local industry gave way to regulations for the protection of foreign investors. This economic policy implemented under the guidelines of the International Monetary Fund (IMF) and the World Bank placed greater emphasis on direct foreign investment in achieving the objective of export-led growth, with numerous more than attractive concessions being offered to foreign investors (Heward, 1997). The first free trade zone (FTZ) was established at Katunayake (near to the airport and capital Colombo) in 1978.

Today the garment industry is one of the fastest growing industries in Sri Lanka. Since 1989 exports have increased six fold to a value of 3 billion US dollars in 2000. Garments account for 52 per cent of all exports from Sri Lanka. According to the Ministry of Industrial Development, at the end of 1998 there were more than 280,000[1] garment workers employed in 890[2] factories producing for export across Sri Lanka. This figure does not include workers in the informal sector or those working for factories producing for domestic consumption; 34 per cent of garments produced for export are sent to the European Union (64.2 per cent to the United States). It is worth noting that codes do not apply to factories producing for domestic consumption.

Garment factories are located both inside the various FTZs, industrial parks and estates, and outside in the villages and districts. In 1992, President Premadasa declared the whole of the country an FTZ and simultaneously set up garment factories in each of the districts, including the war-affected eastern districts, under the Garment 200 Factory Programme.

Inside the FTZs over 75 per cent of workers are single women. These women have migrated from their villages in rural areas to work in the zones, and are mostly aged

Box 1 Transnationals Information Exchange-Asia (TIE-Asia)

TIE-Asia is a non-profit, politically independent, regional labour network, founded in 1992 in Asia to encourage and support the development of democratic workers organizations, new forms of organizing and broader social coalitions in the export-oriented industries of South and South-East Asia. Its aim is to promote and implement the rights of mainly women workers and to bring about improvements to the livelihoods of women workers, their families, communities and to society.

TIE-Asia's vision is achieved through:

- encouraging women into leadership positions within the broad labour movement at the local, national, regional and international levels;
- identifying, documenting and analysing new issues, trends and developments including the changing processes of production of transnational corporations (TNCs) and their impact on workers and the labour movement;
- ensuring information is accessible to workers, activists/leaders and organizers in their own languages;
- extensive training programmes;
- regional and national seminars;
- supporting and initiating campaigns from the factory floor and broad labour issues at the national, regional and international levels;
- facilitating (in workers' own languages) the sharing of information, experiences and strategies through focused regional exchange programmes;
- re-establishing links between urban and rural workers through internal exchange programmes;
- networking with other labour and related organizations.

TIE-Asia Regional Office
141 Ananda Rajakaruna Mw
Colombo 10
Sri Lanka
Phone and Fax: +94 74 617 711
Email: tieasia@sri.lanka.net

between 20 and 29 years. Women are preferred as workers in the FTZs as they are seen as a more flexible workforce for employers, easily manipulated and less likely to demand their rights. Women working in factories have a poor image and marriage advertisements in major Sri Lankan newspapers often state 'no factory girls'. They are also largely unorganized.

Some examples of conditions for workers inside the zones include:

- being forced to work long hours of overtime to reach unrealistically high production targets;
- denial of legal entitlements, with leave being extremely difficult to take;
- excessive fines and penalties: ranging from being late; sick; not reaching production

targets and refusing compulsory overtime—bonuses, fines and penalties are complex and workers frequently cannot calculate how much they will earn each month;

- repression of the right to organize, form a union or bargain collectively;
- poor or non-existent occupational health and safety practices;
- frequent sexual harassment and imposition of inhumane restrictions such as a time limit per week for going to the toilet;
- lack of transportation, especially after late night shifts;
- misrepresentation by the Board of Investment (BOI) of labour law and frequent attempts to circumvent the law or to make it more 'flexible' for employers.

Conditions outside the factory in the FTZs are no better. There is a lack of adequate infrastructure and housing, transport and medical facilities remain poor. Sexual harassment is also an issue. Workers live in a single cramped room, in a boarding house, often 10 or 12 women share a 10ft × 12ft (3m × 3.5m) room, and cook as well as sleep there (AMRC, 1998, p.141). Frequently there is no electricity and a shortage of fresh water. Ventilation and sanitation systems are usually inadequate.

Outside the FTZs, conditions for workers are poor and wages are often lower than in the FTZs; however, there is more freedom for unions to be formed and the living conditions are generally better as workers tend to stay within their village community.

Workers' wages are spent on survival: food; accommodation; transport to and from the factory; and a small amount remitted to their family; sometimes, over several years, workers save some money for marriage. Pay levels are based on the minimum wages concept and are between US$1.04 to US$1.49 per day, these are further reduced by remittances and the continual devaluation of Sri Lanka's currency, the rupee. The World Bank defines extreme poverty as US$1.00 per day.

In the eastern district town of Batticaloa workers can earn as little as US$5.70 per month (19 US cents per day). Anton Marcus, Joint Secretary of the Industrial Transport and General Workers Union (ITGWU), visited Batticaloa and learnt that a substantial number of workers were being paid this training wage for up to one and a half years.[3] In Myhayanganar, a remote area of Sri Lanka, workers are regularly paid below the legal minimum wage.[4] These two examples are typical of an emerging trend in Sri Lanka where major brand labels are being produced for export in remote or isolated areas, where workers are unaware of their basic rights or how to organize, unions are non-existent, there is no knowledge of codes and few job opportunities. This trend presents serious challenges for monitoring supply chains and codes in the garment industry.

Codes and the right to organize: what to do?

Codes can be an important tool to use when campaigning for the right to form unions and have them recognized. This is only effective if it is a central focus of campaigning around the code and only if campaigns recognize the need for democratic unions (as difficult as this is to achieve) as an essential prerequisite for all other worker developments. To relegate freedom of association to the 'too hard' basket is not only rendering codes ineffective, it is a violation of basic human rights.

The formation of the Free Trade Zone Workers Unions (FTZWU), established in January 2000, is the result of over 20 years of organizing in the FTZs by the Industrial

Transport and General Workers Union, the Women's Centre and the Joint Association. It is the first independent and democratic union to be formed for FTZ workers. Since its inception it has formed 11 branches, six in the garment industry, of which only one has been recognized legally and by the employer. Following the example of the FTZWU other democratic unions have formed in the FTZs.

Recognition for the remaining FTZWU branches is being pursued through the courts and through campaigns. Despite the union following legal processes, the Cosmos Macky factory has stated in writing that the company follows the rules and regulations of the Department of Labour and the BOI, 'and not instructions from any Trade Unions, because trade union activities are prohibited by the BOI [Board of Investment] in the zone.'[5] The union has written to the BOI asking them to clarify their position, but they have not yet responded. Letters have also been sent by the union to the Minister of Labour and to the ILO Office, Colombo, asking them to intervene and ensure that the laws of Sri Lanka are upheld. Cosmos Macky is a Korea/Sri Lanka joint venture company, producing sports- and skiwear for export, under the Cosmack trade mark, located in the Katunayake FTZ.

Of the ten FTZWU branches awaiting recognition, four have been smashed. In the case of Fine Lanka Luggage Ltd, 858 workers lost their jobs for forming a union and the factory closed in March 2000. The factory reopened in May 2001, employing a smaller number of non-unionized staff and 60 of the original and unionized employees under stringent conditions. The conditions were that they withdraw their names from the current court case against the factory, agree to a probation period and do not claim backpay for the period that they were locked out of the factory. Fine Lanka produced labels for: Federated Department Stores (Charter Club and Metopolis labels); Sears Roebuck (Forecast Mendocino); J.C. Penny and Co (Protocol and Support Tech); R. H. Macy and Co Inc; High Sierra Sports Co (High Sierra); additional labels included Travel Gear, Atlantic, Jeep and Sports Plus.

The FTZWU launched an international campaign including a solidarity appeal to support Fine Lanka workers. As part of the campaign, letters were also sent to owners and buyers of the brand labels above in October 2000 explaining that their codes had been breached and requesting them to intervene and force the management of Fine Lanka to resolve the dispute in accordance with the labour laws of Sri Lanka and their code. To date no response has been received by the owners or buyers.

At Joy Lanka Pvt Ltd 107 union members lost their jobs for forming a union. The company sought permission from the Department of Labour to terminate these workers on the grounds that the company was losing profits.

On 6 September 2000, 410 workers of Venture International in Kotmale (located approximately 125km east of Colombo) producing for major brand labels—Marlboro Classics; AE77 Performance; Mountain Trek Sport & Athletic; Old Navy; Etam; Gap DPP; Marks and Spencer; Catalina and Outdoor Wear—were dismissed under emergency regulations for taking strike action. The strike, banned under emergency regulations, was in support of worker demands for a pay increase, awarded under the same emergency regulation and because their employer had failed to deposit money forcibly deducted from their wages into a savings account, as promised. Again a mass campaign and a court case were launched, however workers remain unemployed.

Using codes as a tool to pressure companies into respecting and implementing the right to organize, freedom of association, collective bargaining, labour laws and ILO conventions has not, in the experience of TIE-Asia in Sri Lanka, been successful yet.

This strategy also relies on unions and activist organizations in developed countries being prepared to make these rights central to any campaign. Unions and campaign-based organizations in developed countries—whilst agreeing with this position—express difficulties in gaining popular support for a campaign of this nature.

The Clean Clothes Campaign strategy and evaluation meeting held in Barcelona in March, 2001, attended by unionists and activists from over 29 countries, overwhelmingly agreed to a major campaign on the right to organize, form and join unions using codes as a tool. This is an exciting development.

Campaigning for effective codes

There have been successful campaigns around codes of conduct that have benefited factories, regions or groups of workers. But there are millions of workers worldwide who have not benefited. As mentioned previously, in Sri Lanka alone 750,000 precariously employed women workers stand to be disadvantaged through the misuse of codes.

For majority world countries effective campaigning requires links internationally with unions and well-organized campaign groups in developed countries. However, campaigns devised in developed countries around a specific company or companies, designed to assist workers in producing countries, without consultation with those that they are likely to affect, are problematic. Unions and worker organizations are frequently left to deal with the often disastrous results of these campaigns on the ground, without an awareness of the campaigns nor any input into their implementation. Effective campaigns also need to be long-term and sustainable.

TIE-Asia believes organized workers need to both generate and understand campaigns, including the role and possible positive and negative consequences that information provided by them will play. This is critical if workers are to be empowered. Without this, improvements, if there are any, will be eroded away as TNCs continue to find a way around codes.

Misuse and manipulation of codes

As described above, buyers, suppliers and investors of the major brand labels often choose to overlook blatant and repressive violations of codes with respect to the formation and operation of unions. However, they are quick to force other provisions of codes on factory-based management and governments if it benefits production and profit. This manipulation of codes by TNCs on governments and workers of producing countries and the manipulation of codes by government to reduce workers' entitlements under the law can be illustrated through the prevailing situation with regard to overtime in Sri Lanka.

The current legislation in Sri Lanka for the private sector states that the maximum number of overtime hours women can work is 100 hours per year. Within this legislation no more than six hours per week should be worked. The total number of weeks that overtime is worked should not exceed 25 per year. There is no corresponding legislation prescribing overtime limits for men.

In July 2000, the government of Sri Lanka sought to amend the overtime legislation to 100 hours of overtime per month. This was subsequently reduced to 80 hours per month.

In media releases the chairperson of the BOI, Mr Thilan Wijesinghe, claimed these changes needed to be made so Sri Lanka would remain internationally competitive. He claimed it would be necessary especially when quotas under the Multifibre Arrangement (MFA) are removed in 2005. Wijesinghe inferred the changes were also needed to conform to the codes of major brand labels/retailers who do business in Sri Lanka. This is contrary to most codes that recognize that the labour law and/or a stipulated number of hours should prevail, whichever is better.

Most codes state that overtime should be voluntary. This is not reflected in the proposed changes to legislation nor in statements made by the BOI. A newspaper article by Wijesinghe (2000) announcing that Marks and Spencer was creating a South Asian distribution hub in Sri Lanka appeared at the same time as the changes to overtime legislation, submitted by the Presidential Secretariat (to whom the BOI report), were being considered by the labour department. The FTZWU and TIE-Asia believe that major brand labels were behind these amendments. Marks and Spencer have denied any involvement in the proposed amendments. However, when asked to reaffirm their commitment to the labour laws of Sri Lanka, including freedom of association and the right to organize, they refused to do so.

Employers, investors and the BOI of Sri Lanka justify legislative changes on the basis that workers want extra overtime, citing as evidence the high number of overtime hours that are worked, albeit that these are often forced. Yet workers constantly say that, although they need to work long hours to earn enough money to survive, they still want some control over the overtime hours that they work. In addition, if they received a living wage they would not need to, nor want to, work excessive hours of overtime.

The overtime amendment was eventually postponed in Parliament due to pending elections in October 2000, but with elections over the issue will be raised again. The main reason why democratic and independent unions protested against the overtime amendment is that the law as it exists, although routinely violated, offers some protection for workers if they need to refuse overtime work, as should be their right for whatever reason. The very real fear is that if overtime hours were increased to 80 hours per month, then 80 hours would be the amount of 'compulsory or forced' overtime that women workers would be required to work.

This fear is reinforced by a number of judgments from the Supreme Court of Sri Lanka, which state that in certain circumstances overtime is not voluntary. These judgments have applied to the need to meet production orders. Other judgments recognize that an employer has a right to ask an employee to do overtime for a reasonable reason and that the employee has the right to refuse overtime for a reasonable reason.[6]

Positions vary among unions on the provisions that should be contained within the overtime legislation. TIE-Asia's position is that there must be real consultation and discussion with unions before changes are made. Any changes must reinforce the position that all overtime is voluntary and will be remunerated at overtime rates.

Technically, forced overtime would be a violation of most codes, but how can this violation be dealt with? There is no mechanism apart from 'naming and shaming' through protest campaigns and actions to deal with violations. If this amendment is passed, government and the BOI will have succeeded, by using codes to satisfy local and foreign owned suppliers, major retailers, buyers and investors, in reducing the entitlements of an estimated 750,000 women workers. Workers have virtually no redress through a legal system that is already biased against them when it is legal to force extra overtime hours on workers and where precedents support this.

A major campaign is currently underway opposing these changes. The campaign involving unions, labour organizations and women's groups in Sri Lanka so far has obtained the support of the ILO, which has written to the government. Separate letters have also been sent to government and major retailers. Unions and NGOs internationally have responded to urgent appeals by sending protest letters to the Sri Lankan government and solidarity messages to workers.

On 19 March 2001 the government of Sri Lanka signed a memorandum with the International Monetary Fund covering economic and financial polices and technical aspects, without any parliamentary debate or public consultation, committing Sri Lanka to various reforms including reform of the labour market designed to 'facilitate greater labor mobility' (IMF, nd). This agreement was signed in order to receive additional loans. Concurrently relevant government authorities are examining documents recommending changes to labour legislation, including overtime legislation, that are regressive for workers.

Making codes work

Training programmes and access to information are central to raising awareness. They enable workers to participate in the debates around codes and to decide for themselves whether they are a relevant tool to use in their strategies for bringing about change in the workplace and society.

TIE-Asia has conducted leadership training programmes for factory floor leaders and organizers in Sri Lanka for the past four years. Topics covered include: labour laws; organizing (includes campaigning and networking); negotiation and grievance settling; health and safety; women in the workforce and labour movement (including barriers to participation) and globalization. Participatory methodologies are used including a mix of presentation, questions, small group discussions and problem solving. For the past two years information and analysis of codes has been included in these programmes, focusing on using codes as a possible tool in the context of organizing, negotiation, campaigning and globalization.

The Women Working Worldwide (WWW) information and education packs on codes and related issues, developed and trialled by WWW with organizers using a participatory approach in Sri Lanka in 1999, have been invaluable resources for training programmes, and taught two important lessons (WWW, 1998). First monitoring and evaluation has confirmed that training related to codes is best located within broader programmes on workers' rights. Often separate training on codes makes it seem as if codes are something different to, rather than complementary to, labour rights/organizing. Second, TIE-Asia Training Programmes have been successful in educating workers on their rights and how to obtain these through organizing as well as improving general knowledge on issues such as globalization. They have also led to an increased number of democratic trade unions that have women taking an active role in leadership positions. The Industrial Transport and General Workers Union (ITGWU), FTZWU and TIE-Asia all have 50 per cent or more women on their Executive/Board.

However, despite being well organized and initiating campaigns, it is still not uncommon for these unions to be crushed and workers left unemployed. If the factory reemploys workers there is a huge disincentive to organize another union. Likewise dismissed workers, if they are lucky enough to find work, are often discouraged from organizing. This reinforces the need for campaigns and codes to deliver on freedom of association, the right to organize and collectively bargain. Union leaders in Asia also need education on codes. Many unions are active in organizing workers, but have not had access to information and training on codes, which they in turn can use to educate their members and develop positions and policies.

The complexities of the codes debate are perhaps most apparent in the monitoring and verification processes. Central to effective monitoring and verification is: worker involvement through unions; transparency of the supply chain, including the disclosure of suppliers; and transparency in the audit reports of factories. However, monitoring activities around codes involving either private companies or company employed compliance officers vary in their degree of effectiveness.

Another worrying trend is auditors becoming involved in worker education and competing with unions and/or non-government organizations (NGOs) for involvement in worker training. Late in 1999 a US-based audit company identified the need for combined training of both workers and management (including supervisors) in preventing sexual harassment in the workplace at a factory producing for Tommy Hilfiger in Sri Lanka. The auditor then approached several NGOs, seeking their involvement. Unions were not allowed to contribute. At this time there was an active union in the factory and a major campaign by unions, women's and human rights groups on harassment in the workplace was gathering momentum, both of which the audit company were informed about. Unions pointed to the dangers of combined training of workers and management, and also that training alone would not address the serious issue of sexual harassment in the factory.

Conclusion

It is often stated that as labour laws, ILO conventions and constitutions are routinely violated a new approach is necessary. Essentially, regulation has not worked. While to some extent this is true, TIE-Asia does not believe the answer lies in abandoning regulation. After all, if these regulations are mandatory and are not enforced, what hope is there that voluntary legislation will be? Self-regulation or regulation outside existing frameworks (such as legislation, laws, constitutions and so on) can lead to the privatization of labour standards. Voluntary regulation focusing on a specific area, such as clothes, has its uses in spotlighting particular abuses and raising awareness. Where it can reinforce or strengthen existing mandatory regulation its uses are obvious. However, it is doubtful that this will occur on any widespread scale in Asia in the foreseeable future. It may be more productive to ensure that regulation is effective and applies to everyone. This should be done through strengthening existing regulatory mechanisms.

Transnational corporations, as well as speculative investment, need to be regulated and binding. Governments worldwide, in both the developed and majority world, should be pressured to implement ILO conventions that they have signed and—where they have not signed—be pressured to do so. The enforcement capacity of the ILO needs to grow to develop the capacity to force governments and TNCs to implement ILO conventions.

Some UN agreements exist that have the potential to rein in global corporations, but these too are under attack by corporations and the US government (Karliner, 1999).

The UN needs to maintain its role as a watchdog and remain an independent enforcer of human rights, including workers' rights. It cannot do this if it is in partnership with TNCs. Governments should also be pressured to implement existing labour legislation in its entirety and, where necessary, for improvements to be made to existing legislation. National labour law and ILO conventions need to be extended to cover areas of the workforce that are not covered at present.

Codes may have some relevance to the workers of Sri Lanka if they can deliver the right to form and join unions, organize, collectively bargain and strengthen existing regulatory frameworks. If codes can assist the mostly women workers of Sri Lanka's FTZ, currently struggling to have their unions recognized at the factory level, then codes will be relevant. Unions, once established and recognized, can then address the multitude of other issues such as the implementation of labour law, a living wage and ILO conventions.

Where strong organization of workers exists at the factory level then codes can be an effective tool for workers to use when putting forward demands for improvements to their wages and conditions. This requires education on codes to be situated within locally conducted broad worker training programmes. Our most important efforts and energy must go into this and continuing to build genuine international trade unionism and real solidarity at the factory floor level.

Notes

1   The numbers employed in the largest FTZs are: Katunayake (60,409), Biyagama (24,432) and Kogalla (14,000).
2   There are approximately 84 industrial parks in Sri Lanka.
3   This visit took place in February 2001 as part of a TIE-Asia and CWGW District Leadership Training Programme.
4   Information collected during a TIE-Asia District Level Leadership Training Programme in Myhayanganar, August, 2000.
5   Letter dated 12 March 2001 on Cosmos Macky letterhead and signed by a Company Director.
6   Conversation with Attorney at Law, Mr S. Sinnathambi (Sri Lanka).

References

Asia Monitor Resource Centre (AMRC) (1998) *We in the Zone*, AMRC, Hong Kong.
Heward, S (1997) *Garment Workers and the 200 Garment Factory Programme*, Centre for the Welfare of Garment Workers, Colombo, citing Fernando, L. (1988) 'The Challenge of the Open Economy: Trade Unionism in Sri Lanka' in R. Southall (ed.) *Trade Unions and the New Industrialisation of the Third World*, Zed Books, London, pp. 164–81.
IMF (nd) 'Sri Lanka Letter of Intent, Memorandum of Economic and Financial Policies and Technical Memorandum of Understanding', http://www.imf.org, accessed 14 May 2001.

Karliner, J. (1999) *Kofi Annan's Corporate Gambit*, http://www.corpwatch.org, accessed 28 June 2000.

Wijesinghe, T. (2000) 'We Should not Fear the Crisis of Garment Quota in 2005', *Lanka Deepa Daily Newspaper*, 10 May, Colombo, Sri Lanka.

Women Working Worldwide (WWW) (1998) *Company Codes of Conduct: What Are They? Can We Use Them? – An Education Pack for Worker Activists*, WWW, Manchester.

CHAPTER FIVE

Engagement, transparency and trust

A new style of interaction?

A T THE HEART of much of the concern over the social and environmental responsibilities of contemporary business lies a feeling that much of what occurs is developed under a cloak of relative secrecy and in many cases misinformation. With greater emphasis upon corporate responsibility has come increased pressure on firms to disclose far greater levels of information to stakeholders, and significant danger for firms who find that campaign organizations are disclosing information that they had not themselves made public.

The transition towards corporate social responsibility represents not only a challenge to the way in which companies undertake business activity, but also a change in the way corporate activity is communicated and evaluated. As Lord Holme noted, we have moved from a 'trust me' to a 'show me' world (Lord Holme 1999: 2). In confronting these challenges, companies have sought to present a more open and accountable image of themselves, often through the development of detailed environmental and social reporting strategies and by greater engagement and dialogue with a broad range of stakeholders. Companies, it appears, are now more than at any previous time keen to demonstrate a greater level of transparency in their actions and activities and a greater enthusiasm for listening and engaging with the views and criticisms of others.

At the heart of much of this transition in communication has been the change in focus from shareholders to stakeholders, as Archie Carroll's reading in Chapter three highlighted. The challenge for the contemporary business, it is argued, is to incorporate within modern management strategies a particular focus upon the identification and management of relationships with stakeholders beyond the traditional confines of shareholders and employees (see Blair 1998; Donaldson and Preston 1995). By successfully understanding and incorporating the diverse perspectives and concerns of stakeholders, it is argued, a company can avoid the risks of damaging publicity, and potentially increase its 'social capital' as it gains greater respectability and credibility.

Finding out what exactly the concerns of stakeholders are has therefore become a key aspect in the development of an effective corporate responsibility strategy. One of the primary starting points for this process has been through the dissemination of a broader range of information regarding company practice, often through social and environmental reporting. A SalterBaxter report in 2006 noted that 59 per cent of FTSE 100 companies now provide some form of CSR report either in printed form or via the internet.

CSR reporting has expanded rapidly in recent years. Initially many of the reports were fairly general in their coverage and focus, amounting in many cases to little more than a company public relations exercise focused upon good news stories and restricting data to areas of company progress in the social and environmental fields. However, the process of releasing information has undoubtedly opened up the debate regarding what information a company should be reporting and how it should be presented. Through this process we have witnessed an evolution in the depth and nature of CSR reporting. Companies have thus been challenged to go much further with regard to the level of detail and information they release to stakeholders through the reporting process as well as seeing greater concern placed upon the verification, comparability and accuracy of the data. As David Owen (2003: 7) notes, the reporting field has seen a significant evolution involving

> an improvement in structure and content, with fewer blatant public relations exercises, a willingness to convey bad, as well as good, news, continual improvements in the reporting of performance against stated quantified targets, an increased prevalence of verification statements and the steady development of industry wide performance indicators enabling intra-sectoral comparisons to be made.

A key question therefore is what exactly should a CSR report seek to deliver, who should it seek to provide information for, and how should that information be collated? At the heart of the process is the recognition that the reporting process is a foundation stone for how a company can seek to share information and engage with its stakeholders. Although a report gives the corporation a better understanding of its stakeholders' expectations, it also gives the stakeholders a better understanding of the reasons behind the corporation's behaviour. According to Hess (1999), the dialogue required to create a social report and the disclosure of the report to the public transfers information in a variety of directions: from the stakeholders to the corporation; from the corporation to the stakeholders; and from stakeholder to stakeholder. Providing information to stakeholders develops their trust because they can see if their concerns are being addressed. Transferring information between stakeholders is also necessary as various stakeholder groups will often have conflicting views. Through the social report, the various stakeholder groups can see where their expectations match one another, and where they are in competition, enabling their understanding. In addition, by understanding each other's perspective, the stakeholders can work on their points of disagreement.

Public disclosure of the report also promotes corporate accountability. Stakeholders may often believe that corporate claims of ethical behaviour are reputation enhancers or public relations strategies; however, the publication of an externally verified social report, it is argued, means that stakeholders can actually evaluate these claims themselves. What is important here is that disclosure requires that corporations stand behind their actions and give justifications for what they have done, i.e. their actions must speak louder than words.

However, while the reporting process has undoubtedly increased the levels of information becoming available to the public there still remains a significant amount of criticism of what is being produced within these reports, as the readings from Christian Aid, George Monbiot and Deborah Doane suggest. In particular, a number of key issues are highlighted. First, there is concern over the level of independent verification of information within the reports and the suggestion that stakeholder groups should have greater involvement in the verification process. Second, the diversity in both style and content of reporting raises concerns about the comparability of the reports. For example, if one chooses to compare the social and environmental performance of two different oil companies, will their respective CSR reports provide the necessary comparable data from which to make any assessment of performance? Given that companies tend to report in different ways, employing different statistics and measurements and focusing upon different issues and themes, comparability becomes a key challenge. In some cases comparability can even be problematic when considering CSR reports from one company over a period of time. Again, the evolution of reporting and the changing nature of the field can mean that company reports vary quite dramatically year on year.

Third, to what extent do the reports actually provide the reader with an overall picture of the social and environmental impact of a company's activities? At present few companies are either advanced enough in their reporting processes or brave enough in their outlook to try and give the reader an overall assessment of their total environmental and social footprint. Finally, there is a concern that the reporting process becomes almost an end in itself. Almost a case of 'we report, therefore we are a socially responsible company'.

These concerns, among other issues, suggest that there is still some way to go before CSR reporting may be said to really provide a transparent picture of a company's social and environmental impact. It should be noted however that companies are faced with a significant challenge in this field. On the one hand they are faced with a broad range of different stakeholders, all of whom are seeking different levels and types of information regarding company activity. On the other, they have to try and present this information in a manner that is accessible and comparable. In many cases, they are also confronted with the challenge of measuring and reporting on issues for which there are no easy ways to collect or quantify data. The ongoing challenge for companies therefore is to find effective ways in which to demonstrate that their CSR commitments are more than skin-deep and that the values which they espouse in their reports are embedded within all company activities and not just within a selectively identified group of good news stories and statistics.

While CSR reporting undoubtedly raises the level of information available regarding company activity and impact, many critics also suggest that as a process of stakeholder interaction, reporting processes reflect a relatively weak form of engagement. By focusing upon dissemination rather than interaction, it is argued, companies can largely define for themselves the information their stakeholders require rather than reacting to the issues and concerns actually being raised by the stakeholders themselves. In addition, as Crane and Livesey (2003) suggest, one-way forms of information dissemination also pose potential problems in themselves, given that 'the fundamentally dialogic nature of meaning-making is in fact implicit in every act of communication, whether it is explicitly recognised or not' (Crane and Livesey 2003: 46). Even where companies are merely seeking to disseminate and communicate information, they argue, the meanings attached to these messages by other stakeholders provide them with an active role in shaping and interpreting the information, which is often not perceived by the companies themselves.

In going beyond these forms of information dissemination, some companies have sought to undertake far more interactive forms of stakeholder engagement (for a more detailed discussion of this process see Burchell and Cook 2006). In particular, increased emphasis has been placed on the concept of stakeholder dialogue. Payne and Calton (2002) describe this transition in manager–stakeholder relations as going from 'the need for unilateral managerial cognition and control to a perceived need by some for reciprocal engagement and new dialogic forms of collective cognition' (Payne and Calton 2002: 121).

Dialogue is therefore identified as an important channel through which to transcend beyond traditional conflictual processes of communication between organizations and develop a more progressive form of engagement and understanding. Waddock (2001) argues for a similar conception in her work on stakeholder dialogue, claiming that firms are increasingly moving towards engagement strategies focused upon processes of mutual responsibility, information-sharing, open and respectful dialogue and an ongoing commitment to problem-solving. This form of dialogue inevitably implies a changing relationship between a company and the stakeholders involved within the dialogue process. Payne and Calton, for example, argue that through stakeholder dialogue, 'preconceived relationships between self and others change as new learning occurs' (Payne and Calton 2002: 133).

Dialogue between companies and stakeholders, therefore, is seen as a far more interactive two-way process of stakeholder engagement involving the breaking down of existing assumptions and the development of new ways of learning. As Lawrence suggests from her analysis of Royal Dutch/Shell's highly publicized stakeholder dialogue processes, constructing and implementing successful dialogues

> encourage both companies and stakeholder organisations to engage more often in the difficult, but productive, task of listening to and learning from one another.
> (Lawrence 2002: 199)

Jem Bendell (2003) suggests that there are a range of reasons why a company should seek to engage in dialogue with its stakeholders. These he classifies into eight 'dialogue intention levels' outlined as follows:

- *Dialogue as manipulation*: Companies engage to disarm critical stakeholders.
- *Dialogue as therapy*: Companies use dialogue to achieve support for new initiatives or educate stakeholders.
- *Dialogue as information*: The company provides information about its activities but is not seeking to learn from stakeholders or change their views.
- *Dialogue as consultation*: Companies access stakeholder opinions.
- *Dialogue as placation*: Dialogue is used to engage with key critics, often bringing them on to advisory boards and so on.

- *Dialogue as partnership*: Companies work with stakeholders to develop new processes and practices, sharing information and decision-making processes.
- *Dialogue as delegation*: Companies delegate responsibility for decision-making to stakeholders in certain fields.
- *Dialogue as democracy*: All stakeholders have an equal say in company decision-making (Bendell 2003).

Without doubt, the primary focus for much of what has been identified as stakeholder dialogue so far falls into the first five of Bendell's categories. In many cases companies have engaged with stakeholders because of external pressures forcing them to engage with their critics. However, many companies are now recognizing the value of engaging more directly with their stakeholder community, rather than relying on a process of information dissemination. In recent years we have witnessed companies such as Shell and British Nuclear Fuels conducting lengthy and costly processes of dialogue and engagement with some of their fiercest critics.

However, the challenge in this sphere for companies is not just to undertake these processes of dialogue, but to ensure that these dialogues produce tangible results, even if they are not necessarily the ones that the company was hoping to achieve. In some cases there is a lack of clarity regarding what exactly dialogue involves, leading companies to enter into processes with a misunderstanding of exactly what the process is like or is likely to produce. The result of this is that there are far more examples of failed dialogues than there are of successful dialogue processes. Often this has resulted from a difference in expectations among stakeholders and the company regarding the actual aims and objectives of the dialogue. While arguably even failures mark an attempt to engage and a learning process, there is also a danger that many stakeholder groups will eventually stop engaging in these forms of dialogue if they do not perceive any gains to be emerging from them. Indeed, Burchell and Cook's (2006) study noted that, especially within the NGO community, many groups were now reluctant to engage in dialogue processes with companies due to what they perceived to be an uneven process of asymmetrical learning. Companies, it was felt, were keen to gain information and to use dialogue as a system to restrict criticism and public campaigning but were reluctant to really develop meaningful processes of exchange which might have a direct impact on their business activities.

With both the reporting processes and the more complex forms of stakeholder engagement and dialogue, a key aspect to their effective development is the creation of a level of trust and transparency. Given the often conflictual relationships that have evolved between the business community and civil society and the tradition of secrecy that has accompanied business practice, it is no surprise that there is a level of scepticism displayed when companies start to discuss transparency and openness and seek to talk to those they have often previously ignored. However, effective engagement and dialogue can be a key process in changing those relationships and establishing new channels for communication and discussion.

The readings selected in this chapter provide both a positive and negative picture of the engagement process. An excerpt from a CSR network study highlights the challenge of company reporting in this field while the excerpts from CSR reports by both Cadbury and Vodafone provide a flavour for the types of approaches that companies are employing in outlining and measuring their social and environmental impacts. The Cadbury excerpt high-lights the connection between CSR and company values, while the Vodafone example shows how they seek to address awkward issues within their report. They also serve to highlight some of the positive engagement processes that are ongoing and the innovative ways in which CSR can be approached.

At the same time, however, articles by Deborah Doane, George Monbiot and a report by Christian Aid have been included which suggest that there remains a significant gap between company words and deeds and which subsequently raise question marks over the accuracy and validity of company CSR claims. The first reading, however, highlights the challenges of engaging in stakeholder dialogue and looks at Shell's attempts to engage with its critics.

GUIDE TO FURTHER READING

The nature and effectiveness of CSR reporting and stakeholder dialogue has been a key theme within the literature in this field. See, for example, Maurrasse, D. (ed.) (2004) *A Future for Everyone: Innovative Social Responsibility and Community Partnerships*, New York, Routledge; Andriof, J., S. Waddock, B. Husted and S. Rahman (eds) (2003) *Unfolding Stakeholder Thinking 1: Theory, Responsibility and Engagement*, Sheffield, Greenleaf; Andriof, J., S. Waddock, B. Husted and S. Rahman (eds) (2003) *Unfolding Stakeholder Thinking 2: Relationships, Communication, Reporting and Performance*, Sheffield, Green-leaf; Bendell, J. (ed.) (2000) *Terms for Endearment: Business, NGOs and Sustainable Development*, Sheffield, Greenleaf; SalterBaxter (2006) *Is Corporate Responsibility in Your Company's Blood?*, SalterBaxter Report. For recent research into the developing processes of stakeholder engagement and dialogue between companies and NGOs see Burchell, J. and J. Cook (2006) 'Assessing the Impact of Stakeholder Dialogue', *Journal of Public Affairs*, Vol. 6, Nos 3/4, pp. 210–227.

WEB-BASED RESOURCES

A large number of companies now produce CSR reports and it is worth looking at a few different examples to see just how varied the approaches can be. Good starting points for examining CSR reporting and stakeholder dialogue include:

- www.globalreporting.org/ReportsDatabase – The Global Reporting Initiatives Reports Database provides a good source of different reports to examine.
- www.the-environment-council.org.uk/bnfl-national-stakeholder-dialogue – Detailed coverage of British Nuclear Fuels' extensive stakeholder dialogue programme facili-tated by the Environment Council.
- www.globalactionplan.org.uk – Global Action Plan website. Organization that seeks to engage businesses and communities in discussion regarding practical tools for improving environmental performance.

REFERENCES

Bendell, J. (2003) 'Talking for Change? Reflections on Effective Stakeholder Dialogue', in J. Andriof, S. Waddock, B. Husted and S. Rahman (eds) *Unfolding Stakeholder Thinking 2: Relationships, Communication, Reporting and Performance*, Sheffield, Greenleaf.

Blair, M.M. (1998) 'For Whom Should Corporations be Run? An Economic Rationale for Stakeholder Management', *Long Range Planning*, Vol. 32, No. 2, pp. 195–200.

Burchell, J. and J. Cook (2006) 'Assessing the Impact of Stakeholder Dialogue: Changing Relationships Between NGOs and Companies', *Journal of Public Affairs*, Vol. 6, Nos 3/4, pp. 210–227.

Crane, A. and S. Livesey (2003) 'Are You Talking to Me? Stakeholder Communication and the Risks and Rewards of Dialogue', in J. Andriof, S. Waddock, B. Husted and S. Rahman (eds) *Unfolding Stakeholder Thinking 2: Relationships, Communication, Reporting and Performance*, Sheffield, Greenleaf.

Donaldson, T. and L.E. Preston (1995) 'The Stakeholder Theory of the Corporation: Concepts, Evidence and Implications', *Academy of Management Review*, Vol. 49, No. 1, pp. 65–91.

Hess, D.W. (1999) 'Social Reporting: A Reflexive Law Approach to Corporate Social Responsiveness', *Journal of Corporation Law*, Vol. 25, No. 1, pp. 41–84.

Holme, Lord (1999) 'Corporate Social Responsibility', Speech given at conference organized by Norsk Hydro, 28 April.

Lawrence, A.T. (2002) 'The Drivers of Stakeholder Engagement: Reflections on the Case of Royal Dutch Shell', in J. Andriof, S. Waddock, B. Husted and S. Rahman (eds) *Unfolding Stakeholder Thinking: Theory, Responsibility and Engagement*, Sheffield, Greenleaf.

Owen, D. (2003) *Recent Developments in European Social and Environmental Reporting and Auditing Practice: A Critical Evaluation and Tentative Prognosis*, ICCSR Working Paper, University of Nottingham.

Payne, S.L. and J.M. Calton (2002) 'Towards a Managerial Practice of Stakeholder Engagement: Developing Multi-stakeholder Learning Dialogues', in J. Andriof, S. Waddock, B. Husted and S. Rahman (eds) *Unfolding Stakeholder Thinking: Theory, Responsibility and Engagement*, Sheffield, Greenleaf.

Waddock, S. (2001) 'Integrity and Mindfulness: Foundations of Corporate Citizenship', in J. Andriof and M. McIntosh (eds) *Perspectives on Corporate Citizenship*, Sheffield, Greenleaf.

Anne T. Lawrence

THE DRIVERS OF STAKEHOLDER ENGAGEMENT
Reflections on the case of Royal Dutch/Shell

A SMALL BUT significant number of corporations today are moving towards greater engagement with stakeholders. The term 'stakeholder' refers to persons and organisations that affect, or are affected by, a corporation's actions—that is, all those that have a stake in what a firm does. Stakeholders include such diverse groups as customers, employees, creditors, the media, governments, professional and trade associations, social and environmental activists, and non-governmental organisations (Freeman 1984; Post *et al.* 2002). In the stakeholder model of the firm, business organisations are seen as enmeshed in a network involving many participants, each of which shares to some degree in both the risks and rewards of the firm's activities (Donaldson and Preston 1995).

A venerable tradition in the study of business and society has sought to classify variations in the relationship between firms and their stakeholders. In an early and classic formulation, Preston and Post (1975) posited a progression of strategies of corporate response to public constituencies ranging from reactive to proactive, to interactive. Frederick (1978) described an evolution of firm behaviour from corporate social responsibility to corporate social responsiveness; he later (1986 and 1987) added corporate social rectitude—a stance in which corporate behaviour was deeply influenced by societal values, Logsdon and Yuthas (1997) classified companies according to their stage of moral development, with more ethically advanced firms actively promoting the welfare of stakeholders. More recently, theorists have proposed a stage model in which individual firms increase their level of engagement with stakeholders over time. In this view, in the first stage, companies identify or map stakeholders and their interests; in the second stage, they attempt to manage stakeholders and the social issues of concern to them; and, in the third stage, they actively engage stakeholders for long-term value creation. Stakeholder engagement, in contrast to earlier stages, involves a stance of mutual responsibility, information-sharing, open and respectful dialogue, and an ongoing commitment to joint problem-solving (Svendsen 1998; Waddock 2002).

Although we now know a good deal about variations in the corporate-stakeholder relationship and the stages through which it may progress, we know less about the factors that drive firms forward through this process. Certainly, most firms are still in stages one or two; firms in stage three remain the exception. What external or internal factors increase the likelihood that corporations will embrace greater engagement with stakeholders? That is, what are the key drivers of stakeholder engagement? What are the necessary and sufficient conditions for companies and their stakeholders to attempt engagement? Once undertaken, what factors facilitate the success or failure of the process?

This reading examines these questions in the context of a discussion of the experiences of a single firm: the multinational oil company Royal Dutch/Shell. Shell has been widely recognised by academies and practitioners alike as a leader in the process of stakeholder engagement. Since 1995, Shell has taken a series of interrelated initiatives to improve the company's social and environment performance as well as to enhance the public's perception of its corporate citizenship. These initiatives have included a study of society's expectations; revision of the company's business principles; and adoption of a triple-bottom-line approach to auditing and verifying its social and environmental, as well as financial, performance, Shell has also entered into a series of interactive dialogues with a number of stakeholder organisations, including human rights groups, shareholder activists, community groups and environmentalists, on matters of mutual concern. Arguably, Shell is further along in the transition to full stakeholder engagement than any other major multinational corporation. The company is of theoretical interest not because it is typical but, on the contrary, precisely because it is not.

Over an 18-month period from 1999 to 2000, I was part of a team that conducted a study of the transformation of Shell, under the auspices of the Council on Ethics in Economics (CEE). Our immediate purpose was to produce a two-part multimedia case for use by business students and executives. As part of this process, we conducted videotaped interviews with around two dozen Shell executives, leaders of stakeholder organisations, consultants and academics in the United States, the United Kingdom, the Netherlands and Nigeria. These interviews ranged in duration from half an hour or so to several hours; they were professionally transcribed and reviewed for accuracy by the interviewees. We also reviewed a wide range of written and videotaped documentary evidence provided by Shell and its stakeholders. This effort produced two teaching cases, which were published online by the CEE under the titles 'Shell in Nigeria' and 'The Transformation of Shell'.[1]

In this reading, I draw on the interviews and documentary evidence collected during this project to reflect on Shell's experience and that of its stakeholders. My intention, in the tradition of inductive, grounded research, is to help build our theoretical understanding of the conditions that drive corporate–stakeholder engagement. My method, to the extent possible, is to allow the participants in the dialogue process to speak for themselves, to reveal the patterns of meaning by which they understood their own experiences. I focus, in particular, on the parties' **motivation** to seek engagement; their **goals** in the engagement process; the **organisational capacities** they employed; and the **dynamics** of effective dialogue. In constructing my argument, I draw mainly on one particular example of stakeholder engagement: Shell's productive ongoing dialogue with two human rights organisations, Amnesty International and Pax Christi International. I conclude with a discussion of the implications of the Shell case for stakeholder engagement theory.

Shell's crisis of reputation

In the mid-1990s, Shell faced a serious crisis of reputation. At the time, the Royal Dutch/ Shell Group was the world's largest fully integrated petroleum company. 'Upstream', the conglomerate controlled oil and gas exploration and production; 'midstream', the pipe-lines and tankers that carried oil and gas; and 'downstream', the refining, marketing and distribution of the final product. The company also had interests in coal mining, forestry, chemicals and renewable energy. In all the Anglo-Dutch conglomerate comprised over 2,000 separate entities, with exploration and production operations, refineries and mar-keting in scores of countries. Royal Dutch/Shell was, in both its ownership and scope, perhaps the world's most truly transnational corporation. In 1994, Royal Dutch/Shell made more money than any other company in the world, reporting annual profits of US$6.3 billion and, with 106,000 employees worldwide, had the largest workforce of any oil company.

The events that gave rise to the reputational crisis of this major global corporation have been extensively described elsewhere. Briefly, the key developments were these:

- **The Brent Spar incident**. The Brent Spar was an ageing oil storage buoy in the North Sea. In 1991, Shell took the Brent Spar out of service and began looking at options for disposal. In April 1995, after extensive study, Shell announced its inten-tion to sink the Brent Spar in the Atlantic, and British authorities approved the plan. Some environmentalists expressed concern, however, that toxic residue in the Brent Spar's tanks could harm the marine environment. On 30 April activists from the environmental organisation Greenpeace boarded and occupied the abandoned buoy and remained there for three weeks. The Greenpeace occupation and resulting media coverage galvanised public opinion, especially in Europe. Government offi-cials of Belgium, Denmark, Sweden, the Netherlands and Germany asked Shell to postpone sinking the Brent Spar, and a consumer boycott gathered force, especially in Germany. On 20 June Shell abruptly changed course, announcing that it had decided to abandon its plan to sink the Brent Spar at sea and to look at various alternative methods of disposal.[2]

- **Human rights in Nigeria**. Just a few months later, the execution of Ken Saro-Wiwa and eight colleagues in Nigeria on 10 November 1995 led to further wide-spread public criticism of the beleaguered company. Saro-Wiwa was a leader of the Ogoni people of Nigeria and a charismatic environmental and human rights activist. In a series of campaigns, Saro-Wiwa had charged that Shell's operations had despoiled the ecology of the Niger River delta, and that revenue-sharing practices that returned little to the people of the oil-producing regions were unjust. In 1995, the Nigerian military government had brought Saro-Wiwa and several colleagues to trial before a special tribunal on what many believed were trumped-up charges that he had ordered the murder of political opponents. In the wake of Saro-Wiwa's execution, environmentalists and human rights activists criticised Shell for failing to intervene with the authorities to stop the execution and called for an international boycott of Shell's gasoline and other products.[3]

In the wake of the Brent Spar incident and the Saro-Wiwa execution, Shell found itself the object of intense public scrutiny. Environmentalists, human rights activists and churches joined a chorus of criticism. Institutional shareholders in the UK, including public employee pension funds and religious organisations, called for reforms of the company's corporate governance. These campaigns against Shell interacted in a synergistic way to produce what many viewed as a profound challenge to the company's public image as a socially and environmentally responsible corporation. Shell was particularly vulnerable to attacks on its reputation because it marketed a well-known branded product—Shell gasoline sold under the familiar red and yellow seashell logo—in scores of countries. Consumers disappointed with Shell's environmental or human rights performance or responsiveness to its stakeholders could often easily switch allegiance to another brand of gasoline.

Changing course

Coincidentally, at the time that these campaigns against Shell erupted, a managed internal change process was already under way at the company. In 1994, the chairman of Shell's committee of managing directors (CMD), Cor Herkströter, had initiated a review of the firm's organisational structure by management consultants McKinsey and Company, aimed at improving the company's financial performance relative to its competitors. Although Shell was highly profitable, other big oil companies—including rivals British Petroleum, Exxon and Mobil—enjoyed significantly higher returns on capital. In March 1995, Shell concluded the first phase of its internal review by announcing a plan to abandon its complex matrix structure and to reorganise into five worldwide business units. This restructuring was intended to enable the company to focus more efficiently on the needs of its business and retail customers.

Even as Shell announced its intended organisational redesign, however, external pressures on the company had the effect of shifting the focus of the change process to the 'softer' issues of the company's reputation and relations with stakeholders. In a series of executive retreats held in late 1995 and early 1996, consultants retained by Shell asked participants to develop a 'diagnosis of current reality' to serve as a starting point for further changes aimed at improving corporate profitability. To the apparent surprise of both the consultants and Shell's top leaders, discussion began to shift from strictly business matters to the company's social and environmental performance. Many participants at the retreats wanted to talk not about profitability but about the fact that Shell was being pilloried in the press for its failures of social and environmental responsibility.

Mark Moody-Stuart, then a managing director, framed Shell's problem as the need for a new mind-set that paid greater attention to societal expectations. One of the consultants present, Philip H. Mirvis, later observed:

> Mark Moody-Stuart should be credited with the intellectual framing of this. Shell was an engineering-type company . . . a very technical organisation and essentially a very bureaucratic organisation . . . What [Moody-Stuart] said was that the technical mind-set, our rational, logical approach, is blinding us to a world out there of human rights activists, of environmentalists, of governments with different wants and interests and changing customer tastes, expectations of the public, etc. We are so internally focused, so technical, that we are missing a whole set of opportunities and a whole new reality out there

. . . We are not talking any more about a structural change in the organisation; we are not even talking about new leadership per se. We are talking about a new Shell.[4]

The crucial insight, for Shell's leaders, was that meeting the expectations of the 'world out there' was a *business* imperative. The company's reputation was a valuable asset that had to be managed, along with other commercial risks and opportunities. Moody-Stuart, who succeeded Herkströter as chairman of the CMD, described the company's motivation for moving towards greater interaction with civil society:

> [C]ommunication between ourselves and society [was] obviously not optimum, and in some areas it plainly wasn't working. Now, if that is the situation, it is a major situation that needs to be addressed, because, if an organisation is not in communication with society, it is not in communication with its customers. It is a commercial matter, because society is your customers. It is not a soft and woolly thing, because society is what we depend on for our living. So we had better be in line with its wishes, its desires, its aspirations, its dreams and so on.

Later, contrasting the social and commercial obligations of the company, he underscored this point:

> You can't divorce the two. People sometimes try to do that. They say, all this societal stuff is woolly, we should stick to commerce. The two are absolutely linked . . . These soft issues are really business issues, because we are part of society, and members of society are our customers. So, our impact on society really matters commercially.

Once the CMD became convinced of this critical point—that meeting society's expectations was a *business* necessity—the directors undertook a series of interrelated initiatives to improve the public's perception of its corporate citizenship. Shell commissioned a major survey to provide its leaders with information about society's changing expectations in all regions of the world in which it did business. It established a board-level committee, allocated additional staff and resources to its external affairs department, and began exploring other ways to improve its social and environmental performance to meet its customers' expectations.

Seizing an opportunity

As Shell struggled to understand and respond to society's changing expectations, several non-governmental organisations (NGOs) recognised Shell's crisis as an opportunity to pursue their own objectives.

In December 1995, in the wake of Saro-Wiwa's execution, Pax Christi International (PCI)—a Catholic lay organisation devoted to promoting world peace, human rights and economic justice—wrote to Shell asking the company to speak out on human rights in Nigeria. Herkströter replied, responding to specific points and inviting the NGO to engage in further discussion. Independently, Amnesty International (AI) branches in both the United Kingdom and the Netherlands had also approached Shell to express concerns about Shell's actions in Nigeria. At the time, Amnesty International was probably the best-known human rights organisation in the world, with over a million members internationally. Herkströter met with AI representatives in January 1996 and indicated that the company was prepared to review its business principles. When the relevant leaders of the two NGOs discovered they were pursuing a similar agenda, they decided to draft a joint memorandum to Shell. Over the following three years, these two organisations engaged jointly in an ongoing discussion with Shell, involving face-to-face meetings, an exchange of position papers and debate in public forums.

Both Amnesty International and Pax Christi had recently developed an interest in working directly with the business community to promote human rights. Traditionally, these organisations had focused on pressuring governments—through grass-roots campaigns and other methods—to uphold their espoused commitments to the Universal Declaration of Human Rights and other international covenants. Many people in both organisations were fundamentally hostile to the business community. In the 1990s, however, some activists within both NGOs had increasingly sought to work directly with multinational corporations to promote their objectives. In 1991, a group of individual members of Amnesty International–UK, most of whom had industry experience, formed an internal Business Group with the objective of encouraging companies to adopt human rights policies and practices. Geoffrey Chandler, a former Shell executive who had been instrumental in drafting Shell's first Statement of General Business Principles, became chair of the group.[5] Pax Christi had also begun work in this arena, with a department of economic relations undertaking various corporate initiatives.[6]

A core group of activists in Amnesty International and Pax Christi recognised that both protest and persuasion were necessary components of a successful strategy to influence corporate behaviour. Unlike governments—which were constrained to some degree by international human rights agreements they had signed—most corporations could not be *legally* compelled to support human rights, beyond compliance with the laws of the nations in which they operated. As Gemma Crijns, a staff member of Amnesty International in the Netherlands who was active in the dialogue with Shell, put it to us plainly: 'There is no law that says that companies have to be concerned about human rights.' Crijns was convinced that the activist campaigns against Shell had been critical to bringing the company to the table. She put it this way: 'It is more efficient if you work with a company that is in trouble . . . A kind of urgency . . . is very important in this work.'

At the same time, she believed 'that just organising demonstrations or shouting before the door' was insufficient. Her British colleague, Geoffrey Chandler, similarly observed:

> I think very strongly that protest raises an issue, [but] . . . it cannot win the argument. You can only win the argument by engagement and discussion . . . Protest has a role. Protest and engagement are essentially complementary . . . In the end, there is gain from protest, [and] there is gain from argument, as long as it is honest.

Dialogue, unlike protest, offered the NGOs an opportunity to engage Shell, as well as other companies, in an extended discussion of specific actions they might take to improve their human rights records. Chandler commented:

> Companies are not stupid. They are pragmatic. Once they had accepted the problem, and recognised in themselves that they were at fault, they then sat down and said, what do we do? So, we then began to discuss with them how they might incorporate human rights into their own principles.

Risks and rewards

Engaging in an open, interactive dialogue carried risks and rewards for both Shell and its NGO stakeholders. In order for the participants to enter and to continue a dialogue, all parties had to perceive the balance between risk and reward as favourable.

For the company, dialogue offered the potential benefits of learning about society's expectations, drawing on outside expertise, generating creative solutions and achieving stakeholder support for implementing them. It also could potentially disarm or neutralise dangerous critics and improve its reputation for taking constructive action. When asked to describe the benefits of stakeholder engagement, Robin Aram, Shell's vice president for external relations and policy development, commented:

> If you anticipate, and you get into dialogue, and you listen more carefully to those signals, and you become engaged with people, then you will . . . learn a lot of things which you can apply more generally, you'll get closer to your customers, and indeed your business will do better.

The risk of *not* engaging stakeholders, Aram noted, was the converse: the company would fail to meet society's expectations, thereby undermining its licence to operate. 'If the company operates in a way that is not acceptable in the communities and the society in which it operates,' he commented, 'over the long term it would not be allowed to operate.' Of course, dialogue also carried the risk of public failure, loss of control and of raising expectations beyond what the company could deliver. Egbert Wesselink, an officer of Pax Christi Netherlands, expressed his understanding of Shell's risk this way:

> The moment you make a promise you will be attacked ten times harder: that is their [the company's] fear. They fear they will be attacked ten times harder when they promise something and do not do it, than when they have the same behaviour but have never spoken out that they will not do it.

On this point, Geoffrey Chandler added: 'An additional risk in engagement to companies is the degree of disclosure that NGOs demand [when] there is real engagement and, even more, when there is partnership in looking at a problem.'[7]

For their part, the human rights organisations were also acutely aware of the potential risks of a dialogue strategy. Wesselink told us that he had been strenuously criticised for talking with Shell, an organisation that many of his colleagues viewed as 'a symbol of what a multinational enterprise should not do'. Chandler, who organised a series of meetings in the United Kingdom to facilitate dialogue between NGOs and multinational corporations on the topic of human rights, reported that he had been 'vilified' by other activists who thought he was, in effect, consorting with the enemy. In Chandler's view, this criticism was unwarranted:

> The criticism comes from a very narrow focus . . . [from] NGOs who are ideologically opposed to what they call the capitalist system. They would say, you are getting into bed with the transnationals; this is insufferable. My reply is, if we achieve what they are after, which is to get a commitment to the Universal Declaration of Human Rights, . . . [we] are helping them in what they are doing.

The NGOs also expressed concern that their names might be misused to give a kind of seal of approval to company action.

Amnesty International and Pax Christi, like many NGOs, are voluntary organisations that depend to a great extent on the financial support of their members. A tension exists in the rank-and-file between those who support engagement with multinational corporations and those who oppose it. In order for those leaders who favour engagement to maintain membership support, they must achieve measurable results. Crijns, for example, told us that she would have to withdraw from the dialogue process if it showed no progress.

> If there was only the dialogue for the dialogue, if you couldn't show to a member—because Amnesty is a membership organisation—that it is worthwhile to talk to a company, and you talk for a year or two years, and you don't see any worthwhile concrete improvement, you have to stop a dialogue.

The supporters of dialogue on both sides had to be able to show results: for Shell, benefits to the company's reputation; for the NGOs, a change in the company's human rights performance.

The dynamics of successful dialogue

Despite the potential risks, the dialogue between Shell and the two human rights organisations proceeded. The discussion focused on several issues. The two NGOs criticised the vagueness of Shell's Statement of General Business Principles (SGBP) and urged the company to revise them to incorporate explicit support for the Universal Declaration of Human Rights. They recommended that Shell should appoint a director for human rights and undertake independent auditing of its human rights practices. Other portions of the discussion focused specifically on the situation in Nigeria, including Shell's security practices, its relationship to the military authorities, and its role during and after Saro-Wiwa's trial.[8]

As the dialogue continued, Shell took a number of actions that were responsive to the NGOs' recommendations. For example, the company undertook a revision of the SGBP. In the revised principles, published in 1997, the company declared its support for 'fundamental human rights in line with the legitimate role of business'. The principles also clarified the company's stand on political activity. The earlier formulation, which emphasised abstention from politics, was replaced with language stating the company's intention to abstain from *party* politics, while emphasising its right and responsibility to make its position known to governments on matters affecting the company or its stakeholders. Shell also reviewed its rules of engagement for security personnel and made specific changes to bring them into compliance with United Nations standards. It also initiated independent auditing of its social and environmental performance.

In other respects, in contrast, Shell did not act on the NGOs' recommendations. For example, the company did not explicitly endorse the Universal Declaration of Human Rights in its revised principles (although it did endorse them elsewhere). It declined to appoint a director of human rights, saying that its current governance procedures were sufficient.

What characteristics of the **dynamics** of this dialogue kept the process moving forward? I believe that four elements of this particular dialogue were critical to its success; I will call these elements affinity, legitimacy, trust and incrementalism.

One important success factor, in this instance, was a basic cultural **affinity** between the parties. Royal Dutch/Shell was, of course, an Anglo-Dutch firm. This particular dialogue took place between company representatives and the British and Dutch offices of the two NGOs. Amnesty International's chief spokesperson in these talks was Geoffrey Chandler, who, prior to heading up AI's Business Group in the United Kingdom, had been a Shell executive for over two decades. With experience in both the business and human rights communities, he proved extremely effective in bridging the gap between them. Crijns made the point that she felt it had been easier for AI to initiate dialogue in the Netherlands, with its low-hierarchy culture, than it would have been in some other nations:

> It is cultural. I think that the way that I can get in touch with companies here is possible because in Holland our relations are not very hierarchical. It is easy for me to get in touch with the people [corporate executives]. It is much more difficult for my colleagues in the US or in France, for instance. These are really cultural differences.

In short, it helped that at least some individuals on both sides felt reasonably comfortable talking with one another, either because of shared experiences and assumptions, or because of a low-hierarchy setting that put them on a more level playing field. Although they differed on many points, the two parties had enough in common that they were able to work together productively.

Both sides acknowledged the **legitimacy** of the other party and the integrity of its people. Chandler made this point this way:

> We are dealing with human beings here. We don't uniquely have the moral high ground. Shell can only survive as a commercial entity if it can recruit the most intelligent [people] who also have ideals and principles . . . I think we are dealing with people who are increasing [their] belief in these principles in order to survive in the critical world.

Later, he added, 'If one is negotiating with someone, I think you have to assume their integrity is as good as yours, until they prove otherwise.' Similarly, Shell implicitly seemed to acknowledge the legitimacy of Amnesty International and Pax Christi as representatives of a broader community of concern about human rights. The tone of the dialogue, throughout, was respectful.

Both sides in this dialogue demonstrated a willingness to keep talking, even when progress was slow or obstacles emerged. **Trust** had to be earned, as the result of an ongoing process of making and keeping commitments. Relationship building took time. Aram, who participated in many dialogues on Shell's behalf, commented:

> Trust is something that is crucial and takes time to be learned. That's why dialogue needs to be a sustained process. It needs give and take on both sides. There are risks. There are risks, and people get surprises along the way. I think the key thing is to recognise, as you go in to these processes, that there will be surprises, there will be disappointments, and to keep your eye on the long-term ball, and to keep the process going trust is the key. But trust takes a long time to develop, so stick at it.

The human rights activists we spoke with indicated that, as the conversation proceeded, their trust in the company's motives had been enhanced. Crijns stated:

> I have been dealing with Shell . . . [for] four or five years now. I do have a feeling that they really are trying to do it in the right way. Human rights never can be a core issue of a company . . . But I have a feeling that really they are working very hard to do it in [the] right way.

Wesselink of Pax Christi Netherlands similarly described his growing confidence in the process as he participated over time: 'Many people [in the human rights community] . . . said it [stakeholder dialogue] was only window dressing . . . They are fooling you. Well, we did not really get the impression that we were being fooled.'

A final success factor was that both sides seemed willing to accept **incremental progress** towards their goals. Neither side got everything it wanted. Both sides clearly felt, however, that they had met at least some of their objectives and that they could continue to build on these partial successes. Crijns told us that she felt that Shell's commitment to human rights in the revised SGBP was an important 'first step':

> Talking with a company about a code of conduct was new. Quite a lot of [activist] organisations do have the feeling that a [corporate] code of conduct, a piece of paper, is worthless. If there are human rights in them, or not, does not matter. It does not change anything . . . In a sense, I agree with them. But, knowing that human rights are a very alien issue for Shell and other companies, I feel as though we need a piece of paper in which the company itself says, 'we are concerned with human rights'. That would be a first step. Later on, we could come back to them and say, 'you said that you are concerned about human rights . . . Look at what you are doing.'

Both sides saw this dialogue as a first step, with others to follow.

Shell's dialogue with AI and PCI, described here, was only one of a great many initiatives taken by the company after 1995, including several extended dialogues with other stakeholder organisations. Of these, the human rights dialogue was widely viewed as one of the most successful. It is beyond the scope of this reading to discuss Shell's other stakeholder initiatives. But this model, I believe, may help to illuminate failures as well as successes. A number of commentators have observed, for example, that Shell's efforts at dialogue in Nigeria itself were generally unproductive.[9] In contrast to the instance discussed here, Shell Nigeria and its Ogoni critics were separated by vast cultural differences, failed to acknowledge each other's legitimacy, seemed unwilling to accept incremental gains and (in the case of Saro-Wiwa's trial) faced enormous time pressures that prevented the gradual emergence of trust. In short, none of the dynamics of successful dialogue present here was operative in the Nigerian situation. A painful paradox is that dialogue seems most productive where the parties have much in common and plenty of time to talk; yet it may be most needed where the parties have little in common and face a difficult and urgent problem.

Drivers of engagement

Drawing theoretical conclusions from the particulars of a single case is inherently risky. Nevertheless, I will offer some modest conclusions about what Shell's dialogue with its human rights stakeholders reveals about the factors that drive forward the process of stakeholder engagement.

Stakeholder engagement is, at its core, a **relationship**. Dialogue is a multi-party event: the participation of one focal business organisation and at least one stakeholder organisation is necessary, by definition, to constitute engagement. Thus, any analysis that seeks to explain what drives engagement forward that examines only one side of the relationship—whether the corporation or the stakeholder—is necessarily incomplete. As the common expression goes, 'It takes two to tango.' In this instance, I suggest, both Shell and its human rights stakeholders possessed the **motivation** to engage one another in a dialogue, a **goal** that could only be met with the participation of the other party, and the **organisational capacity** to engage with each other. Moreover, the **dynamics** of the dialogue process itself contributed to its success. Table 1 summarises the motivation, goals and organisational capacities of the two parties to this particular dialogue.

Motivation

Shell, for its part, was motivated largely by a serious crisis of reputation, caused by strenuous public criticism of its behaviour by environmentalists, human rights activists and institutional shareholders. These groups had had considerable success in focusing negative media attention on the company. In a process of internal discussion, Shell leaders concluded that its reputation was a core commercial asset and that it needed to act assertively to better meet society's expectations. Understanding society's expectations required dialogue with stakeholders. The two NGOs, for their part, were motivated by a growing realisation that meeting their objective of promoting human rights required the active involvement of corporations. A strategy focused exclusively on pressuring governments to uphold their commitments under international law had proved insufficient. Moreover, in the NGOs' view, while protest might motivate companies to act, it was ultimately inadequate because it did not help them to understand what specific actions to take.

Table 1 Corporate and stakeholder perceptions of the engagement process: Shell and human rights organisations

	Company (Shell)	Stakeholders (AI/PCI)
Motivation	Reputational crisis; Shell perceives it is not meeting society's expectations	Governmental campaigns, protest perceived as inadequate to change corporate behaviour
Goals	To improve corporate reputation; to earn licence to operate; to win approval of society	To change corporate behaviour; to obtain corporate support for human rights principles and practices
Organisational capacity	Managed change process; leaders committed to dialogue; well-funded department of external affairs	Economic relations units in place; experienced staff; core group of activists committed to dialogue

Goals

Shell, for its part, sought to understand and meet society's expectations. As a commercial organisation, the firm needed its customers' trust and confidence in order to market its products successfully. In short, it needed a licence to operate. It felt that by winning the support of legitimate representatives of stakeholder interests it could further this objective. In contrast, Amnesty International and Pax Christi wanted Shell to change its behaviour to better support human rights. They wanted the company to endorse the Universal Declaration of Human Rights, to make specific changes in the way it provided security for its overseas operations, and to undertake changes in its corporate governance and reporting to its stakeholders.

Organisational capacity

Each side had the organisational capacity to engage the other in a productive dialogue. At the time of its crisis of reputation, Shell, quite coincidentally, was involved in a managed change process focused on improving its bottom-line results. As managers involved in this process struggled to make sense of growing public criticism of the company, the organisational change initiative was, in effect, deflected from its original course and redirected to a goal other than the one for which it was intended. Moreover, Shell moved quickly to augment its organisational capacity to respond to stakeholders by allocating resources to its department of external affairs, by assigning top executives to reputation management, and by undertaking intensive environmental scanning initiatives. For their parts, both Amnesty International and Pax Christi had organisational units dedicated to business initiatives, and both had a core group of individuals committed to a corporate dialogue strategy and willing to assume the internal political risks it posed.

As is evident from Table 1, the stakeholder engagement process here was fundamentally **asymmetrical**: that is, the motivation, goals and organisational capacities of the two parties were very different. Yet they complemented each other in a way that made interaction attractive to both.

This case offers an opportunity for commentary on earlier theoretical work on collaborative partnerships. In a review of this literature, Wood and Gray (1991) defined collaboration as occurring 'when a group of autonomous stakeholders of a problem domain engage in an interactive process, using shared rules, norms, and structures, to act or decide on issues related to that domain'. This instance of stakeholder engagement may be considered collaborative to the extent that it did indeed constitute an interactive process among autonomous actors, with the aim of producing tangible results. Yet it was unlike a conventional collaboration in that the parties arguably were able (at least partially) to accomplish their objectives without ever accepting a common definition of the problem domain. To Shell, the problem was a faltering reputation; to the NGOs, the problem was corporate disregard for human rights. Prompting this dialogue was not a common problem but rather an interdependent set of problems: each side needed the other to advance its own agenda. In this respect, this case appears to confirm Logsdon's (1991) finding that collaborations are most likely to emerge where the parties perceive that their problems are both salient and interdependent. It is also consistent with Gray's (1989) conclusion that parties are most likely to collaborate when they see no other way to solve an intractable problem.

Process dynamics

Finally, the process of dialogue itself, in this instance, favoured success in several respects. The parties to the dialogue shared certain common cultural values and assumptions. They were committed to taking the time necessary to build a relationship of trust. Both accepted incremental progress as positive and were able to make enough gains to satisfy the potential critics in their own camp that the process was worth pursuing. And both parties fundamentally respected the other side's legitimacy and integrity.

In short, Shell's dialogue with these human rights organisations suggests that engagement between a business firm and a stakeholder organisation or organisations will be most likely to emerge under the following conditions:

- The business firm faces a **crisis of reputation**. Significant public criticism highlights a gap between society's expectations and the firm's behaviour. Such crises are most likely in firms that sell or provide a branded product or service directly to the public.
- The company perceives that **it cannot improve its reputation unilaterally**. Rather, this requires winning the support of representatives of stakeholder interests. Moreover, these representatives are organised and are perceived by the firm as legitimate.
- The business firm possesses sufficient **organisational capacity** to engage with stakeholders. This may include support from top leadership and an adequately funded external affairs or similar department with a reporting relationship to top executives. It may also include a managed change process that provides an opportunity for leaders to identify and respond quickly to shifts in the external environment.
- The stakeholder organisation perceives that a core **goal** cannot be met without the

active participation of the business firm. Unilateral action has not been effective in meeting its objectives.

- The stakeholder organisation possesses sufficient **organisational capacity** to engage with the business firm. This may include leadership or a significant faction that supports dialogue and an organisational unit with expertise in working with the business community.

- Both sides share a **cultural affinity**, recognise the other side's fundamental **legitimacy**, are able to dedicate considerable time to the process of building **trust**, and are willing to accept **incremental progress** towards their goals.

The stage model implicit in much recent work in stakeholder theory is correct in one sense: it accurately describes the sequence in which various types of stakeholder interaction occur. That is, stakeholder mapping generally precedes stakeholder management, and stakeholder management generally precedes stakeholder engagement. But using stage models to describe social phenomena is risky because the biological analogy can be taken too far. Stage models imply a developmental sequence: that is, one stage inexorably leads to another. A child, if properly nurtured, will pass through a series of physical and emotional stages as he or she becomes an adult. Unless illness, accident or some other catastrophe intervenes, these developmental stages are generally predictable—within limits—to paediatricians, child psychologists and experienced parents. Biology establishes a baseline.

In contrast, organisations are not biological entities, and there is nothing automatic about the process by which stakeholder mapping becomes stakeholder management, or by which stakeholder management becomes stakeholder engagement. On the contrary, the Shell case suggests that the transition from stakeholder management to stakeholder engagement is problematical and contingent. Full stakeholder engagement is likely, for now at least, to remain the exception, because it depends on a number of conditions that can be expected to occur simultaneously only infrequently. In this instance, a series of public relations debacles, a managed change process, the presence of NGOs prepared for dialogue, and some skilled and experienced participants all converged somewhat serendipitously to help drive forward engagement between Shell and its human rights stakeholders. In this sense, the experience of Shell, Amnesty International and Pax Christi must be considered a deviant case.

On the other hand, over time stakeholder engagement is likely to become more, rather than less, common. Companies that see others struggling with a crisis of reputation may elect to address stakeholder concerns proactively to avoid this eventuality. Or, they may do so simply because they become convinced that it is morally right or that it will confer a competitive advantage. NGOs and other stakeholders may see others like themselves succeed in influencing corporate behaviour and conclude that the political risks of engagement are worth taking. The globalisation of markets and the rapid dissemination of information technology will certainly accelerate the rate at which both business firms and stakeholder organisations are able to generalise from each other's best practices. Successful dialogues, such as the one described here, will encourage both companies and stakeholder organisations to engage more often in the difficult, but productive, task of listening to and learning from one another.

Notes

1   Funding for the multimedia case project was provided by a grant from Shell to the Council on Ethics in Economics. Under the terms of agreement between the two organisations, Shell had the right to review for factual accuracy material provided by the company and its executives, but had no authority to edit the final cases. I am deeply grateful to my colleagues on this project, David C. Smith, Joel V. Copeland and John Drummond. However, the conclusions of this reading, as well as any errors it contains, are solely my own. Quotations from the interviews are used here by permission of the Council on Ethics in Economics. The two multimedia cases produced by the project are available for classroom adoption and use, and may be previewed online at www.j-case.com.

2   These events are further documented in 'The Transformation of Shell' (Lawrence 2000b). See also: 'The Brent Spar Incident: A Shell of a Mess', Harvard Business School Case 9–597–013 (1996), and 'Shell, Greenpeace and Brent Spar', Stanford University Graduate School of Business Case P-19 (September 1995).

3   These incidents are further documented in 'Shell in Nigeria' (Lawrence 2000a). See also: 'Royal Dutch/Shell in Nigeria (A) and (B)', Harvard Business School Cases N9–399–126 and N9–399–127 (1999).

4   All quotations, unless otherwise noted, are taken from the interviews conducted for the multimedia cases. Full transcripts of all interviews are included with the cases and are available online.

5   Private correspondence with Geoffrey Chandler. The website of AI–UK's Business Group may be found at www.amnesty.org.uk/business.

6   The growing interest of human rights organisations in engaging multinational corporations in a discussion of their ethical obligations to uphold human rights is explored by Garth Meintjes (2000).

7   Private correspondence with Geoffrey Chandler.

8   Pax Christi International later published a collection of letters, position papers and other documents exchanged by Shell and the two NGOs during their dialogue (Pax Christi International 1998).

9   See, for example, the thoughtful analysis of Shell's continuing difficulties in Nigeria by David Wheeler and colleagues (2000).

References

Donaldson, T. and L.E. Preston (1995) 'The Stakeholder Theory of the Corporation: Concepts, Evidence, and Implications', *Academy of Management Review* 20.1 (January 1995): 65–91.

Frederick, W.C. (1978) *From CSR1 to CSR2: The Maturing of Business-and-Society Thought* (Working Paper 279; Pittsburgh, PA: Graduate School of Business, University of Pittsburgh).

—— (1986) 'Toward CSR3: Why Ethical Analysis is Indispensable and Unavoidable in Corporate Affairs', *California Management Review* 28.2 (Winter 1986): 126–41.

—— (1987) 'Theories of Corporate Social Performance', in S.P. Sethi and C.H. Falbe (eds), *Business and Society: Dimensions of Conflict and Co-operation* (Lexington, MA: Lexington Books): 142–61.

Freeman, R.E. (1984) *Strategic Management: A Stakeholder Approach* (Boston, MA: Pitman).

Gray, B. (1989) *Collaborating: Finding Common Ground for Multiparty Problems*, San Francisco: Jossey Bass.

Lawrence, A.T. (2000a) 'Shell and its Stakeholders: Shell in Nigeria' (multimedia case; Columbus, OH: Council on Ethics in Economics, www.i-case.com).

—— (2000b) 'Shell and its Stakeholders: The Transformation of Shell' (multimedia case; Columbus, OH: Council on Ethics in Economics, www.i-case.com).

Logsdon, J.M. (1991) 'Interests and Interdependence in the Formation of Social Problem-Solving Collaborations', *Journal of Applied Behavioral Science* 27.1: 23–37.

Logsdon, J.M. and K. Yuthas (1997) 'Corporate Social Performance, Stakeholder Orientation, and Organizational Moral Development', *Journal of Business Ethics* 16.12–13: 1213–26.

Meintjes, G. (2000) 'An International Human Rights Perspective on Corporate Codes', in O.G. Williams (ed.), *Global Codes of Conduct: An Idea whose Time has Come* (Notre Dame, IN: University of Notre Dame Press): 83–99.

Pax Christi International (1998) *Multinational Enterprises and Human Rights: A Documentation of the Dialogue between Amnesty International/Pax Christi and Shell* (Utrecht: Pax Christi Netherlands).

Post, J.E., A.T. Lawrence and J. Weber (2002) *Business and Society: Corporate Strategy, Public Policy, Ethics* (New York: McGraw-Hill, 10th edn).

Preston, L.E. and J.E. Post (1975) *Private Management and Public Policy: The Principle of Public Responsibility* (Englewood Cliffs, NJ: Prentice Hall).

Svendsen, A. (1998) *The Stakeholder Strategy: Profiting from Collaborative Business Relationships* (San Francisco: Berrett-Koehler).

Waddock, S.A. (2002) *Leading Corporate Citizens: Vision, Values, Value Added* (Boston, MA: McGraw-Hill).

Wheeler, D., H. Fabig and R. Boele (2000) 'Paradoxes and Dilemmas for Aspiring Stakeholder Responsive Firms in the Extractive Sector: Lessons from the Case of Shell and Ogoni', paper presented to the *Conference on Corporate Governance and Corporate Responsibilities in Developing Economies*, York University, Toronto, April 2000; also accepted for publication in *Journal of Business Ethics*.

Wood, D.J. and B. Gray (1991) 'Toward a Comprehensive Theory of Collaboration', *Journal of Applied Behavioral Science* 27.2: 139–62.

Vodafone

2006 CSR REPORT
Mobile phones, masts and health

Significant reviews and research published during the 2006 financial year

Publications from the INTERPHONE study: Results from a number of the collaborating INTERPHONE national study groups have been published during the financial year 2006, which conclude that there is no evidence of an association between short-term (up to 10 years) mobile phone use and risk of acoustic neuroma, meningioma or glioma. There was insufficient data for firm conclusions to be made on long-term usage. www.iarc.fr/ENG/Units/RCAd.html

May 2005 France: Report to the AFSSE (Agence Francaise de Securite de l'environnement et du Travail) on mobile telephony and health 2004–2005 edition. The AFSSE could not make definitive conclusions regarding health effects caused by the electromagnetic fields generated by mobile phones. On base stations they concluded ". . . no new study has shown convincing evidence of such effects. In the current state of scientific knowledge, such effects have not been conclusively demonstrated." www.afsse.fr

November 2005 Netherlands Health Council of the Netherlands (HCN) – Electromagnetic Fields: Annual Update 2005. The HCN reviewed the scientific evidence in relation to 3G signals, base stations and cancer, mobile phones and brain tumours, laboratory studies on DNA damage and electrical hypersensitivity in their 2005 update. The HCN found no evidence of adverse health effects from exposure to radiofrequency fields below internationally recognised limits. www.gr.nl

December 2005 Sweden Recent Research on EMF and Health Risks: Third annual report from SSI's (Swedish Radiation Protection Authority) Independent Expert Group on Electromagnetic Fields. Regarding the scientific evidence for the effects of radiofrequency fields on DNA strand breakage, the blood-brain barrier, cognitive function and alterations of sleep in human volunteers as well as recent epidemiological evidence on mobile phone use and possible association with brain tumours, the SSI concluded there is no evidence of adverse health effects. The SSI call for more research on long-term health effects. www.ssi.se/english/lank_symbol_Eng.html

December 2005 World Health Organisation (WHO): Electromagnetic Hypersensitivity Fact sheet No 296. The WHO concludes that "EHS is characterized by a variety of non-specific symptoms that differ from individual to individual. The symptoms are certainly real and can vary widely in their severity. Whatever its cause, EHS can be a disabling problem for the affected individual. EHS has no clear diagnostic criteria and there is no scientific basis to link EHS symptoms to EMF exposure. Further, EHS is not a medical diagnosis, nor is it clear that it represents a single medical problem." www.who.int/mediacentre/factsheets/fs296

Vodafone intends to lead the industry in responding to public concerns regarding mobile phones, masts and health. Safeguarding the health and safety of our customers, the public and employees is paramount. We support research to resolve scientific uncertainty and are committed to reducing public concern by making objective information widely available to our stakeholders and by engaging in open, transparent dialogue.

In brief

- The WHO and the latest expert reviews have not suggested any adverse health effects from exposure to low level RF Fields.
- Based on Vodafone's research, levels of concern among the general public remain largely unchanged.
- The WHO concludes that symptoms attributed to electromagnetic hypersensitivity cannot be scientifically linked to exposure to RF fields.
- In January 2006, the WHO updated its future RF field health research needs to focus on children, long-term exposure and social issues.
- Vodafone has extended external engagement and employee awareness programmes.
- Vodafone now requires mobile devices to be tested for use against the body.

The rapid growth of mobile phones has brought personal, commercial and social benefits. However, some people are concerned about the health effects from the radio frequency (RF) fields emitted by handsets and base stations. We believe that introduction of 3G technology may have increased this concern.

We recognise the concern and are addressing this by:

- Engaging with local communities as part of our responsible network deployment process.
- Offering guidance to those who are concerned about how best to limit their RF field exposure from handsets.
- Providing easy-to-understand information through a variety of channels including websites and brochures to help people reach informed views.
- A commitment to inform customers and the general public of significant new developments in published research. We advocate the publication of scientific research in peer-reviewed journals.
- Supporting independent research at arm's length so that areas identified by the WHO as priorities are properly funded.

The handsets we sell and our network of base stations comply with international standards for limiting human exposure to RF fields. Our website explains how mobile phones work and contains links to independent authoritative research organisations, see www.vodafone.com/responsibility/mpmh.

We said

We would directly engage with the public, customers, key opinion formers and employees on mobile phones, masts and health.

We would provide advice to address the concern of customers who wish to reduce exposure to RF fields from their handsets.

We have

Engaged with a wide range of external and internal stakeholders

Our external engagement programme focused on improving communications with a range of stakeholder groups including customers, the general public, national politicians and opinion leaders, investors and analysts and doctors and health agencies.

In the 2006 financial year, we developed a contact programme for government officials and opinion formers to keep them up to date with developments in mobile phone health research. Key medical doctors were identified and a contact and education programme initiated. We produced a standard set of messages and answers to frequently asked questions to ensure anyone contacting Vodafone receives consistent, relevant, up-to-date information. We also reviewed all local operating company websites for consistent messaging.

We commissioned a major research study into public opinion in 18 countries. The study, conducted by MORI, surveyed 17,000 members of the public to understand levels of public concern and the reasons for it. It found that:

- RF is an important issue, but not a primary health concern. This low level of unprompted concern mirrors the findings seen in MORI's research for Vodafone in 2003.

- In most markets the majority believe that "there is no conclusive information regarding the effects of mobile phones and/or masts upon health".
- The single most important trigger leading to concern is information on health effects that people have gathered from the media.
- The public do not think that network operators are taking the RF issue seriously enough. Fewer than half in all markets (except Egypt) think any operator "takes its responsibilities for mobile phones, masts and health seriously".
- Many believe that the industry is withholding important information and many would view their operator more favourably if it proactively supplied information.

Summary of current and forthcoming research on RF and health

Radio frequency (RF) fields are generated by a wide variety of modern devices including mobile phones, TV remote controls and wireless security alarm systems. For the past 60 years, scientists have been monitoring the situation to see if exposure to RF fields at different frequencies has had any effect on human health.

The widespread use of mobile technology has caused particular scientific interest and extensive research has been conducted into the possible health effects of exposure to many parts of the frequency spectrum. As scientific evidence grows, some gaps in knowledge have now been widely addressed.

The World Health Organisation (WHO) concludes that "All reviews conducted so far have indicated that exposures below the limits recommended in the International Commission on Non-Ionizing Radiation Protection (ICNIRP) (1998) EMF guidelines, covering the full frequency range from 0–300 GHz, do not produce any known adverse health effect. However, there are gaps in knowledge that still need to be filled before better health risk assessments can be made." www.who.int/peh-emf/research.

Worldwide there has been a total investment of over US$250 million in scientific research on the possible health effects of EMF. The WHO will review the entirety of the RF field research data and report on its findings in two to three years.

Vodafone Group recognises and supports research aligned to the WHO priorities. We base our position and policies on the guidance of panels of experts considering peer-reviewed sources, conducted under the auspices of national or international health agencies, such as the WHO. While we rely on these experts' reviews, we also monitor new science published in peer-reviewed literature on an ongoing basis.

We will

- Set targets, track and report stakeholder opinion on how responsibly Vodafone is acting regarding mobile phones, masts and health by March 2007.

Future significant reviews and research

2006: INTERPHONE will analyse the totality of data from national studies in 13 countries in order to ascertain whether there is an association between mobile phone usage and an increase in the incidence of tumours of the head. The report is anticipated in late 2006.

2007: The International Agency for Research on Cancer (IARC) will conduct a review of the science leading to a formal classification of the cancer potential of RF fields. IARC routinely conduct reviews of materials in common use to provide scientific advice.

2008: The WHO RF health risk assessment will review the scientific evidence on all health outcomes arising from human exposure to RF fields. The IARC classification will be a key input.

This year our internal communications on health focused on raising appropriate awareness among customer-facing employees and top management teams in local operating companies as well as among employees in general. Some operating companies ran training programmes, for example Vodafone Egypt trained 80% of its employees.

We plan to continue building the level of internal knowledge of health issues by regularly communicating with employees through our employee magazines, intranet and internal TV channel.

Provided advice to customers who wish to reduce exposure to RF fields from their handsets

We published a set of guidelines that are consistent with WHO advice, and have posted these on the Vodafone Group website and on all local operating company websites. Retail and customer-facing staff have been informed about the guidelines and advised to direct customers and members of the public to them.

Increased availability of information on base station RF field strength values available for independently-selected locations

Last year we reported that 14 operating companies published these values on their own websites or provided data for publication by an independent organisation. In July 2005, Hungary started to publish independent field monitoring information and Japan continued with its trial. We extended this information in Portugal through home visits while in Italy the Borodoni Foundation funded a bus visiting places where there is public concern. Plans will be developed to make this information available in our newly acquired companies.

Facts about mobile handsets and health

Mobile phones work on the same principle as television and radio by using RF fields to communicate information. A mobile phone network requires a large number of base stations to connect calls to all our customers' handsets.

The handset RF power adjusts automatically to the minimum needed to communicate with the base station. Generally, the nearer the base station the lower the handset RF power.

When switched on but not in use, handsets send only brief infrequent signals to maintain contact with the network. These are made a few times every hour as a short transmission lasting just a couple of seconds.

Guidelines on field strength

When a person is exposed to an RF field it penetrates a few centimetres into the body and is absorbed as heat. This is measured using specific absorption rate (SAR) values.

The ICNIRP has issued guidelines for SAR values from handsets (measured in watts per kg). These set a maximum SAR value of two watts per kg. All handsets sold by Vodafone in 2005 have maximum SAR values between around 0.24 and 1.05 watts per kg when tested against the head and 0.25–1.94 watts per kg when tested against the body. The maximum value is only reached at the limits of reception, for example in rural or poor coverage areas and typical levels in use are lower. All handsets sold by Vodafone comply with the ICNIRP guidelines. SAR values for many handsets are available on the Mobile Manufacturers Forum site, www.mmfai.org/public/sar.cfm.

Led the industry in measuring RF exposure from equipment worn next to the body

Vodafone now requires manufacturers to test for specific absorption rate (SAR) compliance of their handsets when used against or near to the body. We are continuing to work with international standards bodies to establish global test protocols for new technology and device uses.

Continued to defend four legal actions in the United States

Vodafone, along with various other carriers and mobile phone manufacturers, is a defendant in four actions in the United States alleging personal injury, including brain cancer,

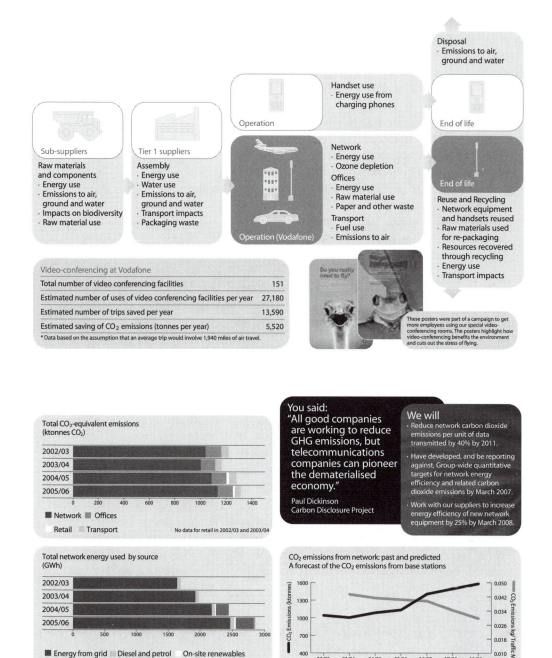

Figure 1 Environmental impacts of our operations: lifecycle diagram showing the direct and indirect impacts of our operations

from mobile phone use. These personal injury claims have not been substantiated and we will be vigorously defending them. For further information, see our Annual Report at www.vodafone.com.

A consequence of our business growth is increasing energy demand to run our network. This is one of Vodafone's most significant environmental impacts and limiting our contribution to climate change is therefore a priority. In partnership with equipment manufacturers we are improving the energy efficiency of our network so that data and voice can be transmitted with less climate impact.

In brief

- Decreased carbon dioxide emissions per unit of data transmitted by 10%.
- New Group target set to reduce carbon dioxide emissions per unit of data transmitted by 40% by 2011.
- Total energy use increased by 23% this year.
- Energy sourced from renewables increased by 22% this year.
- Local operating companies monitoring network energy use prior to setting local reduction targets.
- Working with suppliers to make network equipment more energy efficient.
- Onsite renewable energy technologies trialled.

Our operations fall into three main categories: networks (base station sites that send and receive radio frequency signals, switching centres and data centres to route calls and capture information); offices and call centres; and our retail outlets.

This section of the report focuses on one of our most significant environmental impacts – energy use associated with the operation of our network. This accounts for more than 85% of the carbon dioxide emissions from our total energy use (by our network, retail outlets, offices and transport).

Waste from our network and the reuse, recycling and disposal of used handsets are also significant issues (see page 218). Our other environmental impacts, such as ozone-depleting substances (mainly used in sealed network cooling systems), paper use and water use, are reported on our website.

Environmental impacts occur at every stage of the network equipment life-cycle. Vodafone has direct control over the operating and network equipment end-of-life stages. We use our influence to work with network equipment and mobile phone manufacturers to achieve more energy-efficient designs and to source materials and manufactured products in an environmentally responsible way.

We said

We would develop and report against Group-wide quantitative targets for network energy efficiency and related carbon dioxide emissions by March 2007.

We have

Used more energy

In the 2006 financial year, continuing business growth contributed to a 23% increase in our total energy use to 3,198 GWh. This resulted in a total of 1.31 million tonnes of carbon dioxide emissions, a 3% increase from the previous year. We are implementing a number of measures as part of our strategy to limit our impact on climate change (see below).

Average carbon dioxide emissions per subscriber from our network were approximately 9.55kg in the 2006 financial year, an 11% increase from 8.57kg the previous year. This is roughly equivalent to a single 60km journey in a modern family car with a 1.6 litre petrol engine.

Established a Group-wide target for network carbon dioxide emissions backed by local operating companies' programmes to improve energy measurement and forecasting

Our new 2011 target is to reduce network carbon dioxide emissions per unit of data transmitted (megabits of traffic) by 40%. Working towards this, in the 2006 financial year we expanded existing energy programmes in all local operating companies and intend to undertake a programme of energy audits, remote energy monitoring, energy forecasting and target setting by March 2007. This will increase data accuracy, which will help us identify further areas where we can reduce energy use and eliminate wastage.

Worked with suppliers at group level to improve energy efficiency of network equipment

Our goal is to increase efficiency by 25% compared with current network equipment by March 2008. While it is technically and financially impossible to replace all existing network equipment at once, a 25% improvement in the energy efficiency of all of our current equipment would save around 300,000 tonnes of carbon dioxide emissions, based on current levels. This saving is equivalent to the annual domestic electricity consumption of a city with a population of approximately 360,000.

We have identified the following ways to reduce energy use in base stations:

- Relocating the power source closer to the antenna to reduce power loss – this system (known as remote radio heads) reduces power requirements by 20%. We will begin to install this technology at our base stations next year and we are encouraging all our network equipment suppliers to offer remote radio heads.
- More efficient amplifiers – new power amplifiers will be 10% more energy efficient than the previous generation.
- Reducing the energy needed for cooling through a range of design improvements (see below).

Implemented more energy-efficient network cooling

Network cooling helps to extend the life of batteries and reduce the chance of network failure. Cooling accounts for an estimated 25% of energy used in our network. We are working on a number of initiatives to reduce energy used in cooling. Average energy consumption in some units can be cut by more than 10% (depending on the climate conditions on-site) by increasing the ambient temperature of our base stations from 21°C to 25°C.

In another initiative, Vodafone Germany has installed 1,555 base stations with free cooling since 2001. This system uses fresh air to cool network equipment, reducing the need for energy-intensive air conditioning. The estimated total energy consumption for these free cooling systems since installation is 12.3 MWh, 80% less than the estimated 69.5 MWh if the units were fitted with standard cooling systems. However, this 80% increase in efficiency is not possible in all base station units and can only be achieved in cool climates.

Vodafone Germany plans to install free cooling in 96 out of the 120 units planned for installation in the coming year. Other local operating companies are also developing plans to use free cooling and the Vodafone Group Supply Chain team is working with our global suppliers to find ways to increase equipment suitability to free cooling.

Green base station pilot in Greece

In the 2006 financial year, we created a pilot 'green' site in Greece to explore ways to reduce the costs and environmental impacts of producing power at our network sites. The continuously running diesel generator that powered the site was replaced by solar panels and a wind generator. A fuel cell was also installed to boost the power if there is not enough sunlight or wind.

The three-month trial showed that the system can work at sites with low power loads in remote locations. The system not only reduces environmental impacts but also significantly cuts maintenance costs. We are currently investigating how to use these green technologies at other sites.

Promoted renewable energy technologies

In remote locations not served by an electricity grid, on-site renewable electricity can be a viable alternative to diesel generators. For example, Vodafone Greece installed solar panels at 12 additional base stations in 2005/06, which have reduced generator running time by 60%. There are now 123 solar base stations in Greece and 70 in Egypt.

Renewable power from on-site sources accounts for 0.04% of the total energy used by our network. We buy a greater proportion of network energy from renewable generation sources via electricity grids. In the 2006 financial year, we sourced 30GWh of our grid energy from renewables. Together, on-site and grid renewables make up 10% of Vodafone's total network energy use.

Campaigned to increase video-conferencing among employees

Video-conferencing reduces the number of trips made by Vodafone employees and min-imises travel impacts such as climate change. There are video-conferencing facilities at all local operating companies and we have set up dedicated video-conferencing booths at Group headquarters and other key sites. In the 2006 financial year, we promoted the service among our employees and an estimated 2,265 video conferences were held per month, reducing transport-related emissions by approximately 460 tonnes per month (5,520 tonnes per year).

The fast pace of technology in the mobile phone industry means phones and networks rapidly become obsolete. Most handsets and network equipment can be reused or recycled into new materials and products. For example, refurbished handsets enable low-income customers to buy mobile phones relatively cheaply in emerging markets where mobile phone ownership is helping to drive economic development.

In brief

- Initiatives launched to raise awareness and encourage recycling.
- Recycling programmes established at all local operating companies.
- 1.37 million mobile phones collected for recycling.
- 97% of network equipment waste reused or recycled.

Consumers in high-income countries typically replace their mobile phones every 18 months. In Western Europe, over 145 million phones are sold each year, often to replace old phones still in good condition. If these phones (along with accessories such as batteries, chargers and headsets) are returned, we can arrange to refurbish many of them for reuse in lower-middle-income countries. This means more people can afford mobile

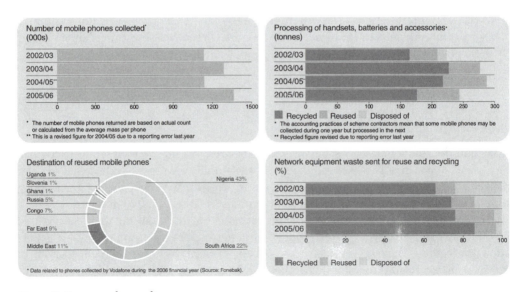

Figure 2 Reuse and recycling

phones and enjoy the social and economic benefits they bring. When a phone cannot be refurbished, it can be broken down into component parts for recycling.

We don't manufacture mobile phones or network equipment, but we are encouraging suppliers to design handsets that are easier to recycle and made from environmentally preferable materials. The Restriction of the use of certain Hazardous Substances in electrical and electronic equipment (RoHS) directive will come into force in July 2006. We continue to work with suppliers to phase out the substances restricted by the directive.

Our fully owned and operated stores and franchise retail stores place us in a good position to collect used handsets when a new phone is sold. We have recovery programmes covering all local operating companies with collection points in all of our offices and the majority of our fully owned retail stores. We continue to expand our return programmes into our franchised stores. The success of these schemes relies on consumers handing in their used mobile phones. Currently only a small proportion of phones are returned to us – millions of handsets are lying unused in people's drawers and cupboards. We have conducted research to help us understand why consumers do not return these phones and have introduced incentives to encourage consumer handset recycling.

We said

- We would have return schemes in all our operating companies by March 2007.
- We would increase the number of phones collected by 50% by March 2007.
- We would actively support development of programmes in at least three developing countries to repair, reuse and recycle mobile phones by March 2007.
- We would continue to send for reuse or recycling 95% of network equipment waste during the year from April 2005 to March 2006.

We have

Established a handset return scheme in all local operating companies

Recycling schemes are now in place at all of our local operating companies, implemented through Vodafone offices and the majority of our owned and operated retail shops, one year ahead of our target. We introduced a return scheme this year at Vodafone Albania, the only operating company without a recycling programme already in place. We launched a campaign to raise awareness among employees in Albania that included training for retail and call centre staff to encourage consumers to return their phones.

How to recycle a base station

Advances in telecommunications technology mean we often need to replace network equipment at our base stations. We resell used equipment where possible, or recycle it through recycling partners such as Shields Environmental.

At the end of a base station's useful life, Shields technicians identify and test the parts that can be sold for reuse. Vodafone's used network equipment makes modern technology affordable to network operators in emerging and developing countries, helping to improve communication in these countries.

Equipment that cannot be resold is broken down into separate materials for recycling. The first step in recycling is to identify and remove any hazardous substances from the equipment. Materials from lead acid batteries are separated to produce bullion (which can be refined into lead alloys), gypsum and a copolymer that can be sold. The remaining materials (acids) are neutralised. Some components contain the hazardous material beryllium oxide which cannot be recycled at present. Shields has a zero landfill policy, so it is storing the beryllium oxide safely while it works with other organisations to find a way to recycle this material.

The remaining non-hazardous materials are then separated. Cardboard, aluminium and steel are recycled and returned to productive use; plastics are incinerated to produce energy; circuit boards are sent to a specialist refiner to recover precious metals including palladium, copper, gold and silver. Vodafone receives a share of the revenue from the sale of these precious metals.

You said

"Reusing phones increases access to communications in emerging economies. The industry must increase handset returns and Vodafone's 50% increase target is very welcome."

James Goodman

Forum for the Future

We will

- Increase the number of phones collected for reuse and recycling by 50% by March 2007 (from the 2004/05 level).
- Support development of programmes in at least three developing countries to repair, reuse and recycle mobile phones by March 2007.
- Send for reuse and recycling 95% of network equipment waste during 2007 financial year.

Raising awareness among employees

Our internal recycling campaign encourages employees to hand in their old handsets, highlighting the environmental and social benefits of reusing and recycling phones.

Collected 1.37 million phones for reuse and recycling

In the 2006 financial year we collected 1.37 million phones for reuse and recycling. This is a 20% increase on last year's figure and we are making progress towards our challenging target to increase the number of phones collected by 50% by March 2007. Although the number of phones collected through our own return programmes is increasing relatively slowly, this does not mean that old phones are all going to waste. Many phones are recycled through other schemes, for example those associated with charities.

In our European markets the Waste Electronic and Electrical Equipment (WEEE) directive requires companies to take back and recycle electronic and electrical equipment. We have handset recycling programmes in place at all our EU companies in 10 countries to comply with the directive. We have also worked with our suppliers of electronic and electrical equipment to ensure that the appropriate labelling is provided on products sold through Vodafone.

Continued to support reuse and recycling in emerging and developing countries

Developing countries often do not have the skills or infrastructure to deal with handset waste safely. We are making good progress towards our target to support handset recycling programmes in at least three emerging and developing countries by March 2007. We have launched programmes in Egypt and Albania and are in the process of setting up a scheme in Romania. The phones are collected through our fully owned stores in these countries and will be sent for recycling.

In the 2006 financial year, we commissioned research by the NGO Forum for the Future into environmental and waste management capacity and mobile phone recycling in emerging economies. The research will assess existing facilities in several African countries, as well as looking at how consumer behaviour affects mobile phone recycling. The project aims to identify how to increase capacity for recycling used mobile phones and how Vodafone and other companies can contribute.

Offered incentives to encourage handset recycling

Many consumers are reluctant to hand in their old phones. We have focused on promoting recycling and making it easy for consumers to return their phones. Our research in Australia and the UK found that offering charity donations or financial incentives encourages people to recycle.

These are some of the ways our local operating companies encouraged handset recycling in the 2006 financial year:

- Vodafone Germany donated €5 to wildlife charity NABU for every handset returned as part of a four-year partnership with the conservation organisation.
- Vodafone Ireland donated all proceeds from recycled handsets to the Conservation Volunteers Ireland Nature Fund, which funds environmental projects around the country.
- Vodafone Italy piloted a programme at retail outlets in four regions offering customers free air time or points if they returned their old phone. Around 9,400 handsets have been collected in these regions since the trial was launched in October 2005, increasing the average number of phones collected at each point of sale from five to 40 per month. The campaign will be extended to all stores in Italy in the 2006 financial year.

Raised awareness of handset recycling among employees

We ran a campaign to encourage employees to hand in their phones for recycling or reuse. We published an article in the employee magazine and produced videos, posters and other promotional material. The campaign highlighted the environmental and social benefits of reusing and recycling phones. The campaign was particularly successful in New Zealand, where more than 2,300 phones were handed in by the 1,300 employees within two weeks.

Promoted handset recycling for corporate customers

We have programmes in Australia, Ireland, Italy, Japan, the Netherlands, Spain and the UK to help our corporate customers increase handset recycling. We supported campaigns to raise awareness among their employees and provided returns bins and freepost envelopes. In the UK, for example, funds generated from recycling are donated either to Vodafone's selected charity or to the customer's chosen charity. In the 2006 financial year, we collected over 200,000 phones from corporate customers in these seven countries.

Continued to participate in the mobile phone partnership initiative (MPPI)

Vodafone is participating in the MPPI, part of the UN Basel Convention on waste. It brings together mobile phone companies, waste and recycling experts, and NGOs. The MPPI has four project groups that are developing guidelines on phone refurbishment and collection, materials recovery and recycling, awareness raising and environmentally responsible design.

Reused or recycled 97% of network equipment waste

We produced 2,950 tonnes of equipment waste in our network in the 2006 financial year. This includes 1,804 tonnes of non-hazardous waste (such as radio equipment, metal and cables) and 1,146 tonnes of hazardous waste (mostly lead acid batteries). Of this, 2,849 tonnes were sent for reuse or recycling, exceeding our ongoing commitment of 95%. Other waste streams where we do not have reliable data include wood, concrete and some plastics.

Cadbury Schweppes

2006 CSR REPORT
Our CSR vision and strategy

C ADBURY SCHWEPPES IS committed to growing responsibly. We believe responsible business comes from listening and learning, and having in place a clear CSR vision and strategy. It also comes from having the processes and systems to follow through and an embedded commitment to living our values.

Our business vision: working together to create brands people love

'Working together to create brands people love' is at the heart of our Purpose and Values statement. For us, it captures the positive, collaborative aspects of doing business and recognises the emotion, attachment and values associated with our brands.

In the past few years, like many other companies, we have been thinking again about what it means to act responsibly in a changing world. We have introduced new policies and new systems to meet the changing expectations that society has of business. New thinking and innovation have strengthened our approach and this has proved an enduring point of difference for Cadbury Schweppes.

We see CSR as a positive contributor to our competitive strategy. Increasingly we think of it as more about doing responsible things profitably than just doing the profitable things responsibly.

Our CSR strategy

It is acting responsibly that has allowed us to grow and create enduring value for shareowners. It is the desire to continue acting responsibly that has led us to drive new energy and thinking into our CSR strategy and what we call our Five Pillars of CSR: marketing, food and consumer issues; ethical sourcing and procurement;

environment, health and safety; human rights and employment standards; and community investment.

We have renewed our goals and commitments for responsible business growth. They set the scene for the next stage of our CSR journey, and we call them our '*Goals and Commitments on Sustainability.*' There are specific goals and commitments for each Pillar and you can find them described on page 227.

All the pillars are firmly underpinned by our commitment to good governance and *Our Business Principles*.

Our business principles

We take our ethical business practices very seriously and have defined our commitment to these in *Our Business Principles*. They describe the high standards of conduct we set for ourselves and act as a guide for turning our values into action. The principles take into account global standards, such as the Universal Declaration of Human Rights and the International Labour Organisation conventions. Please visit our corporate website to read a full copy of *Our Business Principles* at www.cadburyschweppes.com

We expect each employee to uphold our ethical business practices. Every manager receives an annual communication on the principles and each is expected to be responsible for ensuring the same behaviour of those they manage. We ask our managers to sign up to *Our Business Principles*, which includes affirming that they have communicated the principles to their staff. In 2006, we used an electronic IT communication and sign-up process for our senior executives. Our Human Resources department confirms sign-up by our senior executives to our Group Company Secretary and the Chief Executive's Committee.

We asked the Sustainability Team at Deloitte & Touche LLP (Deloitte) to provide assurance on our 2005 and 2006 communication and sign-up process and for sign-up of our 160 most senior executives in 2005.

Our commitment to ethical business practices is underpinned by our global confidential *Speaking Up* process and helpline run by a third party organisation. Through *Speaking Up* colleagues from around the world can raise any concerns they have related to ethical business practices.

Shared responsibility for CSR

At Cadbury Schweppes we all take responsibility for realising the Company's vision and strategy, but it begins at the top. Championing CSR requires leadership both internally within our own organisation and externally where our history and heritage, combined with our strong market position, means that we are well placed to offer that leadership.

Our Board Corporate and Social Responsibility Committee addresses all key aspects of CSR. It has been chaired since its inception by Baroness Wilcox, one of our non-executive directors.

CSR issues also regularly feature on the agenda of the Chief Executive's Committee (CEC) and the Board. Senior steering and working groups oversee and review progress. At a Group level, these groups are:

- Food Issues Strategy Group and Food Issues Strategy into Action Group
- Environment Health and Safety Steering Group
- Human Rights and Ethical Trading Working Group
- Diversity and Inclusiveness Leadership Team
- The Cadbury Schweppes Foundation (which reviews corporate giving)
- Compliance Steering Group

CSR risks and opportunities are also taken into account through our *Business Risk Review Process* and through our annual *Business Contract Process*.

At Cadbury Schweppes it is the job of our management teams throughout our business to bring these commitments to CSR to life at local level and to embed them within the fabric and day-to-day operation of the business.

Our approach to CSR

Values, principles, systems and processes alone are not enough to ensure continued commitment and progress. We constantly look to learn from and better understand the world around us. We share what we learn across our businesses and use it to inform our collective thinking and decision making. We continue to embed this learning in our plans and activities, our business systems and processes.

We recognise that the world is constantly changing and that there will be new CSR challenges and opportunities. We also know we will have to tackle long-standing issues in new ways.

To help us do this, we draw on the collective experience of our colleagues throughout the business. The input of the non-executive directors of Cadbury Schweppes has been particularly helpful. We benchmark ourselves against peers and competitors. We learn from leading companies in other business sectors. We listen to the concerns of NGOs and local communities. And we contribute to and learn from outside organisations such as Forum for the Future, The Corporate Citizenship Company, Business for Social Responsibility, Business in the Community, the Institute of Business Ethics and the International Business Leaders' Forum.

We take an active leadership role in cross-country industry key initiatives such as the International Cocoa Initiative, the Roundtable on Sustainable Palm Oil and the International Business Leaders' Forum, Healthy Eating and Active Lifestyle (HEAL) programme.

The success of each business unit depends upon understanding its consumers and the communities it serves. Our regions and local companies must look to live our CSR values in ways that make sense for their business and brands, and to the needs of their local community.

Embedding CSR

Between 2001 and 2003 we established clear CSR policies and commitments. We built processes to support *Our Business Principles* and we strengthened those of our programmes which focus on sourcing and community, and on ethical marketing and consumer impact. We established measures for our CSR performance. Over this time we have evolved a number of tools and building blocks, the first of which was our Five Pillars of CSR. We report our progress against each of these pillars in the pages that follow.

The Responsibility Pyramid

As we continue to embed CSR practice within the organisation, we have recognised some important strategic levels [the Responsibility Pyramid]. Straightforward risk avoidance is the first step of most companies' journey in CSR, and we are progressing beyond simple reputation enhancement and issue management. We believe that acting responsibly will fuel sustainable growth and advantage for our brands and see CSR as a positive contributor to our competitive strategy.

Living our Values – leadership imperatives

In our Leadership Imperatives programme for managers we include an important section on *Living our Values*. This highlights the values and behaviours we expect of our people in our businesses around the world and ensures our CSR agenda is embedded into local plans.

We ask our people to put Cadbury Schweppes' values into action in the things they do and say every day. We expect all of our people to recognise and value the full range of individual contributions, ideas and cultures and work with them to create maximum value for the organisation and its stakeholders.

We expect all of our managers to live up to our values and assessment of performance in this area is included in our individual performance reviews each year. Increasingly we have come to view CSR as providing a set of essential guiding principles and valuable ways of working.

Assurance

Assurance is an important milestone on our journey. It helps affirm that our policies are durable and that we have the systems and processes in place to deliver our business responsibly. It also helps us manage our performance and inform our decision-making.

We have started our assurance journey by asking the Sustainability Team at Deloitte to provide assurance on key areas of our CSR programme:

- Our Business Principles
- Ethical Sourcing
- Environment, Health and Safety
- Employee Climate Survey
- Community Investment
- CSR report compilation process

. . . For the future we plan to develop a broader and deeper assurance programme of continuous improvement and performance measurement.

Table 1 Our goals and commitments on sustainability 2006–2010

	GOAL	COMMITMENTS (BY 2010 – GLOBALLY – WE WILL . . .)	
Marketing, Food, Consumer	● Contribute to consumer diet, health and lifestyle solutions.	● Improve nutritional labelling information for consumers including responsible consumption messaging, and support initiatives that promote physical activity.	● Increase product choices for consumers including reduced fat, sugar and salt alternatives, for core brands.
Ethical Sourcing	● Maintain ethical sourcing standards, and develop sustainable agriculture programmes.	● Ensure our suppliers meet our ethical sourcing standards.	● Sustainably source at least half of our key agricultural raw materials, such as cocoa, sugar, palm oil, and gum arabic, for core brands.
Environment, Health and Safety	● Minimise the environmental impacts of our business, and embed a zero accident culture.	● Develop reliance on renewable energy, reduce use of carbon-based fuels, and use 100% recoverable or biodegradable packaging.	● Achieve top quartile performance for workplace health and safety.
Human Rights and Employment Standards	● Nurture our Company as 'The Place to Be', where diverse colleagues are proud to work, and are committed and engaged.	● Consistently achieve top quartile Employee Climate survey results.	● Attain 25% female representation in our executive management.
Community	● Help create prosperous, educated, inclusive and healthy communities.	● Contribute at least 1% pre-tax profit for Community Investment as a group and per region, year on year.	● Build on and develop partnerships across the business to help address global social, economic, and environmental concerns linked to the Millennium Development Goals.

What others say about our CSR performance

Our CSR performance is rated by various external indices and this helps us assess how we are progressing. Indices include:

- **Dow Jones Sustainability World Index.** In 2005 we scored 73%, up from 71% in 2004. Our scores have gradually increased since our initial participation in 2001, reflecting our progress.
- **FTSE4Good.** We are included in this index which measures the performance of companies that meet globally recognised CSR standards.
- **Business in the Community Corporate Responsibility Index.** In 2005, our overall score was 92.5%, up from 89% in 2004, 87% in 2003, and 73% in 2002.
- **Carbon Disclosure Project (CDP).** In 2005 CDP's annual Climate Leadership Index of Fortune 500 companies included Cadbury Schweppes in the top 60 companies highlighted as global leaders in carbon management.

Case Study

Making it real: Integrating CSR strategy in Cadbury Schweppes Americas Beverages

In May 2004, Cadbury Schweppes Americas Beverages formed a CSR Council of senior leaders representing each of our five pillars of CSR and the different geographies and functions of the business. The aim of the Council is to align the regional approach with that of the overall Group and to embed CSR into the business, taking account of local market conditions. Following a strategic review of existing CSR activities and consulting widely with colleagues, the Council set out a new approach for working with customers, suppliers, communities, colleagues, and the environment. The Council reports progress to its Regional Leadership Team on a quarterly basis.

Christian Aid

LIVING ITS VALUES
Coca-Cola in India

At the heart of our business is the trust consumers place in us. They rightly expect that we are managing our business according to sound ethical principles, that we are enhancing the health of our communities, and that we are using natural resources responsibly.

> (Douglas N. Daft, Coca-Cola chairman and chief executive)[1]

SITTING AT THE factory gates, villagers from Plachimada in the southern Indian state of Kerala wait patiently for a change of heart from the mighty multinational Coca-Cola as its delivery vehicles trundle back and forth.

Through the crushing heat of the day and the oppressive dark of the night they sit, and have done for more than a year. Members of their community pass by, some stop to give support or food. The sitters sacrifice their vital working time and scant resources to keep hammering home their message: Coca-Cola, the factory's owner, is depriving them of one of their most basic human rights – water.[2]

Mylama, a 55-year-old woman, leads the protest. She says that rainfall has been scarce for the past two years. 'But the availability of water in the well has no relation to rain,' she insists. 'Even when we had less rain before the company came, we still had no shortage of water.'

Another protestor, 64-year-old Shahul Hameed, has been farming since he was born and his land runs up to the Coca-Cola factory confines. 'According to my traditional measures, the water in my well used to be 22 mola[3] deep. Now it's only one mola deep,' he says. 'I was able to run my pump for 14 hours every day. Now it will only run for 30 minutes. That shows you how my agriculture has suffered.'

As they sit, day after day, the community's water is drawn up from the ground by the factory's pumps and processed by its machinery into cola, other fizzy drinks and even, ironically, a carbonated water called 'Kinley'. It then leaves the factory in bottles on the back of trucks. From Plachimada it is transported to Indian towns and cities where it is bought by those who can afford bottled water. From the wells of Mylama and Shahul, to the tables of the urban elites, courtesy of Coca-Cola.

It's not just people from the local community who are angry and claim that Coca-Cola is threatening livelihoods. A retired hydrologist, Dr Achuthan Avittathoor, who lives in Kerala and has investigated the impact of the Coca-Cola factory on the surrounding communities' water, says: 'I want the truth. I am not against Coca-Cola. But it's about priorities. When there is a shortage of drinking water, this must come first.'

Coca-Cola maintains that it is not depleting ground water in Kerala. In a statement emailed to Christian Aid, the company blamed lower-than-usual rainfall in the past two years for the lowering of the villagers' wells. But the company's arguments have not impressed the High Court of Kerala. In December 2003, it ruled that Coca-Cola must stop drawing ground water from Plachimada and gave the company one month to find an alternative source of water.[4] Coca-Cola plans to appeal against this decision.

Coca-Cola says it is fully committed to corporate social responsibility. Its citizenship report, *Living Our Values*, reviews the company's 'initiatives and accomplishments as a corporate citizen', and opens with the words: 'The Coca-Cola company exists to benefit and refresh everyone it touches. *This is our promise* [their italics].'

In India, where it has operated since 1993, Coca-Cola also, significantly, boasts that 'several of our bottling plants provide safe drinking water to local villagers through the organisation of water tankers, bore wells and hand pumps.'[5] But at Plachimada, according to those who sit outside the plant, the values the company is living are not those it lauds in its public statements. The company's 'promise' to 'refresh everyone it touches' has, they say, both literally and figuratively been broken.

Since the Coca-Cola factory opened in 2000, however, people living in the surrounding villages have complained that their wells are almost empty, when previously there had been enough water for everyone. Their claims threaten to make a mockery of Coca-Cola's statement that: 'We will conduct our business in ways that protect and preserve the environment. We will integrate principles of environmental stewardship and sustainable development into our business decisions and processes.'[6]

Although water levels in some wells were dropping before Coke opened its gates, the factory's heavy use of water has, according to people living and farming near the factory, exacerbated the situation and made their lives dramatically more difficult. Many local women now spend much of their day walking to and from distant wells to collect water for drinking, cooking and bathing because nearby water sources have dried up. Most of the 1,200 or so people who live around the factory gates have been affected.

When Dr Avittathoor visited the plant and saw the size of its wells, he estimated the company could use 1,100 cubic metres of water per day. Coca-Cola says the Plachimada plant pumps an average of 400 cubic metres a day and that it was told by the state of Kerala that it could draw up to 880 cubic metres per day.[7]

Oamjie John, a former Jesuit priest who now works as an activist in Kerala, says that the local wells are not only supplied by the immediate rainfall, but also by the aquifer, deep reserves of water which are fed by rainfall over thousands of years. These reserves would not, claims John, have dropped substantially after just two years of unusually poor rainfall – unless they were being depleted in other ways.

Local people also say that the quality of the water left in the wells has deteriorated. It has an unpleasant taste and chalky consistency, making it undrinkable and useless even for cooking. Vasanda, a 15-year-old tailor, says that rice cooked in water from the village well now becomes hard and unusable within a few hours, whereas traditionally the food would be prepared in the morning and kept until the evening meal, when it was still fresh and good to eat. 'I can't cook with the water from the wells. I have to get water from two kilometres away,' she says.

Worse still, many of those in communities surrounding the bottling plant told Christian Aid the same story during its investigation: while the water used to be fine to drink, now what is left at the bottom of their wells gives them severe stomach pains and headaches.

A study conducted by the district medical officer at a local health centre has confirmed the villagers' suspicions about water quality. It concludes: 'This water is unfit for drinking and the people should be made aware of that.' It also includes the opinion of a water analyst: 'The hardness and chloride [level] of the water is very high. The water is unfit for drinking purposes.'[8]

Water samples have also been analysed by Dr Mark Chernaik, a biochemist from Environmental Law Alliance Worldwide (E-Law) – a network of American lawyers, scientists and environmental experts working to promote environmental protection. He found high levels of dissolved salts in the water, commensurate with rapid depletion of the aquifer.

'Water from the two wells would be classified as "very hard",' says Dr Chernaik. In his report, he concludes that: 'Use of this water for bathing and washing would cause severe nuisance and hardship.'[9]

Refreshing Plachimada

> We believe that being part of communities around the world is a privilege; one we must earn every day by making responsible, effective decisions and investments that benefit our company and our communities alike.[10]
>
> (Coca-Cola citizenship report 2002)

While maintaining that it is not depleting the ground water, Coca-Cola has confirmed to Christian Aid that it is currently bringing water into the Plachimada plant from other sources. 'We took a conscious decision not to put stress on water sources at a single location and decided to source water from surplus areas,' said a company statement.[11]

Coca-Cola has also acknowledged – albeit by implication – that the surrounding villages have a problem; it has been paying for tankers to distribute drinking water to the area. This water comes from surrounding villages within four to five miles of Plachimada. According to Mumbai-based Christian Aid partner Vikas Adhyayan Kendra (VAK), which has been supporting the protest outside Coke's gates, no survey has been conducted to ascertain whether people in these villages are also suffering water shortages.

Arychami Krishnan, president of the *panchayat* – the village-level council serving the area – is more vociferous about the company's attempts to provide the communities living around the bottling plant with emergency water. 'These are just symbolic gestures,' he says. 'They don't distribute this water evenly. Some get more, some get less. This just creates a division.'

Villagers add that the water from the company does not come on a regular basis and, therefore, cannot be relied upon, even though Coca-Cola says its tankers visit the communities daily. There are also complaints that when water is provided, it is in insufficient quantities. Mylama, leader of the sit-down protest, says that only six to seven litres per person is distributed, compared with the minimum of 15 litres needed for drinking, cooking, washing and sanitation per person, per day.[12]

Coke has publicly dismissed the protests and vigils of local people as the agitation of Marxists. This allegation was at one time posted on Coca-Cola India's website, but following international media interest, has now been removed.[13] However, in its statement to Christian Aid, the company, while keen to point out that it is 'sympathetic to the plight of the local community accessing water at a time of shortage in rainfall', said: 'The small number of protestors and their organisers are self-declared Marxists and communists and they are dealing with what they perceive to be a high-profile, American "capitalist" company.'

Villagers say that even during previous droughts, they did not run short of water and that water quality did not suffer in the way that it has since the bottling plant opened. However, there is no reliable historical data for water usage, quality or depletion that can substantiate their claims. It is now difficult to gauge empirically to what extent Coca-Cola is to blame for the fall in water levels.

The only study carried out in the area prior to the opening of the plant was an environmental impact assessment (EIA), conducted by Hindustan Coca-Cola itself. However, despite local organisations' persistent requests for a copy, the company has failed to produce one. Such a failure, states one lawyer, is illegal because according to the Kerala government, EIAs are public documents.[14]

Christian Aid asked Coca-Cola if it could see the EIA and was told that the document was part of a larger, commercially sensitive paper that the company was not prepared to copy. After several requests, Coca-Cola faxed a document to Christian Aid entitled *Report on the Integrated Groundwater Surveys Conducted in the Coca-Cola Factory Site at Moolathara, Chitoor Taluk, Pallakkad District, Kerala State*. The document is not dated.

Coca-Cola also says that it harvests rainwater and usually returns around 50 per cent of the water it uses. The company blames the *panchayat* for blocking its plans to expand rainwater harvesting. However, Dr Avittathoor challenges this reasoning. 'The company claims that it is putting back into the aquifer through water harvesting. But whereas the pumping is from the deep aquifer, the recharge water goes to the gravity zone [the sub-soil level]. Therefore, pumping causes depletion of groundwater continuously,' he says.

'Conduct beyond question'

> Our business is built on relationships – relationships based on respect for each other, for our partners, for the communities where we do business and for the environment.
>
> (Douglas N. Daft, Coca-Cola chairman and chief executive)

The Palakkad district in which the plant is situated has long been known as the 'rice chest' of Kerala. In the past, it has produced 35 per cent of the state's rice. Coconuts, ground-nuts and okra, as well as rice, have all been farmed there for generations, the work mostly carried out by the poorest people in Indian society – around 60 per cent of those living in the district are *adivasis*, or tribals.

This famed fertility has endured in spite of the area's historically low rainfall compared with the rest of lush Kerala. Palakkad lies in a region known as a 'rainshadow' where

Coke adds life

'The esteem in which Coca-Cola bottlers, customers, consumers, share owners, employees, suppliers and communities hold our company – even when we falter – speaks to the strength of our principles as business assets.'

Douglas N. Daft, Coca-Cola chairman and chief executive

Coca-Cola not only faces allegations and protests from local people angry at the depletion of their water supplies, it now stands accused of selling toxic waste from the factory – what the company calls 'biosolids' – to local farmers, billing it as fertiliser. Farmers using the waste have complained of skin infections and sores – as well as poor crop yield.

During a recent BBC investigation,[15] however, samples of the waste were taken to the UK and analysed by the University of Exeter. They were found to contain dangerous levels of carcinogen, cadmium and lead. David Santillo of the University of Exeter says the results are very worrying: 'The presence of high levels of lead and cadmium is of particular concern. Lead is particularly noted for its ability to damage the developing nervous system. Cadmium is especially toxic to the kidney, but also to the liver – it is classified as a known human carcinogen.'

Following the BBC's findings, the Kerala State Pollution Control Board (KSPCB) ordered a new study to be carried out on the waste and the well water. It found that, while cadmium and lead levels were not, in its view, hazardous, the waste should not be used as fertiliser.

However, as activist Oamjie John points out, the cadmium levels found in the samples the second time they were tested by the KSPCB (36.5mg per kg of dry weight) are significantly lower than the levels the chair of the KSPCB, Paul Thatchil, announced in August 2003 (202 mg per kg). 'This is a very large difference within just a couple of months,' says John.

Coca-Cola denies its 'biosolids' are toxic, although the company does not deny that they do contain both cadmium and lead 'within the limits prescribed by the State Pollution Control Board [in Kerala]'. However, following the BBC's investigation, the company stopped distributing them as fertiliser because of 'concerns in the minds of some of the local community'. Coca-Cola says it will now dispose of the 'biosolids' by treating them as hazardous waste.[16]

precipitation is notoriously scarce. But now, since the Coca-Cola factory opened, crops have failed and jobbing agricultural labourers have been forced further afield to look for employment.

Ajit Muricken of Christian Aid partner organisation VAK believes the damage caused by the factory's water extraction will take a long time to put right. 'It takes many years for coconut trees to reach the stage when they yield,' he says. 'The lack of water is very likely to seriously affect the livelihoods of marginalised farmers for years to come.'

Even the State Ground Water Department of Kerala, which attributed the depletion of some of Plachimada's open wells to 'below normal rainfall in the area', noted: 'Since there is a drastic fall in rainfall, it is necessary to restrict the exploitation of groundwater at least till the status has improved.'[17] In others words, at the very least it is inappropriate for Hindustan Coca-Cola to be extracting water when people living around the factory have insufficient to drink.

The Keralan government actively encouraged Coca-Cola to open a plant in Plachimada, giving the company a 15 per cent rebate on its capital investment of Rs80 crore (£10m), because Palakkad is a poor, or 'backward', area. Such incentives have proved successful in attracting foreign investors. According to UN figures, flows of foreign direct investment in India rose from US$0.4bn in 1990 to US$5.5bn in 2002.[18] Coca-Cola says it has invested more than US$1bn in India since 1993, making it one of the top investors in the country.

But a court action against Coke by the tiny *panchayat* of Palakkad is threatening one of the company's major investments in India – the Plachimada bottling plant. The Kerala High Court's ruling that Coca-Cola can no longer draw ground water from the area will come as a serious blow to the company and will cast doubt over the future of the plant. The court's ruling also challenges the company's statements that it has not contributed to the depletion of ground water and the findings of a report commissioned by the company and carried out by a retired scientist from the National Geophysical Research Institute in Hyderabad. The report claims there is: 'No field evidence of overexploitation of the groundwater reserves in the plant area.'[19]

Dr Achuthan Avittathoor is clear how water should be used when it is scarce. 'In times of shortage, the priority must be domestic need, then small industry, then essential large industries, and the non-essential industries must come last,' he says.

Perhaps Coca-Cola, and its subsidiary in Kerala, would do well to heed the company's own fine words. As Stephen J Heyer, Coca-Cola's president and chief operating officer, says in its 'Citizenship Report': 'Our goal as leaders is to unlock the enormous reservoir of talent, capability and passion that resides in the people of this system – to tear down the barriers that prevent us from working together in a collaborative environment to make great things happen for all of us.'

Notes

1   http://www2.coca-cola.com/citizenship/index.html.
2   The plant is owned by Coca-Cola's wholly owned Indian subsidiary Hindustan Coca-Cola Beverages Private Limited (HCCBL).
3   A traditional measure. One mola is approximately the length from fingertips to elbow.
4   BBC World Service News, 16 December 2003.
5   http://www2.coca.cola.com/ourcompany/cfs/cfs_include/cfs_india_include.html, accessed in July 2003. The Coca-Cola website for India has now been radically changed.
6   *Living our values*, Coca-Cola Citizenship Report, 2002.
7   Coca-Cola email to Christian Aid, 17 December 2003.
8   The report analysed water samples taken from three wells near the factory. Report dated 13 May 2003.
9   *Interpretation of results of water sample analysis performed by Laboratory Services Division of Sargam Metalas Private Ltd*, Dr Mark Chernaik, US environmental NGO E-Law, 5 March, 2002. Chernaik also consulted Phil Richerson, a hydrologist with the Oregon Department of Environmental Quality.

10   *Living our values*, Coca-Cola Citizenship Report, 2002.

11   Coca-Cola email to Christian Aid, 17 December 2003.

12   15 litres of fresh water per person per day is generally considered to be a necessary minimum to meet drinking and sanitation needs alone according to the Sphere Project's *Humanitarian Charter and Minimum Standards in Disaster Response* handbook.

13   The new Coca-Cola website for India can be accessed at http://www.myenjoyzone.com/index1.php3.

14   *Notification Requiring Environmental Impact Assessment for certain projects in Kerala*, issued by the government of Kerala, 13 January 1978.

15   *Face the Facts*, broadcast 25 July, 2003, BBC Radio 4. http://news.bbc.co.uk/2/hl/south_asia/3096893.stm.

16   Coca-Cola email to Christian Aid, 17 December 2003.

17   *Report on the ground water extraction in the Coca-Cola factory, Plachimada, Palakkad district and water level trends in the area*, Ground Water Department, government of Kerala, January 2003.

18   However, during the same period foreign direct investment flows to China rose from US$3.5bn to US$52.7bn, and several liberal commentators, including the IMF, want foreign direct investment to be deregulated much faster in India. There are still strict ownership rules, for instance foreign ownership of between 51 per cent and 100 per cent of equity still requires a long procedure of government approval.

19   *Water management at the Coca Cola plant at Moolathara village, Palakkad district, Kerala State, India*, RN Athavale, National Geophysical Research Institute (Hyderabad, India, October 2002).

csrnetwork

CSR REPORTING – EXAMINING THE UNPALATABLE ISSUES

'Until food sector companies start to address corporate responsibility issues in a balanced and meaningful way, rather than just another positive PR opportunity, the trust they are seeking will remain elusive.'

RESEARCH BY CORPORATE social responsibility consultancy csrnetwork has taken an in-depth look at how major food companies and food retailers approach corporate accountability, providing some revealing insights into what is, and is not, recorded in their annual reports.

By analysing the social, environmental and economic impacts that face producers and retailers, through independent research and through its Accountability Rating, csrnetwork concludes that until food sector companies start to address corporate responsibility issues in a balanced and meaningful way, the trust they are seeking will remain elusive.

The research reveals, for example, that at first glance Tesco's Corporate Responsibility Review 2003/04 looks impressive – but upon closer examination has some clear gaps. Although McDonald's stands out as covering a high percentage of relevant issues in its 2004 Worldwide Corporate Responsibility Report, it achieves a relatively low score in the Accountability Rating, developed by csrnetwork and AccountAbility.

Furthermore, only three food sector companies covered in csrnetwork's Accountability Rating of the world's largest 100 companies produced reports that were subject to independent assurance.

"Interest and concerns in the foods that we eat are increasing rapidly," says csrnetwork director Jon Woodhead. "The chain of responsibility is coming under intense scrutiny – the stores where we buy the food, how food has been produced, what has gone into the food, what effects the food will have on us.

"Clearly the issues most relevant to a company will vary according to their role as a producer, manufacturer or retailer, but there is increasing pressure for companies to look up and down the supply chain 'from farm to fork' to demonstrate their responsibilities", he continues.

"At the centre of these concerns is the issue of 'trust' – who can consumers trust to meet their expectations? All companies have long understood that trust is central to financial success, but when you take a close look at the ingredients of their glossy corporate social responsibility reports, the 'recipe' adopted by different companies to achieve this trust is highly variable, and in many cases actively avoids the unpalatable issues."

The scores achieved by the majority of companies assessed using the Accountability Rating, make sober reading, compared to the glossy, upbeat tone set by most corporate reports.

Out of the food sector companies in the G-100 (the world's 100 largest companies), Unilever scored highest overall with a score of 53%, closely followed by Carrefour with 52%. Another six companies then scored between 19% and 37%, with the remaining three companies scoring 6% and below. In other words, only two companies scraped above 50%, and the rest were even further behind. Well-known brands outside the G-100 did not fare any better either: Coca-Cola achieved an overall score of 31% and McDonald's 28%, the only notable exception being Danisco – the Danish food ingredients company, with a relatively high score of 51%.

Within these results, there are some revealing insights into some companies' approach to corporate accountability. For example, only three companies, Unilever, Danisco and Coca-Cola, produce annual reports on their corporate responsibility performance that are subject to independent assurance (a third party scrutiny of data and claims).

"This speaks volumes about the willingness of food sector companies to accept the challenge of transparency and the need to move beyond mere PR towards honest accountability," observes Jon.

Under the 'strategic intent' area of the scoring, Carrefour (100%), Nestlé (96%), and McDonald's (85%) stand out as scoring particularly well. This is because these companies show how non-financial issues are embedded into core business strategy and how these issues have affected strategic business decisions. Under the 'performance management' area, companies including Danisco 69%, Coca-Cola 63% and Tesco 69% score well due to evidence that company-wide systems are in place for managing and reporting non-financial issues, that senior managers are trained and involved in issues management and that there is innovation in products and processes related to non-financial issues.

So what do these reports say about the real issues that characterise 'corporate responsibility' for food sector companies?

Social, environmental and economic impacts were analysed through a mixture of internet-based research, direct stakeholder dialogue, business intelligence and outputs from the Accountability Rating research.

The reports by two companies currently in the news are particularly revealing in terms of 'responsibility' issues addressed: Tesco and McDonald's. As a supermarket, Tesco sits at the top of the chain, which stretches between the food producers and consumers, but (on the face of it at least) its report covers much more than just the impacts of its stores. Tesco's Corporate Responsibility Review 03/04 covers issues ranging from local sourcing, environmental impacts of their stores, charitable giving, employee retention, to labour conditions in the supply chain.

At first glance, this is very impressive. But when you look a little closer, the gaps start to appear. Over £6bn of Tesco's sales are now outside the UK, including countries where legislation on environmental and social issues is far less stringent that in the UK, and yet their report covers only the UK in any systematic way, with only a few good news articles on international operations selected for inclusion. Tesco's employs thousands of staff in the UK alone, and yet the report contains no information on the number of lost time accidents during the year, or the amount of time lost through work-related ill health for example.

Commendably the report does include information on Tesco's approach to ethical trading, including how suppliers are audited, but disappointingly there is no information about the results of these audits – how many problems were identified and what has happened since? Is any of this fine posturing actually having an effect in the places that matter?

McDonald's is one company that does stand out as its reporting covers a high percentage of relevant issues but it achieves a relatively low Accountability Rating score. This position is a function of the evolution of McDonald's' approach to corporate accountability over recent years; there is recognition of the breadth of issues facing the company and yet consolidated company-wide reporting is limited by an autonomous business unit structure and franchise restaurant ownership model.

The first McDonald's report in April 2002 attracted considerable criticism from cynics and activists alike, both for ignoring major issues such as nutritional balance and impacts in the supply chain. Their latest report, McDonald's Worldwide Corporate Responsibility Report 2004, covers many more issues reflecting "evolving stakeholder interests".

Unsurprisingly perhaps, the McDonald's report addresses the issue of obesity mainly through euphemisms like 'balanced lifestyles'. The emphasis on 'choice', 'physical activity' and 'information' all place the ball very firmly back in the consumer's court, and all the talk of 'salads plus' seems rather hollow without any evidence that these initiatives are having any real effect on consumer eating habits. The risk McDonald's takes is that by producing a report with such strong positive positioning on these issues of concern, the gap between perception and reality is widened.

The issue that really stands out in all of these food sector companies reports as being conspicuous by its absence or cursory treatment is that of *how* corporate responsibility principles are applied in supply chain relationships.

What incentives are there for food producers to implement costly social or environmental improvements if their customers (other food product producers and retailers) are only interested in price, quality and delivery? Worse still for those companies which supply the supermarkets, delays to payments, forced loyalty payments to cover marketing costs and unreasonable terms of contract have all been identified as commonplace by the Office of Fair Trading in its recent review of the Supermarket Code of Practice.

"Until food sector companies start to address corporate responsibility issues in a balanced and meaningful way, rather than just another positive PR opportunity, the trust they are seeking will remain elusive. What is needed is a greater level of real accountability – building trust through transparent discussion of the issues and dilemmas facing food sector companies," concludes Jon Woodhead.

George Monbiot

MONBIOT.COM
Still drilling

FOR A COMPANY that claims to have moved "beyond petroleum", BP has managed to spill an awful lot of it onto the tundra in Alaska. Last week, after the news was leaked to journalists, it admitted to investors that it is facing criminal charges for allowing 270,000 gallons of crude oil to seep across one of the world's most sensitive habitats.[1] The incident was so serious that some of its staff could be sent to prison.

Had this been Exxon, the epitome of sneering corporate brutality, the news would have surprised no one. But BP's rebranding, like Shell's, has been so effective that you could be forgiven for believing it had become an environmental pressure group. These companies have used the vast profits from their petroleum business to create the impression that they are abandoning it.

Shell's adverts feature photos of its technologists in open-necked shirts and showing perfect teeth (which proves they can't be real greens). They tell stories of their brave experiments with wind power, hydrogen, biofuels and natural gas. The chairman of Shell UK was one of the 14 signatories to a letter sent by businesses to Tony Blair a week ago, calling for the government to exercise "bold leadership on domestic climate change policy" in order to speed "the transition to a low carbon economy".[2]

BP's adverts tell the same story, illustrated with its logo – a kind of green and yellow sunflower which looks rather like the Green Party's. So what on earth was it doing in Alaska, messing around with crude oil? Don't its filling stations now dispense pure carrot juice?

Admittedly BP's latest campaign, "exploring new ways to live without" oil, was prefaced with adverts boasting about its new means of finding the stuff. "By developing innovative technology like BP's Advanced Seismic Imaging, we've been able to make discoveries that were unthinkable only a decade ago."[3] But even this campaign seeks to answer an environmental concern. For the past two or three years, environmentalists (myself included) have been publicising the idea that global oil production might soon peak and then go into decline. This possibility helps to demonstrate, we argued, that our dependence on oil is unsustainable, and we must find means of giving it up. The oil companies have seized our arguments and are using them for the opposite purpose: if oil supplies are in danger, they must be permitted to prospect in new places.

Whatever happens, they can't lose. If they invest in new exploration and production, they secure lucrative control over a diminishing asset. If they fail to invest, as they have done over the past 10 years, the price rises and they do even better. In either case they make so much money that they can throw a few billion into developing alternative technologies without gulping, thus cornering the future energy markets as well.

Please don't misunderstand me. I am glad they are spending some of their money this way. They are among the few companies able to achieve the economies of scale required to bring down the price of expensive new technologies, such as solar power and hydrogen fuel cells. The problem is that they are developing these new capacities not in order to replace their production of oil, but in order to supplement it. Their share price depends on the current and future value of their assets. To sustain the future value, they aim for a "reserve replacement rate" of 100%. In other words, however much oil they produce, they seek to replace it with new discoveries. BP has – so far – managed to meet this target.[4] Shell's desperation to do the same led to the scandal two years ago over the mis-stating of its reserves. The impression they have created in some of their adverts – that they are seeking to move out of petroleum and into other products – is misleading.

And though they have become more transparent, more responsive, less aggressive in their engagement with the public, the impact of their core business is much the same. BP has gone ahead with its extraction of natural gas from Tangguh in West Papua, even though this means collaborating with the Indonesian government, which annexed the territory and controls it by means of a vicious military occupation.[5] Three weeks ago, a demonstration outside BP's headquarters in London reminded us that some of the land seizures, environmental damage and human rights violations associated with its pipeline from Baku in Azerbaijan to Ceyhan in Turkey (which came onstream on May 27th) have been neither acknowledged nor addressed.[6] BP admits that the oil and gas it extracts produce around 570 million tonnes of carbon dioxide a year,[7] roughly the same as the UK emits.[8] This is after it changed its methodology to exclude some of its operations: otherwise it would have been responsible for over twice that amount.[9]

Shell's practices look even worse. Though the flaring of gas from oil wells in Nigeria was banned in 1969,[10] it is still burning hundreds of millions of cubic feet a day, wasting a precious resource and producing more carbon emissions than every one else in sub-Saharan Africa put together.[11] The surrounding communities are plastered with sticky soot. In April Shell was ordered by a court in Lagos to stop the flaring,[12] but does not intend to do so until 2009.[13] It has also been fined $1.5 billion for polluting the Niger delta, but won't pay pending its appeal.[14]

Last year it took five men from the Bog of Erris in Ireland to court for refusing to allow its high pressure gas pipeline to cross their lands. They were jailed for 94 days.[15] Green groups have begged it not to extract oil from the seas around Sakhalin Island off the east coast of Siberia, where a spill could wipe out the world's last 100 Western Pacific grey whales, but it won't back down. To boost its reserves, it has just invested another

$2bn in extracting petroleum from oilsands in Canada.[16] It would be hard to devise a more polluting business.

Both companies are cleverer than they used to be. They have stopped pretending that climate change does not exist or that no one ever gets hurt by their projects. Shell even publishes a list of its recent convictions.[17] But this doesn't mean they have stopped spinning. Shell's new sustainability report, for example, says it will reduce its carbon dioxide emissions "by up to 2.5 million tonnes a year" by burying the gas in old oil fields in the North Sea.[18] But it is using it to drive inaccessible oil out of the reservoirs. It fails to explain whether the 2.5 million tonnes is a gross saving or a net saving (after the burning of the new oil has been taken into account). I suspect the former, but until the UK has some effective corporate reporting rules, companies can continue to give us only the information that suits them.

BP and Shell are to Exxon what New Labour is to the old Tories. The language has changed, but the policies are pretty similar. The denial and aggression which characterised Shell's approach at the time of the Brent Spar campaign and the hanging of Ken Saro-Wiwa have gone. But it seems to me that this only makes them more dangerous.

Notes

1   Terry Macalister, 9 June 2006. BP admits it faces criminal inquiry into Alaskan spill. *Guardian*; Bloomberg, 8 June. BP Faces Grand Jury Probe Over March Alaska Oil Spill. http://www.bloomberg.com/apps/news?pid=10000102&sid=aB0f2Gu.sFZU&refer=uk.

2   The Corporate Leaders Group on Climate Change, 5 June 2006. Letter to Tony Blair. Text of letter sent to me by the BBC.

3   For example, advert in the *New Statesman*, 8 May 2006.

4   BP, 2006. Making Energy More: sustainability report 2005, p.3. http://www.bp.com/liveassets/bp_internet/annual_review/annual_review_2005/STAG1.

5   See George Monbiot, 3 May 2005. In Bed with the Killers. *Guardian*. http://www.monbiot.com/archives/2005/05/03/in-bed-with-the-killers/.

6   http://www.bakuceyhan.org.uk/about.htm. See also George Monbiot, 3 September 2002. Trouble in the Pipeline. *Guardian*. http://www.monbiot.com/archives/2002/09/03/trouble-in-the-pipeline/.

7   BP, 2006, ibid., p.41.

8   HM Government, 2006. Climate Change: The UK Programme 2006, p.31. To convert tonnes of carbon into tonnes of CO_2, you multiply by 3.667. http://www.defra.gov.uk/environment/climatechange/uk/ukccp/pdf/ukccp06-all.pdf.

9   Ashley Seager and Simon Bowers, 21 April 2006. BP attacked over CO_2 emissions. *Guardian*.

10   http://www.foe.co.uk/campaigns/corporates/case_studies/shell/index.html.

11   Terry Macalister, 12 April 2006. Shell ordered to stop flaring off excess gas. *Guardian*.

12   Ibid.

13   Shell, 2006. Meeting the Energy Challenge: The Shell Sustainability Report 2005, p.27. http://www.shell.com/static/hongkong-en/downloads/news_and_library/shell_sustainability_report_2005.pdf.

14   Howard Lesser, 24 May 2006. Shell Oil Company Refuses to Pay Fine.

http://www.voanews.com/english/Africa/2006–05–24-voa55.cfm;   Rory   Carroll,
25 February 2006. Shell told to pay Nigerians $1.5bn pollution damages. *Guardian*.

15   See   http://www.corribsos.com/index.php?id=1&type=page   and   http://
www.indymedia.ie/newswire.php?story_id=70547.

16   Terry Macalister, 2 June 2006. The next big thing or a risky gamble: Shell looks to turn
sand into oil. *Guardian*. Shell is already the major partner in the Athabasca development.

17   Shell, 2006, ibid., p.17.

18   Ibid., p.10.

Deborah Doane

GOOD INTENTIONS – BAD OUTCOMES?
The broken promise of CSR reporting

T HE PROMISE BEHIND corporate social responsibility (CSR) is a broken one. Conventional wisdom holds that 'what's good for business is good for society'. But not only has CSR failed to bring us the vision of leadership we expected, it has also fallen short in delivering more sustainable companies.

The New Economics Foundation (NEF) was a pioneer in the field of social auditing and reporting during the early 1990s, with a view that it would ultimately lead to companies that considered their social and enviornmental impact to be as important as their financial outcomes. 'The challenge is to create the conditions where social and environmental benefits go hand in hand with competitive advantage', remarked NEF in a study for the Association of Chartered Certified Accountants (ACCA) on the subject during the late 1990s (Gonella *et al.*, 1998). Certainly, over the past couple of years – especially since the establishment of the pensions legislation two years ago – we've witnessed the conditions under which reporting appears to have taken off. From fewer than 25 reporters in the UK just two years ago, consultancy group Econtext reports that there are now 103 reporters from the FTSE250 (Saltbaxter and Context, 2002), and SustainAbility finds 234 reporters globally. But the quantity says very little about quality. Repeated studies, including SustainAbility's *Global Reporters Survey* released in November 2002, confirms that there is little meaningful reporting out there that really grapples with the triple bottom line (TBL) question (SustainAbility and UNEP, 2002).

Perhaps this has been due to the limitations of CSR. Its incentives are the market, and market incentives will mean that a company uses certain levers such as reputation, as the leading driver. Consequently, rather than NEF's (and others') original aim of seeing companies rewarded for making a more positive contribution to society and the environment, the results of reporting have, instead, brought us a litany of oxymorons: British American Tobacco is being considered part of the Dow Jones Sustainability Index, in part because it issues a social report. Apparently, the long-term impacts of tobacco on health are good for society. In a similar vein, British Petroleum is hailed as the most socially responsible oil company – despite its strong-arming the Turkish government to develop an oil pipeline and despite the fact that it aims to increase oil production and sees no immediate profitability in renewable energy.

Most absurd is that British Aerospace (BAE) is now trying to be the world's most responsible arms manufacturer, having just issued its first social and environmental report. In it, it talks about exemplary environmental initiatives – for example, reducing harmful chemicals on guns. At the same time, a new advertising campaign touts its remote bomb-dropping technology (named 'Nora', or 'nagging Nora', to the fighter pilots) as just one of the ways in which BAE makes the world a safer place. This isn't just silly: it's absurd.

Corporate social reporting was not about trying to mask the negative impacts of a company by turning them into a 'good' – that is, a safe war; it was about trying to ensure that we hold companies to account for their wider impacts and, in the long run, about rewarding those companies who genuinely contribute to a sustainable society.

Yet, in spite of the increasing uptake in reporting, we have not exactly been led down the so-called 'virtuous path'. In fact, we appear to be going in the opposite direction. Certainly, a plethora of CSR initiatives have been introduced since reporting was in its infancy, and the consultancy basis for CSR programmes and triple bottom line reporting is growing. But while the number of papers, programmes, seminars, conferences and consultancies on the subject grows in size, the depth of these approaches has not kept pace. Sadly, reporting remains an exercise in managing public perceptions of a company, with the outcome being a company 'doing what it can', rather than 'what it should'.

It should be no surprise, then, that civil society groups, among others, are getting impatient and not waiting for the market to deliver quality reports. Thus, 2002 saw the launch of the Corporate Responsibility Coalition (CORE), calling for mandatory social and environmental reporting of all top businesses. Since early in 2003, around 40 leading organizations, from Amnesty International UK, to Christian Aid, Friends of the Earth and the New Economics Foundation, support the coalition, while 287 MPs signed an early day motion (EDM) supporting CORE's aims.

But while legislation is certainly a way to facilitate more meaningful triple bottom line reporting, it will likely only go so far in terms of delivering sustainable development. It's time that we asked ourselves: does business really have the power to change behaviour, or are we caught in an endless cycle that more often rewards bad outcomes over good?

Business being business

When we see an increasing number of companies wanting to report openly on their impacts, joining initiatives such as the UN Global Compact or the UK's Business in the Community benchmarking club, we assume, rightly or wrongly, that the market is working. Indeed, in some cases, the market is managing to bring about more active consciousness about CSR, as with B&Q's sustainable wood products. But while the market delivers consciousness, it does so within the confines of 'shareholder value'. Thus, it rewards behaviour that will have a direct impact on profitability. Companies that can deliver a business case for CSR are far more likely to invest in sustainability programmes, including transparent and honest reporting.

But the outcomes of this can often be perverse. Public relations-driven incentives – which the business case tends to lean towards – may not actually result in real changes in behaviour, as per a few of the examples cited earlier. And we should be wary of assuming that consumers will make decisions based simply on the transparency commitment of a company, let alone their ethical stance. Most research on 'ethical consumption' shows that while a minority of consumers are active in their purchasing decisions, the vast majority are relatively passive – and most are generally only concerned with price. The 2002 Ethical Purchasing Index does confirm that 'deep green' and ethical businesses are growing at a faster rate than the overall market; but they still continue to capture less than 1 per cent of the market in key areas (Co-operative Bank and the New Economics Foundation, 2002). A recent study by the Institute of Grocery Distribution shows that 70 per cent of food shoppers base their purchasing decisions on price, taste and sell-by date (Mason and Jones, 2002).

Socially responsible investment (SRI) is also a growing field. But the trend towards 'ethics-lite' investment – investing in the 'best of the baddies' – is increasingly common, and consumers don't generally look below the SRI surface. The recent inclusion of British American Tobacco in the Dow Jones Sustainability Index makes a mockery of CSR and gives evidence to the fact that, at the end of the day, triple bottom line is more like a pyramid scheme, with profit firmly ensconced at the top. Even SRI funds that aim to keep closer to the intentions of socially responsible investment are limited in the companies that they have to choose from. Thus, banking and mobile phones become the norm for many of the leading SRI funds. But the mobile phone industry has yet to come to grips with the health concerns of mobile phone masts and the use of handsets, taking a defensive stance that is reminiscent of the tobacco industry not too long ago. And banking investments only mean that investment in non-sustainable industries is one step removed – with the banks themselves holding investments in companies that the SRI industry would most likely shun. A handful of companies are trying to get to grips with these issues. Morley's Asset Management issued its sustainability matrix recently, which aims to differentiate between those companies who positively contribute to major social or environmental issues, versus those that are more reactive in this area (Morley Vision, 'Socially Responsible Investing', at www.morleyfm.com). But they still continue to be limited in what they can do from a sustainable development perspective. Cable and Wireless is considered one of the top sustainability performers within Morley's matrix. But they're currently being dragged over the coals as they risk losing monopoly-power concessions in developing countries who have held poor people at ransom, but delivered substantial profits to investors. So, investors are pulling out (John, 2002).

The problem is that the short-term incentives of the stock market are simply not compatible with the long-term objectives of sustainability. Consistent drives for quarterly profit figures won't reward companies who are prepared to make long-term and, indeed, expensive investments in things such as poverty eradication or sustainable energy. Nestlé is taking the Ethiopian government to court for US$6 million in spite of the country's current famine crisis. Nestlé's chief executive has in the past, however, vowed to contribute as a business to sustainable development (Crooks, 2002).

Companies themselves are not necessarily to blame. The limitations of the market-based model to deliver are, quite simply, inadequate. We've been led to believe that there is an immediate business case for CSR and real triple bottom line reporting; but the business case extends little beyond arguments that result in gloss over substance. Thus, SustainAbility's findings confirm that while the size of reporting has increased, companies have yet to take on board the more critical triple bottom line issues (SustainAbility and UNEP, 2002).

Government limitations

A level playing field would certainly make a measurable difference in the way in which companies report on and manage these issues. In the UK, the Company Law Review and its subsequent output, the Government White Paper on Company Law, attempted to reach a compromise on the issue of non-financial reporting. By calling for companies of a certain size to report on social and environmental issues, where it is 'material' to a company's operations, it argues that adequate pressure will be brought to bear on companies to fully disclose their impacts.

But not only would this approach be limited in terms of delivering more sustainable impacts (what is material to business is not commensurate with what is material to society); international pressure, and certainly business pressure from various industry lobby groups, would make it difficult for government to go any further. Perceptions about 'red tape' and yet another layer of bureaucracy see government consistently leaning towards the lowest common denominator approach to regulation on corporate accountability. This is in spite of the fears over repetitions of the various US-style corporate debacles of the past year.

The dance of the slaves

In summary, we're locked into a pattern for which there doesn't appear to be an immediate exit. Government is reluctant to regulate in favour of mandatory reporting and is insistent that business should only report on those impacts that are 'material' to the business. Furthermore, none of the leading CSR-practising companies are prepared to break ranks with their Confederation of British Industry counterparts to support the introduction of a level, accountable playing field to encourage more honest reporting that could ultimately lead to more sustainable performance of business.

The SRI industry can only influence behaviour to a limited extent because it has to make reasonable returns on our investments. And consumers will always only be active for a small part of the time; certainly, the motivations of consumers rarely fall within the altruistic realm. Tony Golding, a leading writer on the City, calls this the 'chain of pressure' (Golding, 2003). I call this a 'dance of the slaves', where no one is prepared to take the lead.

Breaking ranks

The failure of CSR reporting to lead to any measurable change is partly a problem of design; reporting has been about process, rather than performance. We also have to continuously remind ourselves that reporting itself is not an end – it is a means. While the CORE campaign advocates for mandatory reporting and stakeholder accountability, people have wrongly assumed that this has led the argument astray. People who are really concerned about the quality of reporting are more concerned about what businesses and others do with this information, once out there. Will they hold the company to account for its actions? Will the behaviour and outputs actually change? Or is it just a discursive method of belying the truth?

The real reason for the current failure of CSR is that we've been fudging the case for triple bottom line reporting. We have to be honest and 'fess up', as they say. It's time that we openly acknowledge that corporate social reporting, and, indeed, CSR as a whole, is about a *public good* outcome – not necessarily a business outcome. While these two may occasionally align themselves, this will not always be the case.

Thus, for any reporting to be meaningful, there has to be some commensurate accountability mechanisms in place to hold company reporting in check. Civil society groups and other stakeholders should be able to ensure that companies don't overstate their claims and, similarly, include issues that may just be a little bit uncomfortable for the company to accept. Public policy – certainly on mandatory reporting – is one way that would immediately deliver more informed, transparent and honest reporting. Perhaps this shouldn't be linked to business reporting ('the business case'); it should be about something wider.

More boldly, it seems, we should return to our original reason for developing reporting in the first place: to tackle big global problems, rather than see business being more 'profitable' by 'doing good'. And with this in mind, one could argue that the reporting prescription itself has led us down a myopic approach that aims to minimize business impacts on society, rather than having more marked effects on the way that businesses operate. To this end, perhaps triple bottom line reporting could only enable us to support 'best in class' of the baddies, rather than anything more.

The corporate social responsibility agenda should be looking to provoke a far more challenging new agenda for business in society. The real question is: what kind of business and institutions do we need in the 21st century to deliver sustainable development? Public concerns – from poverty to health and the environment – become the master, rather than the servant, to business. In asking this question, we are led down an entirely different road than either the hard-nosed approach to regulation or the process-driven reporting prescriptions of the last decade that have become 'CSR'. Not only would such an examination revolutionize our investment in certain types of industries, it could alter the very incentives we use to reward business today. Different forms of corporate governance would most likely emerge, and the monolithic multinational-sized company could well become obsolete.

Critical qualities for sustainable business would be the following:

Transparent and accountable

By transparent and accountable, I'm not referring to the issuing of a 'glossy' report, for which business may mask its negative impacts simply through excluding information from a report. British Petroleum (BP) engaged in an arguably transparent and accountable 'stakeholder dialogue' in Indonesia, regarding the Tangguh liquefied natural gas project. In the stakeholder analysis, comments such as 'We were forced and tricked into selling our land' and 'The potential for BP to benefit is much greater than that for villagers' came up; yet, any negative feedback from the exercise is eliminated from BP's environmental and social report (2001) and there is no opportunity for stakeholders to actually challenge the outcome of the analysis. The project is expected to proceed.

Equally important is for meaningful and accessible information to be made available to all stakeholders, from minor shareholders to communities. If the outcome of a 'stakeholder dialogue' is, on balance, a negative one, and not in the interests of the wider community, then we should be able to hold business to account for this. Yes, profits and shareholders should be taken into consideration, but not at the expense of others with less power.

At the same time, accountability should also extend to business being willing to hold itself open to the appropriate checks and balances entailed in regulation – not simply letting the market work for itself. Business must recognize that if it is to balance the needs of wider stakeholders, a level playing field and a role for government is, indeed, legitimate.

Trustworthy

A trustworthy business is an extension of the transparent and accountable company. But 'trust' isn't something that's done; it is earned. Immediate and honest responses to disasters or product failure are more likely to build trust and retain customers than defensive actions or ones that hide the truth. If a company finds out that it has 'done harm', as in the case of Unilever in India in 2001, then it should immediately disclose the information and aim to mitigate against negative impacts (Corporate Watch, 2001). Of course, more and more, businesses are recognizing this to be the case; but there remains a plethora of examples where the opposite holds true.

Social and environmental goods versus financial ones

I'm not arguing that business shouldn't be profitable; but profits should not be made off the backs of products and services that aren't delivering sustainable outcomes. Sustainable business is not about minimizing the 'bads'; it's about producing 'goods'. Yes, we need an energy company. No, we don't need, in the long run, those that are harmful to the environment. Yes, we need pharmaceutical innovations. No, we don't need those that are only accessible to a small minority, while excluding the majority.

Companies would require having a much more integrated understanding of how their business impacts upon the outside world – and, in turn, how they can have a positive impact on outcomes. To do this requires a real shift in how we measure intangible assets and how we 'internalize' our 'externalities'. Are companies, consumers and government prepared to give equivalent value to non-financial returns? Is this the real triple bottom line? And can we penalize companies who don't? One way is for us to break down our intangible asset base and include 'tangible' social and environmental measures that would see us moving more towards triple bottom line decision-making, rewards and returns.

Stakeholder driven

A radical redefinition of the 'stakeholder' company would seem to be in order. Companies are now operating based on the primary concerns of shareholders. Although the Centre for Tomorrow's Company tried to redefine this by arguing that those companies who considered their stakeholders would ultimately benefit the shareholder, it would seem that the 'enlightened shareholder value' approach continues to produce limited results when it comes to more sustainable outcomes. We don't want companies who just listen to stakeholder concerns, but dismiss these when it contradicts the shareholder value model; we want companies who are prepared to make difficult choices – real trade-offs between financial and social outcomes. Companies must, therefore, be governed by a wider set of stakeholders. But our current form of corporate governance doesn't yet provide for this and directors' duties continue to be focused primarily on the singular bottom line.

Conclusions: corporate social responsibility and sustainable development

With the public's trust in business increasingly on the decline (MacGillivray, 2002), there seems to be an urgent need to restore not only our faith in business, but in the ability of leaders to address the larger sustainable development problems of our time. However, the current deadlock between individual businesses, financial markets, government and, indeed, consumers is unlikely to bring about a change in the way forward.

Two things are essential. Firstly, leading businesses need to break ranks with the lowest common denominator and give government the green light to bring about relevant legislation that would facilitate more rapid change in this area, from encouraging real transparency and reporting to paying for the full costs of environmental and social degradation. Secondly, and perhaps more importantly, business should turn its strategic thinking regarding corporate social responsibility on its head and ask the question: what are the kinds of businesses we need in the 21st century to deliver sustainable development? And in asking that question, business should be shaped in such a way as to really provide the most positive outcomes, as mapped out above. In short, the 21st century needs companies that lead the future – so that others may share in it.

References

British Petroleum (2001) *BP Environment and Social Report.*

Co-operative Bank and the New Economics Foundation (2002) *Ethical Purchasing Index 2002.* Manchester and London.

Corporate Watch (2001) 'Unilever's Mercury Fever'. www.corpwatch.org.

Crooks, E. (2002) 'Nestle Claiming $6 Million. Compensation against Ethiopia', *Financial Times*, 19 December 2002.

Golding, T. (2003) *The City: Inside the Great Expectation Machine.* London, Prentice Hall.

Gonella, C., A. Pilling *et al.* (1998) *Making Values Count: Contemporary Experience in Social and Ethical Accounting, Auditing and Reporting.* London, Chartered Accountants Educational Trust.

John, P. (2002) 'Cable and Wireless to Exit FTSE 100 Index', *Financial Times*, 10 December 2002.

MacGillivray, A. (2002) *What's Trust Worth?* London, New Economics Foundation.

Mason, J. and S. Jones (2002) 'Food Shoppers Appear to Shun Ethical Goods', *Financial Times*, 21 November 2002.

SustainAbility and UNEP (2002) *Trust Us: The Global Reporters 2002 Survey of Corporate Sustainability Reporting.* London, SustainAbility Ltd.

CHAPTER SIX

The future of CSR

What next for the responsible company?

THROUGHOUT THIS BOOK we have seen the diversity of opinion that surrounds the development of corporate social responsibility and the question of whether or not companies are able to function in a socially and environmentally ethical manner. It is apparent that the transition towards socially responsible business is still in its relative infancy, but what sort of future is there for CSR? Does the emergence of such an emphasis upon corporate responsibility actually mark a significant transition in the way in which companies are organized and behave or is this another management fad that will soon dissipate when other more pressing issues take precedence on the business agenda?

Are we witnessing the evolution of more ethical consumers with strict ideas about how they expect their companies to behave or are we talking about a minority of consumers with the economic ability to place ethics above cost? Similarly, can we believe that companies are changing and that social responsibility will become ingrained in their value commitments and in all aspects of business activity? Will a successful CSR strategy represent the defining feature of tomorrow's successful businesses or will we continue to see companies succeeding in the absence of any such commitments? Without doubt the current status of CSR leaves many more questions than answers regarding its future and sustainability. At the real heart of all these questions however lies the issue of whether it is even possible or for that matter 'responsible' to expect businesses to function under the rubric of social responsibility.

As many of the readings in this book suggest, there are grounds to be optimistic about the future. The notion of corporate responsibility has definitely come to the fore and, with the ongoing challenges of climate change and environmental sustainability putting an ever-increasing spotlight on company activity and production processes, there is certainly a greater impetus for companies to take their social and environmental responsibilities more seriously.

CSR is not purely about the business community, however, and there is clear danger in companies thinking that they can simply control the CSR agenda and select what issues and information they choose to provide. The extent to which companies are free to determine how far their commitments to CSR can be largely PR rhetoric or a more credible attempt to be more open and transparent may not necessarily be completely within their own control. How much information companies may *want* to reveal about themselves may not necessarily equate to how much they may *have* to reveal in order to avoid the potential risks of damaging publicity which the closer scrutiny of inaccurate claims may produce. Thus, companies may indeed find themselves having to travel significantly further down the CSR road to benefit from the badge of 'Corporate Citizenship' (Burchell and Cook 2006).

Certainly, the expansion in both the number of companies undertaking CSR activities and the increase in the nature and extent of these activities suggest that maybe CSR can become a concept that may help to reshape the values of the contemporary company and the subsequent behaviour and practice that such values engender. However, there is still significant scepticism over whether or not CSR actually marks a deep-rooted value change in company activity, or whether the changes we are witnessing are little more than surface window dressing.

This question in itself raises another matter for consideration. We need to ask whether CSR has to be necessarily values-driven in order to achieve significant change. Whether or not companies are really sincere in their commitments to both the environment and society, the pressure to be 'seen' to be doing something, it could be argued, has resulted in a significant increase in resources being channelled from companies towards civil society. Given the current economic climate and the constant pressure on government finances to effectively resource public requirements, this additional set of resources from the private sector is fast becoming a necessary component of public funding.

Under these conditions, one could argue that whatever the underlying motivations, CSR is pushing companies into providing resources that would otherwise not become available. So while we may question the motivation behind a campaign such as Tesco's 'Computers for Schools' scheme, it nevertheless provides invaluable resources for schools which they currently lack the funding to provide for themselves. Similarly, McDonald's funding of the Ronald McDonald Houses to help families with critically ill children is an essential resource that provides vital assistance for families which again would not currently be available without the funding of a company such as McDonald's.

Examples such as these do raise the question of how far we really have to believe the underlying motivation for the action if the practical outcome can provide a justification in itself. If CSR is just about companies making themselves look good in the eyes of the public, can we accept this as the price to pay for the additional public resources becoming available through this process?

There is also a strong case, however, for questioning whether or not it is right that companies should seek to gain respectability through, in many cases, helping to provide resources to solve problems to which they have been one of the primary causes. Can we, for example, start to praise oil companies for looking towards alternative fuel technologies when their previous reluctance to do so and constant emphasis upon oil has arguably led to the current predicament in the first place? Can a tobacco company possibly compensate for the damage that its principal product causes by providing other contributions to civil society? One might argue that the consumer is bright enough to see beyond the rhetoric and to view company activities within this sphere with a significantly critical eye. Otherwise, it could be suggested, we are allowing companies to buy a clearer conscience rather than actually seeking to gain a more ethical form of business practice.

From a more critical perspective, therefore, it would seem that unless CSR has a strong values-driven momentum to it, it is likely to remain a relatively short-term issue; important while public attention is focused upon it, but easy to scale down when the focus of public and media interest moves elsewhere. Similarly, without a level of deep-rooted commitment, when the economic environment becomes more pressing upon companies it is likely that CSR issues will be one of the first areas jettisoned in order to make cut-backs. Under these conditions, if as Clive Crook suggests in his *Economist* article, CSR is 'little more than a cosmetic treatment', the concept could arguably do more harm than good. Companies tend to suffer much more when they expound their virtuous nature and are then subsequently seen to be misleading the public than if they remain relatively silent and make few claims regarding their social responsibility.

On the other side of this debate is the feeling that CSR is an unnecessary process which is forcing companies to try and justify a position which should actually, in itself, require no real justification. This reflects back upon the earlier position highlighted by Milton Friedman's article in Chapter three; namely that the primary social responsibility of any company is to ensure that it continues to make a profit, provide goods and services to society and is a constant source of employment opportunities. The notion of providing a more 'human face' to the capitalist economy, it is argued, is largely an unnecessary task. As Martin Wolf noted in the *Financial Times*, 'a dynamic international economy already has a human face. Its humanity derives from the economic opportunities it offers to ordinary people' (8 December 1999). CSR within this context can only ever be an unnecessary process which directs resources away from the central aims and objectives of the company to the longer-term detriment of society at large.

In many senses the differing perspectives on the development of CSR reflect differing views regarding what our expectations of companies and their roles should be. Should companies be expected to contribute more to the development of civil society than merely through the provision of goods and services? As we have seen throughout this Reader, there is undoubtedly a strong argument to say that as companies benefit through, and indeed are reliant upon, their relationship with society there must inevitably be some level of payback in return for the 'licence to operate'. Given the increasing environmental pressures confronting contemporary society, there is undoubtedly a strong case to suggest that companies have a responsibility to contribute to alleviating the problems which have been created by capitalist society's recent obsession with economic growth and ever greater consumption. As the business community has played a leading role in the creation of these problems, one might argue, it undoubtedly has a responsibility to take a similar role in seeking solutions.

However, this also raises the question of exactly how far corporate responsibility should stretch. One might even suggest that CSR is merely a process of deflecting responsibility for action away from national governments and towards companies. First, in terms of encouraging private investment into public sector activities and to use CSR as a means to plug the gaps in funding towards social improvement strategies. Second, by using CSR as a method to avoid the challenge of creating stricter legislation to control the actions of companies. Without doubt, encouraging companies to undertake more environmentally and socially responsible strategies voluntarily represents a far easier option than to seek to enforce these processes by creating a strong regulatory framework. However, given the increasing concern over the process of climate change and global warming and the relatively slow pace of change that has so far been apparent among industrialized nations, one may easily question whether or not relying on companies to voluntarily live up to their social and environmental responsibilities is enough to create the levels of change that may well be required.

One should also question how far we as consumers are actually ready to take greater responsibility for our purchasing activities. At one level it is easy to condemn companies for the use of sweatshop labour and so on, but this does not always lead to the equivalent level of commitment to not buying products manufactured in this way. Similarly, in recent years there has been considerable criticism and concern raised regarding some of the practices within the food industry. However, there is still a large demand for low-cost products and a criticism that organic and fair trade produce is too expensive. It would appear that for the majority it can be a case of 'out of sight out of mind' and that the connections between the products we purchase and the processes required to produce them do not always present themselves at the forefront of our minds. If, as has been suggested, companies follow the demand of the market, then maybe it is the consumer who needs to take a lead in social responsibility and be more prepared to define what is and what is not acceptable and to purchase accordingly. Much of the literature within the CSR field talks about an increasingly ethical consumer driving companies to become more responsible. Currently, however, it would appear that the ethical market remains relatively small overall. One might also suggest that we as consumers should not be responsible for having to make ethical judgements every time we want to buy something, and in this sense a greater responsibility should again rest upon the producer. Ethical, responsible behaviour should be the norm rather than the exception.

The future for CSR is therefore open to much debate and discussion. The final set of readings provides a range of perspectives as to how CSR might be perceived and where the future may lie for the concept. All offer differing scenarios for how companies might best understand what their roles and responsibilities should be in contemporary society. Simon Zadek (Reading 6.5) offers a relatively positive reflection on the future for CSR, suggesting that we approach its development with an air of 'sceptical optimism'. He notes a level of inevitability that companies must increasingly adapt to their social and environmental responsibilities if they are to sustain themselves in the long term. Blowfield and Frynas (Reading 6.4) provide a broader international perspective and raise some important critical questions for how CSR must develop if it is to seek to have an effective role within developing nations.

The readings by Henderson (6.1) and Crook (6.2) take a far more sceptical approach to the development of CSR, suggesting that the increased focus on the concept has been misplaced and has resulted in companies seeking to justify their roles and activities through unnecessary processes which have had a negative impact for business development. By contrast Allen White (Reading 6.3) provides a set of different scenarios for the future of CSR which reflect the open-ended position the field is currently faced with. As he suggests, all of the scenarios are possible and none are inevitable, leaving the future of CSR still wide open.

REFERENCE

Burchell, J. and J. Cook (2006) 'Confronting the Corporate Citizen: Expanding the Challenges of Corporate Social Responsibility', *International Journal of Sociology and Social Policy*, Vol. 26, Nos. 3/4, pp. 121–137.

D. Henderson

COMPANIES, COMMITMENT AND COLLECTIVISM

Corporate standards

IN **ONE OBVIOUS** respect, the evidence presented here raises a question about the standards that many leading companies now set and maintain. A striking feature of the continuing debate on corporate social responsibility is the often low calibre of the contributions made by businesses and business organisations in general, and in particular by those that support CSR. What emerges on this front is a picture of inadequacy – one might almost say, of market failure. From the evidence presented here, two main aspects stand out.

First, international business today shows a reluctance or inability to argue a well-constructed and vigorous case for itself against unjustified criticisms and attacks. It has failed to present an informed and effective set of arguments in defence of the market economy and the role of companies within it. In some instances, it is clear that the issues are simply not understood: the executives or organisations concerned are in the same state of innocence as many of their critics.

Second, many large corporations that have come out for CSR, whether directly or through organisations which they have created and continue to finance, have lent support to ideas and beliefs that are dubious or false. On behalf of business, they have been ready to endorse uncritically ill-defined and questionable objectives; to confess imaginary sins; to admit to non-existent privileges, and illusory gains from globalisation, that require justification in the eyes of 'society'; to identify the demands of NGOs with 'society's expectations', and treat them as beyond question; to accept overdramatised and mislead-ing interpretations of recent world economic trends and their implications for businesses; and in some cases, to condemn outright the economic system of which private business forms an integral part. Substantial numbers of leading corporations and top executives have acted in this way, while some have linked themselves to causes and organisations which are opposed to economic freedom and the market economy. In these respects, the conduct of many MNEs and those who speak for them falls short of acceptable professional standards.

The basis for these observations is to be found in what has already been quoted or referred to above. A final illustration will serve to round off the picture. It is drawn from WBC2000 itself.

As noted already, the report carries on its opening page two specially highlighted quotations . . . The first, presumably chosen as reflecting the deep convictions of WBCSD member firms, comes from a speech by Kofi Annan. It reads as follows:

> We have to choose between a global market driven only by calculation of short-term profit, and one which has a human face. Between a world which condemns a quarter of the human race to starvation and squalor, and one which offers everyone at least a chance of prosperity, in a healthy environment. Between a selfish free-for-all in which we ignore the fate of the losers, and a future in which the strong and successful face their responsibilities, showing global vision and leadership.

That these glib false antitheses should be formally endorsed, by senior executives representing a large group of prominent international companies, is a commentary on the quality of much present-day business leadership in the sphere of public affairs.

It is not inevitable that the contribution of international business to public debate should be so predominantly inadequate and flawed. Some of the businesses and business executives that are reluctant to align themselves with the cause of CSR could consider joining together to ensure that the issues are treated in a more responsible way. This is not at all a matter of lobbying: there are many business organisations across the world, most of them unmentioned here, that are already performing this function well; and in any case, *what is in question is the general welfare and not the interests of companies as such.* Nor is it a matter of propaganda for laissez-faire and free markets, or of pushing a particular economic or political party line. To the contrary, any such new business-led initiative should be, and be seen to be, neither sectarian nor doctrinaire. What is needed is a flow of timely, readable and well-informed publications, statements and presentations of various kinds – some immediately topical and others more general and reflective, and with different blends of analysis, commentary and research – that would promote greater knowledge and awareness of the working of today's market economy and the place of business within it, and better understanding of current issues that bear on businesses. Such a programme does not demand a lavish budget, so that the number of supporting businesses would not have to be large. But any new venture on these lines should be global in its interests and its vision.

True commitment

From the evidence presented here, it is apparent that, for many of the firms that have endorsed it, the concept of CSR appears as much more than a convenient form of words. It is not a pose, nor is it just a reluctant concession to outside critics and pressures. Of course, and rightly, there is a strong element of calculation in the thinking of all these firms, on this as on other issues. The influence of fashion is also to be seen. But the examples and quotations cited here, which could easily have been multiplied, give evidence of genuine and widespread conviction. The business commitment to CSR, where it has been explicitly made, goes well beyond window-dressing and opportunism. Admittedly, these latter elements are often to be seen. But in the wording of many business reports, statements and resolutions that bear on CSR, there are clear signs that the drafting has been undertaken by enthusiasts or even zealots, rather than hard-faced uncommitted calculators.

That there should be this genuine business support is not at all surprising. Both internal and external influences are at work, and they are mutually supporting.

As to the former, there are to be found, especially but not only within large enterprises, well-defined groups of executives, including board members, who are liable to favour policies and courses of action that fit well into the framework of CSR. For instance, it is to be expected that, for professional reasons, the general argument for higher uniform standards will be backed by the managers concerned both with environmental aspects of a firm's operations and with occupational health and safety. Again, the case for policies based on principles of 'diversity' and 'equal opportunity' is now widely accepted by those responsible for the human resources policies of businesses, while the need to keep on the right side of both officialdom and NGOs, and to present a positive image of the company to the outside world, has to remain a constant preoccupation for executives who are in charge of external and government relations, and who are rightly sensitive to criticisms of their firms' conduct. CSR can thus hold out attractions for all of these four groups.

A further and growing element comprises new categories of professionals whose responsibilities and expertise lie in defining and giving effect to CSR. These include board members and executives specifically charged with responsibility for CSR, 'ethics officers', and managers who are responsible for the design and operation of new and more complex accounting and reporting systems installed in the name of 'stakeholder engagement' and 'meeting the triple bottom line'. Last but perhaps not least, many CEOs have a natural wish to make their own distinctive mark on company policies, and visibly committing their firms to CSR may be a way to achieve this. As against these combined internal forces, which march together with the more generalised idealism about to be described, there may be little effective opposition within a typical international business, at any rate unless and until it becomes apparent that CSR is bringing with it commercially damaging consequences. Viewed in this way, the growth and spread of CSR-type thinking in these companies appears as more than just a reaction to outside pressures: it may have a strong basis of willing internal support.

As to more general influences, CSR is in large part an expression, a reflection, of the prevailing climate of opinion, which affects people within companies as well as outside: these are not two separate worlds. Positive and negative ways of thinking reinforce one another. On the one hand, there is general approval for the appealing notion of sustainable development, and for its stated complementary goals of safeguarding the environment, promoting social justice and advancing human rights; and for many, this goes with acceptance of global salvationist ideas. Almost equally widespread, at the same time, is distrust of the profit motive together with a disparaging view of the standards of conduct that currently prevail in private business. The function of prices and profits, as indispensable signalling mechanisms and hence as means of guiding and facilitating a host of continuing individual choices, goes largely unrecognised. Against such a background of ideas, CSR has clear attractions for many people. It holds out the prospect of a new role for companies in society and on the world scene, a role which appears as both more constructive and more honourable than the mere pursuit of wealth for owners and top executives. It is not surprising to learn that the adoption of CSR by firms has been well received by their employees as well as their outside critics. Even company directors and senior managers, whose view of business past and present is naturally more favourable than that of the average person, have responded enthusiastically to the proposal that for the future their firms should accept a new mission and embrace corporate citizenship.

Alternative paths

The idea of such a transformation of business goals and conduct, from narrow private to wider public concerns, is not new. In the past, it was the main single element in the case for taking private businesses into state ownership. Moreover, the now faded arguments for nationalisation have something in common with the case for CSR today, in that they contain two distinct and disparate elements. For some advocates, the rationale of public ownership was that it would improve the working of the market economy. For others, the purpose of nationalisation was to insulate and liberate the industries concerned from market forces. A parallel can be drawn with the campaign for CSR today.

At first sight, this may seem surprising. After all, the case for CSR is often put in terms of ensuring the future of the market economy, by improving its working in ways that will make it acceptable: on the surface, at least, there is no question of repudiating it. However, the far-reaching measures for improvement that are proposed by supporters of CSR bear little relation to long-established ideas on the subject.

Since the days of Adam Smith, it has been widely recognised that a reliable way to make capitalism serve the public interest more effectively, and to enable enterprise profits to become a better indicator of social welfare, is for economies to become more open, market oriented and subject to competition. It is in an open and competitive environment that companies are best able and most strongly motivated to act in ways that will further the general interest – by responding to the demands of their customers, by keeping down costs and prices, and through timely and well-judged innovation. Not only does such an environment make for better enterprise performance, but at the same time, as noted above, it opens up opportunities for ordinary people, including the poorest: prosperity and economic freedom go together. One important aspect of this nexus was well summarised by Martin Wolf in his column in the *Financial Times*. Apropos of the notion that capitalism and the market economy need to be given a human face, he wrote (8 December 1999): '. . . a dynamic international economy already has a human face. Its humanity derives from the economic opportunities it offers to ordinary people.' Wolf's argument in fact applies more generally, within as well as across political boundaries.

So far as my reading goes, this well-recognised line of thought is rarely found in the writings of CSR supporters.[1] The notion that the domain of competition and economic freedom might be further and progressively widened, and that this would both cause businesses to function better and enlarge opportunities for people in general, plays little part in their thinking. Instead, the working of markets is to be improved through the actions of companies in embracing sustainable development, meeting self-chosen goals and targets in relation to environmental norms and 'social justice', bringing in stakeholders, and playing an active part in 'global governance'. Capitalism has to be born again.

In formulating their radical programme of change, the CSR adherents have taken a position which they do not make explicit and of which they may not be fully aware. *Defending the market economy is identified with making businesses more popular and more respected.* This is to be achieved by meeting 'society's expectations', through making a manifestly genuine commitment to CSR. How this response may affect competition and economic freedom is not directly considered . . There are good reasons to expect that both will be impaired, while at the same time the performance of enterprises will suffer. The likelihood of such an outcome is the greater because the strongest and most effective pressures for change come from organisations that are anti-business and hostile to free markets, while their arguments find support from the enthusiasts and zealots within the business world: these are the views that are attributed to 'society'. It may indeed be true, or eventually become true, that a general adoption of CSR would promote the objective of making MNEs better liked and appreciated, and thus help to keep them alive and profitable in an unfriendly world. But this would come at the cost of accepting false beliefs, yielding to unjustified attacks, and impairing the functioning of the market economy.

New millennium collectivism

Why is it that so many businesses – together with prominent business organisations and what appears to be a dominant majority among writers on business responsibilities, both in business schools and outside – disregard or even reject the idea that the rationale for private business is linked to the case for economic freedom? Three related influences can be seen at work. One is a lack of acquaintance with economic ways of thinking, which in some cases goes with hostility to economics as such. Second is a failure to see the point of a competitive profit-driven economy, as a result of which it seems natural to define business goals in a way that makes profitability a means to higher things rather than a primary objective. Third is the strongly held intuitive notion that market economies, which are taken to be anarchic and amoral, are heavily populated with non-beneficiaries and victims – the deprived, condemned, excluded or marginalised – whose wellbeing depends on collective action, by 'society' or 'the international community', to bring deliverance from above.[2]

These ways of thinking are by no means confined to the business milieu. The ideas that underlie CSR can best be seen as forming part of what I have termed *new millennium collectivism*, in which mistrust and misunderstanding of markets goes with acceptance of global salvationist ideas and a strong intuitive bias towards interventionism. In effect, there is today an informal but wide-ranging alliance of those who share this view of the world and broadly agree on what needs to be done. Besides many businesses and some business organisations, it comprises trade unions, the moderate NGOs, commentators and public figures, including parliamentarians, political leaders and civil servants in a good many government departments, a range of interventionist quangos, and most UN agencies. Along with the more recent elements in global salvationism, CSR is a new variation on a standard collectivist theme.

Rival verdicts

Widely different assessments of CSR are possible. Four rival verdicts might be labelled, in ascending order of approval, as hostile, dismissive, moderately approving, and enthusiastic. The first and last of these, the extremes, have been outlined already: the arguments for CSR, and the reasons for questioning these, have constituted the main subject-matter of this reading. But a word is in order on the two intermediate or qualified assessments.

A dismissive or sceptical view is that, while the general adoption of CSR would admittedly be a matter for concern, the significance of this whole recent development has been overblown. The chief grounds for scepticism are (a) that present-day challenges to business and the market economy are no more serious than in the past, (b) that the CSR of today is in fact not new, (c) that it has been endorsed by businesses for tactical reasons only, and (d) that market pressures and common sense will in any case limit its potential to do harm. When it comes to the point, therefore, and despite the prevailing rhetoric, neither the objectives nor the practices of firms will be much changed. On this interpretation, CSR will prove to be no more than a short-lived fad.

I believe that the first three of these reasons for being dismissive are not well founded. First, the pressures of public opinion on businesses generally and MNEs in particular have clearly become more serious in recent years, largely because of the growing power and influence of the NGOs which the sceptics underrate. Many recent and current episodes provide evidence of this. Second, CSR is novel, and newly influential, (1) in the breadth of public support for the general idea of corporate social responsibility, (2) in the radical implications of the doctrine itself, and (3) in the extent to which businesses generally, and MNEs in particular, in many countries and growing numbers, have sub-scribed to the latter. Whereas previous exercises in corporate social responsibility were largely undertaken by individual companies acting on their own account, CSR has become an international creed and movement. Finally, for many companies the com-mitment to CSR is a matter not just of tactics and opportunist calculation, but also of conviction.

An alternative in-between verdict, positive though not strongly committed, is that judicious and well-publicised moves by firms in the direction of CSR are almost unavoid-able today, and can be expected to do more good than harm. Like the sceptics, those who take this selectively favourable view, the moderates, are inclined to think that the com-mitment to CSR by businesses is often more apparent than real. But they consider that the current challenge from NGOs and other critics is not to be ignored or played down, and that, now more than ever, business and business executives have to deal with outside pressures and concerns in a non-dismissive and resourceful way. This applies especially to the MNEs, and among these to firms involved in mining, energy products, pharma-ceuticals and other activities that render them chronically exposed to attacks.

The moderates hold that companies must be able to show that they are neither blinkered nor insensitive; that they treat people, including local communities and indigen-ous groups, in ways that are fair and humane; that their activities are not generating damaging external effects; that they are aware of current concerns about environmental and 'social' issues; and that, where such concerns appear to them well founded, they are ready to contribute, in ways which are both practicable and consistent with their primary purpose and obligations as commercial entities, to the common efforts that are being made to remedy the situation. Failure to act in this way would be hard to defend in public, and would run the risk of loss of reputation and market share. It would therefore be contrary to the interests of their shareholders.

From such an assessment, it is not a long step to forming the view that, in taking deliberate and well-advertised steps along the path of CSR, companies are doing little more than adapting intelligently to a new and more demanding situation. In any case, the moderates, like the sceptics, think that markets will punish those that go too far.

Stated in such general terms, this view of issues and events has much to be said for it. In effect, it points to a positive version of the defensive and business-focused response to pressures . . . . Within such a company strategy, whether or not the language of corporate social responsibility is adopted appears as a matter of tactics rather than principle. Even if the phrase is deployed, it can be separated from the questionable excess baggage that comes with CSR, including intensive stakeholder involvement, the 'triple bottom line', global salvationist assumptions, the preoccupation with deliverance from above, and collaboration with anti-business elements. The term 'corporate social responsibility' then becomes a useful portmanteau description for a well-considered present-day business response to suspicions, pressures and attacks. It is more than a formula, but much less than a blueprint for a new model of capitalism.

Since a strategy of this kind appears to them to be sound, the moderates are tempted to believe that businesses have in fact adopted it. They imagine that, despite some admittedly extravagant language here and there, it represents the path that most companies expressing allegiance to CSR have actually followed. Such an assessment, however, takes too rosy a view of events. It gives too little weight to the many explicit high-level business endorsements of CSR, because it wrongly sees them as not to be taken at face value. Like their dismissive counterparts, the moderates underrate both the influence of the NGOs and the range and depth of genuine commitment to CSR which is now to be found in and around the business world; and both groups fail to appreciate the extent to which many of the enthusiasts and zealots, within business as well as outside it, have embraced radical ideas and causes. Hence they underestimate both the likelihood that CSR will bring substantial changes to the conduct of enterprises and its potential to do harm. At the same time, both moderates and sceptics may overestimate the power of market pressures and incentives to contain the potential damage, because they do not allow sufficiently for the anti-competitive possibilities and tendencies which, as noted above, go with the adoption of CSR, and which could confirm and reinforce the adverse effects on welfare of worsened performance within firms.

CSR is often presented, by moderates and enthusiasts alike, as a sober and judicious response to challenges that have to be met and new developments on the world scene. Such a description does not fit the facts. Many of the alleged new developments have not in fact taken place: they are part of the mythology of global salvationism. Because the myths are largely believed, because the rationale and functioning of a market economy are not well understood, and because of widespread acceptance of the need for deliverance from above, the assessment of current issues and events by many international businesses, and by others in the business milieu, appears as neither judicious nor informed. Appeasement, and the wish to disarm opposition, go together with a large measure of sympathy with, and acceptance of, a collectivist perspective. The views and demands of NGOs and other hostile critics are treated as more soundly based and more representative than they really are. A misleading view of the world is uncritically accepted.

CSR is flawed in its prescription as well as its diagnosis. What it proposes for individual businesses, through 'stakeholder engagement' and giving effect to the 'triple bottom line', would bring far-reaching changes in corporate philosophy and practice, for purposes that are open to question and with worrying implications for the efficient conduct of enterprises. Across economic systems and political boundaries, it would strengthen existing tendencies to regulate transactions, and to limit competition, in ways that would further restrict the opportunities and freedom of choice of people and enterprises. These various effects, both within firms and beyond them, would undermine the market economy and reduce welfare. Despite the attractions of the phrase and the hopes that it appears to offer, the adoption of CSR marks an aberration on the part of the many businesses concerned, and its growing hold on opinion generally is a matter for great concern.

Notes

1   In a WBCSD report of 1997, however, 'freer and more open markets' are listed as among the conditions enabling businesses to contribute more effectively to sustainable development.
2   The reader may care to note the use of the collectivist first person plural in the quotation given from Kofi Annan (above). This is a typical specimen of a large genre. 'We' are in duty bound to bring deliverance from above, to those who are otherwise condemned to exclusion.

Clive Crook

THE GOOD COMPANY

THE MOVEMENT FOR corporate social responsibility has won the battle of ideas. That is a pity, argues Clive Crook (interviewed *here*)

Over the past ten years or so, corporate social responsibility (CSR) has blossomed as an idea, if not as a coherent practical programme. CSR commands the attention of executives everywhere – if their public statements are to be believed – and especially that of the managers of multinational compaines headquartered in Europe or the United States. Today corporate social responsibility, if it is nothing else, is the tribute that capitalism everywhere pays to virtue.

It would be a challenge to find a recent annual report of any big international company that justifies the firm's existence merely in terms of profit, rather than "service to the community". Such reports often talk proudly of efforts to improve society and safeguard the environment – by restricting emissions of greenhouse gases from the staff kitchen, say, or recycling office stationery – before turning hesitantly to less important matters, such as profits. Big firms nowadays are called upon to be good corporate citizens, and they all want to show that they are.

On the face of it, this marks a significant victory in the battle of ideas. The winners are the charities, non-government organisations and other elements of what is called civil society that pushed for CSR in the first place. These well-intentioned groups certainly did not invent the idea of good corporate citizenship, which goes back a long way. But they dressed the notion in its new CSR garb and moved it much higher up the corporate agenda.

In public-relations terms, their victory is total. In fact, their opponents never turned up. Unopposed, the CSR movement has distilled a widespread suspicion of capitalism into a set of demands for action. As its champions would say, they have held companies to account, by embarrassing the ones that especially offend against the principles of CSR, and by mobilising public sentiment and an almost universally sympathetic press against them. Intellectually, at least, the corporate world has surrendered and gone over to the other side.

The signs of the victory are not just in the speeches of top executives or the diligent reporting of CSR efforts in their published accounts. Corporate social responsibility is now an industry in its own right, and a flourishing profession as well. Consultancies have sprung up to advise companies on how to do CSR, and how to let it be known that they are doing it. The big auditing and general-practice consulting firms offer clients CSR advice (while conspicuously striving to be exemplary corporate citizens themselves).

Most multinationals now have a senior executive, often with a staff at his disposal, explicitly charged with developing and co-ordinating the CSR function. In some cases, these executives have been recruited from NGOs. There are executive-education programmes in CSR, business-school chairs in CSR, CSR professional organisations, CSR websites, CSR newsletters and much, much more.

But what does it all amount to, really? The winners, oddly enough, are disappointed. They are starting to suspect that they have been conned. Civil-society advocates of CSR increasingly accuse firms of merely paying lip-service to the idea of good corporate citizenship. Firms are still mainly interested in making money, they note disapprovingly, whatever the CEO may say in the annual report. When commercial interests and broader social welfare collide, profit comes first. Judge firms and their CSR efforts by what the companies do, charities such as Christian Aid (a CSR pioneer) now insist, not by what they say – and prepare to be unimpressed.

By all means, judge companies by their actions. And, applying that sound measure, CSR enthusiasts are bound to be disappointed. The 2004 *Giving List*, published by Britain's *Guardian* newspaper, showed that the charitable contributions of FTSE 100 companies (including gifts in kind, staff time devoted to charitable causes and related management costs) averaged just 0.97% of pre-tax profits. A few give more; many give almost nothing (though every one of them records some sort of charitable contribution). The total is not exactly startling. The figures for American corporate philanthropy are bigger, but the numbers are unlikely to impress many CSR advocates.

Still, you might say, CSR was always intended to be more about how companies conduct themselves in relation to "stakeholders" (such as workers, consumers, the broader society in which firms operate and, as is often argued, future generations) than about straightforward gifts to charity. Seen that way, donations, large or small, are not the main thing.

Setting gifts aside, then, what about the many other CSR initiatives and activities undertaken by big multinational companies? Many of these are expressly intended to help profits as well as do good. It is unclear whether this kind of CSR quite counts. Some regard it as "win-win", and something to celebrate; others view it as a sham, the same old tainted profit motive masquerading as altruism. And, even to the most innocent observer, plenty of CSR policies smack of tokenism and political correctness more than of a genuine concern to "give back to the community", as the *Giving List* puts it. Is CSR then mostly for show?

It is hazardous to generalise, because CSR takes many different forms and is driven by many different motives. But the short answer must be yes: for most companies, CSR does not go very deep. There are many interesting exceptions – companies that have modelled themselves in ways different from the norm; quite often, particular practices that work well enough in business terms to be genuinely embraced; charitable endeavours that happen to be doing real good, and on a meaningful scale. But for most conventionally organised public companies – which means almost all of the big ones – CSR is little more than a cosmetic treatment. The human face that CSR applies to capitalism goes on each morning, gets increasingly smeared by day and washes off at night.

Under pressure, big multinationals ask their critics to judge them by CSR criteria, and then, as the critics charge, mostly fail to follow through. Their efforts may be enough to convince the public that what they see is pretty, and in many cases this may be all they are ever intended to achieve. But by and large CSR is at best a gloss on capitalism, not the deep systemic reform that its champions deem desirable.

Does this give cause for concern? On the whole, no, for a simple reason. Capitalism does not need the fundamental reform that many CSR advocates wish for. If CSR really were altering the bones behind the face of capitalism – sawing its jaws, removing its teeth and reducing its bite – that would be bad: not just for the owners of capital, who collect the company's profits, but, as this survey will argue, also for society at large. Better that CSR be undertaken as a cosmetic exercise than as serious surgery to fix what doesn't need fixing.

We are an equal-opportunity employer

But this is not the end of the matter. Particular CSR initiatives may do good, or harm, or make no difference one way or the other, but it is important to resist the success of the CSR idea – that is, the almost universal acceptance of its premises and main lines of argument. Otherwise bones may indeed begin to snap and CSR may encroach on corporate decision-making in ways that seriously reduce welfare.

Private enterprise requires a supporting infrastructure of laws and permissions, and more generally the consent of electorates, to pursue its business goals, whatever they may be. This is something that CSR advocates emphasise – they talk of a "licence to operate" – and they are quite right. But the informed consent of electorates, and an appropriately designed economic infrastructure, in turn require an understanding of how capitalism best works to serve the public good. The thinking behind CSR gives an account of this which is muddled and, in some important ways, downright false.

There is another danger too: namely, that CSR will distract attention from genuine problems of business ethics that do need to be addressed. These are not in short supply. To say that CSR reflects a mistaken analysis of how capitalism serves society is certainly not to say that managers can be left to do as they please, nor to say that the behaviour of firms is nobody's concern but their own. There is indeed such a thing as "business ethics": managers need to be clear about that, and to comprehend what it implies for their actions.

Also, private enterprise serves the public good only if certain stringent conditions are met. As a result, getting the most out of capitalism requires public intervention of various kinds, and a lot of it: taxes, public spending, regulation in many different areas of business activity. It also requires corporate executives to be accountable – but to the right people and in the right way.

CSR cannot be a substitute for wise policies in these areas. In several little-noticed respects, it is already a hindrance to them. If left unchallenged, it could well become more so. To improve capitalism, you first need to understand it. The thinking behind CSR does not meet that test.

Allen L. White

FADE, INTEGRATE OR TRANSFORM?
The future of CSR

C SR IS AT a crossroads. After a decade of evolution, the pathway forward defies easy prognosis. Will external events and company choices relegate CSR to a passing fad, leading to its fading from corporate and public agendas? Or will CSR reach full fruition as it becomes aligned, integrated and fully institutionalized in company strategy and operations? Or, alternatively, is something more transformational on the horizon as CSR morphs into a deeper change mode, becoming a force for altering corporate purpose at the most fundamental and systemic level? These questions have profound implications for the future of all corporate enterprises. Exploring possible futures yields insight into where we find ourselves today and provides guidance about where we would like to be and how to get there.

Virtually all large companies pursue some form of scenario planning to optimize deployment of their financial and human capital. In a globalizing world where capital, technology, information and trade flow are increasing freely across borders, prudent management requires nothing less for building a healthy, competitive business in the 21st century. In an interconnected world, companies operate not as discrete, atomistic entities, but rather as elements of a global system characterized by complexity and rapid change. It is the struggle to define and manage the opportunities and risks of this new world that has fueled the emergence of CSR during the last few years, and will continue to do so in coming decades.

This reading frames three potential scenarios, intentionally designed with stark differences in content and implications for companies and their stakeholders. All scenarios are plausible, but which will—or should—materialize is not yet clear. Following the scenarios is a brief chronicle of the CSR movement and an assessment of how its history may inform its future.

Three visions

What does the future hold? To frame an answer to this question, consider three scenarios for the year 2015.

Scenario 1

Dateline: San Francisco, 2015
At the BSR Annual Conference, keynoters proclaim the passing of the CSR movement. A severe economic global downturn is occurring, triggered by energy shocks, over-capacity in many extractive and manufacturing sectors, withdrawal of foreign creditors from U.S. bond markets, prolonged and widespread security crises, and failures of several global financial institutions and investment funds. A wave of multinational company downsizing and consolidation is underway, affecting thousands of suppliers and workers worldwide. The obituary is grim: CSR, once viewed as irreversibly destined to become integral to corporate strategy, management and governance, has proven to be fragile and transient. Attention of business and government turns to basic economic survival and recovery from the crisis. CSR moves quietly into hibernation with an uncertain future, characterized by practices associated with its earliest phase, namely compliance and philanthropy. This is the *fad-and-fade scenario*.

The fad-and-fade scenario paints a picture of CSR falling victim to a series of developments that lead to a retreat to its earliest and most superficial form. While the hypothetical developments associated with this scenario are largely beyond the control of any one sector, company or constituency, the combination is not implausible. Certainly the last decade has seen versions of each development in some form and degree—a financial meltdown in Asia in the 1990s, fragility of hedge funds and savings and loan organizations, and an apparent inflection point in the upward surge of oil prices during 2005.

While the combination of these conditions may not be probable, the decline of CSR in this scenario is not wholly dependent on external forces. The fad-and-fade scenario would be as much a reflection of CSR's own failing to address social, environmental and governance challenges of business, most of which will persist as challenges for many years to come. Regardless of macro-economic and political trends, companies will be faced with issues of transparency, labor standards, human rights, political lobbying, climate change and many other aspects of the CSR agenda. The difference between the fad-and-fade scenario and others is that government mandates and regulation emerge as the dominant remnants of a former vibrant movement, replacing business innovation as the primary driver of best CSR practices. This, needless to say, would be a sorry outcome after years of progress toward continuous company-led innovation in creating strategies, methods and tools for advancing the CSR agenda.

Scenario 2

Dateline: San Francisco, 2015
At the BSR Annual Conference, keynoters applaud the triumph of the CSR movement and the demise of its skeptics and naysayers. In a mere two decades, CSR moved from the extraordinary to the expected, embedded in company strategy and operations. Boards of Directors, CEOs and top managers no longer ask for the business case for CSR; it has

been persuasively demonstrated across a wide range of sectors and companies. Continuous enhancement of CSR practices is generally accepted, ranging from adherence to leading norms such as the Global Compact, GRI and ILO core labor standards, to internal management standards such as the new ISO CSR guidance. For large and small, public and private companies alike, CSR is the rule; the small fraction of firms that fail to grasp this find themselves increasingly at a competitive disadvantage. This is the **embed-and-integrate scenario**.

This scenario constitutes the deepening and broadening of CSR integration. Early leaders have been joined by thousands of companies worldwide in melding business values with a strong sense of moral and ethical commitment to CSR from the margins to the core of company business units and functional areas. R&D, product and service design, manufacturing, marketing, finance and accounting embrace CSR as integral to their execution and success. Corporate directors understand that CSR issues—social reporting, environmental stewardship, fair wages, consistency between company policies and lobbying practices—are not only wise business but integral to fiduciary duty.

The embed-and-integrate scenario has materialized because CSR has shed its add-on, dispensable characterization in the company and become entrenched in decision-making and culture. It has proven its worth to shareholder value, reputation and brand, and now enjoys the embrace of multiple champions throughout the ranks of executives, managers and employees. The scenario is characterized by a continuing dynamic of learning, experimentation and implementation of new ideas built on a platform of generally accepted standards of good governance, labor practices, reporting and environmental stewardship. While some of the external conditions of the fad-and-fade scenario are evident, the embed-and-integrate scenario provides CSR resilience amidst adverse conditions such as those described in Scenario 1.

Scenario 3

Dateline: San Francisco, 2015
At the BSR Annual Conference, keynoters reflect on the productive yet ultimately unfulfilled promise of CSR and the ascendance of a wholly different approach to corporate responsibility. While incremental progress was achieved in human rights, labor and environmental performance of corporations, intensifying ecological stresses and social inequalities spurred a fundamental rethinking of the purpose of the corporation. Frustration and disillusionment set in across a broad group of stakeholders, spurring the formation of an improbable coalition of civil society, labor and corporations into a movement in support of "corporate redesign." The notion of "shareholder value," discredited for its "short-termism" and social vacuity, has been replaced by "wealth creation" and "stakeholder governance." These concepts are rooted in the idea that all company stakeholders—employees, communities, suppliers, shareholders—are "investors" in the company and deserve to participate in its governance and benefit from its surplus. Received wisdoms such as the primacy of the shareholder, traditional fiduciary duty and limited liability remain the subjects of ongoing debates, instigating efforts to legally alter the nature and purpose of corporations to reflect a broader social function. This is the **transition-and-transformation scenario**.

Something bigger than any one company, or group of companies, is unfolding. Public confidence in the business community continues to decline amidst sharpening differences among winners and losers in the globalization process. A wave of mergers and acquisitions that benefit a limited few feed a public and civil society backlash against "churning" in the capital markets. A number of retired business leaders step forward, joined in coalition by labor and civil society groups, to challenge the prevailing wisdom concerning the rights and obligations of corporations. Spurred by proliferating initiatives at the state level,[1] a movement to redefine the purpose of the corporation gains momentum among employee groups and civil society organizations, and is fortified by a well-organized group of legal and business scholars.

By 2010, a focus on corporate purpose has moved into the political and policy arena, challenging "shareholderism" as incongruent with 21st-century needs and expectations of business. But unlike earlier incremental and fragmented corporate reform efforts, this movement is attracting broad support among progressive members of the corporate community itself. Disillusionment with short-term motivation is broad and deep, and the concept of companies as "team production" entities dependent on the joint investment of employees, communities, customers, shareholders and other stakeholders has captured the public imagination.[2]

The beacon of this movement is embodied in a new set of "design principles" that strives to foster the innovation and competitive instincts of companies while elevating social purpose as the preeminent goal of the corporation. Its six principles are:[3]

1   The purpose of the corporation is to harness private interests in service to the public interest.
2   Corporations shall accrue fair returns for shareholders, but not at the expense of the legitimate interests of other stakeholders.
3   Corporations shall operate sustainably, meeting the needs of the present generation without compromising the ability of future generations to meet their needs.
4   Corporations shall distribute their wealth equitably among those who contribute to its creation.
5   Corporations shall be governed in a manner that is participatory, transparent, ethical and accountable.
6   Corporate rights shall not infringe on the right of natural persons to govern themselves, nor infringe on other universal human rights.

These principles diffuse quickly to major emerging economies such as Brazil, South Africa, India and China, which themselves face the dual challenges of compering internationally while addressing the acute social inequities that persist despite rapidly expanding economies. Gradually, the principles find their way into law, governance and practice, giving rise to a new vision of the role of corporations in developing societies.

Meanwhile, multinationals, drawn to the emerging South for its labor (skilled and unskilled) and burgeoning consumer markets, find themselves held to these corporate design principles alongside the suite of other prevailing international norms (e.g. Global Compact, GRI, ILO Core Labor Standards) as conditions for doing business.

How plausible is this post-CSR, transformational scenario? For some, no doubt, it stretches credulity given its departure from the prevailing norm of shareholder-driven corporate law and practice. But in historical perspective, major shifts of this magnitude—including the modern environmental, women's and civil rights movements—have occurred with regularity, spurred by grievance, galvanized by a handful of visionaries, and driven by the intersection of crisis and opportunity.

The contemporary pace of social change is certainly not diminishing and is arguably accelerating, owing to the forces of globalization. Revisiting the historical roots of the corporation and the trajectory of CSR is important for framing where we have come from, and for thinking about where we are headed.

Genesis of the modern corporation

A glimpse of the origins of the modern corporation is helpful for understanding CSR in the late 20th and early 21st centuries. Imagining the next phase of CSR invites consideration of the birth of the corporation as we know it. Therefore, an understanding of what has come before provides insight into the range of possibilities for the corporation.

From its genesis in the early Industrial Revolution, the joint-stock corporation took root as the heir to the private-partnership organization, wherein close owner-capitalists maintained high levels of familiarity with the workings of the companies that they partially owned. As the scale of companies grew, so did the need for capital well beyond what the original entrepreneur and close partners could provide. Thus, the idea of passive investors purchasing equity shares emerged, and by the end of the 19th century this would come to dominate the industrial landscape and become a central driving force of the economic expansion of Western nations.

This development was not warmly embraced by all. Indeed, as early as the late 18th century, Adam Smith harbored doubts about the social repercussions of the joint-stock company. Notwithstanding his seminal observation that individuals working to advance their self-interests is the surest route to aggregate societal well-being, Smith understood the threat of business monopoly, privilege and protection to societal interests. His concern with business power to "intimidate the legislature" was a premonition of contemporary corporate political influence, the future scale of which he could not have possibly imagined.

U.S. court decisions in the late 19th century fueled the rise of shareholder supremacy, a notion built on the premise that shareholding entitles shareholders to be the dominant recipients of surplus generated by corporate wealth creation. This view, while upheld in the courts, met with opposition, even among business leaders. Henry Ford and Owen D. Young, GE's chairman in the 1920s, questioned the supremacy of shareholders relative to other parties that contribute to wealth creation.[4] Ford was sued by two shareholders for suspending dividends in favor of plant expansion. When asked what is the purpose of his corporation, Ford responded: "To do as much good as we can, everywhere, for everybody concerned . . . and incidentally to make money." Ford lost his case in a Michigan court. A few years later, Young rhetorically asked: "To whom do I owe my obligations?" His answer: the company owes "a fair rate of return to shareholders" at the same time as it serves the interests of employees, customers and the public.

Notwithstanding this ubiquitous view of corporate purpose, shareholderism intensified during the ensuing decades, subject only to slight modifications by subsequent court rulings.[5] Reinforced by "stock market capitalism"—the unwavering focus on short-term share price at the expense of other performance indicators—shareholder primacy reached its pinnacle after the 1980s. This was evidenced during the wave of mergers and acquisitions (M&As) that swept the business community in the name of maximizing short-term shareholder value. Though the magnitude of long-term benefits—even to shareholders—of the 1980s and subsequent waves of M&As remain contested, the period solidified the supremacy of shareholder rights vis-à-vis the rights of other stakeholders.

Today, the received wisdom of shareholder value as the central purpose of business poses a continuing challenge to CSR. The conflict begins with management education and is entrenched deeply as to be the core driver of board and executive decision-making. Such is the case even though, as Sumantra Ghoshal observes: "If the value creation is achieved by combining the resources of both employees and shareholders, why should the value distribution favor on the latter? Why must the mainstream of our theory be premised on maximizing the returns to just one of these various contributors?"[6]

In a fundamental sense, the emergence of CSR may be viewed as a modest corrective mechanism to shareholderism. Its emphasis on stakeholder rights and participation opposes the unrelenting focus on shareholder interests, especially those that place short-term share price above all other goals.

Outside the Anglo-American business culture, questions about the nature and purpose of the corporation are heard with some frequency. In Germany, for example, where labor is represented on corporate boards, equity ownership is traditionally far more concentrated than in the U.S. and UK. Market dominance rather than share price is viewed as the core performance indicator. The distaste for shareholderism was expressed recently by the chairman of the German Social Democratic party, referring to the failed effort of Deutsche Börse to buy the London Stock Exchange: "Financial investors . . . have no face; they descend upon companies like locusts, destroy everything [for short-term gain] and move on."

In India, South Africa and Brazil, skepticism of shareholderism has cast CSR as an antidote or preemptive mechanism. In India, the Gandhian model of voluntary commitment to public welfare and social needs is at least as influential in shaping attitudes toward corporate purpose as are imported doctrines associated with Friedman and other Western thought leaders that equate corporate purpose with private gain.[7]

Many multinationals, of course, are well aware of these differences as they navigate relationships with host governments and business partners who may hold different views on such critical issues as labor standards, transparency and engagement of indigenous peoples. But with the globalization of business likely to continue unabated, the challenges of understanding and reconciling different CSR cultures will persist for many years to come.

CSR emergence

No single historical event marks the birth of CSR. Some observers date its origins to the early environmentalism of the 1960s, when the first serious regulations were put in place in North America and Europe. At the same time, the long tradition of corporate philanthropy in the U.S. has remained a standard component and expectation of "responsible business" since the early days of the large American industrial firm.

Juxtaposed with the ascendance of shareholder value as the core purpose of business were the early precursors of CSR that took root some 25 years ago. Distilled to its basics, the CSR story is a chronicle of gradual redefinition and expansion ranging from "must do" legal compliance blended with traditional philanthropy, to "should do" based on traditional benefit/cost analysis, to "ought to do" based on emerging global norms of integrity, ethics and justice.[8] These phases form a continuum, implying a process of building toward a more complex and nuanced framework for defining CSR in concept and practice.

Despite its uneven and disjointed evolution, it is fair to say that one identifiable thread in CSR history is a three-fold shift in focus from what is legally required and charitable to what is financially justified and, most recently, to what is morally expected. Each step along this continuum mirrors an evolving definition of the parties to whom corporations are responsible and accountable.[9]

Since 2000, CSR has entered yet another phase often called "integration." This stage reflects a maturation of the CSR idea and recognition of the inherent limits of distancing CSR from core business strategy and operations. The leading edge is now characterized by the idea of seamlessness—identifying and implementing actions that make CSR everyone's business and ending its isolation as a useful but dispensable add-on to "real" business activities. Paradoxically, companies pursuing integration see CSR becoming less visible as it penetrates not only strategy and operations, but corporate governance.

What is emerging in the integration phase is actually multifaceted, comprising:[10]

- *Alignment* with business objectives within overall company strategy
- *Integration* across business entities and functional areas
- *Institutionalization* by embedding strategies, policies, processes and systems into the fabric of the organization.

Though integration is far from the norm, it is clearly moving to a level of best practice among companies who understand the rich opportunities of shifting CSR from the margins to the core of business practice.

The bastions of mainstream business such as *The Wall Street Journal* and *Fortune* now often report on a range of CSR issues such as sweatshops, climate change and fair trade. Another barometer of integration is the extent to which leading companies are blending financial and CSR reporting.[11] Recent reports by Novo Nordisk, Novartis, Dofasco and BC Hydro (Canada), GSK (UK), SAS, Natura (Brazil) and DSM (Netherlands) illustrate this trend. Reading the Novo Nordisk report, for example, one is hard-pressed to distinguish a CSR issue from a business strategy issue. Sections in the Novo Nordisk publication include Defeating Diabetes, Innovation, Business Ethics, and People and Industry Under Fire. In a sector under intense scrutiny for its drug trials, transparency, pricing and post-commercial safety assessment, Novo takes a direct, unflinching approach to reporting. The topics that it grapples with are of no less interest to investors than they are to civil society groups, medical professionals and consumer groups. In the contemporary phase of CSR, integration of this nature is likely to intensify as the confluence of CSR and standard business practices continues to make headway in corporate strategy and operations.

Integration in its various forms will continue unabated. The blurring of CSR with issues of corporate strategy, management and governance seems destined to continue in the next few years to include issues like corporate lobbying, business taxes paid to government, and product stewardship issues that are only now emerging.

In the coming years, will a steady state emerge in which CSR is effectively absorbed into the business mainstream, interwoven with most or all aspects of strategy, management and governance? For many practitioners, this would be the most satisfying of outcomes.

Seeing a dramatic shift in relatively few years from the narrowness of philanthropy to the point of seamless invisibility within the corporation would be nothing short of remarkable. For companies that have embraced CSR, this future would vindicate their efforts. At the same time, this trend would challenge the skeptics who continue to dismiss CSR as a costly, unjustified deviation from business' principal purpose of creating share-holder value.[12] For those who have resisted CSR, it would lay bare the foolishness of coloring CSR as diversionary and immaterial to core business concerns.

Of course, it is premature to judge exactly when—or if—this full integration will occur across a broad band of companies or, alternatively, whether the field will become increasingly stratified among firms that strive for continuously deeper integration and those that remain stuck in the business-case and philanthropic mindsets. Pondering this question logically leads to an even longer-term one: Even if integration does shift from an extraordinary practice to the exceptional and eventually the expected, will such mainstreaming end the evolution of CSR as we know it?

Why ask "what's next?"

Envisioning the future of CSR presents both a challenge and opportunity for companies seeking to maintain prosperity in an increasingly complex business environment that is fraught with risk and rich in opportunity. We are in a moment when we are cognizant of CSR's impressive progress in relatively few years, yet uncertain about its future. It's time to question how the vast resources and unparalleled ingenuity of corporations can be harnessed to build maximum long-term wealth for all stakeholders.

What, specifically, underlies this moment? Three conditions come to mind. The first is *scale*. The reach of the largest multinationals is unprecedented. We already have wit-nessed companies—Wal-Mart, ExxonMobil, BP, Shell—with revenues in excess of a quarter *trillion* dollars (US), a turnover inconceivable even a decade ago. In the case of Wal-Mart, for example, scale of this magnitude is associated with domination of vast networks of suppliers, over a million U.S. workers, and enormous influence on product pricing, labor practices and community impacts. Inevitably, scale at this level gives rise to questions as to whether such corporate influence is matched by commensurate standards of corporate responsibility.

Transience is a second condition. The pace of change in the global economy is exemplified by waves of mergers and acquisitions, fleeting ownership enabled by new investment instruments such as hedge funds, and dislocation associated with frenetic restructuring of where and how goods and services are produced. Large segments of the shareholder population are immune to the repercussions of these rapidly shifting tides. But for workers and communities, the uncertainty is unsettling at minimum and ruinous at worst. For shareholders, transience is simply the modern manifestation of "creative destruction," enabling the market to relentlessly drive toward near-term shareholder returns often, though not always, in the name of efficiency and competitiveness. For workers and communities, however, transience is the embodiment of the amorality of business and the market economy in general, bowing to near-term returns at the expense of broader long-term, non-shareholder interests.

Finally, *disparities* constitute a third condition that contributes to the anxiety over the direction of global companies. Disparities come in many forms—the ratio of executive pay to average wages; the inequalities between shareholder returns and non-shareholder (employee, community, environment) returns; and imbalances between how corporations are governed and who is affected by such governance. Disparities are also present in significant segments of capital markets, exemplified by investment banking firms that accrue extraordinary profits while shifting the risks to other parties. This has been termed the "Heads we win, tails you lose" strategy.[13] Lastly, disparities are evident in the flat or declining real wages of workers versus the steady, sometimes dramatic increases of the wealth of CEOs.

Scale, transience and disparities—these conditions conspire to infect the public perception of business and to prompt questions about what the corporate future holds. The erosion of the safety net that corporations once provided in terms of health coverage, pension funds and job tenure further feeds unease that the business-society social contract is unraveling. These developments, combined with the sense that CSR may be approaching its limits, cloud the corporate future. But clouds need not lead to paralysis. Indeed, all signals point to a moment of opportunity for companies to shape—not just react to—the future of CSR.

Reflections

Few would doubt that the global future is inextricably linked to the corporate future. As such, CSR is not an option; it is a reality. The sheer weight of the corporate role in wealth creation and the footprint associated with this creative process makes responsibility inevitable. We may argue about the degree and proper responses associated with such responsibility, but there can be little argument about the fact itself.

The core question facing companies is how to harness the full potential of business to serve the public interest while preserving and enhancing core assets—creativity, innovation and competitive drive. In some sense, this has always been the central challenge of CSR. We see more than ever that the opportunities for individual, company and collective action are plentiful. Companies coming together—often prodded by external parties—to tackle climate change is a living example of this.

But for every opportunity realized, dozens remain untapped. Why, for example, do we not see U.S. companies rallying for universal health care in the face of the enormous cost burdens that threaten their financial future? Or, in the case of the airline and transport services industry, both buffeted by petroleum price hikes and uncertainties, why do we not see collective action to vastly accelerate alternative fuels research? Why is there a paucity of initiatives like Nike's challenge to apparel makers to create common standards and audits for contract manufacturers? Is it a question of political will? Legal impediments? Or just blind competitiveness that obscures the potential payoffs?

Two centuries ago, social purpose was central to the charter of U.S. corporations. One hundred years ago, well into the era of the large, investor-owned companies, industrialists like Ford and Young understood the concept of harnessing the private interest to serve a broader public purpose. With the right mix of wisdom and will, the next decades may well witness a turn away from the deleterious effects of single-minded shareholderism toward next-generation CSR that meets the dual goals of prosperous corporations and prosperous societies.

Notes

1   Current examples of state initiatives to redefine directors' duties and/or establish special charters for responsible companies have occurred in California, Minnesota and Maine.

2   Blair, Margaret M. and Stout, Lynn A., "A Team Production Theory of Corporate Law," *Virginia Law Review*, Vol. 85, No. 2, pp. 248–328, March 1999, http://ssrn.com/abstract=425500.

3   These principles, in draft at this writing, reflect the collective thinking of a forum of individuals in law, business, labor, civil society, government and journalism, who have begun an initiative to advance corporate redesign. See www.corporate2020.org.

4   Michael Skapinker, "Only the Strong Survive," *Financial Times*, June 11–12, 2005, W1.

5   The courts tended to dodge the question of the distinction between long-term profit maximization and short-term profit and share price maximization, generally upholding the right of companies to take non-maximizing actions in the short term as long as they would achieve long-term maximization.

6   Sumantra Ghoshal, "Bad Management Theories are Destroying Good Management Practices," *Academy of Management Learning & Education*, 2005, Vol. 4, No. 1, 75–91.

7   N.K. Balasubramanian *et al.*, "Emerging Opportunities or Traditions Reinforced: An Analysis of the Attitudes Towards CSR and Trends of Thinking About CSR in India," *Journal of Corporate Citizenship*, 17 (spring 2005), 79–92.

8   Another characterization of CSR's evolution is its transition from public relations to managing reputations, and operational risk to strategic differentiator. Simon Zadek, *Third Generation Corporate Citizenship: Public Policy and Business in Society*, The Foreign Policy Center, 2001.

9   This framework is a variant on Lynne Sharpe Paine, *Value Shift*, New York, McGraw-Hill, 2003, 123.

10   Boston College Center for Corporate Citizenship, *Integration: Critical Link for Corporate Citizenship—Strategies and Real Cases from 8 Companies*. 2005. For an alternative but compatible framework of the transition from pre-compliance to post-strategic, see also Simon Zadek, "The Path to Corporate Responsibility," *Harvard Business Review*, Dec. 2004, 125–132.

11   Allen White, "New Wine, New Bottles: The Rise of Non-Financial Reporting," June 20, 2005, http://www.bsr.org/Meta/200506_BSR_Allen-White_Essay.pdf.

12   The recent *Economist* piece, and the furor it triggered, attests to the durability of this view. "The Good Company," *Economist*, January 22, 2005, 3–22.

13   Philip Augar, *The Greed Merchants*, Cambridge, England: Portfolio, 2005.

Michael Blowfield and Jedrzej George Frynas

SETTING NEW AGENDAS

Critical perspectives on Corporate Social Responsibility in the developing world

THE THEME OF this special issue is Corporate Social Responsibility (CSR) in the developing world, and the need for more critical perspectives to understand what CSR does and could mean for the poor and marginalized in developing countries. Numerous claims have been made about the contribution CSR can make to poverty alleviation and other development goals. However, the contributors to this issue have reached the conclusion that current CSR approaches do not warrant such claims. Their work shows the need for a critical approach to the strengths and limitations of CSR, one that poses questions that hitherto have been unasked or neglected. In this editorial we outline what such a critical agenda might look like, drawing on the work of our fellow contributors and the many others who have been invited to comment.

A critical agenda is needed because many policy-makers see business as important in meeting development challenges: not just those of economic growth, but also in areas such as combating HIV/AIDS, reducing poverty and building human capital. Moreover, government, civil society and business all to some extent see CSR as a bridge connecting the arenas of business and development, and increasingly discuss CSR programmes in terms of their contribution to development. Implicit in this view is that developing economies are different from developed ones, and require particular attention. This broadly complements the premise of international development theory that there are unique aspects to issues such as poverty and sustainability in the developing world that demand different solutions from those that might be implemented in developed economies. However, as many of the articles in this issue make plain, the challenges of development are complex. Therefore, to understand the relationship between CSR and development we need to go beyond the issues identified within the field of CSR itself, and look at how that field is helping business develop and address the central issues identified by the international development community.

In order to understand the potential and limitations of CSR's contribution, we need first to have a working understanding of what we mean by CSR; accordingly, in the next section of this editorial we provide a short overview of how CSR is defined. We then examine the various criticisms made of CSR, and consider whether they are valid in a developing-country context. On the basis of the articles in this special issue, we explore several ways in which CSR affects international development, and ask what we know and need to know about how the ideas, norms and values that underpin CSR theory and practice relate to developmental goals. We make no apology for the fact that we raise many questions to which we do not have answers; however, we conclude with some next steps that policy-makers, CSR practitioners and researchers might usefully consider.

What is CSR?

While 'corporate social responsibility' is a recent term, a preoccupation with business ethics and the social dimensions of business activity has been around for a very long time. Business practices based on moral principles and 'controlled greed' were advocated by pre-Christian western thinkers such as Cicero in the first century BC and their non-western counterparts such as India's Kautilya in the fourth century BC; Islam and the medieval Christian Church publicly condemned certain business practices, notably usury. The modern precursors of CSR can be traced back to nineteenth-century boycotts of foodstuffs produced with slave labour, the moral vision of entrepreneurs such as Cadbury and Marks, and the Nuremberg war crimes trials after the Second World War, which saw the directors of the German firm I. G. Farben found guilty of mass murder and using slave labour.[1] From a historical perspective, then, CSR is simply the latest manifestation of earlier debates on the role of business in society. What is new, according to Fabig and Boele, is that 'today's debates are conducted at the intersection of development, environment and human rights, and are more global in outlook than earlier in this [the twentieth] century or even in the 1960s'.[2]

There is no agreement among observers on why the concept of CSR has risen to prominence in recent history, or on the definition of what companies should be responsible for and how. As Michael Blowfield argues in this issue, there are discernible common elements to managing CSR, and these significantly influence how companies view their responsibilities. However, this does not stop CSR from being interpreted differently by different people. It can, for example, mean different things to practitioners seeking to implement CSR inside companies and to researchers trying to establish CSR as a discipline; it can also mean different things to NGOs and to companies. Although these differences are an inevitable and potentially fruitful element of the innovation process, they can be frustrating, not least to company managers who might prefer a bounded concept similar to quality control or financial accounting. Instead, managers find themselves wrestling with issues as diverse as animal rights, corporate governance, environmental management, corporate philanthropy, stakeholder management, labour rights and community development. To complicate matters further, the vocabulary of business-society debates is being expanded to include new terms such as corporate accountability, socially responsible investment and sustainable development, aimed variously at replacing, redefining or complementing the CSR concept.

Institutions and individuals can also change their interpretations of CSR. For instance, the World Business Council for Sustainable Development (WBCSD) has changed its definition over time. Initially (1998), it referred to CSR as 'the continuing commitment by business to behave ethically and contribute to economic development while improving the quality of life of the workforce and their families as well as of the local community and society at large'. But that definition was later changed (2002) to 'the commitment of business to contribute to sustainable economic development, working with employees, their families, the local community and society at large to improve their quality of life'.

CSR as culture

One way of looking at CSR is in terms of its cultural roots, reflecting the belief, expressed by writers from Max Weber to Charles Turner, that culture affects capitalism. While notions of corporate responsibility are not unique to the West, the most publicized approaches to CSR today may be regarded as specifically Anglo-Saxon, since the rediscovery of 'social' concerns of business in Anglo-Saxon countries stems from a more rigid division between 'social' and 'economic' affairs and the stress on individualistic—rather than communitarian—values. Continental European, Asian or African societies may not have the term CSR in their vocabularies, yet some of these societies may have had a longstanding social contract whereby business has social obligations to employees or wider society, such as exists in Japan.[3]

While the origins of the current CSR concept may have been Anglo-Saxon, the meaning of CSR can differ from one society to another. When asked by the WBCSD what CSR means to them, people from different countries emphasized different issues: for instance, environmental issues were stressed in Thailand, while Ghanaians stressed empowering local communities.[4] At the same time, the ethical concerns of business managers differ among nations,[5] and managers in multinational companies can find themselves juggling the perhaps contrary expectations of their local and head offices.[6] These differences render any common or comprehensive definition of what constitutes corporate responsibility elusive, especially when new initiatives seem to be continually emerging.

CSR as an alternative to government

For many proponents and critics, a key distinguishing feature of CSR is the voluntary nature of the initiatives companies undertake in its name, in contrast to the formal regulatory mechanisms historically used to govern business.[7] Few hold that business should not be legally accountable, but in certain circumstances a voluntary approach to regulating business behaviour might be beneficial. For instance, where there is a strong system of governance, voluntary approaches might be a way of extending company accountability without the need for new legislation—a complementary approach encouraging business to act responsibly but not an alternative to the rule of law. Equally, where the rule of law is weak, voluntary approaches can encourage multinational companies to introduce higher levels of performance than those required for local legal compliance.

'Voluntary CSR' can also be interpreted as part of a wider revisiting of the role of government, and an increasing focus on enabling legislation that encourages certain behaviours rather than simply attempting to codify every detail of compliance. Examples include the UK Pension Fund Act 2000 or the French Economic Regulations Act 2001, both of which require companies to report on CSR without attempting to define what that means.

However interpreted, the broad idea of 'voluntary' mechanisms to regulate business behaviour is winning support from policy-makers in national governments and inter-governmental organizations, underpinned by the assumption that firms are capable of policing themselves in the absence of binding international and national law to regulate corporate behaviour. The European Commission's Green Paper of July 2001 defined CSR as 'a concept whereby companies integrate social and environmental concerns in their business operations and in their interaction with their stakeholders on a voluntary basis'.

Yet this perspective on CSR is not shared by everyone, and there are reservations about the emphasis on voluntarism. Indeed, many 'voluntary' initiatives also have a 'mandatory' aspect, and there are already many intersections between CSR and the law, including actual new legislation (as passed by Ghana to require logging companies to secure a Social Responsibility Agreement with customary landowners) as well as legal aspects to some CSR initiatives (as when a code of conduct by a multinational firm is incorporated into a contract with a supplier, becoming legally binding).[8] Effective CSR may well require good government (e.g. to draft regional development plans), and some policy-makers see CSR as a stepping-stone towards legal codification. World Bank staff, for example, have argued that CSR can be a useful step on the way to better national legislation in countries that have failed to enforce their laws.[9] Therefore, important as voluntaryism may be, it is not necessarily appropriate to see it as the lowest common denominator of CSR.

CSR as an umbrella term

It will be apparent from the above discussion that CSR is not the homogeneous, coherent concept that it is often presented as being. Indeed, one concern is that the use of the term CSR has become so broad as to allow people to interpret and adopt it for many different purposes. This vagueness restricts CSR's usefulness both as an analytical tool and as a guide for decision-makers. The various contributors to this special issue have different understandings of what CSR represents and, rather than offering yet another definition at the start, we have left it to them to set out what they each mean by CSR in their articles. But their views are not entirely disparate, and, rather than looking for an inclusive definition, it may be more useful to think of CSR as an umbrella term for a variety of theories and practices all of which recognize the following: (a) that companies have a responsibility for their impact on society and the natural environment, sometimes beyond legal compliance and the liability of individuals; (b) that companies have a responsibility for the behaviour of others with whom they do business (e.g. within supply chains); and (c) that business needs to manage its relationship with wider society, whether for reasons of commercial viability or to add value to society.

Some of the ambiguity about CSR arises because the term has been used to refer both to a research agenda and to corporate practice. In this special issue we are concerned with both, but we primarily hope to advance a new research agenda and a debate on the business-society relationship. We feel that the current research agenda on CSR lacks systematic rigour and fails to tackle key questions. At the same time, while CSR is a broad church, the research questions tend to be surprisingly narrow. For example, in business schools much of the research on CSR focuses on issues related to the stakeholder view of the firm and the potential contribution of CSR to profitability.[10] Even within such a restricted research agenda, moreover, vital questions are not being asked. For example, while dozens of studies have investigated the correlation between firms' social commitment and profitability, a key causal question remains unanswered: does social commitment drive a firm's profitability, or does profitability allow the firm to invest in social initiatives?

A particular concern of this special issue is to stimulate more profound questions related to the role of CSR in international development. When CSR emerged as a distinct field in the early 1990s, most of the initial work was focused on developed economies or the adoption of universal norms such as basic workers' rights. Although there were initiatives—such as those from the fair trade movement—that were specific to the developing world, by the time empirical studies started to be commissioned to investigate whether CSR could benefit the poor and marginalized,[11] certain conventions and orthodoxies had already been established. Consequently, research into CSR and development has tended to be normative, based on issues and approaches that are taken for granted. As we discuss below, this leaves unasked important questions about the structural biases of CSR, and means that the ways in which ideology informs and influences the possibilities of CSR are either unacknowledged or regarded as unproblematic. Yet, as can be inferred from the discussion of voluntarism above, there are strong ideational elements to different ideas about CSR, and what we mean by CSR and its consequences for the role of business in development will differ significantly depending on whether the goals, instruments and agents of CSR conform with, for instance, social democratic, libertarian or neo-conservative development agendas. These differing agendas are likely to affect not only what values are promoted, but also the way CSR is implemented.

Criticisms of CSR

Along with the greater attention paid to the role of business in developing economies since the 1980s have come frequent complaints that companies exploit the social and environmental conditions of such countries. In this light, efforts intended to tackle corporate abuses with the backing of companies themselves should be welcomed. CSR is proposed as benefiting both companies and the societies in which they operate. It is presented as a universal good that can be embraced by different sections of the political spectrum. Moreover, in the context of international development and poverty alleviation, CSR is recommended as beneficial to both the North and the South, contributing simultaneously to universal human rights, equity and economic growth.

The contributors to this special issue embrace the multiple potentials of CSR, yet each of them has concerns both about CSR in its current form and about its implications for international development. These concerns were not the starting point of their analyses, but rather the result of discussions among the contributors; nonetheless, despite the different methods and disciplines represented here, those concerns have much in common.

Criticism of CSR is by no means unique to the authors gathered here. In addition to the many companies still resistant to CSR, and the politicians and academics who see it as a barrier to trade, civil society advocates are increasingly questioning its benefits. Broadly speaking, most criticism falls into two camps: one could be characterized as the 'CSR is bad capitalism' school,[12] the other as 'weak CSR is bad development' school.[13]

The 'CSR is bad capitalism' school, associated with traditional business management theory, echoes Milton Friedman's famous statement that there is 'only one social responsibility of business: to use its resources and engage in activities designed to increase its profits'.[14] According to this view, CSR is inherently misguided in principle. By pursuing social and environmental objectives, firms may ultimately hurt shareholders by generating lower profits. Furthermore, firms are said to lack the expertise to engage in solving social problems. Nonetheless, business scholars have tried to reconcile profit-maximizing objectives with social objectives by suggesting that CSR can lead to higher long-term profitability. Margolis and Walsh found that, between 1972 and 2002, at least 127 published empirical studies examined the relationship between socially responsible behaviour on the part of companies and their financial performance, the majority of them pointing to a positive relationship between the two variables.[15]

The 'weak CSR is bad development' school, associated with civil society organizations and critics of business behaviour, argues that companies should take responsibility for the broader impacts of business activity, but that current CSR practice is simply inadequate for this purpose. According to this view, the planning and implementation of social programmes by firms is generally deficient, although the evidence is often drawn from the worst abuses, which may not be a fair test of CSR's effectiveness. Many of these critics consider the provision of social justice the domain of state regulation or argue that, at a minimum, the state has an obligation to monitor corporate social programmes. They point out that—in the absence of state involvement and proper monitoring—CSR initiatives such as corporate codes of conduct tend to lack precision and uniformity across firms and industries, and that there are few, if any, sanctions for non-compliance. Nonetheless, it should be noted that although its criticisms of CSR can be strident, this school treats CSR as capable of reform, for instance through improved partnerships, or better constructed and implemented codes of conduct.[16]

Two other critical schools should be acknowledged: one that disputes that capitalism can make any contribution to social and environmental justice,[17] and another that views CSR as nothing more than good capitalism and therefore not worth thinking about in its own right.[18]

All of these critiques have something to offer in terms of understanding CSR, but they have not invested sufficient effort in analysing the actual impact of CSR on those it claims to benefit. Indeed, one of the common concerns of the authors in this special issue is that dogmatic positions are being taken about what is right and wrong on the basis what amounts to little more than ad hoc case-study evidence. Beyond this, we are concerned that CSR is becoming a field of passionately felt answers and too many unasked questions. What unites the contributions in this special issue is the search for the right questions to be asking in the first place. These questions can be broadly divided into four areas: the meaning of CSR for developing countries, its relationship to international governance, its analytical limitations, and the consequences of thinking in terms of the business case for CSR.

What CSR means to developing economies

Some (including some of the contributors here) would argue that CSR is a work in progress and that, rather than condemning the good for being imperfect, we should examine the processes under way and explore whether they are likely to fulfil their promise. Yet the fact is that we know very little about the impact of CSR initiatives in developing countries, and what we do know raises questions about both the efficiency of CSR approaches and the tangible benefits for the poor and marginalized. As Newell puts it, the most we can confidently say about CSR's impact at the present time is that it benefits some people and some companies in some situations.

To the extent that thought is being given to the consequences (both theoretical and actual) of CSR for the developing world, this tends to be at the micro level, looking at what particular companies or initiatives are doing. There has been some theoretical work on the relationship between CSR and national competitive advantage that can be extended to developing countries,[19] but do we know enough about big-picture issues such as the effect of social and environmental standards on foreign direct investment and trade? Some major development challenges, such as HIV/AIDS, are part of CSR discussions, not least because they affect company efficiency, but this has not yet resulted in anything like concentrated intercompany/interindustry campaigns, and we do not know where the tipping point is between isolated and concerted action.

The success of CSR initiatives is often linked to stakeholder dialogue and stakeholder engagement, ideas that occur repeatedly in discussions of best CSR practice. Stakeholder engagement brings together representatives of business, non-governmental and public sectors in order to identify and address aspects of corporate responsibility, and has the added advantage that it has gained legitimacy among both business and development practitioners. As with many elements of CSR practice, it is represented as being ideationally neutral. But stakeholder engagement presents particular challenges in a developing-country context where factors such as language, culture, education and pluralistic values can all affect the process of negotiation and decision-making. In addition, we need to consider whether some of those thought of as stakeholders, such as workers and local communities, can participate directly or are dependent on the services of proxies such as trade unions and NGOs. If the former is the case, are the voices of those known to have little influence being heard? If it is the latter, are the issues raised really the priorities of the poor and marginalized, or rather those that have the most resonance with the civil society organizations and their funders? For instance, homeworkers in the clothing industry and smallholder farmers were for a long time overlooked by ethical sourcing initiatives,[20] and the priority issues for workforces dominated by women have not been addressed in these initiatives.[21] Such examples indicate that civil society organizations are less likely to press firms for improvements to the working conditions of groups that are either not a priority for these organizations or simply not recognized. The question of who gets represented is not merely an academic nicety, but has profound implications for the well-being of certain members of society in developing countries.

Those groups whose issues are not taken up by civil society organizations may also be ignored by firms since they are not considered 'primary stakeholders'. Unlike organized labour, homeworkers will rarely present a threat to a firm's productivity, nor is the firm's dependence on them likely to be high. Ironically, a firm's commitment to CSR can actually lead to these marginalized groups being seen as a threat to the company's claim to responsible operation. Some major sporting goods companies, for instance, have reduced the amount of outsourcing to smaller producers in part because it is difficult to monitor those facilities.[22] Since inclusion in or exclusion from stakeholder status is not based on either legal rights or moral obligations, a stakeholder's recognition is contingent upon the business case for that recognition. Consequently, the well-being of some groups in developing countries may be jeopardized by the very pursuit of CSR.

Beyond the question of inclusion or exclusion of certain groups or issues, neither CSR theory nor its practice adequately addresses questions about the relationship between companies and others. For example, should the stakeholder relationship be based on accountability, disclosure, claim or entitlement? Can the concerns of society about business be disaggregated into typically single-issue-oriented stakeholder groups? How and by whom are competing claims by those groups to be addressed? As things stand, CSR promotes an approach the effectiveness of which clearly depends on how power is located and exerted, and yet the insights of power relations theory have not been widely used in the CSR context.

CSR and governance

We noted above that voluntarism is one recurring feature of contemporary CSR, and in the context of international development one of the most important sets of questions is about how CSR relates to changing models of national and international governance. CSR is frequently advocated as a means of filling gaps in governance that have arisen with the acceleration of liberal economic globalization. But should CSR be regarded as a stopgap measure while ways are sought to give social and environmental issues a similar degree of international protection to that enjoyed by capital and intellectual property? Is it a stepping-stone on the path to better national regulation in developing countries? Or is it part of a longer-term project for overcoming the weaknesses of territorially prescribed judicial and welfare mechanisms, that is, addressing the limitations of the nation-state in regulating a global economy?

We are concerned that such questions are not being widely asked at a time when CSR is presented by some as a means of exercising control over the behaviour of business without resort to formal jurisprudence. The UK's Department for International Development has stated that 'international legally binding frameworks for multinational companies may divert attention and energy away from encouraging corporate social responsibility and towards legal process'.[23] While initiatives such as the King Report on Corporate Governance in South Africa suggest that developing countries might not object to this trend, the view expressed by DFID is not dissimilar to that of various business leaders and business writers who advocate CSR as a means of reducing the need for formal regulation. As Freeman and Reed, pioneers of business-centred stakeholder theory, state: 'If this task of stakeholder management is done properly, much of the air is let out of critics who argue that the corporation must be democratised in terms of increased direct citizen participation.'[24] Yet, even as these prescriptions are made, there is scant discussion of the implications of a shift towards a new regulatory regime for the developing world and indeed international development policy.

It is not that new approaches fail to put demands on companies: corporate-led bodies such as the WBCSD seek to improve the effectiveness of CSR practice within firms, and international organizations such as the World Bank and the United Nations have emphasized the need to build corporate and developing-country government capacity to engage in CSR.[25] But how can this be achieved if the underlying dimensions of CSR are not made clear? What are the implications of voluntarism for the developing world?

At the same time, NGO appeals for more international regulation seem to ignore the many historical failures of formal regulatory approaches to international social and environmental justice. Certainly it seems to make sense to explore further the role of national legislation and enforcement, even though some companies with a stated commitment to CSR are lobbying aggressively against suggested legal models such as the US Alien Tort Claims Act.[26] We need to learn more about the optimal balance of voluntary and mandatory, national and international, prescriptive and enabling regulation. Will the role of national and regional government move from that of enforcer to that of facilitator? Will CSR be another channel whereby business influences the substance of formal justice? Are the concept of 'stakeholder' and the notion of 'multi-stakeholder engagement' rigorous and inclusive enough to complement or even be an alternative to representative democracy in the governance process?

Analytical limitations of CSR

The above questions related to international development and governance have far-reaching implications. Yet, while finding answers to them is of course important, we also need to consider why the questions themselves are only now being asked. We cannot understand how CSR is developing only by examining what has happened; equally important is to explore who and what are being overlooked, taken for granted, ignored or excluded. We have already mentioned some of the people in developing countries who are ignored or marginalized by CSR, not because they do not have a valid claim to be considered stakeholders, but because they were either not acknowledged or were too difficult to manage. This is recognized by some CSR researchers, but typically the proposed solution is to improve the taxonomy of stakeholders. What this technical response fails to ask is whether there is anything inherent within current approaches to CSR that causes certain entities and aspects of justice and well-being to be excluded in the first place.

Going beyond technical responses that simply reinforce existing norms about why and how to conduct CSR requires us to introduce historical and ideational perspectives into our analysis. These are all missing from research at present, even as CSR is increasingly viewed as a discipline in its own right. Consequently, while CSR is presented simultaneously as a response to and a product of globalization, nowhere is there any recognition that globalization is a highly contested concept strongly influenced by ideological interpretation, and this in turn makes it difficult to understand any inherent possibilities, biases or limitations in contemporary approaches. In other words, CSR as a discipline lacks the means reflexively to consider its own orthodoxy.

Such a capacity is a prerequisite for understanding or predicting CSR's impact, especially when applied in societies that do not share the same cultural and societal norms, values and priorities that underpin CSR. Without it, CSR is likely to treat particular norms as universal, and particular approaches as globally applicable. In doing so, there is a strong possibility that CSR will legitimize and reproduce values and perspectives that are not in the interests of developing economies or the poor and marginalized.

CSR practice does not, of course, lack ideational or historical dimensions, but these are almost entirely absent from any discussion about CSR. Cutting across this absence of a structural understanding is an inability or unwillingness to consider causality. Thus, for instance, poverty is presented as a regrettable fact rather than a consequence of any causal conditions and events. The advantage of this is that it allows poverty to be presented to business as something undesirable and soluble on a par with, for instance, a malfunctioning valve or a quality control problem. However, it does nothing to encourage examination of the complexity of multilayered, structurally rooted problems or of the role of business within them.

An unwillingness to tackle causality is not unique to CSR, and it is possible to argue that one of the reasons why CSR and international development practice have moved closer together is that they share and reinforce assumptions that poverty and marginalization are fundamentally matters of geography, identity or difference, rather than structural phenomena. The shift evident in development theory from seeing poverty as something systemic to seeing it as a matter of function/dysfunction falls outside our scope here, but it is worth noting that CSR and development share certain beliefs or myths about the developing world. For instance, both treat the geographical separation of North–South, developed and developing, as valid distinctions in understanding where and why poverty exists. Both treat civil society as a valid, unproblematic and largely positive category, despite the many differences among civil society organizations and the questions their roles raise about contemporary democracy. Above all, by ignoring any structural dimension to poverty, they reinforce the belief that it can be solved by discrete, identifiable actors.

It is not necessarily that the assumptions found in CSR are wrong; but at present they are simply not acknowledged, and this has real consequences both for international development and for companies. In Litvin's historical study of corporations that were harmed or destroyed because of their behaviour in foreign countries, a recurring theme is the tragic consequences of failing to invest in understanding and addressing the complexities of their relationship with society.[27] One of the concerns about contemporary CSR is that, rather than encouraging more detailed understanding, it may be reinforcing the misguided belief that for every complex problem there is a simple solution.

The business case for CSR

Anyone wondering how the above assumptions get reproduced and legitimized need look no further than the emphasis placed on 'the business case for CSR'. Throughout this editorial we have cited examples of business thinking influencing the language and practice of CSR. For example, we have quoted Freeman and Reed's belief that stakeholders are something to be managed by companies (seemingly little different from a product or a brand), and we have alluded to the use of techniques rooted in financial management to manage social and environmental performance. Perhaps above all, we have repeatedly used the term 'business' as if it were a homogeneous category, rather than an arena where the often conflicting interests of managers, other employees, investors and other entities are acted out.

Nowhere is acceptance of business homogeneity more apparent than in the numerous attempts to make the business case for CSR. The business case is partly driven by business schools, where CSR is usually justified as enabling managers either to protect firms from external threats (e.g. risk management) or to benefit from external opportunities (e.g. new product development through partnerships with NGOs)—as illustrated by the many studies on the contribution of CSR towards firm profitability or those on stakeholder mapping in top business journals such as the *Academy of Management Review*. At the extreme, firms are advised to consider a group as a stakeholder only if they depend on its resources.[28] Such work has an effect far beyond business schools, as it has the potential to influence CSR practitioners and future managers who translate ideas about CSR into practice.

However, if consideration of a social, economic or environmental issue depends on there being a business case for such consideration, what happens to those issues where that case cannot be made? Is the paramountcy granted to the business case influencing which issues get addressed and which ones ignored? Can corporations, built on a western economic model, recognize values rooted in other cultures? Is CSR in some way allowing business to appropriate the meaning of ethics?

If we look at CSR standards such as those for workers' rights and natural resource management, it is certainly possible to conclude that important issues for people in developing countries have been inadequately addressed. For instance, labour codes of practice are far more likely to outlaw slavery and child labour (practices where there is little direct financial motivation to continue, especially compared to the potential consequences of a consumer backlash) than to recognize the right to a living wage or freedom of association (both of which many companies fear might work to their commercial disadvantage). But we should also be aware of what has not been included at all in such standards. One may ask, for example, why crucial economic issues (as opposed to labour issues) are always excluded from the contents of CSR standards, and whose interests are served when no mention is made of the right to invest and disinvest at will or the supremacy of the market as a determinant of price.

The business case is not necessarily a bad thing, and it is an important aspect of getting senior management engaged in CSR. But we need to consider how far the business case shapes not only the choice of issues or relevant constituents, but also the very discourse that delineates the boundaries of CSR. This influence is evident in the unquestioned adoption of business measurement and management techniques to address social and environmental issues, something that Michael Blowfield claims in this issue contributes to business's redefining of the meaning of development. These techniques determine, to some extent, who or what is a stakeholder, and what issues are addressed. In other words, participation in the CSR discourse is disciplined by the need to use a language and modes of thinking acceptable to the business community.

Notes

1   Joanne B. Ciulla, 'Why is business talking about ethics? Reflections on foreign conversations', *California Management Review* 34: 1, 1991, pp. 67–86; Scott Pegg, 'An emerging market for the new millennium: transnational corporations and human rights', in Jedrzej George Frynas and Scott Pegg, eds, *Transnational corporations and human rights* (London: Palgrave, 2003); R. C. Sekhar, *Ethical choices in business* (Delhi: Response Books, 2002).

2   Heike Fabig and Richard Boele, 'The changing nature of NGO activity in a globalizing world: pushing the corporate responsibility agenda', *IDS Bulletin* 30: 3, 1999, p. 63.

3   Charles H. Turner and Fons Trompenaars, *The seven cultures of capitalism: value systems for creating wealth in the United States, Britain, Japan, Germany, France, Sweden and the Netherlands* (New York: Doubleday, 1993), ch. 8.

4   World Business Council for Sustainable Development, *Corporate social responsibility: making good business sense* (Geneva: WBCSD, 2000).

5   Terence Jackson, 'Management ethics and corporate policy: a cross-cultural comparison', *Journal of Management Studies* 37: 3, 2003, pp. 349–69.

6   John Stopford and Susan Strange, *Rival states, rival firms: competition for world market shares* (Cambridge: Cambridge University Press, 1991).

7   K. Andrews, 'Can the best corporations be made moral?', *Harvard Business Review*, May–June 1973, pp. 57–64; Christian Aid, *Behind the mask: the real face of corporate social responsibility* (London: Christian Aid, 2004). See also the set of largely critical articles published in *The Economist*, 20 Jan. 2005.

8   Halina Ward, *Legal issues in corporate citizenship* (London: International Institute for Environment and Development, 2003).

9   Michael Klein and Tim Harford, 'Corporate responsibility: when will voluntary reputation building improve standards?', *Public Policy Journal*, Washington DC, accessed at http://rru.worldbank.org/ PublicPolicyjournal/Summary.aspx?id=271, accessed 15 Feb. 2005.

10 For a review see Joshua D. Margolis and James P. Walsh, 'Misery loves companies: rethinking social initiatives by business', *Administrative Science Quarterly* 48: 2, 2003, pp. 268–305.

11 See e.g. Natural Resources and Ethical Trade Programme, 'Ethical trade and sustainable rural livelihoods', in Diane Carney, ed., *Sustainable rural livelihoods: what contribution can we make?* (London: Department for International Development, 1998).

12 See e.g. Theodore Levitt, 'The dangers of social responsibility', *Harvard Business Review* 36: 5, 1958, pp. 41–50; Milton Friedman, *Capitalism and freedom* (Chicago: University of Chicago Press, 1962); David Henderson, *Misguided virtues: false notions of corporate social responsibility* (London: Institute of Economic Affairs, 2002); 'Two-faced capitalism', *The Economist*, 24 Jan. 2004, available at www.Economist.com.

13 See e.g. Christian Aid, *Behind the mask*; Stephanie Barrientos, Catherine Dolan and Anne Tallontire, 'A gendered value chain approach to codes of conduct in African horti-culture', *World Development* 31: 9, 2003, pp. 1511–27; Jem Bendell, *Barricades and boardrooms: a contemporary history of the corporate accountability movement*, Technology, Business and Society Programme Paper 13 (Geneva: United Nations Research Institute for Social Development, June 2004); Dara O'Rourke, 'Outsourcing regulation: non-governmental systems of labor standards and monitoring', *Policy Studies Journal* 31: 1, 2003, pp. 1–29.

14 Friedman, *Capitalism and freedom*, p. 133.

15 Margolis and Walsh, 'Misery loves companies'.

16 Steve Waddell, 'Complementary resources: the win-win rationale for partnership with NGOs', in Jem Bendell, ed., *Terms for endearment: business, NGOs and sustainable development* (Sheffield: Greenleaf, 2000); Alex Wawryk, 'Regulating transnational corporations through corporate codes of conduct', in Frynas and Pegg, *Transnational corporations and human rights*.

17 See e.g. Marjorie Kelly, *The divine right of capital: dethroning the corporate aristocracy* (San Francisco: Berrett-Koehler, 2001).

18 See e.g. Tom Sorell and John Hendry, *Business ethics* (Oxford: Butterworth-Heinemann, 1994); Richard E. Freeman and David Reed, 'Stockholders and stakeholders: a

new perspective on corporate governance', *California Management Review* 25: 3, 1983, pp. 88–106; Richard E. Freeman, *Strategic management: a stakeholder approach* (Boston: Pitman, 2004).

19   Tracey Swift and Simon Zadek, *Corporate responsibility and the competitive advantage of nations* (London: Institute of Social and Ethical Accountability with the Copenhagen Centre, 2002).

20   See e.g. Jedrzej George Frynas, 'The transnational garment industry in South and South-East Asia', in Frynas and Pegg, *Transnational corporations and human rights*, p. 167; Michael E. Blowfield, 'Ethical supply chains in the cocoa, coffee and tea industries', *Greener Management International* 43, Autumn 2004, pp. 15–24; Dena Freeman, 'Homeworkers in global supply chains', *Greener Management International* 43, Autumn 2004, pp. 107–18.

21   Barrientos et al., 'A gendered value chain approach to codes of conduct'.

22   Michael E. Blowfield, 'Corporate responsibility and voluntary labor codes in the context of globalization and labor in developing countries', paper presented at the conference on Globalization and Labor at Brown University, Watson Institute for International Studies, Dec. 2004.

23   DFID, *DFID and corporate social responsibility* (London: Department for International Development, 2003), p. 9.

24   Freeman and Reed, 'Stockholders and stakeholders', p. 96.

25   See e.g. Georg Kell and David Levin, 'The Global Compact network: an historic experiment in learning and action', *Business and Society Review* 108: 2, 2003, pp.151–81. *Journal of Corporate Citizenship* issue no. 11, Autumn 2003, examines the United Nations Global Compact in detail.

26   See Jedrzej George Frynas, 'Social and environmental litigation against transnational firms in Africa', *Journal of Modern African Studies* 42: 3, 2004, pp 363–88.

27   Daniel Litvin, *Empires of profit: commerce, conquest and corporate responsibility* (London: Texere, 2003).

28   See I. Jawahar and G. McLaughlin, 'Toward a descriptive stakeholder theory: an organizational life cycle approach', *Academy of Management Review* 26: 3, 2001, pp. 397–414.

Simon Zadek

HOW CIVIL CAN CORPORATIONS BE?

Unearthly beings

A **LITTLE KNOWN** utopian fairy tale written by Carl Ewald during the Weimar period in Germany, *A Fairy Tale About God and Kings*, tells of a group of citizens who, fed up with the kings that rule them, trek to heaven to appeal directly to God. Having talked their way past the heavenly guards, they present their petition. If you are indeed good and all powerful, they plead, you must do something about these kings. God consults extensively with advisers, and goes so far as to commission senior angels to research the matter. Days go by, and the citizens group waits patiently, sure that justice will be done. Eventually, they are called again before God who, flanked by teams of celestial counsellors, gives an answer. Commanding the citizens to return back to earth, God explains, 'Kings were not my idea. They are your own invention, so there's nothing I can do for you; you will have to sort it out yourselves.'[1]

This short, political fable is neither about gods nor kings; nor is it about good, bad or evil. It is about our ability to create the futures that we want, and where necessary to remould the institutions that govern our lives to suit the purpose for which they were intended, or for which they are now needed. This is as true for businesses as for any other aspect of our future. Businesses are run by people for people. They are no more or less than a human invention for making things out of other things and getting them into use; using and making money; and for making people variously happy, satisfied or simply able to survive.

Institutions can certainly be changed, but that does not mean it is easy to do so. People in positions of power have vested interests in keeping them as they are. They build and maintain mechanisms that protect and indeed nurture historic patterns. Some of this is laudable and even virtuous; some is destructive and unacceptable, even when it is within the law. Many people quite unknowingly, and sometimes uncaringly, perpetuate institutional bad habits by virtue of their investing or buying patterns. This is rarely because they consciously seek to do others harm. Even the meanest, leanest, short-term investor rarely sets out to support a corporation *because* it undermines human rights or creates environmental havoc. It is simply that they do not take or want to take responsibility for the bigger picture, and therefore are satisfied in taking what they can, given the way things are.

Sceptical optimism

Sceptical optimism is a productive stance to take in assessing the potential and pitfalls of corporate citizenship. Scepticism is, after all, not only an appropriate foundation on which to base penetrating enquiry, but also guards against today's pervasive, all-too-safe cynicism. Optimism is scepticism's crucial accompaniment in that it offers vision and direction, and so guards against the passivity that comes with its pessimistic alter ego.

This book has taken a sceptically optimistic stance in exploring the critical issue of the role of business in society. It has considered, firstly, the strategic question of what we can and should expect from the business community in addressing the imperatives and aspirations underpinning sustainable development. Secondly, it has delved into the more operational question of whether and how these expectations can in practice be realized. On the first question, the exploration has concluded that there are cautious grounds for optimism. The emerging New Economy does offer corporations greater opportunities for securing significant competitive advantage by addressing social and environmental challenges. The viability of such strategies depends largely on two factors: the economic strength of adopting corporations, and the emergence of institutional arrangements that serve to guide and stabilize progressive market norms as they emerge. For the first, those corporations able to lever markets through their size and agility will be more effective in securing competitive advantage from citizenship strategies. Many are able to force their competitors to follow suit, if necessary through the regulatory route. For the second, the emergence of new governance frameworks involving the business community working with, for example, NGOs and public bodies can over time tend to reinforce and support good corporate citizenship in the New Economy.

On the second question, the book suggests that understanding the real potential contribution of the business community requires a shift away from the aspirational architecture of sustainable development to an approach sensitive to the scope for and nature of change. The *civil corporation* is proposed as one that takes full advantage of opportunities for learning and action in building social and environmental objectives into its core business by effectively developing its internal values and competencies. Such a process-oriented approach is not a retreat from vision, but a means of understanding, encouraging and calibrating progress. Working on the *how* is critically dependent on corporations' adoption of appropriate new approaches, tools, and above all values and attitudes. Those discussed in earlier chapters include new forms of measurement and accounting, stakeholder engagement, the standardization and professionalization of disclosure and external verification, and governance. These dimensions of the business process are all elements of how corporations acquire and use knowledge, and can themselves be impacted and transformed in the process.

Corporations that build such internal competencies can align their business more effectively to those social and environmental issues around which market opportunities based on stakeholder interests, loyalty and commitment can be built. These are the civil corporations that will drive markets in more ethical directions. Others will be followers rather than leaders, tending to emulate best practice by adopting emerging standardized approaches. Then there are and will continue to be those corporations that do not develop such competencies. These will seek other means of securing competitive advantage. In so doing they will either fail to survive, or remain or become part of the problem.

Tomorrow's world

The civil corporation can exist in the here and now. Their characterization is not based on a predicted financial, nuclear or environmental meltdown. Similarly, there is no reliance on, for example, radical localization or a global citizens' revolution, virtual or otherwise. Finally, the practicality of the civil corporation does not depend on any fundamental change in people's nature as we generally experience it. A 'modern utopia', insisted H. G. Wells a century ago, 'must have people inherently the same as those in the world'.[2]

Tomorrow has therefore been assumed to be a fundamentally familiar place. But that does not mean that things will stay the same. The unusually public and publicized view of the CIA of the world in 2015 makes salutary reading.[3] It points to what it sees as a wealth of positive potential developments, mainly emerging through the effective application of emerging technological opportunities. However, it also sees an exacerbation of current social and environmental problems as a result of continued population growth, unequal application of new technologies, and constraints in availability of and access to basic resources, notably water. Few people believe, and certainly this includes the host of experts consulted by the CIA, that an extrapolation of current political, social and economic development patterns will deliver the significant improvements needed to underpin a sustainable development pathway.

Not surprisingly, the CIA's public conclusions do not predict any radical shift in the way economic development is guided, whether by governments and international agencies, the business community or other key players. In their future scenario, NGOs become more influential, and national governments in the main become weaker or, for a few, become more powerful transnational players. The CIA is probably correct in its broad view of likely developments for NGOs and governments. Changes in the role of the state over the last two decades are almost certainly little more than a preview of what is to come. NGOs, similarly, are in a period of great change, as they adjust to the extension of the market, the globalization of concerns and opportunities, and the extraordinary rise of their own power into hitherto uncharted waters.

Box 1 Some of the CIA's view of the world in 2015

Demographics

World population in 2015 will be 7.2 billion, up from 6.1 billion in the year 2000, and in most countries, people will live longer. Ninety-five per cent of the increase will be in developing countries, nearly all in rapidly expanding urban areas. Where political systems are brittle, the combination of population growth and urbanization will foster instability. More than half of the world's population will be urban.

Food

Overall food production will be adequate to feed the world's growing population, but poor infrastructure and distribution, political instability, and chronic poverty will lead to a 20 per cent increase in numbers of malnourished people in parts of sub-Saharan Africa.

Water

Nearly half the world's population – more than 3 billion people – will live in countries that are 'water-stressed' (less than 1700 m^3 of water per capita per year) mostly in Africa, the Middle East, South Asia and northern China.

Environment

Contemporary environmental problems will persist and in many instances grow over the next 15 years. With increasingly intensive land use, significant degradation of arable land will continue as will the loss of tropical forests . . . greenhouse gas emissions will increase substantially. The depletion of tropical forests and other species-rich habitats, such as wetlands and coral reefs, will exacerbate the historically large losses of biological species now occurring.

Health

Disparities in health status between developed and developing countries will persist and widen. In developed countries, major inroads against a variety of maladies will be achieved by 2015 as a result of generous health spending and major medical advances. The revolution in biotechnology holds the promise of even more dramatic improvements in health status. AIDS will reduce economic growth by up to 1 per cent of GDP per year and consume more than 50 per cent of health budgets in the hardest-hit countries.

On business, the CIA and its advisers are strangely silent. The assumption made is, quite simply, business as usual. Yet it is the business community that is changing most rapidly and dramatically, and this is likely only to accelerate over the coming years. The business community is undoubtedly becoming more powerful, notably the small number of global corporations that dominate international trade and investment and have unparalleled access to capital and influence over public policy and the media. At the same time, corporations are not a homogeneous group, and are arguably becoming less so as the nature of competition shifts in ways described in earlier chapters. We are witnessing a global experiment in the evolution of the corporate community. Coming decades will see radical shifts in how they are owned, managed and governed; in what they produce, on what terms, and for whom. Their legal rights and responsibilities will be increasingly

fought over; both in the end are likely to grow significantly. As their basis for differen-
tiation becomes increasingly value-based, we may not even call them businesses, but
perhaps *value-webs* or simply communities-of-interest. Most of all, perhaps, the relationships between business, the state and private non-profit organizations (of which NGOs are
only one variant) will transform over the coming years, as the earlier discussion of the
new civil governance suggests.

Today's public concern and often outrage at the growing power and practices of the
corporations is, to be frank, unlikely to be sustained into the future in its current forms.
Increasing insecurity emanating from civil, environmental and financial instabilities may
well make relatively familiar and secure corporations a more attractive proposition to
many, particularly in those societies with rapidly ageing populations that place particular
value on security and stability. Younger generations, similarly, will be the first to grow
up in societies where massive global corporations are the norm. How, or even whether,
their particular radical agenda plays itself out remains entirely unclear at this stage.
They may well be more comfortable with embracing progressive corporations and
setting them against others, rather than challenging the presumptions underlying the
corporate community as a whole. This is certainly not a prediction of the 'end of
history'. But it is a prediction that the frontlines of our concerns with today's institutions, and also our visions for them, will change in the not too distant future, and
dramatically so.

Is being civil enough?

Corporations can be civil. But can they and will they be civil enough? The preceding
chapters here posed and sought to answer the practical questions underlying this challenge. Can even the most enlightened business improve its social and environmental
performance sufficiently to reach universally accepted standards while remaining a viable
business? Even if some could do so by virtue of their visionary leadership and powerful
market position, would they remain worthy but isolated examples within what is otherwise a mass of poor social and environmental performers? Finally and most important,
will all these developments add up to a coherent response to the third generation question
of what roles good corporate citizenship will play in addressing the really big social and
environmental challenges of both today's and tomorrow's world?

The recent history of corporate citizenship offers us insights into the answers to these
questions.

- *Good practices by some corporations, even those that prove sustainable, will not alone ensure
  that the wider business community meets basic social and environmental standards.* Market
  fragmentation, even in those markets where a few players are relatively dominant,
  will limit the extent to which the wider business community follows corporations
  leading in improving their social and environmental performance, even where there
  is a competitive edge gained through such leadership.
- *Powerful dynamics driving the New Economy will tend to undermine good corporate citizenship, as well as those elements that tend to nurture it.* 'Impatient money' will tend to
  penalize those seeking to enhance their longer-term business success through really
  significant enhancements in social and environmental performance. Such attempts

by most corporations will not be sustainable unless they are rewarded in financial terms through the markets in which they operate, or/and supported by enabling legislation.

● *Private standards could be either part of the solution or the problem, and will in practice be both.* Standards may exist along any of the pathways, even those that extend into ethical wastelands. It should not be assumed that private standards push the change process into the positive innovation cycle (Mecca), even where they are technically good standards.

That is, individual corporations acting alone will rarely be able to sustain *significantly* enhanced social and environmental performance for extended periods of time. Another way of looking at this is that if corporations seeking to achieve this are not emulated by their competitors, it either means that the corporation has failed to achieve any competitive advantage through its good practices, or that its competitive advantage exists only within a restricted market niche that has high barriers to entry and does not threaten the broader market (and so will not have extended impact). From this perspective, corporate citizenship based on leadership practices that are not institutionalized beyond the individual corporation is unlikely to deliver adequate social and environmental goods, and offset bads, to meaningfully address the third generation challenge.

To effectively move beyond the Oasis and steer clear of the Desert pathways, the civil corporation will have to take a lead in creating collective processes, and codifying best practice and building adequate oversight to ensure implementation across the wider business community. Two specific inferences can be drawn:

1   *Alliances of corporations have a far greater chance to sustain significant enhancements in social and environmental performance, and also to influence other market players to follow suit. Such alliances may form within sectors.* For this to be worth their while, however, is likely to require multi-stakeholder alliances that bring together public bodies and private non-profit organizations such as NGOs and trade unions.

2   *Such civil alliances and partnerships will over time seek to codify negotiated agreements into more formalized governance frameworks.* The main reasons for this are to reduce transaction and other costs and increase the potential for replication by others. These new civil governance frameworks will in some instances promote public, statutory regulation and at other times seek to regulate through private standards. Those frameworks that fail to effectively codify agreements will, over time, fail and eventually collapse. Public bodies and private non-profit organizations, and indeed civil corporations, will withdraw their support and so remove a critical source of legitimacy as well as operational competencies.

There is no simple template or magic bullet that will secure a progressive role for the business community in addressing the challenges and aspirations underlying sustainable development. That the business community is so powerful does not offset the fact that even its more dominant members have restricted room for manoeuvre, certainly in the shorter term. It makes no sense to promote virtuous corporations that are, as a result, absorbed by their less angelic competitors. This reality partly reflects on business's more powerful stakeholders. After all, business behaviour and performance embodies, codifies and in many ways reinforces *our own* ambivalence as to how we trade off personal and collective interests, both now and into the future.

The propositions underlying the *civil corporation* do offer a route for getting the most out of economy and business in addressing social and environmental aims and challenges. The book has sought to frame how best to identify and guide corporations in developing viable business strategies and practices that deliver against such aims and challenges. Most important, perhaps, it has sought to answer the more daunting question of how much we can expect from business – and corporate citizenship – in overcoming global poverty, inequality and environmental insecurity. The core answer to this critical question is that corporate citizenship will only be effective if and where it evolves to a point where business becomes active in promoting and institutionalizing new global governance frameworks that effectively secure civil market behaviour. Leading civil corporations will be those that go beyond getting their own house in order, and actively engage in promoting governance frameworks that enable, and if necessary enforce, the wider business community to address, effectively and without contradiction, the aspirations underpinning sustainable development.

Notes

1   Ewald, C. (1921) 'A Fairy Tale About God and Kings', in Zipes, J. (ed.) (1990) *Utopian Tales from Weimar*, Polygon, Edinburgh, pp. 34–35
2   Wells, H. G. (1976) *A Modern Utopia*, Bison, London
3   Central Intelligence Agency (2000) *Global Trends 2015: A Dialogue About the Future with Nongovernmental Experts* (www.cia.gov/cia/publications/globaltrends2015/index.html).

Index